TRUCE

MURDER, MYTH AND THE LAST DAYS
OF THE IRISH WAR OF INDEPENDENCE

Pádraig Óg Ó Ruairc

MERCIER PRESS

Irish Publisher – Irish Story

A bundled eBook edition is available
with the purchase of this print book.

CLEARLY PRINT YOUR NAME ABOVE IN UPPER CASE

Instructions to claim your eBook edition:
1. Download the BitLit app for Android or iOS
2. Write your name in **UPPER CASE** above
3. Use the BitLit app to submit a photo
4. Download your eBook to any device

MERCIER PRESS

Cork

www.mercierpress.ie

© Pádraig Óg Ó Ruairc, 2016

ISBN: 978 1 78117 385 5

10 9 8 7 6 5 4 3 2 1

A CIP record for this title is available from the British Library

Printed and bound in the EU.

CONTENTS

To my wife Anne Maria, meeting you was the best thing that ever happened to me.

Acknowledgements

First of all I wish to thank my PhD supervisor, Dr Ruán O'Donnell of the University of Limerick, for his confidence in me, support and assistance during the course of my studies. I also owe a great debt of gratitude to Dr John O'Callaghan of St Angela's College for his invaluable help and advice during my research; Dr John Borgonovo of University College Cork, who has always been very generous in sharing his extensive knowledge and research on the 1916 period; Dr Fearghal McGarry of Queen's University Belfast, who acted as external examiner for my PhD thesis; Dr Gavin Wilk, who was my PhD's internal examiner; Dr William Mulligan of University College Dublin, who was very helpful in giving me direction when I called upon him as a former student; Dr Seán Gannon, who gave me a lot of help and sound practical advice; Dr Andy Bielenberg, who was often my first port of call whenever I got 'stuck' on a query relating to fatalities in Cork; Dr Philip McConway, who shared his knowledge and research on the conflict in the midlands; Dr Daithí Ó Corráin, who bore my unsolicited requests for information with good grace, even when they must have been an unwelcome imposition; Dr Gerard Noonan, who generously shared information from his then-unpublished thesis about IRA activity in Britain; Dr Brian Hanley, who gave me great assistance; Dr Tim Horgan, undoubtedly one of the finest historians that 'the Kingdom' has ever produced and whose wit and humour make every meeting memorable; Dr William Kautt and Commandant Sean A. Murphy (ret.), who gave advice on military matters; Dr Matthew Lewis, who advised me on the history of Armagh and south Down; Fr Brian Murphy, OSB, who was able to give me great insight into the political machinations of the era; John Dorney, a great man to discuss history with; Tommy Graham of *History Ireland* magazine; Las 'Guns&Hoses' and Donal 'CHTM' Fallon, the best father-and-son team in Irish history; Barry Keane, who helped me to understand the local geography of the Ellis Quarry killings; Liz Gillis, a hard-working historian who has a real passion for her subject; Liam Ó Duibhir, an expert on the history of Donegal, who was always willing to help; Donal O'Flynn, one of nature's gentlemen, who has an encyclopedic knowledge of the 3rd West Cork Brigade area; my old pal Cyril Wall, who gave me great advice in my early endeavours; Jim McDermott and Kieran Glennon, two great Belfast historians without whose assistance I would never have been able to write the chapter on Belfast's Bloody Sunday; Gary O'Brien, who gave vital assistance; Seán Enright, who provided a valuable insight into legal matters related to the Hague Conventions; Gerry White, an officer and a gentleman; Phil Flood, who did not bat an eyelid when I arrived on her doorstep unannounced asking awkward questions about the history of Kilcash; and Kathy Hegarty Thorne, for sharing her research on Roscommon. A special thanks also to the Sheehy family of Clonmeen House.

Thanks also to the staff of the Irish Military Archives, in particular Hugh and Noelle, who do a spectacular job and provide a top-class service; the staff of the British National Archives at Kew in London, whose thorough and efficient service make research there a pleasure; to a number of British military museums that gave me assistance, including The National Army Museum, the Argyll and Southern Highlanders Museum, the Keep Military Museum in Dorset, the Worchestershire Regimental Museum; and of course, to Ian Hook at the Essex Regimental Museum and Stanley C. Jenkins of the Soldiers of Oxfordshire Trust, who both went above and beyond the call of duty in their efforts to help me; also to Mike Maguire of the local studies section in Limerick City Library and his counterpart Peter Byrne in the Local Studies Centre in Ennis; and Sean O'Mahony and the 1916–21 Club in Dublin, who have always given valuable assistance and support to my endeavours; and to the members of the Meelick-Parteen and

Cratloe Commemoration Committee (Johnny White, Councillor Cathal Crowe, Tom Gleeson, Éamon O'Halloran, Jody O'Connor, Ger Hickey and Pat McDonough), who have done incredible work in preserving the history of the IRA's East Clare Brigade. Tom Toomey is an inspiration to me and a generation of younger historians – the people of Limerick are lucky to have such a talented scholar at work preserving and promoting their heritage.

To my work colleagues in the OPW, especially those in the Shannon region and Claremorris; William Butler, who is on the cusp of publishing a brilliant book; Michael Houlihan, a font of wisdom and encouragement; Dara Maken, a great friend and pro-prietor of Enniskerry Village Stores – the finest retail emporium in Ireland; Chris Coe, a loyal friend and an extraordinarily talented craftsman; Patrick Fleckenstein and Seán Patrick Donald, two Cape Veterans, of whom the Atlantic prevents me seeing more; Liam Hogan, my comrade in sedition; and Joe, Sham, Farrell, Larkin, Spud and O'Connell: I couldn't have done this without you.

Des and Annette Long do unceasing work to keep the 'spirit of '16' alive in Limerick; Criostoir de Baroid keeps the flag flying in Cork; Cormac Ó Comhraí, I have learned so much from you in the few years of our friendship – I hope some of your regu-lar pupils realise how lucky they are to have such a talented and dedicated teacher; Dr Tomás Mac Conmara has never been given the credit he deserves for the outstanding work he has done to preserve Clare's heritage; and Dr Billy Mag Fhloinn, I want to thank you for the years of help you have given me with so many different things.

A special thanks to my parents, Pat and Monica, for their financial assistance during my time at university, and to my sister Deirdre and my brother Kevin for their support.

Tomás – *mo bhuachaill beag gealgháireach, sonas agus spreagadh nua i mho shaol agus Anne Maria, ar ndóigh.*

1

INTRODUCTION

For decades, nationalist Ireland has told glorious stories of IRA flying columns beating the dastardly Black and Tans. In fact there were few flying columns and an awful lot of … murders … In [July] 1921, with the Truce just hours away, an RIC man named Alfred Needham, aged 20, clearly thought that finally he could marry his sweetheart. But a clerk in Ennis tipped off the IRA that the groom's profession was 'Constable'. So a beaming Alfred and his teenage bride emerged from the registry office and two gunmen shot him dead. Yet … this July our political classes will once again unite around the fiction that 'the War of Independence' was honourable and necessary and largely worthwhile.[1]

This is how newspaper columnist Kevin Myers described one of the last killings of the Irish War of Independence in an article in the *Irish Independent* marking the ninetieth anniversary of the Anglo-Irish Truce, which ended the war on 11 July 1921. Myers dismissed the IRA military campaign of 1919–21, which eventually led to the creation of an independent state in southern Ireland, as part of a 'cycle of psychiatric futility'. Furthermore, he claimed that the 'murder' of Alfred Needham exposed as a fiction the concept of the War of Independence as a necessary and legitimate war.

Ironically, Myers' account of Needham's killing is almost entirely fictional. There was no wedding ceremony, no teenage bride and no clerk who tipped off the IRA. Needham, a Black and Tan from London, was shot standing at the door of a stable with two other armed members of the Royal Irish Constabulary (RIC) – not while leaving a registry office with his new bride. The tale about

Needham being killed immediately after getting married appears to have been invented for melodramatic effect in a propaganda story. Yet different versions of this story continue to resurface every few years masquerading as factual history. Author Richard Abbott, an RUC officer who compiled a history of RIC casualties during the War of Independence, claimed that the IRA had attacked both Needham and his new bride after their wedding ceremony – killing him and hospitalising her.[2] Eunan O'Halpin, Professor of Contemporary Irish History at Trinity College Dublin, stated in a recent television documentary that Needham had married in a church ceremony and was shot dead in front of his new bride just minutes after they had exchanged wedding vows.[3] A common element in most of these accounts is the suggestion that the IRA Volunteers who killed Needham knew a ceasefire had been agreed with the British forces and that this was a motivating factor in the attack.

The stories about Needham's wedding are part of a wider narrative about the War of Independence, which claims that the announcement of the Truce on 8 July 1921 led to a wave of unjustifiable 'eleventh-hour' IRA attacks before the ceasefire began. Supporters of this narrative claim that republicans launched a determined campaign to kill as many people as possible before the war ended and that these final IRA attacks were made mainly against so-called 'soft targets', i.e. unarmed members of the British forces and loyalist civilians. Some historians and commentators allege that attacks on 'soft targets' accounted for the bulk of IRA activity throughout the War of Independence, which they claim was more akin to terrorism than to a military campaign. It has also been asserted that Protestants were targeted as part of a sectarian campaign conducted by the IRA, and that such attacks intensified after the Truce was announced.

A number of stories similar to the one about Needham's wedding are reproduced regularly in histories of the War of Independence to support the idea that the IRA exploited the declaration of the Truce as an opportunity for wanton violence. These include claims that:

- After the announcement of the Truce, the IRA killed up to a dozen alleged spies, most of whom were innocent Protestants with no connection to the British forces.

- Four teenage soldiers, mere boys who had left their post to visit a sweet shop, were abducted and murdered by the IRA for no apparent reason.

- Three Protestant boys were abducted, killed and secretly buried by the IRA in Cork city because of republican paranoia about spies.

- A devout Catholic serving in the RIC was shot dead by IRA gunmen while on his way to Mass on the morning of the ceasefire.

- The IRA in Kerry launched its only attack of the war, killing a soldier and an innocent young woman, just minutes before the Truce started.

- A Black and Tan strolling through a picturesque Wicklow village was murdered by republicans less than an hour after the ceasefire began.

Some of these stories have a grain of truth to them. Others are entirely fictional or are genuine killings taken out of context and with new details invented for propaganda value. For years, Irish and British authors writing about the War of Independence have accepted these stories as truthful, repeating and recycling them without question. Meanwhile the activities of the British forces in the same period have been ignored, with many authors unquestioningly accepting assurances that the British Army, RIC and Black and Tans all ceased hostilities the minute the Truce was announced, leaving the IRA as the sole protagonists in the final violent days of the conflict.

The allegation that the IRA callously took the announcement of the Truce as an opportunity to attack 'soft targets' was first employed as anti-republican propaganda in early accounts of the war written by British authors. The official history of the British Army's 6th Division in Ireland, written in 1922, claimed the IRA exploited the declaration of the Truce as:

> … an opportunity for attacking and murdering people when vigilance would obviously be relaxed, and if they could only postpone these murders to the last moment, the murderers could not possibly be punished. They carried out their programme to the letter. A private of the Machine Gun Corps was murdered on July 10th … four unarmed soldiers were kidnapped and murdered in Cork, and a patrol in Castleisland was ambushed, with results more disastrous to the rebels than even to the patrol itself; and finally, within fifteen minutes of the Truce, the inhabitants of Killarney, who had never summoned up courage to strike a blow for freedom during the progress of the war, attacked two sergeants of the Royal Fusiliers in the street, one of whom died. Thus was the Truce inaugurated.[4]

Walter Phillips, an English historian who published one of the first popular histories of the conflict in 1923, said: 'the weekend before the coming of the Truce was one of the bloodiest on record in Ireland'. Phillips held the IRA solely responsible for this increase in violence and focused on the killings of off-duty soldiers and loyalist civilians.[5] In his memoirs, published in 1924, General Nevil Macready, the former commander of the British forces in Ireland, contrasted the morality of the military campaigns waged by the rival forces in the final days and hours before the Truce began. According to Macready, British forces refrained from any hasty and unnecessary last-minute attacks, while the IRA intensified its military campaign through opportunistic killings:

The Truce would begin at 12 noon on 11th July, 1921, until which time the troops, while taking no risks, should abstain as far as possible from unnecessary activity against the rebels, who, far from imitating such chivalrous forbearance, continued their campaign of outrage and assassination until the clocks struck twelve on 11th July.[6]

Like Phillips, Macready cited attacks on the British forces, the killing of civilians and the destruction of the homes of loyalists as proof of an IRA 'campaign of outrage' prompted by the announcement of the Truce.[7]

Allegations that the IRA engaged in unjustified military operations in the dying hours of the conflict were not confined to British writers. This accusation became a core piece of anti-republican propaganda in the Irish Free State. During the Civil War both sides accused their opponents of cowardice, denouncing them as 'eleventh-hour warriors' and 'Trucileers', i.e. men who joined the IRA at the time of the Truce but who had played little or no part in the War of Independence. The military record of its various supporters and opponents often dominated the debates surrounding the acceptance of the Anglo-Irish Treaty.[8] Free State propaganda defined republican opponents of the Anglo-Irish Treaty as 'Johnny-come-latelys' who 'had never challenged Dublin Castle' or 'ever fired a shot against the British forces'. Furthermore they denounced the guerrilla tactics used by IRA 'Trucileers' and, with no sense of irony or hypocrisy, encouraged them to 'fight fair' even though the exact same guerrilla tactics had been employed during the War of Independence.[9]

In his 1924 book *The Victory of Sinn Féin*, the Free State polemicist P. S. O'Hegarty condemned the anti-Treaty IRA as 'a terrorist army' of 'Tinpikemen' that had shied away from danger during the War of Independence but who had sprung into action at the last moment: 'all the young men in all the counties who had kept aloof of the fighting when it was dangerous were now eager to become heroes, and to be able to tell stories about this and that ambush'.[10] Piaras Béaslaí, the former IRA director of publicity who wrote a biography of Michael Collins shortly after the Civil War, castigated the republican opponents of the Treaty, whom he dismissed as 'Trucileers':

> A great many eleventh-hour warriors, in comparatively peaceful parts of the country, hastened to make up arrears by firing shots at the last moment, and there were attacks on the English forces up to within a few minutes of the Truce. These belated exhibitions of prowess, with no military objective, when the danger seemed past, reflected no credit on Irishmen.[11]

Many of the IRA units responsible for these operations later fought against acceptance of the Treaty, and Béaslaí's comments are likely to have been influenced by his support for the Treaty and his experiences during the Civil War.

Abusive comments about 'Trucileers' were directed in particular against republicans in Kerry, where there had been limited IRA activity in the pre-Truce period but an increase in operations in the last days of the war. In October 1933, following a republican attack on a 'Blueshirt' rally in Tralee, Eoin O'Duffy, leader of the pro-Treaty Fine Gael party, taunted his political opponents in the county by declaring: 'Kerry's entire record in the Black and Tan struggle consisted in shooting an unfortunate soldier the day of the Truce. To hear such people shouting "Up the Republic" would make a dog sick.'[12]

Years later, a number of historians began repeating allegations that the IRA had exploited the announcement of the Truce to commit unjustified and morally questionable attacks, and over time this allegation became widely accepted as historical fact. In his book *The Black and Tans*, Richard Bennett claimed that there was 'a wild flurry of activity' by 'Eleventh hour warriors of the IRA

[who] hurried to get their last shots in'. Bennett cited the IRA execution of civilians suspected of spying and attacks on off-duty members of the British forces as proof of this. He claimed that these 'eleventh-hour' attacks were typical of the IRA's military campaign, which had 'relapsed into a moral anarchy unconnected with any political or social or practical end other than the muzzle of a gun'.[13]

Charles Townshend has claimed that the Truce was 'preceded by one of the bloodiest weekends in the conflict, with the IRA killing some 20 people in the last 36 hours'.[14] Joseph Curran attributed a propaganda and political motivation to the apparent escalation in IRA violence immediately before the ceasefire: 'On July 8 Macready ordered his troops to abstain from unnecessary activity in view of the Truce agreement. The IRA, on the other hand, kept up its attacks until the last moment to demonstrate its capacity and willingness to carry on the fight.'[15] Tim Pat Coogan claimed that the IRA committed 'cold-blooded' killings after the Truce's announcement: 'the IRA kept up the offensive to within minutes of that noontide. On some it had a galvanic effect. Knowing that retribution could not occur after the 11th, many literally eleventh-hour warriors now took the field'.[16] Maryann Valiulis claimed that some bloodlust was to be found on both sides in the last days of the war, but suggested that the republicans were primarily responsible, having provoked British forces through a series of unjustified and gratuitous killings:

> Neither side ... would let the hostilities cease without one last burst of violence before the Truce came into effect. The IRA received word that the British forces would attempt one final action ... The reason for the contemplated action by the British forces was that six soldiers were captured and shot on about 9 July 1921. In addition, records indicate that 11 spies were executed by the IRA just prior to the advent of the Truce.[17]

Peter Hart stated that local IRA units had advance knowledge of the Truce and this led to an increase in republican violence deliberately calculated to inflict fatalities on British forces and to kill loyalist civilians and other 'soft targets':

> The first eleven days in July did bring a last-minute upsurge in political activity … this was partly a product of the impending Truce, allowing IRA units outside Dublin to wreak maximum havoc in the knowledge that they would soon be immune from retaliation … Civilian targets, in fact, offered the only remaining untapped market for IRA operations in early 1921, which guerrillas were already beginning to exploit when the Truce mercifully intervened.[18]

Hart further claimed that anti-Protestant violence perpetrated by the IRA increased continually until the Truce began on 11 July 1921.[19] According to him, the IRA engaged in a spate of unwarranted killings after the ceasefire was announced: 'many guerrilla units had made a point of killing as many enemies as possible up until the last minute (twenty people in the last thirty-six hours)'.[20]

More recently, Marie Coleman has suggested that IRA Volunteers who knew the Truce was imminent might have had a sectarian motive in launching last-minute attacks. Coleman cites the executions of the Pearson brothers, two Protestant farmers at Coolacrease, Co. Offaly, and suggests that their killers were motivated by 'the desire of the hitherto inactive Offaly Brigade to record a success before the Truce'.[21]

Through frequent repetition, the claim that the announcement of the Truce led to a surge in unjustifiable 'last-minute' republican killings has effectively become part of the standard narrative of the War of Independence. Over time, this narrative has become more exaggerated and has been incorporated into an increasingly melodramatic, propagandistic and factually inaccurate history. This repetition and promotion has been part of a wider ideological debate about 'revisionism' in the academic study of Irish history and an ongoing political debate on the legitimacy of physical-force republicanism. The debate on these issues has been conducted in overtly political and moral terms in newspaper articles, and on radio and television, with politicians and polemicists such as Conor Cruise O'Brien featuring prominently.[22]

Newspaper columnist and political activist Eoghan Harris, a self-described anti-republican revisionist, has produced a number of television pieces and articles critical of the IRA's conduct during the War of Independence, which allege that republican violence in that period had a strong sectarian intent. He has insisted that 'the first duty of academic historians is to protect past victims of the IRA who no longer have a voice'.[23] Harris has also made the specific claim that republican 'bloodlust' led to an increase in IRA violence after the announcement of the Truce.[24]

Kevin Myers has made similar claims in his newspaper columns, which regularly feature the War of Independence as a topic. He has frequently repeated the claim that the IRA exploited the announcement of the Truce as an opportunity to indulge in sectarian killings and attacks on 'soft targets'. In *The Irish Times*, Myers alleged that: 'The conference in the Mansion House in Dublin, where the details of the ceasefire were being hammered out, gave three days' notice of the Truce. Those days were filled with bloodshed as killers embarked upon a once-in-a-lifetime Summer Sale of murder, guaranteed without legal consequence.'[25] Claims by Myers and Harris cannot be treated with the same weight as serious historical research by academics, but the media in Ireland plays an important role in shaping perceptions of the conflict and opinion pieces by these commentators have helped to promote and expand the existing narrative of pre-Truce violence.

This book attempts to separate the fiction, myth and propaganda from the facts, and to establish what really happened from 8–11 July 1921 – to find out if there is any truth in the allegations, or if they are just made-up stories that have enjoyed an unnaturally long life. To date, almost all of the books and articles which claim that the announcement of the Truce led to a massive surge in violence have focused entirely on killings carried out by the IRA and ignored the actions of British forces in the last days of the conflict. This has resulted in a biased history of the last days of the conflict, in which those killed by the IRA are remembered as the victims of vengeful and futile militarism while those killed by the British forces are conveniently forgotten. Here, contemporary accounts from newspapers, military and police reports, testimony from Irish loyalists and eyewitness accounts from veterans of both the IRA and the British forces have been used to build up a detailed and accurate picture and to establish for the first time what really happened during the final days and hours of the Irish War of Independence.

2

THE POLITICAL AND MILITARY
ORIGINS OF THE TRUCE

A huge volume of history has been written about the negotiations that led to the Anglo-Irish Treaty – but, in comparison, very little has been written about the peace talks that brought about the Truce which ended the War of Independence. Even after both sides had come to realise that a military cessation was necessary, there was a long and protracted debate between them about the form the ceasefire should take.

Republicans were keen to exact the maximum propaganda value from any agreement with the British and wanted to secure a formal, bilateral military armistice. Such an agreement would effectively bestow 'belligerent status' on the IRA, meaning that the British recognised them as lawful 'combatants' in a 'legitimate' army.[1] It would also involve the British giving tacit political recognition to Dáil Éireann, the Irish republican government. The republicans were determined to ensure that any ceasefire would not involve any major concessions on their part, such as the surrender of IRA arms or the prosecution of wanted IRA leaders.

In contrast, the British aimed to force the IRA to accept an informal truce that imposed harsh military conditions and restrictions on the republicans. This would effectively amount to a military surrender by the IRA, and would deny Dáil Éireann, Sinn Féin and the IRA the propaganda coup and legitimacy they would win as parties to a formal agreement with the British government.

Many of the writers who have claimed that there was an upsurge in IRA violence just before the Truce have mistakenly attributed a degree of foresight to republican combatants that simply did not exist. Supporters of this account wrongly assumed that IRA Volunteers throughout Ireland knew well in advance that the Truce was coming, were motivated to kill as many of their enemies as possible before the war ended and had time to plan new attacks before the ceasefire began. Some of these writers also did not understand the terms and conditions of the Truce or the type of ceasefire it involved. A full understanding of the Truce, its form and political and military origins, is necessary before any attempt can be made to understand the violence that occurred after the ceasefire was announced, or to put those events in context.

The official position of the British government during the conflict was that the IRA was a 'murder gang' and that the republican insurrection was an illegal attempt by a criminal conspiracy to overthrow British rule through terrorism. Some members of the British government even believed that the IRA was the puppet of an international conspiracy, led by Bolshevik Russia, which sought to destroy the British Empire.[2] Because members of the British government continually repeated this position in public, they could not openly encourage any contact or negotiations with Irish republicans. In 1918 the British cabinet insisted:

> as a preliminary to proceeding with the Government policy … of the grant of self-government to Ireland, it was first necessary [to] restore respect for government, enforce the law and, above all, put down with a stern hand the Irish-German conspiracy which appears to be widespread in Ireland.[3]

In 1920 the British cabinet's 'Irish Situation Committee' recommended:

> no person … should in any circumstance be permitted to hold communication with Sinn Féin, except on the basis of the Government's

expressed policy, viz: the repression of crime and the determination to carry through the Government of Ireland Bill on its present main lines.[4]

Despite this hardline public stance, in private the British authorities maintained contact with members of Sinn Féin throughout the conflict in the hope of opening peace negotiations. In March 1920 Alfred Davies, a Conservative MP, wrote to Art O'Brien, Sinn Féin's representative in London, stating that the majority of MPs favoured a political settlement for Ireland. Davies offered to arrange a meeting between the Sinn Féin leader, Arthur Griffith, and the British prime minister, David Lloyd George.[5] In July of that year, Lord Curzon, the British foreign secretary, advised the British cabinet that 'you must negotiate with Sinn Féin. We shall be driven to dominion Home Rule [in southern Ireland] sooner or later.'[6]

In the same month Sir Charles Russell, the English barrister and baronet, was approached by Lloyd George and asked to contact Sinn Féin to begin negotiations. Lloyd George indicated to Russell that a negotiated peace was possible on condition that it excluded Michael Collins and other members of the IRA leadership.[7] Two months later a meeting was arranged in Dublin between Griffith and Sir John Anderson, the joint under-secretary for Ireland. The meeting was aborted at the last moment, apparently because Griffith insisted that the British would first have to recognise Dáil Éireann. Though disappointed by this outcome, Mark Sturgis, the most senior British civil servant in Dublin Castle, interpreted the development as evidence of a split among Irish republicans: 'It looks as if the pressure on the quiet side of Sinn Féin to break away from the gunmen is increasing.'[8] The attorney general was less optimistic: 'the bad element in Sinn Féin would seize on any new statement made by the government [as a weakness] and any Sinn Feiners negotiating would be shot'.[9]

The first peace initiative to suggest a ceasefire between the opposing military forces came from General George Cockerill, a Conservative MP, who proposed in October 1920 that an immediate ceasefire between the IRA and the British forces should be arranged. Cockerill suggested that once this ceasefire began, Dáil Éireann would meet in public with British approval and political negotiations could begin.[10] Responding to this call, Patrick Moylett, an Irish Republican Brotherhood (IRB) member and judge in the Sinn Féin courts, met Cockerill and a number of other influential British politicians, including C. J. Phillips, an official from the British Foreign Office, and Herbert Fisher, the Minister for Education.[11] Despite being a member of Sinn Féin and an associate of Griffith, Moylett was acting on his own initiative.

Shortly after Moylett and Cockerill began these discussions, they took on a new sense of urgency when Terence MacSwiney, the republican mayor of Cork, died on hunger strike at Brixton Prison in England. Moylett was summoned immediately to Downing Street for an additional meeting with Phillips. Phillips proposed that the announcement of an immediate IRA ceasefire would lead to an informal truce between them and the British forces, allowing formal political negotiations to begin.[12] Moylett forwarded this proposal to Griffith, who responded in writing with the following proposals:

(1) The Dáil Éireann should be allowed to meet on the distinct understanding that –

(a) Attacks on the police and soldiers instantly cease.

(b) At the meeting no reference be made to the existence of any 'Irish Republic'. From the point of view of the British Government the meeting would merely be that of representatives of Ireland referred to by the Prime Minister in his speech in Parliament …

(2) The only 'business' of the meeting would be to receive and answer an invitation from the British Government to nominate representatives to a conference called by the British Government for a settlement of the whole Irish question. Sinn Féin's idea of a conference is that it would consist of one or two members representing Ulster, one or two representing Sinn Féin and (say) five others representing England, Scotland, Wales and possibly the two Dominions specially interested in the Irish Question, viz., Canada and Australia.[13]

Whilst secret negotiations with Griffith continued in private, in public the British government engaged in a bout of sabre rattling. Lloyd George made a speech at the Guildhall in London stating: 'We have murder by the throat, we had to reorganise the police. When the government was ready we struck the terrorists and now the terrorists are complaining of terror.'[14] The hardline rhetoric coming from the British government and its public inflexibility frustrated Michael Collins, who asked: 'I wonder what these people with their hypocritical good intentions and good wishes say to L. George's speech yesterday? So much for the peace feelers.'[15]

The willingness of Moylett and Griffith to negotiate a ceasefire gave their British counterparts the impression that the republicans were ready to sue for peace at any cost, which may have influenced the triumphalist tone of the prime minister's speech. It also convinced Phillips that British measures to crush the insurrection and restore order were bearing fruit. On 19 November he wrote to Lloyd George:

I got a very clear impression … that the Sinn Féin leaders realise quite well the hopelessness of their attempts to carry on the struggle on present lines and are seeking a plan by which they may at the same time end the present crisis, save their own faces as far as possible and checkmate the extremist section among their followers.[16]

Within days of Phillips' letter, the IRA scored a series of decisive victories that completely undermined this impression.

In a wave of co-ordinated attacks on Sunday 21 November 1920, the IRA's Dublin Brigade killed twelve suspected British intelligence agents and two members of the RIC Auxiliary Division.[17] A few hours later members of the British forces took their revenge by attacking spectators at a Gaelic football match in Croke Park, killing fourteen civilians. That night, members of the RIC Auxiliary Division at Dublin Castle killed two senior IRA officers and a civilian.[18] According to Moylett, the day that became known as Bloody Sunday gave a new impetus to the negotiations: 'The week following the 21st November I had conferences every day with Phillips. That week … I spent every day in Downing St and we discussed the question of a settlement in detail from every angle.' Phillips assured Moylett that if Dáil Éireann used its influence to get the IRA to suspend their military campaign for a week, it would enable Lloyd George to propose a peace settlement in the House of Commons.[19]

Moylett assured the British that Dáil Éireann could secure a week-long IRA ceasefire. In return he sought a commitment from the British that the Black and Tans and RIC Auxiliaries would be confined to barracks once the cessation began. The proposed truce was intended as a temporary, informal arrangement to facilitate political negotiations.[20] However, efforts to secure a truce were soon frustrated by the arrest of Griffith and another Sinn Féin TD, Eoin MacNeill.[21] A further complication emerged when the British insisted that leading members of the IRA would not be immune from prosecution during the ceasefire. 'They wished to exempt Mick Collins, Dan Breen and one or two others. The truce would not cover these men, meaning that they were reserved for subsequent prosecution.' Moylett's talks with the British faltered on this issue, and his peace initiative fell apart soon after.[22]

On 28 November 1920 the Cork No. 3 Brigade IRA ambushed

a patrol of RIC Auxiliaries at Kilmichael, killing sixteen members of the patrol. A seventeenth Auxiliary initially escaped but was captured and killed shortly afterwards.[23] The IRA victory at Kilmichael was an unprecedented development that came as a great shock to the British government.[24] Apart from the large number of fatalities, the fact that sixteen of the dead were ex-military officers from England and Scotland had an additional impact in Britain, because before Kilmichael the majority of 'British' fatalities in Ireland had been Irish RIC constables. Lloyd George observed, 'The last attack of the rebels seemed … to partake of a different character from the preceding operations. The others were assassinations. This last was a military operation.'[25] By coincidence, on the same date as the Kilmichael ambush, the IRA carried out co-ordinated acts of industrial sabotage in several British cities. In Liverpool and Bootle alone, IRA operations caused £250,000 worth of damage.[26] The British public and press feared these attacks were the start of an IRA campaign in Britain.

Bloody Sunday, Kilmichael and the campaign of sabotage in England generated significant press coverage in the British media.[27] The unprecedented scale of these attacks, coupled with the state funerals at Westminster Abbey of six British officers killed on Bloody Sunday, ensured that the IRA's military campaign made front-page newspaper headlines all over Britain. Mark Sturgis, who was in London at the time, was struck by the public reaction:

> One thing is very sure. We can no longer complain of lack of interest on this side … Liverpool and the murders have made a tremendous difference in the tone. Everyone is talking of Shin [Féin] murder plots and the press is unanimous as far as I have seen it. Even *The Times* wishes us God speed in smashing the murder gang.[28]

These dramatic events were followed immediately by a profusion of new attempts to secure a truce.

Some Sinn Féin politicians were disturbed by the violence of the IRA's military campaign, the most prominent being Roger Sweetman, Sinn Féin TD for North Wexford. In the immediate aftermath of Bloody Sunday and Kilmichael, Sweetman wrote to several newspapers appealing for an IRA ceasefire.[29] He expressed serious reservations about the morality of the use of military force by republicans, and his attempts to arrange a ceasefire appear to have been based on a moral objection to the growing intensity of the IRA's military campaign. Sweetman's appeal was made without the approval of Dáil Éireann or consultation with the IRA's leadership, and had no prospect of success. Nonetheless, it was significant because it was the first time a TD had called publicly for an end to hostilities as a precursor to peace negotiations. Shortly afterwards Sweetman resigned as a TD in protest at the nature of the IRA's continuing military campaign.[30] The British government took notice of Sweetman's appeal and Phillips questioned Moylett about it. Moylett and others in Sinn Féin regarded Sweetman's appeal as premature, damaging and counter-productive.[31]

Following quickly after Sweetman's appeal came the 'Galway Peace Resolution', tabled at a special meeting of Galway County Council on 3 December 1920. The meeting had been called to discuss the council's finances. Because of the number of councillors wanted by the British forces, only six attended. Since a quorum of eight was not present, the meeting did not have the power to conduct any official council business.[32] A discussion of the political situation in Ireland ensued among the assembled councillors, during which Councillor James Haverty, an IRA officer, read the following proposal for peace negotiations:[33]

That we, the members of Galway County Council, assembled on December 3, 1920, view with sorrow and grief the shootings, burnings, reprisals and counter-reprisals now taking place all over England and Ireland by armed forces of the British Empire on one hand and armed forces of the Irish Republic on the other. That we believe this unfortunate state of affairs is detrimental to the interests of both countries in such a crisis in world affairs. We, therefore, as adherents of Dáil Éireann, request that body to appoint three delegates to negotiate a truce.

We further request the British Government to appoint three more delegates who will have power to arrange a truce and preliminary terms of peace so that an end may be brought to the unfortunate strife by a peace honourable to both countries. That we consider the initiative lies with the British Government who should withdraw the ban on the meeting of Dáil Éireann for the purpose of appointing delegates. That we further consider that if either side refuses to accede to proposals such as these, the world will hold it responsible for any further shootings or burnings that may take place.[34]

Haverty's proposal was widely reported in the national and international press.[35] Reacting to these press reports, the acting chairwoman of the council, Alice Cashel, called a meeting of the full council to repudiate publicly Haverty's proposal. However, she was arrested along with several other councillors who were on their way to that meeting.[36] Regardless of its validity, the 'Galway Peace Resolution' resulted in swift condemnation from other republicans. Galway Councillor Pádraig Kilkelly approached the local IRA leadership, asking them to issue a statement denouncing the resolution and highlighting the fact that the majority of councillors were 'on the run' and had not supported Haverty's motion.[37] The IRA in Galway despairingly referred to it as 'The White Feather Resolution' and was anxious to take action to dispel the rumour that 'Galway had been tamed'.[38] When a copy of the resolution was circulated to Clare County Council, Michael Brennan, the council's chairman and leader of the IRA's East Clare Brigade, burned it in protest.[39]

Nonetheless, the British government was encouraged by events in Galway, interpreting them as further evidence of a growing split between republican 'moderates' and 'gunmen'. A meeting of the British cabinet on 6 December described the 'Galway Peace Resolution' as 'the first occasion on which a Sinn Féin County Council had condemned the Sinn Féin policy of murder and outrage'. Lloyd George sent a receptive, yet firm response to Haverty's proposal, stating that negotiations could begin as soon as the IRA declared a ceasefire:

> The first necessary preliminary to the re-establishment of normal conditions is that murder and crimes of violence shall cease. It is to that end that the efforts of the Irish executive have been constantly directed, and until it has been attained no progress can be made toward a political settlement.[40]

Those who supported the 'Peace Resolution' had no authority from Dáil Éireann to enter negotiations with the British. Nor did they have the necessary influence with the IRA to compel it to accept British demands for a unilateral ceasefire as a precursor to negotiations – so it is not surprising that the political manoeuvres that grew from the 'Peace Resolution' came to nothing.

Fr Michael O'Flanagan, who had been appointed 'acting president' of Sinn Féin after Griffith's arrest, launched the next peace initiative. Shortly after the dramatic events in Galway, O'Flanagan sent a telegram to Lloyd George seeking terms: 'You state you are willing to make peace at once without waiting till Christmas. Ireland is also willing to make peace. What first step do you propose?'[41] Like Sweetman, O'Flanagan was acting on his own and held moral reservations about the IRA's military campaign.[42] However, his efforts met with more success, mainly because of his senior position within Sinn Féin and his willingness to compromise on what Phillips called 'the full republican attitude'.[43] O'Flanagan was one of the few republican separatists willing to countenance partition. He believed that Ulster unionists had excluded themselves from the

Irish nation, and republicans could not 'compel Antrim and Down to love us by force'. He believed that it would be hypocritical for Sinn Féin to condemn British coercion of Ireland while attempting to coerce the unionists of Ulster. Furthermore, O'Flanagan was also willing to consider a political settlement based on dominion status.[44]

While relatively few members of Sinn Féin and the IRA were willing to consider partition, many members of Sinn Féin at the time shared O'Flanagan's attitude towards dominion status and were willing to compromise on the demand for a republic because many were separatists seeking Irish independence, rather than idealists committed to the philosophy and ideals of Irish republicanism.[45]

Because of O'Flanagan's senior position within Sinn Féin, the British initially made the mistake of thinking he spoke with full authority and the power to negotiate as an official representative of the republican leadership. Sturgis noted with misguided optimism that O'Flanagan was 'an accredited representative ready to speak as "the man on the bridge" from Dáil Éireann'.[46] However, as time went on they developed doubts about the priest's credentials, and in early 1921 Lloyd George told Sir John Anderson that O'Flanagan represented nobody but himself and that he must deal with someone 'who could deliver the goods'. Consequently Anderson asked O'Flanagan to help him make direct contact with Éamon de Valera, leader of Sinn Féin and president of the Irish Republic, concerning negotiations.[47]

Michael Collins did not appreciate O'Flanagan's efforts to secure an IRA ceasefire, considering them to be an unjustified intrusion imposing on the efforts of others who had greater prospects of success. He publicly condemned O'Flanagan's efforts, saying: 'We must not allow ourselves to be rushed by these foolish productions or foolish people, who are tumbling over themselves to talk about a truce, when there is no truce.'[48] One contemporary recalled that Collins was extremely angry: 'He was very wroth with

Father O'Flanagan ... He said, "That ruins things for us", and he was not surprised when the negotiations broke down.'[49] Likewise, Collins told Jerry Ryan, an IRA officer from Tipperary, that the priest's meddling had prevented a political settlement being reached: 'only for Fr Flanagan [*sic*] and Galway County Council we would have a good settlement, but not a republic'.[50]

Despite the rash of peace initiatives that began in November 1920, the only endeavour that had a realistic prospect of success was that headed by Patrick Clune – the Archbishop of Perth.[51] Clune had a personal interest in Irish affairs because RIC Auxiliaries had killed his nephew, Conor Clune, on Bloody Sunday.[52] On 1 December the archbishop and his secretary, Rev. J. T. McMahon, met the British prime minister at the House of Commons. He recounted his experiences of conditions in Ireland where he had witnessed the aftermath of British reprisals, and Lloyd George asked him if he would go to Dublin and meet the leadership of Sinn Féin to arrange an IRA ceasefire as a precursor to political negotiations.[53] The archbishop agreed, and Art O'Brien forwarded a letter written by him to Collins. Collins favoured a truce and wrote to Griffith on 2 December, stating: 'My view is that a truce on the terms specified cannot possibly do us any harm. It appears to me that it is distinctly an advance.'[54] Collins was willing to support a ceasefire provided the terms were favourable to the IRA: 'It is too much to expect that Irish physical force could combat successfully English physical force for any length of time if the directors of the latter could get a free hand for ruthlessness'.[55]

Clune returned to Ireland, accompanied by Dr Fogarty, the Bishop of Killaloe, and held several meetings with Collins in Dublin. He made contact in Dublin Castle with Andy Cope, the assistant under-secretary for Ireland. Cope arranged for the clergymen to visit Griffith, MacNeill and Michael Staines, a Sinn Féin TD for Dublin, all of whom were prisoners in Mountjoy Gaol. Staines was the most militant of the republican leaders in

Mountjoy. As well as being a TD and a judge in the Dáil Éireann courts, he was an IRA officer and a veteran of the 1916 Rising.[56] Collins had told him that the archbishop was conducting truce negotiations with the endorsement of the IRA and would be visiting the prison to meet him. It is likely that Collins wanted Staines involved in the negotiations as a precaution against the possibility that Griffith and MacNeill would agree to conditions that would have been unacceptable to the IRA. Griffith also regarded Staines as the unofficial voice of the IRA rank and file during the negotiations. Staines recalled Griffith asking him, 'What I want to know is what will the fighting men think about this?' Staines replied, 'the fighting men would be quite happy for a truce, provided there was no surrender of arms'.[57]

Bishop Fogarty recalled that the republican leaders in Mountjoy Gaol were initially receptive to the peace proposal: 'We discussed the proposed truce, which Arthur Griffith welcomed with enthusiasm … Eoin MacNeill … was not so impressed, but was willing to accept it.'[58] Fogarty also claimed that Cope was enthusiastic about the prospects for a ceasefire, describing them as 'a splendid opportunity … for a final settlement'.[59] Both Griffith and Collins were prepared to advise Dáil Éireann to support a truce, provided the terms and conditions attached to it were favourable to the IRA.[60] Collins provided Clune with a general outline of the terms that would be acceptable to the republicans. These were based on a bilateral truce and a commitment that the entire republican government would be allowed to meet in public: 'If it is understood that the acts of violence (attacks, counter-attacks, reprisals, arrests, pursuits) are called off on both sides, we are agreeable to issue the necessary instructions on our side, it being understood that the entire Dáil shall be free to meet and that its peaceful activities not be interfered with.'[61]

With the initial groundwork for negotiations laid, Clune returned to London with a proposal for both sides to agree to a month-long ceasefire. He had a meeting with Lloyd George on 8 December, but quickly realised that during his absence from London the 'Galway Peace Resolution' and O'Flanagan's letter had changed the whole political situation and the British government's attitude to negotiations. After meeting Clune, Lloyd George held aloft Fr O'Flanagan's telegram and a copy of the 'Galway Peace Resolution', proclaiming, 'Dr Clune, this is the white feather and we are going to make these fellows surrender!'[62] Convinced that the republicans were desperate for a settlement, the British prime minister began to impose new demands during the peace negotiations. The British rejected the initial republican proposals delivered by Clune and insisted that TDs who were members of the IRA leadership, specifically Collins and Richard Mulcahy, could not attend the proposed public meeting of Dáil Éireann. Furthermore the British now demanded that the hierarchy of the Catholic Church and the Labour Party be involved in the peace talks.[63] Next, Lloyd George introduced the demand that the IRA would have to surrender their arms as a condition of the ceasefire. Clune objected to this, knowing it would be unacceptable to the republicans.[64] Having reached this impasse, the archbishop returned to Dublin to hold further discussions with the republican leaders in Mountjoy Gaol. Two days later Sir Hamar Greenwood publicly offered the Irish republicans an armistice in the House of Commons, on the condition that the IRA would first have to surrender its arms and turn over members of the republican leadership to the British.[65]

On 11 December the British cabinet met to discuss Clune's request for a month-long ceasefire to facilitate negotiations and drafted the following response, which Sir John Anderson was to deliver to the archbishop in Dublin:

Such a request as you make would deserve earnest consideration of H.M. Government if it was made upon the authority of the constitutional representatives of Ireland. We have already stated that we are willing to facilitate a meeting of the Irish Parliamentary representatives for this or any other purpose likely to bring about an end of the present unhappy conditions. The cessation of murderous attacks upon the loyal servants of the Crown would immediately enable constitutional discussions to begin and peace to be restored ...

1. All arms, ammunition, uniforms, explosives, in area under martial law to be surrendered to the Government.

2. All arms in the rest of Ireland to be handed over to the safe custody of Government, no distinction to be made between the rest of Ireland and Ulster.

3. Sinn Fein to order the cessation of all violence in return for which the government to stop reprisals and shop looting, raids, burnings, floggings, execution without court martial (not admitted) and people only to be executed after due court martial.

4. Sinn Fein M.P.s (except specific list) to be allowed to assemble.[66]

Rejecting the British government's proposals as too punitive, Clune sent another telegram to London, again asking for a month-long truce that did not involve a surrender of IRA arms. During the cabinet discussion that followed, Lloyd George indicated that there had been a shift in public opinion and that the British government's policies were winning the support of 'the decent public in Ireland', citing the Catholic bishop of Cork's condemnation of IRA ambushes in support of this.[67]

Clune met Sturgis and Anderson to tell them that the republicans would not agree to a surrender of arms. Anderson encouraged Clune to persevere with his efforts, stating that even if the republicans would not surrender their arms, 'an unofficial truce, a slacking off on both sides might be arranged'.[68] The archbishop responded favourably to Anderson's suggestion and stated that, if such a situation could be created over the Christmas period, it might induce the necessary conditions for a political settlement. Following his meeting with Anderson, Clune again returned to Mountjoy.[69] Griffith rejected the proposals, stating that 'there would be no surrender, no matter what frightfulness was used'.[70]

Lloyd George's hardening attitude and his insistence on IRA disarmament as a precondition of the proposed truce had by this time damaged Collins' interest in the peace negotiations, since he believed the British were taking advantage of the republicans' willingness to negotiate. On 14 December Collins wrote to Griffith, emphasising that the British terms were entirely unacceptable and that it was preferable for the IRA to continue its military campaign rather than submit to punitive terms:

> I am looking at it from an entirely utilitarian point of view. We have clearly demonstrated our willingness to have peace on honourable terms. Lloyd George insists on capitulation. Between them there is no mean; and it is only a waste of time continuing. It may make it appear that we are more anxious than they … Let Lloyd George make no mistake – the IRA is not broken.[71]

Cope held another meeting with Clune on 17 December. This meeting coincided with a communiqué from London, which reiterated that 'no truce is possible without disarmament'. Clune reported this to the republican leaders at Mountjoy, who again rejected this demand. Clune complained that the British government had 'jumped a step' and were laying down terms for a formal peace agreement while he was merely trying to arrange an informal military truce. The circular argument about the surrender of arms continued.[72]

On 21 December Clune had a meeting with Lloyd George and Andrew Bonar Law, the British Conservative leader, in London. The archbishop appealed to them to drop their demand for a surrender of IRA arms. Clune submitted to them the following proposals, drafted by Griffith and endorsed by Collins, which stated that if the British pledged to ensure their forces complied with the terms of the proposed truce, Dáil Éireann would give the same undertaking regarding the IRA:

> The British Government undertakes that during the Truce, no raids, arrests, pursuits, burnings, shootings, lootings, demolitions, courts-martial or other acts of violence will be carried out by its forces, and there will be no enforcement of the terms of martial law proclamations. We on our side undertake to use all possible means to ensure that no acts whatever of violence will occur on our side during the period of the Truce.
>
> The British Government, on their part, and we on ours, will use our best efforts to bring about the conditions above mentioned, with the object of creating an atmosphere favourable to the meeting together of the representatives of the Irish People, with a view to the bringing about of a permanent peace.[73]

On Christmas Eve Lloyd George informed the British cabinet that he had held further discussions with Clune, and the archbishop had informed him that Collins desired peace and was in earnest about a truce, but that the IRA would never surrender its arms. Clune had enquired whether this condition could be rescinded. In considering this proposal the British cabinet enquired about the current military situation in Ireland and were told that IRA arms had already been surrendered in some districts and that the British forces 'had at last definitely established the upper hand'. Consequently, senior British military officers advised the British cabinet not to do anything that might upset this new favourable military situation. The cabinet decided not to change the demand for a surrender of IRA arms and reflected on whether 'it would not be wiser to postpone any further approaches towards Sinn Fein until the Government of Ireland Act [scheduled for the summer of 1921] has been brought into operation'.[74]

Lloyd George's private discussions with Clune went on, but the issue of IRA arms continued to be the main stumbling block. On 28 December Clune outlined his final proposals for a truce to begin on New Year's Eve:

(1) Cessation of hostilities – acts of aggression and activities on both sides for the period of one month in order to create a peaceful atmosphere.

(2) The meeting of Dáil Éireann to discuss among themselves or with plenipotentiaries of the Government the final settlement of the Irish Question.[75]

Meanwhile, members of the British cabinet had further meetings with their military advisers to discuss the possibility of a truce. The British generals insisted they could crush the IRA within six weeks. Greenwood assured the prime minister: 'The SF cause and organisation is breaking up. Clune and everyone else admits this … there is no need of hurry in settlement. We can in due course and on our own good terms settle this Irish Question for good.'[76] Macready emphasised that there was a danger that an armistice would lead to a strengthening and reorganisation of the IRA. Sir Henry Wilson, chief of the Imperial General Staff, stated that a truce with the IRA 'would be absolutely fatal'. While other members of the cabinet spoke in favour of a compromise, the majority supported a continuation of the war. Accepting these military assurances, the British government rejected the republican proposals for a truce.

On New Year's Eve Lloyd George's private secretary, Philip Kerr, citing the precedent of the surrender of arms by the Boers during the Second Boer War, informed Archbishop Clune that the surrender of arms by the IRA remained an essential precondition to any proposed truce.[77] This brought an end to these negotiations, and the British cabinet did not seriously consider the prospect again until the cabinet meetings of late April and early May 1921.[78]

The Government of Ireland Act had been passed through the British parliament in December 1920. This was due to come into effect in May 1921, by which time it was envisaged that the 'Ulster Question' would be solved through partition and the creation of the new parliament of Northern Ireland, and that these measures would satisfy the Conservatives and the Ulster Unionist members of the British government. If this political situation was implemented successfully and the extremely optimistic predictions of the British government's military advisers came to pass, then Lloyd George would have much greater freedom to negotiate with Sinn Féin concerning the future of 'Southern Ireland' by May 1921. This optimistic political and military forecast was undoubtedly a factor in the British decision to end negotiations. Lloyd George's secretary spelled this out to Clune in late December 1920 when terminating the Truce negotiations, stating:

> the [British] Government had come to the conclusion that it was better to see the thing through as was done in the American and South African wars unless meanwhile the Sinn Feiners surrender their arms and publicly announce the abandonment of violent measures: that the Government felt sanguine that the new Home Rule Bill when studied and understood would be worked, in fact they felt sanguine that within six months all would be working in harmony for Ireland ...[79]

The negotiations came so close to success that one of the principal negotiators on the republican side, Michael Collins, told his comrade Liam Deasy that they 'nearly had a truce' but that General Macready had made this impossible.[80] Herbert Asquith later described it as 'the big missed opportunity'.[81]

Following the failure of the peace initiative launched in

December 1920, the prospect of a truce was briefly raised again in March 1921, when Lord Midleton, leader of the southern unionists, brought up the issue at a British cabinet meeting. This lack of interest in peace was unsurprising, given the overwhelmingly positive security reports that Lloyd George had received in the interim from Ireland, which stressed that a British victory was imminent. Lloyd George was told by Sir Henry Tudor, the inspector general of the RIC, that there had been a noticeable increase in RIC recruits, that RIC morale had been strengthened and that the public were increasingly afraid of the force, with the result that it received greater assistance from the civilian population thanks to a major change in public opinion in favour of the British authorities.[82] However, Midleton poured scorn on the prospect of an impending victory, pointing out that the rate of republican violence had tripled in just seven months. He suggested that prominent Irish businessmen and senior Catholic clergymen should be approached to act as intermediaries with Sinn Féin. Lloyd George rejected Midleton's proposal, citing the favourable reports he had received from military commanders, which suggested that the British forces would soon inflict such heavy losses on the IRA that the republican military campaign would grind to a halt before any elections were held under the Government of Ireland Act:

> We are told by our Military Advisers that by May we should have the rebellion sufficiently under control to justify going on with the elections ... Macready's view was that progress was certainly being made, but the situation was bad at the moment because the desperate men were being driven to the hills. He was confident that they could be subdued, but would not give a date.[83]

Despite the prime minister's assurances that a military victory would soon make the need for a truce redundant, Thomas Jones, deputy secretary to the British Cabinet, was sceptical of the claims made by British military advisers. Jones wrote to Bonar Law on 24 April predicting that the forthcoming elections would result in a republican landslide, necessitating either a truce with the IRA or the imposition of Crown Colony government:

> In the south the Sinn Feiners will be returned without contests. They will refuse to take the oath and the government will have to decide whether to try some sort of truce or Constituent Assembly or Crown Colony. Meanwhile no General will name a date when murder will cease and the Chief Secretary has dropped his optimism of six months ago and now talks of pacification in years rather than months.[84]

At this time an increasing number of influential people in Britain were pushing for an end to the conflict. In April Brigadier-General Francis Crozier, the former head of the RIC Auxiliary Division, wrote to *The Times* calling for a truce with the IRA. A few days later the Anglican Bishop of Chelmsford and a group of senior Protestant clergymen called for the war to end. Lloyd George rejected both appeals.[85]

At a cabinet meeting on 27 April, in an apparent volte-face from his previous position, Sir Hamar Greenwood agreed with Jones' prediction that Sinn Féin candidates would sweep the board at the elections and questioned Macready's and Tudor's claims that the British forces would regain control of the situation within three to four months. He stated bluntly that the British forces had failed 'in breaking the terror' and that a continuation of the conflict 'was not going to solve the Irish question'. Greenwood believed that the only solution was for the British government to negotiate with Sinn Féin and the best way to achieve this was by agreeing a ceasefire with the IRA beforehand. He attached two preconditions to his proposal; that Dáil Éireann would have to drop its demand for an Irish Republic and that the constitutional position of the north of Ireland would not be affected. Greenwood stressed that a British government offer to negotiate should be made in public and the military settlement should be 'a truce – not a surrender'.[86] Edwin Montagu, the secretary for India, backed Greenwood's proposal, but insisted that there should be no amnesty for wanted IRA members. Furthermore, Montagu suggested that the British should offer more generous terms than they had previously and would have to drop their demand for the IRA to surrender its arms.[87]

Sir Arthur Boscawen, Conservative Minister for Agriculture, was hostile to the idea of a truce because of the status that a formal agreement would confer on the IRA: 'I dislike the word truce, which implies they [the IRA] are belligerents whereas they are really murderers.' The cabinet's discussion on Greenwood's and Montagu's proposal for negotiations was dominated by Sinn Féin's demand for an Irish Republic; the members of the cabinet were at that stage willing to offer political and fiscal autonomy, but all were agreed that the demand for a republic was out of the question. Lloyd George suggested that there was a rift within Sinn Féin between de Valera, who was thought to be a pragmatic moderate willing to negotiate, and Collins, who was depicted as a gun-wielding fanatic who would never concede the demand for a republic. Furthermore, the prime minister stated that if the British made a public offer of a truce it would be interpreted as a sign of weakness and used by Sinn Féin 'as a base for further demands'. Lloyd George rejected an appeal for a ceasefire, citing the latest positive military report from General Strickland, commander of the British Army's 6th Division, and reiterating his belief that the IRA was 'gradually being beaten'. He claimed that a truce would be a mistake from a military standpoint as it would give the IRA 'breathing space', and so the proposal for a truce before the elections was rejected.[88]

The Government of Ireland Act came into effect on 3 May 1921 and elections were due to be held later that month for both the northern and southern Irish parliaments created by the act. With these elections looming, the British cabinet met again on 12

May. Several cabinet members were in favour of negotiating a truce with the IRA before the elections but realised that there was by then not enough time to arrange this before the poll.[89] The meeting was entirely dominated by debate over whether or not an armistice was necessary. Furthermore, there was much agonising over what terms should be offered in any potential peace manoeuvre. The issues that had arisen in the Clune negotiations re-emerged. The question of an amnesty for wanted IRA personnel was still problematic. The viceroy, Lord FitzAlan, declared that the idea of Michael Collins' involvement in negotiations to arrange a truce was wholly unacceptable.[90] Edward Shortt, the chief secretary for Ireland, was adamant that there should be no formal offer of a truce and proposed that the military campaign should continue until the IRA was forced to seek terms from the British: 'Nothing will so buck up the IRA as that we should offer a truce they have not asked for … I am against a *public* offer of truce. If they *first* say "We'll stop murder", that's a different story.'[91]

Determined that any arrangement would not confer belligerent status on the IRA, Lloyd George stated that: '[a] "Truce" is rejected by everybody … because they [the IRA] are not an honourable enemy and they have no rights'.[92] At the conclusion of the meeting Arthur Neville Chamberlain, Unionist MP for Birmingham, gave his impression of the favourable military situation in Ireland, declaring that: 'The position of the Crown forces is stronger and is improving every day. To a large extent the offer of the so-called truce would be a confession of failure.' The Liberal cabinet ministers were more sceptical, and Dr Christopher Addison, the Minister for Health, declared: 'The statement the IRA is nearly broken does not carry much weight with me. Such prophecies have been made before.' When a vote was forced on this issue, opinion on the advisability of arranging an immediate truce between the IRA and British forces was divided strictly along party political lines. Consequently, the proposal for a truce was defeated, with the nine Conservatives voting against and the five Liberals being in favour.[93]

As expected, the elections held on 22 May to appoint representatives to the new northern and southern Irish parliaments resulted in a unionist victory in the north-eastern six counties that formed the newly created political entity of Northern Ireland. Unionist candidates won forty of the available fifty-two seats there.[94] Over thirty Sinn Féin and Irish Parliamentary Party (IPP) candidates stood for election in the north, winning just six seats each.[95] In stark contrast, the 'elections' to the southern parliament resulted in a republican landslide. Not a single seat was contested, with 124 Sinn Féin candidates and four unionists being returned unopposed.[96]

Just three days after the election the IRA's Dublin Brigade launched a daring daylight operation in Dublin city, destroying the Custom House. The building was home to a number of British governmental departments for Ireland including the local government board, Inland Revenue, the estate duty control office and the stamp office. The fire that gutted the building also destroyed legal documents being prepared for the establishment of the new parliament of Northern Ireland. The event made international newspaper headlines and proved a major embarrassment to the British government.

Sinn Féin's election success had effectively ensured that the plan to establish a southern parliament was unworkable. The timetable for the implementation of the Government of Ireland Act required that the southern parliament would be established by 14 July. The British cabinet met again on 2 June and decided that, if the act could not be implemented by mid-July, Crown Colony government would be declared and martial law enforced throughout the twenty-six counties of southern Ireland. This would be accompanied by an increase in the number of British troops stationed in Ireland and a military surge against the IRA.[97]

However, by this stage Britain's military and political policies in Ireland were being met with increasing local and international opposition. The British forces had the capacity to absorb the losses inflicted on them by the IRA, but as long as the war continued and British casualties mounted, so did British public opposition to the conflict. During the First World War Lloyd George told the editor of *The Guardian*: 'If people really knew [what was happening] the war would be stopped tomorrow ... But of course they don't and they can't know. The correspondents don't write, and the censorship would not pass the truth.'[98] The problem for the British government was that the British public knew exactly what was happening in Ireland in 1921. English journalists such as Hugh Martin and Wilfrid Ewart were able to record with authority events in Ireland, including British reprisals and assassinations, and their reports were serialised in British newspapers.[99] The censor was powerless to stop them. Furthermore, photojournalism had become an important part of the press and was used to record the aftermath of British reprisals.[100] The intense press coverage of events in Ireland exposed British methods and tactics that were normally obscured by distance, indifference and ignorance, at a time when the British public assumed that British colonial policing and military campaigns were conducted for the noblest motives and employing the highest moral standards.[101]

The fact that some of the conflict's major events, including the hunger strike of Terence MacSwiney, his funeral procession and the funerals of British officers killed at Kilmichael and on Bloody Sunday, occurred in London heightened the British public's consciousness of what was happening in Ireland.[102] Developments in Ireland were relayed to London within a few hours, and the opposition in the House of Commons (Labour, 'Asquith Liberals' and a handful of Irish nationalist MPs) used this information to great effect. Government ministers frequently had to reply to opposition questions without full knowledge of the facts and were then embarrassed when a more accurate and detailed version of events subsequently emerged.[103] Hamar Greenwood reported that press reports from Ireland caused dismay in the British cabinet: 'A sensational Press upsets their nerves & makes them impatient, first clamorous for stern measures and then screams itself into hysterics when it sees what stern measures mean in practice.'[104] The republicans also proved particularly adept at propaganda and soliciting international sympathy for their cause. Their newssheet, *The Irish Bulletin*, was produced five times a week in several languages and became increasingly popular in India, Egypt and other restless British territories. Excerpts were even published in influential British newspapers, including *The Times*.[105] By June 1921 the republicans had established official press bureaux in several European capitals, including Berlin, Madrid, Paris and Rome. These ensured that British reprisals in Ireland were widely reported in the international press.[106]

The United States were also keeping a close eye on developments. While de Valera's tour of the country from June 1919 to December 1920 failed in its objective to secure American recognition for the Irish Republic, it succeeded in rallying Irish-Americans, who purchased several million dollars' worth of Republican Bonds, effectively bankrolling the republican political and military campaigns. De Valera's trip also garnered significant political and media attention for events in Ireland.[107]

By May 1921 republican influence extended far beyond Europe and the Irish diaspora in America. The republicans had established consulates in several commonwealth countries, including Australia, New Zealand and Canada, as well as the United States and a number of South American countries, including Chile and Argentina. One of the most successful republican diplomatic initiatives was South Africa, where the republican envoys enlisted the sympathy of Jan Smuts, the South African premier. At the British Commonwealth Conference in May 1921, Smuts publicly expressed his opposition to British policy in Ireland, making a direct appeal to Lloyd George to negotiate with the Irish republicans by offering them dominion status.

The actions of the British forces were eroding the support of loyalists in southern Ireland for British rule. During the conflict, members of the British military and British RIC recruits never fully grasped who their enemy was. On the one hand they claimed that the IRA had little or no popular support and held sway over the local populace through terrorism; on the other, British troops purportedly charged with 'the restoration of order' readily destroyed private homes and businesses, and killed Irish civilians on the assumption that most of the populace were in league with the enemy and should suffer to atone for IRA activity. This mindset was probably best expressed by Major Bernard Law Montgomery:

> We were not ... [in] close contact with the loyalists ... we did not appreciate their suffering ... Personally, my whole attention was given to defeating the rebels and it never bothered me a bit how many houses were burned. I think I regarded all civilians as 'Shinners', and I never had any dealings with any of them.[108]

The fact that Montgomery was stationed in Cork, which had a very large loyalist population, shows that the British forces' approach to the civilian population in the most active rebel areas was completely ham-fisted and counter-productive. Many neutral civilians, supporters of Home Rule, and even some moderate southern unionists, were driven to support militant republicanism as a result of indiscriminate British reprisals. One loyalist recalled that: 'With the rebels ... you had known where you stood, whereas the Black and Tans ... did not know a unionist from a Republican and hardly bothered to make the distinction.'[109] 'The O'Conor Don', a prominent loyalist landowner, reacted to reprisals by stating, 'Tell Mr Lloyd George, if the Government don't turn these damned Black and Tans out of the country we'll soon all be damned republicans.'[110]

The prospect of continuing a long and costly war with the IRA and the risk of further major political embarrassment on both the domestic and international fronts was important in convincing the British government that a truce with the IRA and political negotiations with Sinn Féin were necessary.[111] Arthur Balfour's unionist opposition to any settlement with the republicans weakened as the conflict wore on: 'Naturally we should wish to end this uphill, sordid, unchivalrous, loathsome conflict – we are sick of it!'[112] Winston Churchill, who had previously championed the Black and Tans and defended British reprisals, now advised that it was 'Of great public interest to get a respite in Ireland [which is damaging] the interests of this country all over the world; we are getting an odious reputation; poisoning our relations with the United States.'[113] Lloyd George later described the situation in Ireland as 'a feud that was costly and embarrassing to us, a feud that brought no credit, no honour and no strength'.[114]

By this time the British Army was in crisis because of a shortage of manpower caused by Britain's international military commitments and an increased demand for troops to quell insurgencies throughout the Empire. The demand for manpower was unprecedented in peacetime; never before had British military resources been stretched so thinly across much of the globe.[115] The end of the First World War was followed by a rapid reduction in the size of the British military. In the twelve months following the end of that conflict the strength of the British Army was reduced from 3,779,825 men to 888,952.[116] By November 1920 the number of troops was reduced further to 369,710.[117] In 1922 the total strength of the British Army was just 218,000 men – far lower than its pre-war strength in 1914.[118] While the British armed forces were rapidly being reduced, the British Empire was enlarged following the Treaty of Versailles by the addition of former German and Ottoman territories, including Palestine and Mesopotamia.[119] Moreover, the British Army had committed troops to the occupation of the Rhineland and had intervened in the Russian Civil War.[120]

In the autumn of 1920 the prospect of rebellion in Egypt resulted in a request for troops to be transferred there from Ireland. General Macready refused this on the grounds that any reduction in military strength in Ireland would ultimately result in a British withdrawal. Following the outbreak of rebellion in Mesopotamia in July 1920, the War Office transferred nineteen battalions (approx. 13,300 troops) from the British-Indian Army to bolster the already 50,000 strong British-Indian garrison there. The transfer of such a large number of troops was considered detrimental to security policy in India, but was deemed absolutely necessary because there were no regular British Army reinforcements available. An appeal was made to 'white' British dominions for additional troops, but only New Zealand could offer assistance.[121] Though the situation had been at its worst in mid-1920 and improved slowly after that, it had still not been fully resolved by the summer of 1921. In mid-1921 the British Army still had 20,000 troops stationed in Egypt, more than three times the number of pre-war troops that had been stationed there.[122] At the same time, the military situation in Palestine began to worsen and was a further drain on the increasingly limited British military resources.[123]

Social unrest in Britain also needed soldiers as an auxiliary force in support of the police. British soldiers had been used to break the Welsh coal miners' strike. Industrial unrest and demonstrations by unemployed ex-soldiers were common, and social upheaval within Britain was considered a real possibility. The availability of a reserve of troops to prevent upheaval on the home front was considered a priority by the British Army's imperial general staff, with Sir Henry Wilson warning Churchill that 'we must secure our base first'.[124] In April 1921 the threat posed by 'Sinn Feiners, Communists and other dangerous elements' at home was considered so great that the British cabinet sanctioned the transfer of eight battalions (approx. 5,600 troops) from operations in Upper Silesia, Malta and Egypt to bolster the level of troops in Britain.[125] In a desperate attempt to address the shortage of troops, the age of enlistment was reduced from eighteen to seventeen years, but the standard of recruits this measure netted was considered very poor and this change did nothing to solve the critical shortage of troops with technical skills including wireless operators, motorcyclists, telegraphists and drivers.[126] In July 1920 General Macready complained that 'many [of the soldiers in Ireland] were young and untrained, and if the strain were doubled you would get very near the danger limit'.[127] The shortage of British reinforcements resulted in the deployment of 800 Royal Navy marines to garrison Irish coastguard stations in May 1920. It was an unprecedented development for naval troops to be committed to on-shore military operations. As the situation deteriorated, the RIC was used increasingly in this role, and in June 1921 a further two battalions of Royal Marines were trained for deployment in Ireland.[128]

By the summer of 1921 the military situation in Ireland was a huge drain on Britain's increasingly limited military resources. There was always the very real possibility that the longer the IRA's military campaign continued, the greater was the prospect that another, similar insurrection could erupt in India, Egypt or elsewhere, for which insufficient troops would be available.[129] Sir Henry Wilson commented:

> We have definite evidence of a worldwide conspiracy fomented by all the elements most hostile to British interests – Sinn Feiners and Socialists at our own doors, Russian Bolsheviks, Turkish and Egyptian nationalists and Indian seditionists. Up to the present time we have been lucky in not having experienced trouble in more than one theatre at the same time.[130]

Apart from the shortage of manpower, the British forces in Ireland were also beset by a rapid decline in morale. Figures for 1920 and 1921 show that 5 per cent of the RIC's total strength (including members of the Auxiliary Division and Black and Tans) had been killed and a further 8 per cent wounded in IRA attacks. The conditions of the conflict and the lack of any respite for members of the RIC had a devastating effect on the force's morale.

A strong indicator of this was the rapidly increasing suicide rate among members of the force. Before the War of Independence, suicide by members of the force was a relatively unknown phenomenon. By 1920 the suicide rate within the RIC had reached 36.36 per 100,000 compared to an average rate of suicide among the civilian population in Britain and Ireland at the time of 5.45 per 100,000. The following year, the RIC suicide rate climbed to 88.88 per 100,000.[131] This was a significant escalation of an already high rate. These increasing rates indicate that the psychological stresses on the RIC during the War of Independence were far greater than those on British military units on the north-western frontier or in Iraq in the same period, as those troops experienced a far lower suicide rate.[132] The RIC district inspector for Lurgan in Co. Armagh, which was then one of the least disturbed counties, reported in January 1921: 'I submit that regular warfare would be less trying than the condition of affairs that prevails at present.'[133]

The situation was little better for British soldiers stationed in Ireland, who experienced social isolation, confinement to barracks, low morale and the stresses resulting from the guerrilla conflict. As an example of this, at least four British soldiers stationed in Co. Clare committed suicide. The real figure may be higher, as these suicides were referred to euphemistically in the press as 'accidental shootings'.[134] The rate of desertion among British troops stationed in Ireland is a further indication of how low their morale was. By 1921 the rate of desertion was up to seven times greater than among their counterparts stationed in Britain (see Table 2.1). By the summer of 1921 Macready warned that the stress on all ranks was 'incomparably greater than ... in time of actual war', and this was having a detrimental effect on British military capability in Ireland.[135]

Table 2.1: Desertion among British soldiers, by month, January to July 1921[136]

Month	Total number of deserters	Number of deserters in Ireland	Number of deserters in Britain
January 1921	70	43	27
February 1921	56	45	11
March 1921	60	53	7
April 1921	79	61	18
May 1921	74	57	17
June 1921	Unavailable	Unavailable	Unavailable
July 1921	56	48	8

Initially, the British authorities had held an optimistic view of the military situation in Ireland based on reports that IRA activity was confined to only a few counties, and the perception that this was manageable and that it was only a matter of time before the British forces restored order. In May 1920 Hamar Greenwood dismissed the IRA as a small band of 'thugs' hired by Michael Collins with funds from Irish factions in America to cause trouble in Cork, Dublin and Limerick. When the British cabinet sanctioned martial law in Munster, Lloyd George assured its members: 'There have been twelve counties in Ireland in which there has been no murder.' Hamar Greenwood felt confident enough to tell the British cabinet that the IRA in Counties Cork, Galway and Tipperary had fled to the hills in desperation and that most of Ireland was unaffected by violence. As late as April 1921, General Macready was advising members of the British cabinet that 'the situation was bad at the moment because the desperate men were being driven into the hills', but British forces would regain control of the situation thereafter.

However, the constant reassurances from senior British officers that the pacification of Ireland was imminent became increasingly hollow as their deadlines for British military victory were constantly breached. Consequently, the British cabinet had become more sceptical of such assurances by the summer of 1921.[137] In preparation for the imposition of Crown Colony government and martial law throughout southern Ireland, the total strength of the British forces in the country was increased by about a third through the deployment of an additional seventeen infantry battalions between 14 June and 7 July.[138] These reinforcements brought the total strength of British military forces in Ireland to approximately 80,000, including Royal Flying Corps and Royal Marines, and 15,000 police, including regular RIC, Dublin Metropolitan Police (DMP), Black and Tans and members of the RIC Auxiliary Division.

Even with this military surge, the assurances of the British government's military advisers that the British forces were on the brink of victory were sounding increasingly hollow by the summer of 1921 as the IRA continued to intensify their campaign (see Table 2.2). The various military measures enacted by the British, including the deployment of the Black and Tans and RIC Auxiliaries, the imposition of martial law, and the policies of executing captured republicans and instituting official reprisals had failed to halt the intensification and spread of the IRA's military campaign. Between 21 January 1919 and 31 May 1921 the IRA killed approximately 367 members of the various British police forces in Ireland including the DMP, the regular RIC, Black and Tans, RIC Auxiliaries and Special Constabulary.[139] In the same period at least 147 members of the British Army, the Royal Marines and the Coastguard were also killed in Ireland.[140]

Table 2.2: British fatalities and IRA 'outrages' by month, January 1919 to June 1921[141]

Month	RIC and DMP fatalities	British military fatalities	Total reported 'outrages'
January 1919	2	0	198
February 1919	0	0	285
March 1919	0	0	168
April 1919	1	0	258
May 1919	2	0	256
June 1919	1	0	250
July 1919	1	0	298
August 1919	2	0	349
September 1919	2	1	346
October 1919	2	0	353
November 1919	1	0	437
December 1919	1	0	483
January 1920	4	0	600
February 1920	2	1	659
March 1920	7	1	Figures unavailable
April 1920	12	1	Figures unavailable
May 1920	12	0	1,400
June 1920	7	0	1,180
July 1920	15	6	1,760
August 1920	16	4	1,324
September 1920	23	4	1,283
October 1920	27	15	1,422
November 1920	37	23	1,335
December 1920	17	5	1,483
January 1921	25	2	1,234
February 1921	36	14	1,283
March 1921	34	34	1,698
April 1921	25	7	1,867
May 1921	54	27	2,188
June 1921	40	20	2,256

The rate of attrition in the war was slowly increasing in favour of the IRA. In the first five months of 1921 the IRA killed 175 members of the RIC – a total almost equal to the annual figure of RIC fatalities for the year 1920.[142] In the same period, eighty-four members of the British Army, British Secret Service, Royal Marines and Coastguard were killed, far exceeding the annual total of sixty-two British troops killed in Ireland the previous year.[143] The month of May saw the highest number of casualties inflicted on the British forces in the entire war, with fifty-five members of the RIC and twenty-eight British soldiers killed by the IRA in that month alone.[144] On top of all this, the number of reported 'outrages' – i.e. IRA ambushes, attacks on RIC barracks, sabotage, arson attacks, agrarian violence, defiance of British proclamations, etc. – continued to rise, forcing Greenwood to admit on 6 June that the previous few months had seen 'a very marked increase in rebel military activity throughout the whole country'.[145]

While the IRA's Dublin Brigade was in difficulty and the IRA nationally were suffering from a shortage of arms and ammunition, analysis of the military situation in the summer of 1921 shows that, despite a military stalemate having set in in some parts of the south-west, the IRA nationally were capable of continuing their military campaign for the foreseeable future.[146] General Macready wrote to the British cabinet on 23 May 1921, stating, 'I am convinced that by October unless a peaceful solution has been reached, it will not be safe to ask the troops to continue there another winter under the conditions which obtained during the last.' His pessimism was shared by many of his fellow officers. Major General Douglas Wimberley of the Cameron Highlanders feared that a draconian suppression of the IRA's military campaign would only be a temporary victory and would not destroy the republican insurrection:

The British government in July 1921 decided to treat and compromise with the rebel leaders. To my mind this was the only course open to them, for though no doubt we, in the Army, given the powers of life and death, and [an] official policy of ruthlessness, could easily have quelled the actual active Sinn Féin revolt, by means of really stern measures backed by the British Government, I feel certain the discontent would merely have smouldered underground. It would have burst into flames as soon as we withdrew. The really brutal measures which Cumberland and his army took in Scotland in 1745, finally to crush the rising there, would never have been tolerated by public opinion in Britain in 1921![147]

Brigade Major Bernard Law Montgomery of the 17th Infantry Brigade was also convinced of the need for more draconian measures to secure victory, but was as sceptical as Wimberley about political and public support for such measures, and ultimately concluded that negotiation was necessary:

My own view is that to win a war of this sort you need to be ruthless. Oliver Cromwell or the Germans would have settled it in a very short time. Nowadays public opinion precludes such methods, the nation would never allow it and the politicians would lose their jobs if they sanctioned it … if we had gone on we could probably have squashed the rebellion as a temporary measure, but it would have broken out again like an ulcer the moment we removed the troops. I think the rebels would probably have refused battles, and hidden away their arms, etc., until we had gone. The only way therefore was to give them some form of self-government.[148]

Basil Thomson, head of the British Police Special Branch Irish Division, warned the British government:

It cannot be conscientiously said that any headway has been made against the Irish Republican Army and there is a feeling among the people that Sinn Féin will win. This feeling is due to the increased prestige gained by Sinn Féin owing to its success in guerrilla warfare especially in the martial law areas. The fear of reprisals is not so great now. The country folk who were opposed to the operations of the Irish Republican Army in their localities do not now mind and although they are for the most part against the murders of individuals they are in favour of ambushes. They are beginning to be proud of the Irish heroes who have gained such victories over the Crown forces in spite of all the restrictions imposed by martial law.[149]

Lloyd George put on a brave front, declaring to the House of Commons on 21 June that 'the British would continue the war, whatever sacrifice, to prevent Irish independence'.[150] However, the British were no closer to defeating the IRA than they had been a year previously. In effect the IRA was winning the war, because to them, their survival meant success. As Henry Kissinger later put it: 'The guerrilla wins if he does not lose. The conventional army loses if it does not win.'[151] As long as the IRA existed, the British government's administration could not function in Ireland – the British forces in Ireland were effectively losing the war because their mission was to restore peaceful conditions under British rule. This was only possible through the complete destruction of the IRA. Therefore the war has to be regarded to an extent as a victory for the republicans because of Britain's inability to destroy the IRA after two and a half years of conflict. The British government had little choice but to broker a meaningful truce to end the conflict as a first step towards negotiating a political agreement with Sinn Féin, because they were not in a position to impose a settlement.

By the summer of 1921 the British authorities in Dublin found it difficult, because of the military situation, to keep their channels of communication with Sinn Féin open. The chief problem they faced was that they were unable to make direct contact with de Valera and instead had to draw conclusions based on interviews he gave to the international press.[152] On 14 June 1921 Tom Casement, brother of the republican leader Roger Casement who was executed after the 1916 Rising, met de Valera in Dublin and succeeded in putting him in direct contact with Jan Smuts, the South African prime minister and former Boer rebel. Casement was a personal friend of Smuts and both had a personal interest in Irish politics.[153] De Valera told the South African leader that he was willing to negotiate with the British but stressed the importance of a military truce between the IRA and British forces before any negotiations could begin.[154] Smuts wrote to Lloyd George on the same day telling him that the situation in Ireland was 'an unmeasured calamity' for the British Empire. He urged Lloyd George to begin negotiations, pointing out that the establishment of the northern parliament effectively copper-fastened partition and would remove this thorny issue from any discussions. Finally, Smuts proposed that the king's speech at the opening of the northern parliament should be used to extend an olive branch to the republicans.[155]

The British government was facing a deadline of mid-July, by which time it either had to enforce 'the restoration of order in Ireland' with unprecedented draconian military measures, or begin political negotiations with Sinn Féin, which they knew would be conditional on a formal military truce with the IRA.[156] The government's Irish Situation Committee met on 15 June and was given a detailed report by General Macready on the military measures that would be necessary if political agreement had not been reached by the mid-July deadline, when Crown Colony government was due to be imposed. Under Macready's proposals, any damage to British government property would be recovered through a levy on the surrounding district. All cars, motorcycles and privately owned motor transport were to be seized, all ports would be closed and compulsory identification cards were to be introduced. Membership of Dáil Éireann, the IRA and IRB was to be considered treason punishable by death, and those caught with arms or ammunition would be tried by a military court martial and hanged. Anyone caught using arms against British forces would be summarily executed without trial. The general estimated that another twenty battalions of British troops would be needed to restore British authority and as many as 100 republicans a week would have to be executed. Macready warned that even if these measures were imposed it still might not be enough to defeat the IRA and could 'land this country deeper in the mire … Anything short of these extreme measures, the present situation might go on for such time that political pressures or political change will cause us to abandon the country and we shall be beaten.' Macready summed up the situation as 'It must be all out or another policy.'[157]

Privately, Macready was willing to admit that a negotiated end to the conflict was the only viable option. On 20 June 1921 he wrote to Lloyd George's secretary, Frances Stevenson, stating that he was not convinced that draconian measures would succeed in quashing the insurrection, or that the British public was willing to support them:

> There are, of course, one or two wild people about who still hold the absurd idea that if you go on killing long enough peace will ensue. I do not believe it for one moment, but I do believe that the more people that are killed, the more difficult will be the final solution, unless while killing is going on a body of opinion is growing up imbued with a strong idea that the Government have made a generous and definite offer to Ireland.[158]

Acting on the suggestion of Smuts and several influential figures in Britain, King George V used his speech at the opening of the northern parliament to call for peace. Privately, the king also urged the British cabinet to capitalise on the favourable atmosphere generated by his speech to begin negotiations with Sinn Féin.[159] By coincidence, on the same date that the king addressed the opening of the northern parliament, the British military arrested de Valera in Dublin. When Lloyd George learned of de Valera's arrest, he ordered his immediate release.[160] De Valera was at that time regarded by the British prime minister as a pragmatist and one of the 'moderates' within Sinn Féin who would be key to negotiations.[161] The day after de Valera's release, Lloyd George wrote to him and James Craig, the northern unionist leader, inviting them to attend negotiations in London. Lord Midleton, who debated the necessity for a truce with Lloyd George a short time later, recalled that even at this late stage the British government was anxious to avoid a formal military truce with the IRA, and its primary objective was to get de Valera to agree to talks, in the hope that an informal cessation of military activities would take place as a result of this.[162]

Craig refused Lloyd George's invitation to the London conference. De Valera replied to Lloyd George on 28 June stating that he had been in consultation with 'the principal representatives of our nation as are available' (i.e. the Sinn Féin TDs who had not been imprisoned by the British forces) and that they were eager to negotiate a lasting peace. However, de Valera stressed that he wanted to meet with unionist leaders in Dublin before giving a final formal acceptance to the invitation. De Valera then wrote to Craig and four of the leading southern unionists – Lord Midleton, Sir Maurice Woods, Sir Robert Dockrell and Andrew Jameson – inviting them to a conference in Dublin.[163] Tom Casement and Smuts' private secretary arrived in Dublin to continue discussions with de Valera, and Casement suggested to Cope that, as a sign of good faith, the British authorities should release five Sinn Féin TDs – Arthur Griffith, Eoin MacNeill, Michael Staines, Éamon Duggan and Robert Barton – from prison to enable them to take part in the negotiations.[164] The release of these five was an important step, given that Griffith, MacNeill and Staines had all been party to previous attempts to negotiate a ceasefire, and that Duggan and Barton, as well as being TDs, were also senior IRA officers. Duggan in particular had worked closely with Michael Collins until his arrest.[165]

Craig refused de Valera's invitation to talks in Dublin, but the four southern unionist leaders had a meeting with him and Griffith at the Mansion House on 4 July. De Valera implored the unionists to persuade Craig to come to Dublin to engage in negotiations, but they replied that they could not convince him to attend. De Valera agreed in principle with the unionists' suggestion that he should go to London and begin negotiations with Lloyd George in spite of Craig's absence, but he stressed the need for a truce before he would commit to talks, adding that he 'did not believe negotiations could well go forward while the two sides were actively engaged in war'.[166] The southern unionists agreed with de Valera on the need for an armistice and undertook to secure an offer of a truce from the British government if de Valera ensured that the IRA would observe any arrangements. At Jameson's suggestion, Lord Midleton travelled to London to secure Lloyd George's support for a truce and the conference was adjourned for four days pending his response. Midleton reported to Lloyd George:

> Mr de Valera was willing to accept the Prime Minister's proposal … Mr de Valera [also] recognises the necessity of stopping all fighting and action likely to produce feeling between the contending parties during the progress of negotiations. He is willing to sign the formula adopted last December if the Government are willing to do the same.[167]

Midleton's mention of 'the formula adopted last December' is a reference to the previous terms that had been proposed by Archbishop Clune whereby a formal, public and bilateral truce would be implemented between the IRA and the British forces before the start of political negotiations; that members of the IRA, Dáil Éireann and Sinn Féin would not be subject to arrest or execution during a truce; and that a surrender of IRA arms was not a precondition of such an arrangement. The truce arrangements agreed in July 1921 were remarkably similar to these.

Midleton returned to Dublin and met de Valera, Griffith, Barton, Duggan and the other three southern unionists.[168] He reported that he had met with 'some difficulty' in getting Lloyd George to agree to a formal truce between the IRA and the British forces, but that the prime minister was willing to do it if it was approved by the British military authorities in Ireland.[169] After receiving this news the conference adjourned at 1 p.m. to enable the southern unionists to approach General Macready and ask him to secure British military agreement for a formal truce. The unionist delegation gave Macready a letter that had been received from Lloyd George and which suggested that 'as soon as we hear that Mr de Valera is prepared to enter into conference with the British government and cease all acts of violence we should give instructions to the troops and to the police to suspend active operations against those who are engaged in this unfortunate conflict'.[170]

General Macready agreed to draft truce terms and submitted these to the Mansion House conference when it reconvened at 4 p.m. that afternoon. Macready then contacted Cope, General Boyd, commanding officer of the British military in the Dublin district, and General Tudor, who commanded the RIC, and all of them agreed to the Truce.[171] At 5.30 p.m. Midleton again contacted Macready, asking if he would agree to minor changes to the terms suggested by de Valera. In response to this message Macready departed for the Mansion House and there announced his approval of the Truce at the peace conference. Final agreement on the terms of the Truce was reached at 8 p.m. on Friday 8 July, and Macready returned to the Royal Hospital in Kilmainham to telephone the result to Lloyd George in Downing Street.

The terms of the Truce were far more favourable to the IRA than those the British government had offered in December 1920, and this represented a significant gain for the Irish republicans.[172] The republicans had secured a number of concessions from the British, which effectively conferred 'belligerent status' on the IRA as lawful 'combatants' in a 'legitimate army'.[173] Initially, the British had opposed any formal public armistice with the IRA and had proposed the public announcement of a formal IRA ceasefire, which would be followed by a private informal British undertaking to follow suit. However, the republicans refused to enter negotiations without first securing a bilateral ceasefire and were adamant in rejecting anything short of a formal public truce, and the Anglo-Irish Truce agreed in July 1921 was a formal public agreement between the IRA leadership and the British military command in Ireland. The demand for a surrender of IRA arms, which had proved the main stumbling block to agreeing a ceasefire previously, was quietly dropped by the British, who also stopped insisting that there could be no amnesty for senior IRA officers and that they had the right to execute IRA prisoners after the ceasefire began. The release of senior republican leaders from prison to facilitate the Truce negotiations and the direct involvement of IRA officers in its final agreement are further examples of just how much the British government had conceded to the Irish republicans in six months.

Had the IRA agreed to halt their military campaign on such unfavourable terms as dictated by the British in December 1920 it would have been tantamount to surrender and an admission of British victory. However the failure of the British forces to defeat the IRA and restore order in Ireland, and the continued escalation of the IRA campaign in the spring and summer of 1921, forced the British to reach a more generous agreement with the IRA, which was negotiating from a position of relative strength. Irish republicans recognised that the favourable terms of the Truce they had secured were an embarrassment to the British government, and Sinn Féin and the IRA were eager to publicise their victory. P. S. O'Hegarty, a member of Sinn Féin at the time, later wrote:

To grasp the full magnitude of it, one only has to compare the terms of the Irish Truce with the terms of the Armistice which Germany accepted at the close of the Great War. She [Germany] had to surrender her arms, surrender territory, and submit to many humiliations. She was treated as a vanquished enemy. Whereas we, on the other hand, were treated as England's equal, and agreed to no conditions for our Volunteers which England did not also agree to for her army.[174]

By continuing their military campaign the republicans had secured favourable terms, which applied equally to their opponents. The first editorial of the IRA newspaper, *An t-Óglach*, published after the Truce said: 'The guns are silent – but they remain in the hands of the Irish Volunteers. From the military point of view we remain exactly where we were; we have lost no advantage.'[175]

The British were conscious that they had ceded a propaganda victory to the republicans by consenting to a public military agreement with the IRA. They attempted to downplay the significance of the Truce retrospectively. Reflecting their earlier hesitation to come to a formal agreement with the IRA, the British made a conscious effort to avoid references to it as a truce, and where the word was used in the British Army's *Record of the Rebellion in Ireland* it was usually placed in inverted commas. British officers preferred to use more ambiguous terms to describe the event. Colonel Maxwell Scott was at pains to explain his contention that 'the words "truce" and "armistice" had no application in the situation where one side [the IRA] had no belligerent rights'.[176] Major General Sir Hugh Jeudwine wrote to his subordinate officers proscribing the use of the term 'Truce':

The word 'Truce' has been applied to this Agreement and the situation which follows from it. This word is generally understood to be applicable to an armistice between recognised belligerents. It is preferable, therefore, that it should not be used by us in this instance, but that the statement of terms should be referred to as the 'Agreement' and its effects as a 'suspension of activities'.[177]

In his memoirs, General Macready attempted to muddy the waters further. While he was willing to refer to the agreement as 'the Truce', he made the false claim that it had a limited geographical scope and that its terms did not apply in the north of Ireland. 'As time went on it was claimed by Sinn Féin that Ulster was included in the terms of the Truce, an absurd insinuation, but in keeping with the vanity and native inaccuracy of the Southern Irish.'[178] This, of course, was nonsense, and Macready knew it, but he was prepared to twist the truth in an attempt to save face.

These efforts to undermine the status of both the Truce and the IRA as participants can best be understood as the actions of military officers who guarded their status jealously, held a supremacist world-view and were used to expressing contempt for their adversaries, whom they frequently dismissed as 'savages'. Their effort to demean the Truce was a statement against both their enemies and their political leaders, whom they felt had failed them.[179]

However, the protestations of senior British officers counted for little when compared to the fact that the Anglo-Irish Truce had been reported to the League of Nations by the British government. This action gave *de facto*, and probably also *de jure*, legitimacy to the IRA as a belligerent army, because an army can only conduct a formal agreement with an equal counterpart.[180] By agreeing a formal truce with the IRA in 1921 the British government effectively recognised the legitimacy of its actions in the preceding years and this legitimacy was copper-fastened when the British later granted amnesty from prosecution for all IRA activities which occurred before the 'operation of the Truce'.[181] Commenting on the situation in Ireland, Lloyd George had famously declared, 'You don't declare war on rebels'; and following this logic he could equally have proclaimed, 'You don't agree peace with a murder gang.'

British references to the IRA as a 'murder gang' soon evaporated, however, and the RIC's *Weekly Summary* newssheet published on the morning of the Truce committed a serious *faux pas* in British eyes by referring to the IRA as 'the Irish Army'.[182]

THE DISSEMINATION OF NEWS ABOUT THE TRUCE

Any analysis of the impact that the announcement of the Truce had on the final days of the military campaigns of the IRA and British forces has first to establish when combatants throughout Ireland learned that a ceasefire was imminent. This is crucial in assessing whether the announcement led to a flurry of IRA attacks on their civilian opponents and British forces, or if these attacks were entirely coincidental and would have occurred regardless of the announcement.

One historian has speculated that the British forces may have known that a ceasefire was imminent as early as May 1921.[183] In fact, the rank and file of the British forces, like their opponents in the IRA, had little or no forewarning that an armistice was imminent. Some senior British officers in Dublin may have been aware of the secret political negotiations – but there was no guarantee that these would result in any military or political arrangements. British historian Charles Townshend has shown that 'From the [British] military standpoint, an armistice during the summer season still represented the height of unwisdom. A truce was not therefore a foregone conclusion when de Valera opened a Dáil conference on 5 July.'[184] General Macready's memoirs also express the doubt and uncertainty that existed, even among the highest echelons in the British forces, over whether a truce could be agreed, saying, 'I had no official information on the subject, nor did I place much faith in it in view of the repeated failures of such conferences in the past.'[185]

Despite the modern radio and telegraph communications available to the British forces, it took some time for news of the Truce to reach their more isolated outposts. This is not surprising given the rate at which news of the Armistice spread among Allied units on the Western Front on 11 November 1918. The Allied communication network during the First World War would have been more reliable and subject to less enemy interference than that used by the British forces in Ireland in 1921, yet some Allied units on the Western Front did not receive a ceasefire order until 4.15 p.m. on 11 November – over five hours after the ceasefire came into effect.[186] In other theatres of that conflict it took even longer to spread news of the ceasefire. Some combatants in German East Africa did not learn about the Armistice in Europe until 25 November, two weeks after the war had officially ended.[187] The experience of the First World War and the widespread republican disruption of the British communications network in Ireland were probably important considerations in delaying the beginning of the Truce for three days after it had been agreed.

The headquarters of the British 5th Division received notification of the Truce by telephone at 10.30 p.m. on Friday 8 July, several hours after it had been agreed.[188] Other British units received less notice. Members of the Oxford and Buckinghamshire Light Infantry learned of the Truce while on manoeuvres in Tipperary the following day.[189] Likewise, Douglas V. Duff, a Black and Tan stationed in Galway city, only received thirty-six hours' notice. After 10 p.m. on 9 July, Duff and his comrades left Galway by boat to assist the Royal Marine garrison at Ballyvaughan coastguard station, which was under attack.[190] Duff first learned of the Truce from Marine W. A. Mungham, a member of the station's garrison who had been shot in the thigh during the attack: 'one of the wounded marines told us they had received a wireless message that a truce had been arranged between the Government and Sinn Féin to become operative within forty-eight hours. We could not believe it.'[191] A detachment of the Buffs Regiment, stationed at Castletownroche, Co. Cork, received news of the Truce about the same time by carrier pigeon.[192]

The official history of the British Army's 5th Division indicates that their IRA opponents were generally unaware that an armistice was imminent, and states that the reason for the three-day delay in implementing the agreement was 'in order to give the rebel leaders time to get instructions out to their own people'.[193] Gossip, press speculation and rumours of a ceasefire had been circulating within the ranks of the Dublin IRA for some time, but by July 1921 these were given little credence. IRA Volunteer Todd Andrews recalled hearing rumours of a ceasefire as early as November 1920 and dismissed these as a British ploy to weaken IRA morale, because 'No one wants to risk death if peace is in sight.'[194] Seán Prendergast, a member of the 1st Battalion of the IRA's Dublin Brigade, described the announcement of the Truce as 'a bolt from the blue'.[195] James Fulham, a member of the 4th Battalion, was equally taken by surprise: 'We had no idea then that there was a Truce near. I don't think any Volunteers had any idea of a Truce at this time.'[196] Joseph O'Connor, commandant of the 3rd Battalion of the IRA's Dublin Brigade, recalled that while 'various peace rumours … were circulated through the city' he did not receive official notification of the Truce from IRA GHQ until a few hours after it had been formally agreed, and had continued planning attacks on the British forces until then in ignorance of political developments.[197] Michael Collins was aware of the speculation within the republican ranks concerning an armistice and felt it was damaging morale. He made a deliberate decision to keep the IRA rank and file in the dark and sent a curt message to members of the Dublin Brigade, ordering them to 'Stop talking and get on with the work.'[198]

Some provincial IRA units had read press reports speculating that a truce was being arranged but they dismissed these as baseless. Tom Barry, the leader of the 3rd Cork Brigade's flying column, had been hearing peace rumours for so long that he put no stock in them and was taken completely by surprise when the Truce was finally announced:

I was standing on a roadside in west Cork and somebody came along and said, 'There's a truce with the British.' I'd been hearing rumours about this for the past twelve months and I didn't believe it, but this fellow went off and got a newspaper which said that de Valera was meeting Macready, the British Commander in Chief, so I had to believe it then.[199]

IRA Volunteer Paddy Donoughue from Ballyvourney was equally taken aback by the announcement of the ceasefire: 'Peace Talk – there was quite a lot ... no one of us ever recognised a peace or thought that it would come until [the news broke] two days before the Truce happened.'[200] Volunteer James Comerford in Kilkenny had a similar experience: 'The newspapers during recent days had been writing about a possible Truce. But no one expected a Truce to take place in the year of 1921.'[201] Tim O'Connor of the IRA's East Connemara Brigade was so loath to believe the stories he had heard about a possible ceasefire that he accused the IRA courier who had brought him a dispatch announcing the Truce of being an agent provocateur and threatened to have him shot.[202] Members of the Tipperary No. 3 Brigade IRA's flying column thought the IRA officer who brought them the news was playing a joke.[203] Their brigade headquarters staff were equally shocked by the sudden end to the conflict, and Seamus Babington, the brigade engineer, stated that the suggestion that the British forces would agree a truce with the IRA was completely inconceivable at the time: 'No one could believe it, for, at the time, no one saw or expected anything but death and burning ... But, far and beyond our wildest hopes and dreams ... the Truce was declared.'[204]

In some cases, IRA units received official dispatches informing them of the Truce, but more often they learned about the agreement through press reports. For example, Michael Brennan, commander of the IRA's 1st Western Division, received the dispatch from IRA headquarters sometime 'on the 9th or 10th of July'.[205]

Brennan immediately sent copies of the dispatch to the units under his command throughout Clare and south-east Galway, but some of these units did not learn about the Truce until after 1 p.m. on Sunday 10 July.[206] The IRA's three Cork Brigades, which had been the most active and effective republican military units during the conflict, received no advance notice of the Truce. The IRA leadership in the county all appear to have discovered that the Truce was imminent from press reports in *The Cork Examiner* newspaper on Saturday 9 July.[207]

In some cases the dispatches and messages sent from IRA GHQ and local IRA commanders barely reached local IRA units before the Truce came into effect. Both the IRA's North Wexford Brigade and the Tyrone Brigade were unaware that a truce had been agreed until late on 10 July.[208] Bill Carrigan, commandant of the 4th Battalion of the IRA's Kilkenny Brigade got word of the Truce at 7 a.m. on the morning of 11 July, just four hours before the ceasefire was due to take effect.[209] A handful of IRA units including the 4th Battalion of the Donegal Brigade received no formal notification of the Truce until after the ceasefire had started.[210] At least one IRA unit, unaware that a ceasefire had begun, carried out a successful ambush near Macroom at 3 p.m. on 11 July and succeeded in forcing the surrender of a group of RIC Auxiliaries and capturing their vehicle. The Auxiliaries were quick to point out that this action was in breach of the Truce, but the IRA personnel involved refused to believe that such an arrangement had been agreed. It was only after they returned to their base of operations that they learned that the Auxiliaries had been correct and that a truce had begun.[211]

The available evidence from contemporary British documents and from the personal accounts of both IRA and British veterans shows that rank-and-file combatants on both sides had no idea that a ceasefire was imminent before the Truce was officially announced at 8 p.m. on 8 July.[212] Despite the modern communication technology available to the British forces, many of their troops did not know that the Truce had been agreed until late on Saturday 9 July, although news of the agreement would certainly have reached all British outposts in Ireland by Sunday 10 July. News of the agreement spread even more slowly through the IRA's communication network, which was reliant on couriers travelling with written dispatches. IRA Volunteers in Dublin city were the first to learn of it, on the evening of 8 July and morning of 9 July. Clearly many of their counterparts in provincial areas only learned of the agreement on the evening of Sunday 10 July or early on the morning of Monday 11 July.

As soon as the Truce was signed, IRA GHQ was under pressure to get news of the agreement to local IRA units before the ceasefire began. The IRA leadership immediately drafted and printed hundreds of copies of the following dispatch for distribution to IRA units all over Ireland:

Oglaigh na h-Éireann 8–7–1921
GHQ, Dublin

To officers commanding all units,

In view of the conversations now being entered into by our government, with the government of Great Britain, and in pursuance of mutual understandings to suspend hostilities during these conversations, active operations by our troops will be suspended as from noon Monday 11th July.

Risteard Ua Maolchata, Chief of Staff[213]

The GHQ dispatch was very matter-of-fact in informing local IRA units that a truce had been agreed with the British forces: it gave the date and hour when it would begin and ordered that its terms were to be complied with in full. However, the order contained no instructions to local IRA units as to what action they were to take in the last days and hours before the Truce began. This effectively left local IRA officers to decide if they should follow through with attacks that had already been planned, or if these operations should be abandoned in light of the impending Truce. The GHQ dispatch did not give any directions to IRA Volunteers as to whether additional operations should be planned to 'tie up loose ends' regarding loyalist activity, suspected spies or members of the British forces who had committed reprisal killings.

Most IRA brigade officers who received the official GHQ order copied it exactly and sent these copies to the local IRA companies they commanded, without adding any clarification on what action should be taken before the Truce began. A handful of brigades issued oral instructions ordering the Volunteers under their command to increase attacks on RIC barracks and British military outposts before the ceasefire started. Only one IRA unit, the 1st Eastern Division, issued a written order that specified exactly what action should be taken in the final days and hours of the conflict. This order was issued by Seamus Finn, the divisional adjutant of the IRA's 1st Eastern Division, on Saturday 9 July 1921 and was circulated to all IRA brigades in Meath, Kildare, south-east Cavan, southern Louth, north-east Offaly and eastern Westmeath, and to the Fingal Battalion of the IRA's Dublin Brigade:

FIRST EASTERN DIVISION GENERAL ORDER 9/7/21

To O/C. No. (7) Naas Brig.

Owing to TRUCE been called at noon on MONDAY next, it is advisable that a good stroke be made at the Enemy before then. Sucs [*sic*] will it is believed strengthen the hands of our representatives in the making of a definite peace. You will therefore hit anywhere and everywhere you can within your area before 12 NOON on MONDAY.

The principal objecti[ve] [s]hould in all cases be members of old RIC or their Barracks.

ALL SPIES of whom you may have already been advised off [*sic*] are to be executed also before said hour on MONDAY.

IMPORTANT

It is definitely understood that all HOSTILITIES cease at 12 NOON on MONDAY THE 11TH OF JULY

Brig. Coms. have power in all cases to execute known SPIES or TRAITORS without consulting D.H.Q.

In order to take advantage of terms of TRUCE and to prevent our O/C from falling into hands of Enemy, the Div. meeting called for Monday is hereby postponed until same hour on TUESDAY 12th July.

Officers to report at Div. H.Q. on Monday night.
SIGNED DIV. ADJ.[214]

Despite the free hand and encouragement this order apparently gave, no civilians suspected of spying were executed by the IRA's 1st Eastern Division between the time the order was issued and the beginning of the Truce. Furthermore, despite the explicit instructions issued, not a single member of the RIC was killed in the 1st Eastern Division's operational area in the same time period. Nonetheless, the 1st Eastern Division's Truce order is significant because it was far more militant and detailed in its instructions than the official dispatch issued by IRA GHQ the previous day.[215]

This order is the only direct documentary evidence supporting the narrative that the IRA exploited the announcement of the Truce as an opportunity to carry out unjustifiable 'eleventh-hour' attacks on members of the British forces, to step up the killing of civilians they accused of being spies and to inflict the maximum number of fatalities on its opponents without fear of retribution. These claims will now be examined in detail to find out exactly what happened during the last days of the War of Independence, beginning with the claims concerning the IRA's intelligence war and the execution of civilians it accused of being spies.

3

THE EXECUTION
OF SUSPECTED SPIES

The battle to win the 'intelligence war' and gather accurate intelligence information that could be used against the enemy was of huge importance to both sides during the War of Independence. For the British forces, the best way to defeat the republican insurgency was to acquire accurate intelligence information about IRA personnel, their supply of arms and their operations. Before the 1916 Rising, the British government had relied on the RIC and the DMP to gather intelligence information about Irish republicans. However, the widespread closure of rural RIC barracks following IRA attacks, the success of Sinn Féin's police boycott and the resulting mass resignation of Irish-born constables meant that the British forces became increasingly dependent on the local population for information and began recruiting civilians for intelligence work.[1]

Given the role of spies and informers in defeating the insurrections of 1798 and 1867, the IRA was acutely aware of the importance of stopping the flow of information to the British by identifying and eliminating their agents.[2] It is common in insurrections that those who co-operate with the authorities, or actively assist them in their operations, are dealt with severely.[3] As a guerrilla army, relying on secrecy and mobility, the IRA was rarely in a position to punish suspected spies by holding them prisoner. Instead, it inflicted a variety of other punishments on these suspects. Some received threatening notices, others suffered economic boycott or were forced into exile. In the most extreme cases, republicans captured and killed civilians they claimed were spies and informers. These killings were sanctioned by the IRA GHQ, with Michael Collins, the IRA director of intelligence, declaring that 'there was no crime in detecting and destroying in wartime, the spy and the informer'.[4] Given the potential threat they posed, the killing of British intelligence agents, spies and informers was a logical and necessary action from a republican perspective, and 184 civilians accused of spying were executed by the IRA during the War of Independence.[5]

Almost a century later, killings related to the intelligence war still remain one of the most controversial features of the conflict. It has been repeatedly alleged that members of the IRA exploited the intelligence war and the execution of spies as a pretext to settle personal vendettas, persecute Irishmen who had served in the British forces and carry out a sectarian campaign against Protestants. These accusations first surfaced in the memoirs of British veterans published shortly after the conflict. Hugh Pollard, a former RIC press officer who produced anti-republican propaganda during the war, claimed that most of the civilians killed by the IRA as spies were innocents murdered because of petty jealousies and rivalry over farmland: 'these were private murders, possibly in pursuit of old faction feuds, but carried out under the all-embracing Irish cloak of patriotism'.[6] The history of the British Army's 6th Division suggested that there was a sectarian motivation to these killings. It claimed 'a large number of Protestant Loyalists were murdered and labelled as spies' and that 'a regular murder campaign was instigated against Protestant Loyalists and anyone who might be suspected of being an informer, quite irrespective of whether he really was one or not'.[7] Sir Arthur Hezlet, a former British naval officer who wrote a history of the 'B' Specials, claimed that most of those killed by the IRA had no contact with the British forces and were murdered solely because they were Protestants or ex-servicemen.[8]

In recent years a number of academic historians have put for-

ward similar theories that echo these claims. Jane Leonard maintained that unarmed ex-servicemen became an increasingly temp-
ting target for the IRA as it struggled to overcome improvements
in the tactics, weaponry and armament of the British forces.[9]
Leonard also noted that ex-soldiers killed by the IRA were usually
accused of spying for the British, but dismissed these assertions as
an 'implausible guise' and claimed that 'evidence to sustain these
allegations is remarkably thin'.[10] Professor David Fitzpatrick of
Trinity College Dublin added a new dimension to these assertions
by suggesting that, in addition to Protestants and ex-servicemen,
the IRA also targeted several other isolated social groups, including itinerants, adulterers and homosexuals:

> … several hundred supposed informers were murdered, sometimes
> in gruesome fashion, their bodies being buried or dumped in the sea.
> Though many of the dead had indeed tipped off the police or the
> Castle, others were the victims of numerous paranoiac assumptions.
> Adulterers, homosexuals, tinkers, beggars, ex-servicemen, Protestants:
> there were many dangerous and potentially lethal labels for Ireland's
> inhabitants in the revolutionary period … The purity of the fight had
> been sullied, even in republican consciousness, well before the Truce.[11]

Fitzpatrick's extraordinary claim that homophobia was a factor in
some IRA killings is very difficult to take seriously, as it is not supported by any examples or references.[12]

Peter Hart, a student of Fitzpatrick's, argued that accusations of
spying made by the IRA in Cork served as a pretext for the intimidation of minorities – 'strangers' and 'outsiders' who 'fell outside the
moral boundaries of respectable Catholic society'. He claimed that
the majority of those the IRA executed for spying were innocent
and that such killings often had more to do with prejudice against
Protestants and ex-servicemen than concerns about military security. Hart even suggested such killings were part of a national

campaign of sectarian violence against Protestants that was tantamount to 'ethnic cleansing'.[13] According to Hart, violence against these civilian targets increased as the conflict drew to a close and eventually became more common than IRA military attacks on the British forces: 'The war continued to escalate right up to the July 1921 Truce, and anti-Protestant violence rose right along with it.'[14] Hart stated that this upsurge in republican violence was timed deliberately to coincide with the advent of the Truce, because the IRA knew it would be immune from retaliation when the Truce began. He alleged that some IRA units attempted to kill as many of their enemy's people as possible before the ceasefire began.[15]

A number of other academics have also attempted to link this increase in violence to IRA knowledge that a ceasefire was imminent and to the announcement of the Truce. Eunan O'Halpin has claimed that some victims were killed by IRA Volunteers who knew the Truce was coming and saw it as an opportunity to increase the body count before the ceasefire started:

> In ... Queen's County ... the decision to execute spies may have arisen partly from a desire to fire a fatal shot for Ireland while there was still time to do so. The IRA killed Peter Keyes, a father of ten ... on 5 July [1921]. John Poynton, who had briefly served in the RIC before resigning for family reasons, was also shot at 4 a.m. on the morning of the Truce.[16]

Marie Coleman claimed that ex-soldiers were 'the softest of targets' for the IRA, and that the shooting of spies usually happened when the IRA came under increasing military pressure from the British forces.[17] Like O'Halpin, Coleman maintains that IRA Volunteers rushed to commit last-minute killings when they learned that the war was ending. According to her, the IRA in Offaly knew that a truce was looming when they killed the Pearson brothers, two Protestants who were shot at their farm in Coolacrease.[18]

However, there is little or no proof to support claims that the motive for any of these killings was the advent of the Truce. The Pearson brothers and Keyes were killed a full week before the Truce began. The ceasefire had not even been agreed at the time of these shootings, and none of the republicans involved knew that the Truce was imminent. While Poynton's killers undoubtedly knew about the Truce, the circumstances of his case (see p. 90) suggest that he had been under suspicion of spying long before and that the timing of his killing on the eve of the Truce was largely coincidental.

It has also been suggested that three other alleged spies – Andrew Knight, John Moloney and William McPhearson – were all killed by the IRA in a knee-jerk reaction to the announcement of the Truce. However, evidence from British military inquests proves that the Truce could not possibly have been a factor in these attacks, since all of those killed were shot before 5.30 p.m. on 8 July, when the Truce was announced, and the IRA rank and file had no knowledge before then that a ceasefire was imminent.[19]

Newspaper columnist Kevin Myers has promoted similar theories in his opinion pieces, making outlandish claims about the killing of alleged spies and suggesting that the IRA exploited the announcement of the Truce as an opportunity to launch a wave of sectarian killings targeting Protestants. According to Myers, Andrew Knight, a Protestant from Dublin, was killed by the IRA in reprisal for the deaths of four Catholics killed by the B Specials in Newry. Myers has also implied that two other Protestants killed by the IRA just before the Truce, Major George O'Connor and John Poynton, were murdered because of their religion.[20] These claims are little more than speculation. Knight was shot on suspicion of spying and had been identified as a British agent by a serving member of the DMP – there is no evidence to suggest that his killing had anything to do with his religion or events in Newry.[21] Myers' contention that O'Connor and Poynton were killed because of their religion ignores other more likely reasons why the IRA would have targeted them, including Poynton's service as a Black and Tan and the fact that both men were staunch loyalists accused of spying for the British forces.

Other claims Myers has made about the announcement of the Truce motivating last-minute killings are equally dubious. According to him, two ex-servicemen – Anthony Foody, a retired RIC sergeant from Mayo, and Thomas Smith, a former British soldier from Meath – were killed by republicans who exploited the announcement of the Truce on 8 July as an opportunity for 'murder without legal consequence'. [22] This is impossible, since both men were killed before the Truce was announced. The body of Smith, an alleged British spy, was found days before the announcement and its state of decomposition indicated that he had been killed in late June.[23] Foody was shot dead on 7 July, apparently in reprisal for his involvement in the killing of Edward Dwyer, an IRA officer from Tipperary who was shot dead at his home by masked men in October 1920. The timing of both killings was entirely coincidental to the Truce, and suggestions otherwise are ill-informed speculation.

Historians and others who support the claim that news of the ceasefire led to a wave of republican killings have consistently overestimated the number of suspected spies killed by the IRA after the announcement of the Truce. In her biography of the IRA Chief of Staff Richard Mulcahy, Maria Valiulis wrote: 'records indicate that eleven spies were executed by the IRA just before the advent of the Truce'.[24] Valiulis based her figure on a document in Michael Collins' papers that purports to list all the spies executed by the IRA during the conflict. However, this document is unreliable and only three of the eleven entries on the list dated 9–11 July 1921 were actually killed after the Truce was announced.[25]

The number of civilians killed as spies in Cork after the announcement of the Truce has also been grossly exaggerated.

In his book, *The Year of Disappearances*, Gerard Murphy made the fantastic claim that the IRA executed three Protestant teenagers after the Truce and secretly buried their bodies on the outskirts of Cork city. According to Murphy, the trio confessed to being spies before they were shot and this sparked an IRA campaign of sectarian murder, 'a whole witch hunt fuelled by suspicion and paranoia that led to dozens of deaths ... and the flight of hundreds of Protestant families'.[26] However, there is no verifiable evidence that these anonymous victims ever existed, much less that the IRA killed them. Murphy cannot name the alleged victims and there is no historical record of three Protestant boys going missing at the time – a fact Murphy attributes to 'a spectacular cover-up' and 'a big conspiracy' involving the press, the British government and even Cork Protestants themselves.[27] He claimed that IRA veteran Connie Neenan had referred to the killing of these three boys in an interview recorded by Ernie O'Malley.[28] However, Murphy misread the document and used an inaccurate transcription of it in his book – in fact Neenan's interview does not mention the alleged incident at all.[29] The only other information Murphy could offer about these alleged IRA victims came from an anonymous source.[30] Murphy states he was told 'the story' about these Protestant boys by an unnamed eighty-nine-year-old man, the son of an anonymous IRA Volunteer from Cork, who had in turn been informed 'by a Volunteer who waited until all connected to the event were themselves dead'. This anonymous third-hand information is completely unreliable as evidence, as it cannot be checked or verified, and so his record of these killings cannot be taken seriously as factual history.

Murphy also claimed that another Protestant youth, Edward Olliffe Jr, was killed by the IRA after the announcement of the Truce. According to a contemporary RIC report, Olliffe was abducted by armed men near his home at Innishannon on 10 July 1921.[31] Murphy wrongly assumed that Olliffe was executed by the

IRA after his abduction on the eve of the Truce.[32] In fact Olliffe was not killed by the IRA and died over half a century after the War of Independence ended. He had indeed been abducted by the IRA and was held prisoner for several months, but emerged from the ordeal unscathed.[33] Olliffe, like all four of his siblings, emigrated to the United States after the conflict ended.[34] In November 1922 he left Liverpool for New York on the passenger ship *Cedric* en route to his uncle's home in California. In December 1979 the *Observer-Reporter* newspaper recorded that Edward Olliffe was still alive and well, and living at Walnut Creek in California.[35]

The number of suspected spies killed at the time of the Truce has consistently been overestimated because there is an automatic tendency, as with Edward Olliffe, to assume that anyone who went missing at the time was killed by the IRA. During the War of Independence some IRA units did occasionally 'disappear' suspected spies, whose bodies were secretly buried instead of being labelled and dumped in a public area for discovery, as per usual IRA practice. The British forces were also known to 'disappear' some of their victims, but it was far more common for the IRA to do so. Even so, the practice was relatively rare and fewer than twenty-five of those executed as spies during that conflict were buried in secret. In fact many of those who went missing for far less sinister reasons during the conflict are often wrongly assumed to have been killed by republicans. Eunan O'Halpin's 2013 television documentary *In the Name of the Republic* concluded with a 'List of the known disappeared', naming fifty-seven individuals supposedly 'known with certainty' to have been 'disappeared' by the IRA. Among those listed was William Shiels, a British spy from Bweeng in Co. Cork, whom O'Halpin claimed was killed by the IRA on the day the Truce began. However, the republicans never captured Shiels and he fled Ireland after the ceasefire. During the Civil War both the IRA and the Free State Army attempted, without success, to locate and assassinate him. It is clear that when Shiels 'disappeared' it was to some far-flung location with the assistance of the British government, and not into a shallow grave dug by the IRA.[36]

A list of missing civilians, issued by the British government, was published in *The Irish Times* on 22 August 1921. The list contained the names of eight people who 'disappeared' between 8 and 11 July 1921.[37] Two of the eight, John H. N. Begley and William J. Nolan, were abducted and executed by the IRA, but it appears that the other six listed survived the conflict.[38] As well as Olliffe, two others listed as 'missing' immediately before the Truce, namely Bridget Burke and Daniel M. J. O'Connell, were abducted by the IRA but were later released unharmed.[39] A fourth missing person, Eugene Swanton, escaped after ten weeks in IRA captivity.[40] No information is available about the fate of two other men – James Gaffney and Francis Boyle – named on the list as having gone missing in Monaghan on 9 July 1921.[41] Neither of these men's families made applications to the Irish Compensation Commission, though it was common for the families of the IRA's victims to do so. Without further information it is futile to speculate as to whether the IRA, or any other party, was responsible for their disappearances and, if so, what fate befell them.

Despite estimates of up to a dozen civilians being shot as spies in the final days of the conflict, and speculation about 'the disappeared' and anonymous victims – the reality is that just six suspected spies were executed by the IRA following the announcement of the Truce. Four alleged spies – David Cummins, Eric Steadman, Major G. B. O'Connor and John Poynton – were executed in the time period between the announcement of the Truce on 8 July 1921 and the beginning of the ceasefire at noon on 11 July. Another two suspected spies – William Nolan and John Begley – were both abducted by the IRA in Cork city on the morning of the Truce and were killed and secretly buried by the IRA a short time later.

DAVID CUMMINS

At 1 p.m. on 8 July 1921 a group of IRA Volunteers from the 2nd Battalion, Tipperary No. 3 Brigade arrested David Cummins at his workplace in Noan, Co. Tipperary.[42] Cummins was executed by a firing squad that night and his body was discovered on the side of a road near Dualla the following day. Cummins was a native of Donegal, but had been employed as a chauffeur for over a decade by Mr Frederick Armitage, a wealthy loyalist landowner who lived at Noan. Cummins was held prisoner at Meldrum House, a large country estate house, which was at that time unoccupied except for a caretaker. The IRA Volunteers who abducted Cummins were under the command of Paddy Byrne, vice-commandant of the local IRA battalion. Shortly after Cummins' capture, Byrne received a signed dispatch from his commandant, Seán Downey, ordering Cummins' execution.[43] Paul Mulcahy, one of the IRA Volunteers guarding Cummins, recalled that Byrne offered the condemned man a chance to receive spiritual aid before his execution:

> In Dualla, Byrne asked him if he wished to see a priest or to make an Act of Contrition, and he replied; 'No, I am not a Catholic.' Later before his execution Byrne again asked him if he wished to see a clergyman or if he had any final request to make, and he replied, 'No.' In my presence, at any rate, there were no other conversations with him.[44]

After his execution, a label was attached to his body at the roadside bearing the text 'Convicted spy. Spies and informers beware.'[45] Cummins was buried in the graveyard of St Mary's Church of Ireland in Tipperary town. At the time of writing his grave is unmarked.

It is difficult to establish on what basis or evidence, if any, the IRA executed Cummins as a spy. Neither of the IRA men who mentioned Cummins' execution in their testimony to the Bureau of Military History were privy to the evidence that had been used to convict Cummins of spying and sentence him to death.[46] IRA

Lieutenant Timothy Tierney, who had delivered Seán Downey's order to execute Cummins, could not recall being given any specific information about Cummins' alleged role as a spy: 'I cannot tell you anything of Cummins' history but I understand that he had been found guilty of spying. What the specific charge against him was, I cannot now recall – perhaps I never heard it.'[47] Paul Mulcahy knew Cummins personally but had no idea why he was suspected of being a British spy:

> I had known him for some time but had no evidence that he was a spy. The Brigade and Battalion Staffs had apparently information about him of which I was not, or am not now, aware … I understand that the decision to execute him had already been made.[48]

Marie Coleman has suggested that, in cases like Cummins', where local IRA veterans did not give specific evidence in their memoirs regarding the guilt of those accused of spying, those killed might have been the innocent victims of IRA prejudice against ex-soldiers.[49] However, it would be wrong to assume automatically that because the reasons for an execution of a suspected spy were not known to those tasked with carrying it out, there was no legitimate reason for the action. That the reason has not survived to the present day does not necessarily imply a lack of contemporary evidence. The IRA was a secretive guerrilla army, where much communication would have been carried out orally and where written communications would sometimes have deliberately been destroyed. Executions were often based on sensitive intelligence information from protected sources and this information was restricted to those who had the authority to sanction an execution. Therefore, in the event that an IRA Volunteer who had taken part in an execution was captured by the British forces, he would not be able to reveal any information during interrogation. For example, members of Collins' 'Squad', which on a regular basis assassinated

British agents and civilians suspected of spying, were rarely told the specific reasons why their target was to be killed.[50] In short, what the condemned were accused of having done to deserve their fate was not the concern of those tasked with carrying out the execution.

Without more detail it is impossible to discern whether the IRA decision to execute Cummins was based on purely military concerns, or if there were other motivating factors. The Ireland Compensation Commission, established in 1922 by the British government and the Provisional Government of the Irish Free State to compensate civilian victims of the conflict, awarded Cummins' mother £600 in compensation for his death. Unlike in the cases of a number of other alleged spies shot at the time, the British government did not accept full responsibility for Cummins' death. Instead the commission ruled that liability in the case was 'Agreed 50/50' in terms of British responsibility.[51] Unfortunately, this ambiguous ruling does not shed any light on Cummins' possible involvement with the British forces. Whatever the motivation for his execution, the timing of David Cummins' abduction and shooting on the advent of the Truce appears to have been a complete coincidence. Cummins was abducted by the IRA at 1 p.m. on 8 July, hours before the Truce had been agreed or announced. According to Paul Mulcahy, the decision to kill Cummins had apparently been made well in advance of the announcement of the Truce.[52] Given that Ernie O'Malley, the commander of the local IRA Division, did not know that a truce had been agreed until the day after this shooting, it is highly unlikely that Cummins' killers would have known about the impending ceasefire when they shot their captive.[53]

ERIC STEADMAN
Shortly after 2 a.m. on 10 July, labourer Michael Buckley discovered the body of an unidentified man at Puttaghaun, Tullamore.[54]

The man's body had been 'riddled with bullets' and a label was affixed to it reading: 'Convicted Spy, Eric Steadman, [E]X Soldier Birmingham. TRIED, Convicted and Executed on July 9th 1921. Sooner or later we get THEM. Beware of the IRA.'[55] The deceased was an Englishman; apparently he was an ex-soldier and, when interrogated by his captors, gave his name as Eric Steadman.[56] However, despite extensive inquiries made by the Birmingham Constabulary, no trace was ever uncovered of an Eric Steadman having lived in Birmingham.[57]

Steadman had been in Ireland for some time, and his IRA captors claimed that he had travelled through the midlands collecting information about IRA activities in return for payments from the British forces. The republicans further alleged that Steadman was not a genuine vagrant but adopted this as a disguise, dressing as a tramp and carrying a 'billy can'. One of his executioners stated that Steadman's hands belied the impression of someone living rough: 'his fingers were long and they had silky indications of a man who didn't do much manual work … a low stout block of a man who seemingly didn't do any manual work … he was not much to look at.'[58] The inquest into Steadman's death confirmed this impression. The deceased was described as being 'about 40 years of age, about 5ft 9in height … slightly built and poorly clad'.

Steadman had been arrested in the first week of July and interrogated. One of his captors, IRA Volunteer Seán Magennis, claimed that he spoke openly under interrogation about his role as a British agent: 'We questioned him and he seemed to be frank enough, he said that he went from house to house in Kildare and Wicklow and that he supplied information to the big houses, and that they paid him.' Steadman's captors held a conference and decided that he should be executed by firing squad. He was held prisoner for a number of days at Ballydaly, Tullamore, Co. Offaly. The IRA attempted to secure a clergyman to provide the condemned man with spiritual aid, but a clergyman from Tullamore refused this request, so his executioners instead baptised Steadman before shooting him and affixing the 'spy label' to his body. After execution, his body was removed to Puttaghaun to prevent the houses of republican activists in Ballydaly being burned.[59] It was unusual to name the deceased on the 'spy labels' and his executioners may have done this because Steadman was not local to the area and would not have been identified otherwise.

As an Englishman and a stranger to the area, Steadman's presence in Tullamore would have immediately made the IRA suspicious of his activities. The British Army sent soldiers disguised in civilian clothes into the countryside, often posing as deserters, to gather intelligence information and scout the countryside.[60] The RIC used a similar tactic. One RIC veteran recalled that during the conflict members of a special unit, organised by a senior RIC officer, 'all dressed like old farmers' while on intelligence gathering operations.[61] Consequently, republicans had a tendency to regard all strangers visiting their areas as potential spies. In November 1920 the IRA's intelligence department warned local units to be on the lookout for strangers in their area and 'those with English accents in particular'.[62] In May 1921 Wilfrid Ewart, an ex-British Army officer turned reporter, was arrested by the IRA near Tullamore on suspicion of being a spy. Though Ewart was an Englishman and a former British Army officer, which would have been evident from his accent and manner, he was subsequently released unharmed, having been searched and interrogated.[63] Sir Kenneth Strong, detachment intelligence officer with the Royal Scots Fusiliers stationed in Tullamore, disguised himself in civilian attire when carrying out intelligence work in the area:

My area of responsibility was so small that unusual happenings soon came to the notice of local inhabitants. Contacts with my so-called agents had to be personal and this could be an exceedingly dangerous undertaking for the informant. To get to a rendezvous I would disguise myself, usually as the owner of a small donkey cart, but my English accent was against me and I had several narrow escapes.[64]

Ewart's and Strong's experiences show that the Tullamore IRA did not automatically condemn to death as spies any strangers and/or Englishmen visiting the area – despite having justifiable grounds for suspecting them. In Steadman's case farmers in the Tullamore area had reported to the IRA that a stranger was looking for work on the bogs. The IRA had apparently arrested Steadman for inter-rogation on a previous occasion, but he had escaped. Local repub-licans alleged that Steadman later returned to the district and was seen alighting from an RIC lorry. He was captured by the IRA for a second time and killed.[65]

If Steadman was not a British agent, then his presence in rural Ireland during the conflict was incredibly dangerous and excep-tionally foolhardy. He was certain to be suspected of being a spy by republicans, thereby putting his life in extreme peril. Moreover, if he was not a British agent, then his persistence in returning to the Tullamore district if he had already escaped from IRA custody defies logic and any regard for his own life or personal safety.

Without further information it is impossible to establish for certain if Steadman had gathered intelligence for the British forces. It is also difficult to establish whether his executioners knew of the impending ceasefire at the time he was killed. Seán Magennis stated that Steadman had been arrested and held 'a couple of days' before his execution on 9 July.[66] This suggests that Steadman was captured and sentenced to death before the Truce had been announced. However, the evidence of Captain Lindsey, the Royal Army Medical Corps officer who testified at the inquest into Steadman's killing, is problematic. Having examined Steadman's body at 9 a.m. on 10 July, Lindsey declared, 'I consider that the deceased has been dead for at least three days.'[67] If this estimate was correct, Steadman would have been executed on or before

7 July and therefore the Truce could not possibly have been a factor in his death. Yet Lindsey's conclusion is at odds with the date on the label attached to Steadman's body, stating specifically that he had been 'Executed on 9th July'. The court of inquiry concluded that 'the deceased … met with his death prior to 9 July'.[68]

MAJOR GEORGE BERNARD O'CONNOR

A few minutes before midnight on 10 July, IRA Volunteers from the Cork No. 1 Brigade called at the home of Major George Bernard O'Connor at Illane, Rochestown, Cork city. They knocked on the door of the house and O'Connor's wife answered. The republicans said they wanted to see her husband and pushed their way inside. Major O'Connor was forced to get dressed and was taken outside by the raiders, who told his wife and the household servants that he would be returning shortly. O'Connor was taken a short distance from his home and shot several times. The following morning his body was found about 100 yards on the Cork side of Hop Island with a label attached reading 'Convicted Spy'.[69]

O'Connor, aged seventy, was a justice of the peace and member of the Cork Chamber of Commerce. He was a former British officer with the 19th Hussars and had been promoted to the rank of major during the Boer War. An active unionist and supporter of Sir Horace Plunkett's Dominion Home Rule League, Major O'Connor had stood for election in the College Green Parliamentary Division of Dublin city, a traditional southern unionist stronghold. He was later nominated as a unionist candidate for the Cork City Division in the 1918 general election, but declined the nomination to stand.[70] O'Connor was also an active and outspoken opponent of Irish republicanism.

Connie Neenan, a local IRA officer, claimed that the major was killed because the IRA believed he was a spy and had been responsible for several setbacks suffered by the IRA in Cork city:

The night before the Truce was signed was a Sunday and the only activity planned in our battalion was the apprehension of a well-known British intelligence agent who was responsible for a great deal of the harm and hardship that befell our men. This assignment came within the activities of [our] Company and the man in question was caught and executed.[71]

The IRA already had a history with O'Connor. On 29 January 1921 the IRA had commandeered a horse and trap at Rochestown that belonged to O'Connor and used it to remove six cases of British Army supplies it had taken from the Cork train. Following three further mail raids on trains at Rochestown, O'Connor made a formal complaint to the British Army, castigating them for not doing enough to protect the rail network.[72] In April 1921 the major had made a legal affidavit to the courts martial of the IRA prisoners captured at Clonmult, two of whom were later executed.[73] O'Connor had been under observation by the IRA for some time. Since early July IRA Volunteers had been posted near his home in preparation for his abduction and on 10 July the leadership of the Cork No. 1 Brigade issued orders for O'Connor's immediate execution.[74]

Mick Murphy, a member of the 2nd Battalion of the Cork No. 1 Brigade IRA, stated that O'Connor was shot because he was a member of a civilian spy ring in Cork.[75] On 9 February 1921 another justice of the peace, Alfred Reilly, was travelling with O'Connor in a pony and trap through Cork city. Armed IRA Volunteers held them up and Reilly was taken from the trap, placed against a wall and shot twice. A label was pinned to his coat reading 'Spy. By order IRA. Take warning'.[76] According to Murphy, Reilly had been shot because he was a member of a civilian spy ring in the city, and O'Connor's connection to him later brought him under suspicion: 'This man [Reilly] was a member of the senior secret service of the Y.M.C.A. ... With Riley [*sic*] that night was a retired British Army officer named Major O'Connor. He, too, was [later] shot and killed.'[77] Shortly after Reilly's killing, the IRA made a failed attempt to kill O'Connor.[78]

Florrie O'Donoghue apparently referred to Major O'Connor's killing, and the evidence used to sanction his execution, in an interview conducted by Ernie O'Malley:

> At the end of the Tan War, Florrie and a number of other officers got out of town every night. They used to go separately to a small cottage … An ex-British officer noticed one or some of them and he gave information. Florrie's wife, [General] Strickland's secretary, saw the note but she had no time [to copy it]. She tried to memorise it. Later that day she got hold of this note, brought it out as evidence. The man was arrested, court-martialled and shot before nightfall.[79]

After his death, O'Connor's family made a claim for financial assistance to the Ireland Compensation Commission. Though the IRA had undoubtedly killed O'Connor, his killing was listed as being 'Accepted as [a] British Liability'.[80] While this was not conclusive evidence that the major was a British agent, the ruling is suggestive that O'Connor was killed because he had an association with the British authorities. O'Connor's connection with Reilly, a suspected spy executed by the IRA, his communications with the British Army regarding IRA raids on the mails, and perhaps most significantly his testimony to the courts martial of the IRA men captured at Clonmult may have led the IRA to conclude that he was providing information and assistance to the British forces concerning IRA activities. It is beyond doubt that his killers knew the Truce was imminent at the time of his killing.

JOHN POYNTON

Shortly before 3 a.m. on 11 July 1921 a group of masked and armed men called at Poynton's farm at Kilbride near Portarlington,

Co. Laois. The men knocked and then called out for the door to be opened. When John Poynton, the youngest son of the family, answered the door, a tall, masked man armed with a revolver entered the house and forced him outside. Poynton's mother attempted to follow them but was ordered back inside at gunpoint. Seconds later she heard five gunshots and went outside to see what had happened. She witnessed two men walking away and found her son trying to follow them. John Poynton had been fatally wounded and his mother and two sisters carried him into the house where he collapsed, dying about twenty minutes later.[81] Poynton was a twenty-three-year-old farmer and a former Black and Tan. He had joined the RIC with his older brother Ambrose, on 6 December 1920. The brothers were in the force for less than two weeks when their father, a retired RIC sergeant, died suddenly. John subsequently resigned, citing 'family affairs', and returned to Kilbride to run the family farm.[82] Ambrose remained in the RIC and was stationed in Belturbet, Co. Cavan.[83]

The local IRA was aware that the brothers had joined the RIC and monitored John Poynton closely after his return. The IRA Volunteers watching Poynton reported that he regularly socialised with members of the RIC in Portarlington and made frequent visits to the RIC barracks there to play cards.[84] These would have been very dangerous activities at a time when a social boycott of the police was widely enforced, even in areas such as Laois, which had seen relatively little republican activity. Local IRA intelligence reported that Poynton 'frequented the Barracks and was absent after curfew being in the habit of meeting patrols on lonely points along the roads'.[85]

As a result of these alleged activities, the IRA came to suspect that Poynton was guilty of gathering information for the British forces. The local IRA believed that Poynton was responsible for a number of arrests made by the RIC in the Kilbride district and ordered him to leave the area.[86] Poynton was seemingly oblivious or indifferent to the danger his life was in as a result of his association with the RIC. According to IRA intelligence, Poynton allegedly boasted on one occasion that, 'He would shop every member of the IRA for a £1 per head [sic].'[87] He continued to ignore the IRA's order to leave the area even after another suspected spy in the district was killed.[88] After Poynton's death, his family made a claim for financial compensation to the Ireland Compensation Commission. Though the IRA had undoubtedly killed Poynton, his killing is listed as being an 'Agreed British Liability'.[89] Again, while it is not conclusive evidence that Poynton was a British agent, this ruling is a strong indication that he was killed because he had an association with, or had given assistance to, the British authorities.

WILLIAM J. NOLAN

Seventeen-year-old William J. Nolan left his family's home at Annmount, Friar's Walk in Cork city to post a letter at 11 a.m. on 11 July 1921.[90] He never returned from this errand and was reported missing to the RIC. Nolan had recently applied to join the RIC, and it appears that he was abducted and executed by the IRA.[91] His recent application could explain his abduction and execution at the hands of republicans. The Nolan family had very strong links to the RIC: William's father was a retired RIC constable and his older brother had also joined the force. At the time of Nolan's disappearance, applicants to join the RIC were being targeted by the IRA in Cork. A number of RIC recruits in Cork had been killed by the IRA, including Michael Finbar O'Sullivan, who was abducted and executed in February 1921.[92] Republicans in Cork had issued a proclamation warning 'prospective recruits that they join the RIC at their own peril. All nations are agreed as to the fate of traitors.'[93]

The fact that Nolan had applied to join the RIC at such a young age may be an indication that he had supplied the British forces with information about republican activities. It was not unusual for young loyalists who aided the British in this manner to join the RIC as a means of protection. For example, Constable Patrick Edward Conway, a sixteen-year-old loyalist, joined the DMP as a 'Temporary Constable' a few days after an informer's information led to the death of an IRA Volunteer in Conway's home area of Broadford, Co. Limerick. The acceptance of such a young recruit into the force was highly unusual.[94] In a similar case, a young woman in East Clare was suspected by the local IRA of spying because she applied to join the RIC Women's Auxiliary Service as a 'searcher'.[95]

It is uncertain whether Nolan was targeted because he was suspected of spying, because he had applied to join the RIC, or both. There is some uncertainty as to his exact fate. However, it would appear that he was abducted by IRA Volunteer Pat 'Pa' Scannell and other members of E Company, 2nd Battalion of the IRA's Cork No. 1 Brigade, executed and his body secretly buried.[96]

JOHN H. N. BEGLEY

At 11.55 a.m. on 11 July 1921, five minutes before the Truce came into effect, the IRA in Cork abducted John H. N. Begley.[97] He had been identified in the city centre by a group of IRA Volunteers led by Seán O'Connell and Tadhg Twohig. According to O'Connell:

> … we received instructions to arrest another ex-British soldier named Begley who was alleged to be an enemy agent. We watched for him and at about noon one day Tadg [sic] Twohig and I tracked him up Patrick Street. We were 'covered' by four or five men from 'G' Company, all of whom were armed with revolvers. We arrested Begley and took him out of the City.[98]

According to O'Connell, their captive was executed a short time later on the instructions of the leadership of the Cork No. 1 Brigade.

Begley was a Catholic ex-soldier who lived at 1 Rock Cottages, North Mall, in Cork city.[99] Connie Neenan stated, 'we had a few ex-British soldiers in Cork who were spies and we shot them and buried them'.[100] Neenan described Begley as 'a young kid, a non-descript type' and claimed that Begley was a spy for the British forces who had been recruited by William Shiels, an ex-soldier who had infiltrated the IRA: 'One of the group broke down in June [sic] 1921 when he was caught outside of Douglas. Begley one of the Shiels crowd, said it was Shiels who got him into this mess.'[101]

William 'Bill' Shiels, an ex-soldier, was a native of Boherbee in North Cork.[102] In February 1920 he approached a member of the IRA, asked to join the Cork No. 2 Brigade's flying column, and was accepted despite the objections of a local IRA officer. It appears that Shiels joined the IRA with the specific intention of gathering intelligence information for the British forces.[103] In February 1921 he supplied them with information that an IRA flying column was stationed at Mourne Abbey, and this resulted in the deaths of six IRA Volunteers.[104] The following month, the British Army raided a republican 'safe house' at Nadd, which resulted in the deaths of three IRA Volunteers.[105] The British Army attributed its success to Shiels, whom they described as 'a man who had deserted from the rebels'.[106] Shiels left the flying column the night before the raid, on the pretext of visiting his sick mother, and was observed entering Kanturk RIC Barracks, but there was a delay in relaying this information to the IRA unit at Nadd.[107] During the raid Shiels was seen wearing a Black and Tan uniform and assisting the British forces.[108] This was apparently a disguise for Shiels, who was working as an 'identifier'.[109]

Shiels recruited other ex-soldiers who worked as paid informers for the British forces in Cork, including a man named Saunders, who identified Shiels as his 'handler' before being executed by the IRA.[110] Shiels may also have recruited a third ex-soldier, William

McPhearson, who was killed by the IRA in Mallow, Co. Cork.[111] Shiels fled to England after the War of Independence and may later have gone to America.[112]

As well as the information about Shiels' activities forced from Saunders, the IRA also received information about his intelligence network from a Black and Tan stationed in Kanturk, Co. Cork.[113] Begley's alleged association with Shiels, Saunders and the British Army intelligence network in Cork would have made his capture, interrogation and execution a top priority. Seán O'Connell, captain of G Company, 1st Battalion of the Cork Brigade IRA, stated that: 'Due to the excellent Intelligence Service set up in each Battalion and Company area, it was possible to bring those informers "to heel" when the evidence against them proved conclusive.'[114] The report to IRA GHQ of Begley's shooting stated that Begley was 'a spy for whom we were on the lookout'.[115] O'Connell's statement to the Bureau of Military History and the IRA's report on Begley's shooting both make it clear that the IRA had been aware of his supposed connection to Shiels and British Army intelligence, and had intended to abduct and interrogate him for some time. The fact that the British authorities accepted liability for Begley's fate and awarded his family £1,500 in compensation may be an indication that Begley had been involved in intelligence work.[116]

THE SHOOTING OF BRIDGET DILLON

There were a number of unsuccessful attempts by the IRA to kill suspected spies between the announcement of the Truce and its implementation three days later.[117] The most serious of these happened at Kilcash, Co. Tipperary, when the IRA attempted to kill Michael-Thomas Dillon, a Catholic ex-soldier, and his younger brother William on the night of 9 July 1921. There are two surviving accounts of this incident recorded in the Ernie O'Malley Notebooks. The briefer of the two comes from Mick Burke, a veteran of the Tipperary No. 3 Brigade IRA, who simply stated:

'A girl, Dillon, [was] shot there [in] Kilcash, in connection with spying. There was some mix up over it, and it was supposed to have been a mistake.'[118] Andrew Kennedy, a member of the brigade's flying column, gave a slightly more detailed account of the affair:

> The night we left the place [Kilcash], a policeman's son, and a daughter, sent in the information to Carrick. He [Michael Dillon, the ex-policeman] fired on the lads that were sent to arrest him and she was shot dead, and the peeler's son disappeared from the country. Some of the Carrick[-on-Suir] men had been sent to arrest him in Kilpatrick, Kilcash.[119]

However, there is no indication that Bridget Dillon was an informer for the British forces, as inferred by Kennedy, and the circumstances of her death were far more complex than either of O'Malley's interviewees indicated.

During the War of Independence several members of the Dillon family came to the attention of the local IRA. Lord Ormonde employed the head of the family, Michael Dillon Snr, a retired RIC constable, as a caretaker.[120] According to Seamus Babington, who knew him personally, Michael-Thomas Dillon had attempted to join the IRA, and was prone to erratic and suspicious behaviour.[121] It is clear that Michael Dillon Snr had given some assistance to the British forces during the conflict, but it is questionable if this was of anything more than peripheral value. In his correspondence with the Irish Grants Committee, he stated definitively: 'I attribute all my misfortune to the fact that I directed British troops in Ireland in 1921.'[122] This could be interpreted as Michael Dillon having been an 'identifier' for the British Army. However, the application of Dillon's son to the same body is more ambiguous. Michael-Thomas Dillon stated that his father was victimised because he had given directions to a British Army patrol that was lost on a mountain road in 1921.[123]

Regardless of whether Michael Dillon Snr gave the British forces relatively minor aid on just one occasion, or consistently gave them more substantial assistance, once the IRA had discovered that he had helped them to any degree he would automatically have come under suspicion.

Babington, who owned a business in the town, also knew Dillon's youngest son, William, a senior pupil at Carrick-on-Suir Christian Brothers College. Babington's shop in Carrick-on-Suir was used to hold IRA meetings and to store arms and ammunition. Babington claimed to have noticed William Dillon loitering outside the premises for hours at a time, and regarded this behaviour as suspicious.[124] He described Dillon as 'not fully normal' – today he would probably be described as having an intellectual disability or behavioural disorder.[125]

In July 1921 a meeting of IRA officers in Kilcash was encircled by British troops stationed at Clonmel, Co. Tipperary, and those attending narrowly avoided capture.[126] Seamus Babington later claimed to have received definite information from republican sympathisers in the post office at Clonmel that William Dillon and his older brother Michael-Thomas, who worked as a postal clerk in Clonmel, were responsible:

> We had friends in the post office at Ballypatrick as well as at Clonmel, the receiving depot. Young [William] Dillon ... who mixed frequently and socially the night before with the column, billeted with families in [the] Kilcash area, 'phoned from Ballypatrick post office to his brother [Michael], who was a postal clerk in Clonmel post office, informing him of the I.R.A. invasion of the area that day and he at once 'phoned the British military in Clonmel. Ears were always on the alert, and word was at once sent from Clonmel to Kilcash and Ballypatrick shortly before the military arrived, and by the narrowest escape imaginable, the I.R.A. men had just got outside the ring.[127]

Local IRA leader Dinny Lacey came to the area on 9 July and ordered the IRA's Ballyneale Company to surround the Dillon house and keep it under observation.[128] According to Babington, the republicans had orders to 'surround the house only'.[129] Having watched the house for two hours, some members of the Ballyneale Company overstepped their instructions and decided to take matters into their own hands. At 11.30 p.m. members of the IRA approached the house, asking for a drink of water as a ruse to gain entry. When this was refused they attempted to force their way in and Michael Dillon Snr threw a glass jug at one of the men who was at a window attempting to force entry.[130] At that moment Dillon's fifteen-year-old daughter, Bridget, appeared at an upstairs window and was shot by one of the IRA Volunteers, who fired a shotgun. She was fatally wounded, suffering eight buckshot pellets to the right side of her head, two of which penetrated her brain.[131] Reports that members of the Dillon family opened fire first are apparently without basis.[132]

Following Bridget's shooting, William and Michael-Thomas went outside and appealed to the IRA to send for medical aid for their sister. Their request was refused and they were forced to stand at the gable-end of the house while the IRA formed a firing squad. William and Michael-Thomas managed to escape while the IRA officer in command of the group was organising the squad. The brothers were fired on as they fled but escaped unscathed. The IRA remained at the Dillon property for around a further hour before departing. Bridget Dillon died of her wounds at about 1.30 a.m. without receiving any medical assistance.[133] In the aftermath of the shooting, Dinny Lacey held an IRA inquiry into Bridget's death to investigate why the IRA company had exceeded their orders. According to Babington, Lacey 'was so upset and so annoyed that he favoured punishment on the company and the man who so foolishly fired on the house'.[134] The Dillon family relocated to Clonmel, but soon suffered further misfortune. On 4 May 1922

William Dillon was abducted by a group of armed men and killed a short time later.[135] Michael-Thomas Dillon left Clonmel for England following his brother's death.[136]

THE CASE FOR AND AGAINST SECTARIANISM

In the five cases where the religion of those executed as spies following the announcement of the Truce is known, three – David Cummins, Major O'Connor and John Poynton – were Protestant, and two – William Nolan and John Begley – were Catholic. The religious denomination of Eric Steadman is unclear. It has been stated that O'Connor and Poynton were both killed because they were Protestants.[137] This claim is supportive of the suggestion that throughout the conflict the IRA was motivated by anti-Protestant sectarianism to kill Protestant civilians alleged to have been spies. Drawing on local histories, veteran testimony and contemporary documents, all of those killed by the IRA as spies during the War of Independence are listed in Table 3.1 in an attempt to establish to what extent members of the IRA may have exploited the intelligence war as a cover for anti-Protestant sectarianism.

Table 3.1: Civilians executed as suspected spies by the IRA, county by county

Name	Date killed	Religion	Previous military or police service
Civilians executed as suspected spies by the IRA in Co. Armagh: 2[138]			
Hugh O'Hanlon	07-06-1921	Catholic	No military service
James Smyth	07-06-1921	Catholic	No military service

Name	Date killed	Religion	Previous military or police service
Civilians executed as suspected spies by the IRA in Co. Carlow: 5[139]			
Patrick Doyle	19-09-1920	Catholic	No military service
William Kennedy	15-03-1921	Catholic	No military service
Michael O'Dempsey	15-03-1921	Catholic	No military service
Frank O'Donoghue	??-06-1921	Catholic	No military service
Michael Hackett	01-06-1921	Catholic	Ex-soldier

Civilians executed as suspected spies by the IRA in Co. Cavan: 2[140]			
Patrick Briody	23-05-1921	Catholic	No military service
Hugh Newman	29-06-1921	Catholic	Ex-soldier

Civilians executed as suspected spies by the IRA in Co. Clare: 3[141]			
Martin Counihan	28-10-1920	Catholic	No military service
John Reilly	21-04-1921	Catholic	Ex-soldier
Patrick D'Arcy	21-06-1921	Catholic	Ex-IRA Volunteer

Civilians executed as suspected spies by the IRA in Co. Cork: 66[142]			
Timothy Quinlisk	20-02-1920	Catholic	Ex-soldier
James Herlihy	20-08-1920	Catholic	No military service
James Gordon	??-08-1920	Catholic	Ex-RIC
John O'Callaghan	15-09-1920	Catholic	Ex-soldier
John Hawkes	13-10-1920	Catholic	No military service
Thomas Downing	24-11-1920	Catholic	Ex-soldier
James Blemens	02-12-1920	Protestant	No military service
Frederick Blemens	02-12-1920	Protestant	No military service
George Horgan	12-12-1920	Catholic	Ex-soldier
Michael Dwyer	22-01-1921	Catholic	Ex-soldier
Tom Bradfield	23-01-1921	Protestant	No military service
Patrick Rae	23-01-1921	Catholic	No military service
Tom Bradfield	01-02-1921	Protestant	No military service
Alfred Kidney	04-02-1921	Catholic	Ex-soldier
Alfred Charles Reilly	09-02-1921	Protestant	No military service
William Johnson	09-02-1921	Protestant	No military service
Robert Eady	11-02-1921	Catholic	No military service
John O'Leary	12-02-1921	Catholic	Ex-soldier
William Sullivan	14-02-1921	Catholic	Ex-soldier
Charles Beale	14-02-1921	Protestant	No military service
Michael Walsh	18-02-1921	Catholic	Ex-soldier
Matt Sweetnam	19-02-1921	Protestant	No military service
Thomas Connell	19-02-1921	Protestant	No military service
William Mohally	20-02-1921	Catholic	Ex-soldier
Michael O'Sullivan	20-02-1921	Catholic	Ex-soldier (applicant to join RIC)
Alfred Cotter	25-02-1921	Protestant	No military service
Thomas Cotter	01-03-1921	Protestant	No military service
Brigid Noble	04-03-1921	Catholic	No military service
John Sheehan	05-03-1921	Catholic	No military service
John Good	10-03-1921	Protestant	No military service

David Nagle	13-03-1921	Catholic	Ex-RIC
Mary Lindsay	19-03-1921	Protestant	No military service
James Clarke	19-03-1921	Protestant	No military service
Cornelius Sheehan	19-03-1921	Catholic	Ex-soldier
Dan Lucey	20-03-1921	Catholic	No military service
Daniel McCarthy	25-03-1921	Catholic	No military service
John Cathcart	25-03-1921	Protestant	No military service
William Good	26-03-1921	Protestant	Ex-soldier
Denis Donovan	29-03-1921	Catholic	Ex-navy
Frederick Stennings	30-03-1921	Protestant	No military service
Denis Finbar Donovan	12-04-1921	Catholic	No military service
John Sheehan	21-04-1921	Catholic	No military service
Stephen O'Callaghan	29-04-1921	Catholic	Ex-soldier
William McCarthy	29-04-1921	Catholic	Ex-soldier
N. J. Harrison	30-04-1921	Catholic	Ex-RIC
Michael O'Keefe	30-04-1921	Catholic	Ex-soldier
James Saunders	05-05-1921	Catholic	No military service
William B. Purcell	06-05-1921	Catholic	Ex-soldier
James Lynch	06-05-1921	Catholic	No military service
Thomas Collins	07-05-1921	Catholic	Ex-soldier
David Walsh	16-05-1921	Catholic	Ex-soldier
Edward Hawkins	20-05-1921	Catholic	Ex-soldier
Francis McMahon	20-05-1921	Protestant	Ex-soldier
Christopher O'Sullivan	27-05-1921	Catholic	Ex-soldier
Warren J. Peacock	31-05-1921	Protestant	Ex-soldier
Dave Fitzgibbon	08-06-1921	Catholic	Ex-soldier
Daniel O'Callaghan	21-06-1921	Catholic	Ex-navy
John Crowley	24-06-1921	Catholic	No military service
John Lynch	25-06-1921	Catholic	Ex-soldier
Patrick Sheehan	28-06-1921	Catholic	No military service
John Sullivan	28-06-1921	Catholic	Ex-soldier
Francis Sullivan	01-07-1921	Catholic	No military service
William McPhearson	07-07-1921	Protestant	Ex-soldier
George B. O'Connor	10-07-1921	Protestant	Ex-soldier
William Nolan	11-07-1921	Catholic	Civilian (applicant to join RIC)
John Begley	11-07-1921	Catholic	Ex-soldier

Civilians executed as suspected spies by the IRA in Co. Dublin: 13[143]			
William 'Jack' Straw	21-10-1920	Unknown	Ex-soldier
Thomas Herbert-Smith	21-11-1920	Protestant	No military service

William McGrath	14-01-1921	Catholic	Ex-soldier
William Doran	29-01-1921	Catholic	Ex-soldier
James 'Skanker' Ryan	05-02-1921	Catholic	Ex-soldier
Patrick James O'Neill	15-04-1921	Protestant	Ex-soldier
Peter Graham	15-05-1921	Catholic	No military service
Stephen Arthur Barden	19-05-1921	Catholic	No military service
Leslie Frasier	22-05-1921	Protestant	Ex-soldier
John Ellard Brady	04-06-1921	Catholic	Ex-soldier
Thomas Halpin	04-06-1921	Catholic	Ex-navy
Robert Pike	18-06-1921	Catholic	Ex-soldier
Andrew Knight	07-07-1921	Protestant	No military service

Civilians executed as suspected spies by the IRA in England: 1[144]			
Vincent P. Fourvargue	21-03-1921	Catholic	IRA Volunteer

Civilians executed as suspected spies by the IRA in Co. Galway: 3[145]			
Patrick Joyce	15-10-1920	Catholic	No military service
Thomas Morris	02-04-1921	Catholic	Ex-soldier (also served in RIC)
Tom Hannon	27-04-1921	Catholic	No military service

Civilians executed as suspected spies by the IRA in Co. Kerry: 8[146]			
Godfrey Jasper	29-10-1920	Protestant	Ex-RIC
Martin Daly	20-03-1921	Catholic	No military service
John 'Sardy' Nagle	25-03-1921	Catholic	No military service
John O'Mahony	07-04-1921	Catholic	Ex-soldier
Arthur Vicars	14-04-1921	Protestant	Ex-soldier
Thomas O'Sullivan	04-05-1921	Catholic	No military service
John Fitzgerald	03-06-1921	Catholic	Ex-soldier
James Kane	11-06-1921	Catholic	Ex-RIC

Civilians executed as suspected spies by the IRA in Co. Kildare: 2[147]			
Michael Power	13-06-1921	Catholic	Ex-soldier
Philip Dunne	16-06-1921	Catholic	No military service

Civilians executed as suspected spies by the IRA in Co. Kilkenny: 4[148]			
William Kenny	27-08-1920	Catholic	Ex-soldier
Michael Cassidy	05-01-1921	Catholic	Ex-soldier
Michael O'Keefe	17-05-1921	Catholic	Ex-soldier
Patrick Dermody	17-05-1921	Catholic	Ex-soldier

Civilians executed as suspected spies by the IRA in Co. Laois: 2[149]			
Peter Keyes	05-07-1921	Catholic	No military service
John Poynton	10-07-1921	Protestant	Ex-RIC

Civilians executed as suspected spies by the IRA in Co. Leitrim: 2[150]			
William Latimer	30-03-1921	Protestant	No military service
John Harrison	22-04-1921	Protestant	No military service

Civilians executed as suspected spies by the IRA in Co. Limerick: 7[151]			
Denis Crowley	26-03-1920	Catholic	Ex-soldier
James Dalton	15-05-1920	Catholic	IRA Volunteer
Patrick Daly	01-08-1920	Catholic	No military service
Michael O'Meara	31-12-1920	Catholic	Ex-soldier
John O'Grady	18-03-1921	Catholic	Ex-soldier
Michael Boland	28-06-1921	Catholic	Ex-soldier
John Moloney	08-07-1921	Catholic	Ex-soldier

Civilians executed as suspected spies by the IRA in Co. Longford: 7[152]			
William Elliot	22-01-1921	Protestant	No military service
William Charters	22-01-1921	Protestant	No military service
Thomas Leacock	15-03-1921	Catholic	No military service
Edward Beirne	05-04-1921	Catholic	No military service
Thomas Byrne	06-04-1921	Catholic	Ex-soldier
John MacNamee	08-04-1921	Catholic	No military service
Sandy Gillespie	Unknown	Catholic	No military service

Civilians executed as suspected spies by the IRA in Co. Louth: 1[153]			
Henry Murray	25-02-1921	Catholic	Ex-soldier

Civilians executed as suspected spies by the IRA in Co. Meath: 4[154]			
Brian Bradley	02-01-1921	Catholic	Ex-soldier
John Donoghue	13-06-1921	Catholic	Ex-soldier
Thomas Smith	26-06-1921	Catholic	Ex-soldier
Patrick Keelan	02-07-1921	Catholic	No military service

Civilians executed as suspected spies by the IRA in Co. Monaghan: 8[155]			
Michael O'Brien	13-11-1920	Catholic	No military service
Joseph Gibbs	??-01-1921	Catholic	No military service
Patrick Larmour	09-03-1921	Catholic	IRA Volunteer
Frank McPhillipps	09-03-1921	Catholic	No military service
Henry Kerr	25-03-1921	Catholic	No military service

Hugh Duffy	01-04-1921	Protestant	Member Ulster Special Constabulary
Kate Carroll	16-04-1921	Catholic	No military service
Arthur Treanor	25-06-1921	Catholic	No military service

Civilians executed as suspected spies by the IRA in Co. Offaly: 8[156]			
Patrick Birmingham	05-05-1921	Catholic	Ex-soldier
John Lawler	26-05-1921	Catholic	Ex-soldier
Patrick O'Connell	17-06-1921	Catholic	Ex-soldier
Michael Reilly	17-06-1921	Catholic	Ex-soldier
Thomas Cunningham	18-06-1921	Catholic	Ex-soldier
Richard Pearson	01-07-1921	Protestant	No military service
Abraham Pearson	01-07-1921	Protestant	No military service
Eric Steadman	09-07-1921	Unknown	Ex-soldier

Civilians executed as suspected spies by the IRA in Co. Roscommon: 9[157]			
Edward Canning	01-11-1920	Catholic	Ex-soldier
Bernard Ward	06-11-1920	Catholic	Ex-soldier
Martin Heavy	31-12-1920	Catholic	Ex-soldier
Francis Elliot	04-03-1921	Catholic	Ex-soldier
John Gilligan	06-04-1921	Catholic	Ex-soldier
John Weymes	06-04-1921	Catholic	Ex-RIC
Martin Scanlon	08-05-1921	Catholic	Ex-RIC
John McCalley	08-05-1921	Unknown	No military service
'Slickfoot' Maher	Unknown	Unknown	Ex-soldier

Civilians executed as suspected spies by the IRA in Co. Sligo: 1[158]			
Thomas Walker	14-04-1921	Protestant	No military service

Civilians executed as suspected spies by the IRA in Co. Tipperary: 16[159]			
Thomas Kirby	08-01-1921	Catholic	Ex-soldier
— 'Looby'	??-01-1921	Unknown	Unknown
Michael Ryan	19-02-1921	Catholic	Ex-soldier
James 'Rockam' Maher	07-03-1921	Catholic	Ex-soldier
Patrick 'Swordy' Meara	07-03-1921	Catholic	Ex-soldier
George Lysaght	07-03-1921	Protestant	No military service
Joseph Brady	26-03-1921	Catholic	No military service
Robert Stone	16-04-1921	Protestant	No military service
Timothy Cranley	23-04-1921	Catholic	Ex-soldier
Fred. Crossley Boyle	13-06-1921	Protestant	No military service

George Wallis	15-06-1921	Protestant	No military service
Robert Healy	15-06-1921	Catholic	Ex-soldier
Patrick Maher	26-06-1921	Catholic	Ex-soldier
David Cummins	09-07-1921	Protestant	Ex-soldier
Jerry Brien	??-1921	Unknown	Unknown
Brian Turpin	??-1921	Unknown	Unknown

Civilians executed as suspected spies by the IRA in Co. Waterford: 1[160]			
William Moran	13-04-1921	Catholic	Ex-soldier

Civilians executed as suspected spies by the IRA in Co. Westmeath: 5[161]			
Martin Lyons	25-11-1920	Catholic	Ex-soldier
James Blagriff	30-12-1920	Catholic	Ex-soldier
George Johnston	11-04-1921	Protestant	No military service
Samuel Lee	11-06-1921	Unknown	Unknown
Unidentified man	02-07-1921	Unknown	Unknown

Civilians executed as suspected spies by the IRA in Co. Wexford: 4[162]			
Jeremiah Newsome	08-02-1921	Catholic	Ex-soldier
James Skelton	21-03-1921	Catholic	Ex-soldier
Thomas Skelton	21-03-1921	Catholic	No military service
James Morrisey	25-05 1921	Catholic	Ex-soldier

The IRA killed a total of 184 civilians accused of spying during the War of Independence. The religious denomination of nine of those killed is unknown. Of the remaining 175 whose religious affinities are known, forty-two (24 per cent) were Protestant and 133 (76 per cent) Catholic, so in terms of religion Protestants were a small but significant minority amongst those executed by the IRA as spies. No Protestants were killed in twelve counties where spies were shot, which rules out any possibility that the IRA in Armagh, Carlow, Cavan, Clare, Galway, Kildare, Kilkenny, Limerick, Louth, Meath, Waterford or Wexford used the issue of spies as a pretext for sectarian activity against, or the 'ethnic cleansing' of, Protestants. If the seven counties where no suspected spies were executed are also taken into account then it can be shown conclusively that no Protestants were executed on suspicion of spying in nineteen of

Ireland's thirty-two counties. Even if Peter Hart's doubtful thesis that the IRA's campaign in Cork was motivated by anti-Protestant sectarianism were accepted as fact, this sample illustrates the dangers of assuming that the experience of one county during the conflict was reflective of the country as a whole. Furthermore, given that only twenty-one (approximately 32 per cent) of the sixty-six civilians shot as spies by the Cork IRA were Protestant, Hart may have overstated the case for a possible sectarian motivation in the killing of civilians by the IRA during the 'intelligence war' in Cork.

Thomas Walker, the only person killed by the IRA in Co. Sligo as a spy, was a Protestant, as were both of the men executed by the IRA in Co. Leitrim. One of the two civilians killed by the IRA on the pretext of spying in Co. Laois was a Protestant. In Co. Tipperary Protestants accounted for about half of those killed whose religious denomination is known, while in Cork, Kerry, Longford, Monaghan, Offaly and Westmeath, Protestants accounted for a third or less of those killed. Although a significant minority of the total number killed (approximately a quarter) were Protestants, it should be remembered that a very significant proportion of Irish loyalists would have been from this religion and they were the most likely section of the Irish population, for historical, political, cultural and social reasons, to be willing to risk incurring the wrath of the IRA by assisting the British forces. However, Catholics suspected of spying were also shot in very large numbers. Overall, the religious make-up of those executed closely mirrored the overall religious constitution of Irish society at that time.[163]

Despite this evidence, there have been repeated claims that IRA executions of Protestants who were alleged to be spies were motivated by sectarianism. Hart suggested that many of the Protestants in West Cork killed by the IRA were targeted because of their religion, but there is evidence suggesting that a hard core of the Protestant loyalist community in the area was actively assisting the British forces. While the British Army's 'Record of the Rebellion in Ireland' states that Protestants in southern Ireland 'rarely gave much information, because, except by chance they had not got it to give', it also acknowledged that the situation was different in West Cork, where members of the Protestant-loyalist community actively assisted the British forces: 'in the Bandon Valley ... there were many Protestant farmers who gave information ... it proved almost impossible to protect these brave men, many of whom were murdered'.[164]

There is evidence that the British forces in Bandon even recruited members of the local Protestant congregation, through their minister, Reverend Lord, to gather intelligence information about the IRA. Tom Bradfield, a Protestant civilian from Bandon, met Peter Monaghan, a Scottish IRA Volunteer, and mistook him for an RIC Auxiliary because of his accent. Having volunteered the location of an IRA arms dump, Bradfield proudly declared that he had gathered intelligence for the British forces: 'The Reverend Mr Lord is my man, and I give him the information.'[165] Another Protestant interrogated by the IRA on suspicion of being an informer told his captors that he was innocent, but that Reverend Lord met members of his congregation every Sunday after church services to gather information for the British forces to pass on to Major Percival of the Essex Regiment, who boasted: 'I have my own intelligence service around here and I know everything'.[166]

The British Army's 'Irish Rebellion in the 6th Divisional Area' stated:

> Martial law had undoubtedly frightened a large number of civilians, and made them more willing to give information to the Crown forces. This fact apparently was realised by the rebel leaders, as, commencing in February [1921], a regular murder campaign was instituted against Protestant-Loyalists and anybody who might be suspected of being an informer, quite irrespective of whether he really was one or not ... it had the result of making information very hard to obtain.[167]

Though this statement accuses the IRA of being less than discerning in targeting suspected spies, it also implies that the IRA's execution of suspected spies was largely motivated by military circumstances, rather than sectarianism or other prejudices, and was ultimately effective in discouraging civilians from assisting the British forces. Lionel Curtis, an adviser to the British government who visited Ireland in June 1921, reported to the government: 'Protestants in the South do not complain of persecution on sectarian grounds. If Protestant farmers are murdered, it is not by reason of their religion, but rather because they are under suspicion as loyalists. The distinction is a fine but a real one.'[168] Some influential southern-Irish Protestants at the time were also quick to dismiss allegations of sectarianism. John Henry Bernard, the Provost of Trinity College and former Church of Ireland Archbishop of Dublin, declared in 1924 that, 'During the melancholy years 1920–1923, there have, indeed, been outbursts of violence directed at Loyalist minorities, but for the most part it has been qua Loyalist and not qua Protestant that the members of the Church of Ireland have suffered.'[169]

At least two Protestants and five ex-servicemen were killed as suspected spies by the IRA in Co. Offaly, and Kenneth Strong, a British Army intelligence officer active in the county, attributed the killing of suspected spies in the county to errors made by the British forces and not to an IRA campaign against Protestants or ex-soldiers:

> If things went wrong I knew that I had always the shelter of the barracks to which to retire. Not so the unfortunate informant. A few shots in the night and the next morning a corpse and pinned to it a label 'Traitor. Shot by orders of the IRA'. I'd had no previous Intelligence training and I was often worried by the fear that my inexperience may have led to some of these tragedies.[170]

Regarding the pre-Truce killings, in David Cummins' case it appears that at the time he was abducted and sentenced to death the local IRA leader may not have been aware of his captive's religious denomination. Paddy Byrne, the vice-commandant of the local IRA battalion initially offered Cummins the chance to see a Catholic priest before his execution. Presumably Byrne did this on the assumption that Cummins, like the overwhelming majority of those who shared his surname in the county, was a Catholic.[171] If this was the case, then it was only when Cummins stated definitively that he was 'not a Catholic', immediately before his execution, that Byrne would have realised Cummins was Protestant. If the IRA military commander who oversaw his execution was unaware of Cummins' religion, it rules out the possibility of a sectarian motive in the IRA's decision to execute him. If the IRA was indeed ignorant of Cummins' religion, it might be interpreted as an indication that the 2nd Battalion of the Tipperary No. 3 Brigade IRA suspected people of being spies based on their activities, and that a suspect's religious denomination was not part of their thought process in attempting to discern a suspect's guilt.

At the inquest into John Poynton's death, his mother, Emily Poynton, stated that: 'My son had no enemies and was very popular and except that for a week he was in the RIC I know no reason why this should have occurred.' Constable W. T. McMullen gave evidence that Poynton 'was no friend to Sinn Féin and was friendly with the police'.[172] This evidence, coupled with the IRA's suspicion that he was acting as a spy and had ignored an IRA order to leave the district, was probably sufficient cause in republican eyes to account for his killing. The inquest did not cite religious sectarianism as a factor in Poynton's death. Given that the only other civilian executed by the IRA in Co. Laois on suspicion of spying was Catholic, it seems unlikely that Poynton's death was motivated by religious sectarianism.

Eric Steadman was a stranger in the Tullamore area and it is extremely unlikely that the IRA would have known what religious denomination, if any, he belonged to. It is likely that suspicions of him as a stranger in the area and a possible spy were more significant factors in his killing. A unique aspect of Steadman's killing was his baptism by his captors shortly before his execution:

> He was a prisoner only for a couple of days ... we had a conscience about it. The brother Jimmy pointed out to him how nice it would be if he could die in the State of Grace, that is from our point of view: and Seamus explained the Catholic Church situation to him. We sent into the Tullamore parochial house for a clergyman as there was a spy to be shot, but no one came out to him. So begod Seamus then got the water and he had him baptised. Then he was shot soon afterwards.[173]

The only other case where a suspected spy was baptised immediately before his or her execution occurred in Co. Roscommon, where a Black and Tan named Harold Round was captured and executed in June 1921. Round told his captors he was an atheist, but at their instigation agreed to see a priest and be baptised.[174] If Steadman's executioners believed he was an atheist or had not been baptised, they may have wanted him to be baptised, based on the Christian belief that the unbaptised cannot enter Heaven.[175] They may also have feared that if they killed an unbaptised man, they may have been condemning his soul to an eternal state of Limbo and even though it is impossible to determine exactly why Steadman's baptism occurred, this seems the most likely scenario. Cummins and Steadman appear to have been the only two of the suspected spies executed immediately before the Truce to have been offered any form of spiritual aid.

While more Protestant suspects were executed as spies than Catholics immediately before the Truce, the IRA also killed two Catholics and attempted to kill at least three other Catholic loyalists, all of whom had been suspected of spying. Despite claims that the IRA was unduly influenced by anti-Protestant bias in their decision to kill suspected spies, the Meath IRA treated C. W. Chaloner, a Protestant ex-soldier, more leniently than Christopher Farrell, a Catholic labourer. Chaloner was punished by merely having his car commandeered, while Farrell suffered abduction and interrogation.[176]

AN IRA CAMPAIGN AGAINST EX-SOLDIERS?

When looking at reasons behind the killing of those executed, it is important to remember that four of the six suspected spies executed by the IRA at the time of the Truce were ex-soldiers: David Cummins, Eric Steadman, Major O'Connor and John Begley. A fifth, John Poynton, was an ex-RIC constable. The final IRA victim, William Nolan, had applied to join the RIC. Table 3.1 shows that at least 'eighty-eight of the 184 civilians killed by the IRA as suspected spies (approximately 48 per cent) were ex-servicemen (eighty-five ex-British Army soldiers and three ex-Royal Navy). A further eight of the total (approximately 4 per cent) were ex-RIC.[177] One of those killed, Hugh Duffy, was a member of the USC, and William Nolan was a civilian, but had recently applied to join the RIC. At least four serving or former IRA Volunteers (approximately 2 per cent) were shot as spies. At least eighty-six of those killed (approximately 46 per cent) had no military or police service.

Jane Leonard has argued that the IRA envied the military experience, pensions and entitlements of ex-soldiers and despised them for having served in the British Army, with the result that many innocent ex-soldiers were killed by the IRA on the pretext that they were British spies: 'Within the nationalist community ex-soldiers weakened the revolution's effectiveness by refusing to join Sinn Féin, subscribe to its funds, or obey the rulings of its courts.'[178] However Leonard's study does not take into account the very large number of ex-soldiers who joined republican organisations during the conflict. Rather than being an object of envy, as Leonard suggested, the experience of ex-servicemen who chose to join the IRA was largely recognised and rewarded.

The presence of large numbers of ex-servicemen in IRA units throughout Ireland implies that the IRA was far less prejudiced against ex-soldiers than Leonard's work has suggested.[179] J. B. E. Hittle's study of the conflict concluded that 'some of the IRA's best men were experienced combat veterans of the British Army. Their knowledge of weapons and tactics proved invaluable to the [IRA's flying] columns'.[180] These included the IRA's director of training, Emmet Dalton; Tom Barry, training officer of the Cork No. 3 Brigade;[181] Ignatius O'Neill, leader of the 4th Battalion of the Mid Clare Brigade's active service unit (ASU);[182] Dan McSweeney, training officer of the 7th Battalion, Cork No. 1 Brigade;[183] and Paddy Horkan, a former member of the Worcestershire Regiment, captain of A Company of the 1st Battalion, West Mayo Brigade.[184] The commandant of the IRA's Athlone Brigade, Jim Tormey, was also an ex-British soldier.[185] The Sinn Féin leaders Erskine Childers and Robert Barton were both former British Army officers, and Barton held honorary rank in the IRA.[186] This shows that ex-servicemen held influence and a percentage of leadership positions within the organisation that were far in excess of their numerical representation. Far from being prejudiced against ex-British soldiers, many IRA brigades actively sought to recruit ex-servicemen because of their military experience. Frank McGrath, commandant of the Tipperary No. 1 Brigade IRA, was known to favour IRA recruits and officers who had seen military service in the British Army.[187]

The RIC reported that, in Belfast, 'many ex-soldiers with good war records become IRA criminals'.[188] Seamus McKenna, intelligence officer of the IRA's Belfast Brigade, claimed that this was because the leadership of the Belfast IRA favoured recruits who were ex-British servicemen over raw recruits with stronger republican credentials.[189] Even IRA support units in England attracted large numbers of British Army veterans and dozens of ex-soldiers joined the London, Liverpool, Nottingham and Sheffield companies of the IRA.[190] A briefing document circulated to British Army intelligence officers in October 1920 stated that the IRA was actively recruiting ex-servicemen.[191] Florrie O'Donoghue, the intelligence officer with the 1st Cork Brigade IRA, stated that 'hundreds of men with British Army service served loyally and well in the IRA, some of them being the foremost among the intrepid fighters'.[192] William Corrie, an ex-British soldier who served in E Company, 1st Battalion of the Dublin Brigade IRA, stated: 'During my service with the IRA I met *hundreds* of ex-servicemen.'[193]

Corrie's experience, and the numerous examples cited above, pose serious questions about Leonard's conclusions and challenge Peter Hart's claim that the reason only a 'tiny minority' of the British Army veterans joined the IRA was because of prejudice against them.[194] More recent research by Paul Taylor has shown that 'the reality was far more complex and multifaceted … intimidation directed towards them [ex-soldiers] during the conflict was mostly for reasons other than war service and … following independence they were not marginalised by the state or the community.'[195]

Nonetheless, the IRA had reason to be suspicious of ex-soldiers who demonstrated strong loyalist sympathies. At least two attempts were made to use ex-soldiers' associations to gather information about the IRA. British intelligence recruited John Byrne, a former leader of the Soldiers', Sailors' and Airmen's Union, to infiltrate the IRA in an effort to capture Michael Collins.[196] A similar British intelligence operation was mounted in Co. Kerry, where John O'Mahony, an ex-soldier who worked in Tralee, attempted to recruit ex-servicemen to gather intelligence for the British military.[197] Both attempts failed after the IRA assassinated the British agents involved.

The economic difficulties of many former ex-servicemen, coupled with their military training and proven record of loyalty to the British crown, made them ideal candidates for intelligence work on behalf of the British forces. Irishmen who had served in the British forces were far more likely to suffer economic hardship after the war than their British counterparts as average unemployment in Ireland among ex-soldiers was 46 per cent compared to just 10 per cent in Britain, although this was largely due to the general high rate of unemployment in post-war Ireland and not to any specific prejudice against Irish ex-servicemen.[198] As early as July 1919, several thousand Irish ex-servicemen engaged in protests about unemployment and inadequate financial provision in their British Army pensions.[199] By February 1920 an estimated 27,000 able-bodied ex-servicemen in Ireland were unemployed.[200] This situation had improved little by the end of that year, with 21,000 ex-servicemen still unemployed.[201] In January 1921 there were 24,000 unemployed ex-soldiers in Ireland, with a concentration of 4,500 former servicemen out of work in Cork alone.[202] In June 1921 the Munster Fusilier Ex-Comrades Association reported 'in the present state of affairs in Ireland, it was very difficult for an ex-serviceman to obtain employment of any kind'.[203] Major General H. S. Jeudwine commanding the British 5th Division in Ireland reported in February 1921 that 'although the peasants and the small farmers in the west of Ireland were the most prosperous they had been within living memory, ex-soldiers were suffering particular hardship. Probably almost the only cases in which there has been want this winter have been among unemployed ex-soldiers and their families'.[204] Since the British authorities in Ireland had publicly offered financial rewards for the supply of intelligence information, some ex-soldiers may have been forced to act as spies and informers out of economic necessity in 1920 and 1921.

Post 1920 approximately 2,500 of the RIC's recent recruits, comprising 20 per cent of the recruits to the Black and Tans and

10 per cent of the recruits to the RIC Auxiliary Division, were Irishmen – the vast majority were ex-soldiers.[205] The RIC Veterans and Drivers Division recruited local ex-servicemen in Ireland because of a shortage of experienced drivers in the RIC, and operated in tandem with the RIC Auxiliary Division, with its members driving vehicles used in their patrols, raids and searches.[206] Local ex-servicemen who joined the Veterans and Drivers Division proved a particularly useful source of intelligence information because of their knowledge of the local populace and geography, and at least one local ex-serviceman, Denis O'Loughlin, who joined the Division was suspected of being a spy and was killed by the IRA.[207] A number of Catholic ex-servicemen who operated as a criminal gang in Co. Limerick joined the RIC Auxiliary Division following an armed clash between them and the local IRA unit in Newcastle West, and were suspected of engaging in intelligence gathering after their enlistment.[208]

Many unemployed Irish ex-servicemen re-enlisted in the British Army in 1919 and 1920. In February 1921 the British government facilitated further recruitment by issuing a directive allowing ex-servicemen to re-enlist in the British Army for short service attachments to British regiments stationed in Ireland.[209] These regiments often recruited local ex-servicemen who could re-enlist for a period of ninety days' 'emergency service'.[210] The 1st Battalion of the Devonshire Regiment recruited local ex-servicemen in Waterford and they performed general fatigue duties, wore British uniform, but lived outside of barracks and were known as the 'Waterford Devons'.[211] Some loyalist ex-soldiers, such as William Shiels, who had officially returned to civilian life, were nonetheless involved in covert intelligence-gathering work on behalf of the British Army while dressed in British uniform.[212]

The re-enlistment of local ex-soldiers into the British regiments serving in Ireland helped to blur the distinction between ex-servicemen and serving members of the British forces, so it was logical for the IRA to assume that, if the British Army were utilising ex-soldiers in Ireland for fatigue duties, they would also seek to recruit them for intelligence gathering. This distinction was further blurred when Irish ex-servicemen donned British uniform to disguise themselves as English soldiers while carrying out intelligence work. Another alleged informer, Thomas Kirby, who was captured, executed and secretly buried by the IRA, though officially a civilian, had worn a British military uniform to conceal his identity when he was acting as a civilian 'identifier' accompanying British military patrols.[213] A number of other ex-soldiers were among the most effective informers in the British forces' intelligence war against the IRA, including Daniel 'Monkey' McDonnell and Patrick 'Croxy' Connors.[214]

The RIC county inspector's reports for July 1921 do not state that any of the ex-servicemen who were executed – David Cummins, Eric Steadman or Major G. B. O'Connor – were killed by the IRA as part of an IRA campaign targeting ex-soldiers.[215] As Steadman was not a native of the area where he was killed, it is unlikely that the local IRA would have been aware that he was an ex-soldier until he was captured and interrogated. Steadman's demeanour, behaviour and, in particular, his English accent would have been enough to draw the IRA's suspicion, even if he had no prior military experience. John Poynton's mother testified that the sole source of his unpopularity was his association with the RIC.[216] Given that he was the only ex-RIC constable executed by the IRA in Co. Laois, it seems likely that it was his continued interaction with the RIC after his return home that led to the suspicion that he was a spy and to his killing, rather than any campaign against former RIC constables.

In many parts of Ireland there was significant hostility between ex-soldiers and the British forces – in some areas the British forces were responsible for killing more ex-soldiers than the IRA. At least five ex-soldiers in Cork city and a further ten ex-servicemen in Limerick who had no association with the IRA were killed by the British forces.[217] Both the IRA and the British forces usually killed ex-servicemen because they perceived them to be active opponents. However, it would be a misleading oversimplification to suggest that either grouping was so blindly prejudiced that they were not interested in harnessing the military experience of ex-servicemen and waged campaigns against them.

In many cases it is simply impossible to know for certain how many of the people killed by the IRA for spying had given information and assistance to the British forces.[218] One of Ireland's leading historians, Diarmaid Ferriter, has described it as 'perhaps an impossible task' to find out.[219] This is because there is no documentation publicly available that can confirm conclusively the 'guilt' or 'innocence' of suspected spies. Letters written to the British forces that provided intelligence information, which were intercepted by the IRA, in most cases have not survived. Contemporary British documents did not name their informants for security reasons and it appears that some British documents relating to intelligence matters during the conflict are still confidential. At the time the British forces rarely confirmed or denied the alleged role of those who had been executed and few members of the British forces who served in Ireland during the War of Independence were willing to talk about the conflict or include information concerning it in their memoirs. Even today the British government will neither confirm nor deny allegations made against alleged spies executed by Irish republicans almost a century ago. In 2015 the British Home Office refused a Freedom of Information request to divulge information about financial payments to Irish informants a century earlier on the basis that 'to do so would undermine British national security and could lead to present-day informants being less willing to come forward in case their names were revealed in 100 years' time'.[220] As a result, historians are overly reliant on the accounts of IRA veterans for information about the supposed guilt or innocence of suspected spies and informers.[221]

The register of the Irish Compensation Commission may give an indication of how many, if any, of those killed by the IRA as suspected spies had actively assisted the British forces. Of the 184 suspected spies killed by the IRA, ninety-four are identifiable on the commission's register. As well as recording the compensation paid to their families, the register frequently commented on the British government's liability for the killing. Since the IRA killed the ninety-four individuals listed in Table 3.2, an admission of 'British Liability' on the register may be an indication that the deceased had actively supported the British forces. The term 'full Liability' was used by British government officials in approving separate claims by members of the British forces, including British soldiers and RIC constables as well as some of the civilians the IRA shot as alleged British spies.[222]

In some cases there is additional evidence to corroborate the indication that suspected spies killed by the IRA and accepted as British liabilities were assisting the British forces. For example, William Latimer, who was killed by the IRA on 30 March 1921, is listed on the register as a 'British Liability'. In her evidence to the Irish Grants Committee, his widow stated that he had supplied information to the RIC before he was killed.[223]

No comment on liability was recorded in thirteen cases (approximately 13 per cent); liability is suggested in a further sixteen cases (approximately 16 per cent of the total) but no more detail is given. Of the remainder, the British admitted partial liability for the deaths of ten (approximately 10 per cent), and fifteen are identified as 'British supporter', which seemingly indicates that the deceased were targeted simply because they were identifiable as loyalists. The forty-one remaining cases (approximately 42 per cent of the total) were recorded as 'British Liability', 'full British Liability' or 'full Liability', which is a strong indication that many, if not the majority, of those identified, had been actively assisting the British forces.

Table 3.2: Suspected spies killed by the IRA listed on the Compensation Commission Register

Name	Date	Acceptance of British liability	Compensation awarded
James Gordon	??-08-1920	'L' [Liability]	£34
William Kenny	27-08-1920	Not Stated	£360
John O'Callaghan	15-09-1920	'L'	£950
Patrick Doyle	19-09-1920	'Accepted British Liability'	£1,200
John Hawkes	13-10-1920	'L – British supporter'	£300
Patrick Joyce	15-10-1920	Not Stated	£3,750
Martin Counihan	28-10-1920	'Agreed to accept as a British Liability'	£2,160
Bernard Ward	06-11-1920	'L – Agreed British Liability'	£2,500
Michael O'Brien	13-11-1920	'Agreed 50/50'	£125
Tom Herbert-Smith	21-11-1920	'L'	£3,500
Thomas Downing	24-11-1920	'L'	£38
Frederick Blemens	02-12-1920	'L'	£56
George Horgan	12-12-1920	'Agreed British Liability'	£900
James Blagriff	30-12-1920	'British supporter'	£1,500
Martin Heavy	31-12-1920	'Agreed to accept as British Liability'	£400
Michael O'Meara	31-12-1920	'L – Agreed to accept as British Liability'	£2,850
William Charters	22-01-1921	'L – Agreed British Liability'	£1,500
William Elliot	22-01-1921	'Agreed British Liability'	£1,000
Michael Dwyer	22-01-1921	'L – Agreed to accept as British Liability'	£1,600
Tom Bradfield	23-01-1921	'British supporter'	£6,000
Patrick Rae	23-01-1921	'L'	£2,000
William Doran	29-01-1921	'L – British supporter'	£1,750

Tom Bradfield	01-02-1921	'British supporter'	£5,000
Alfred Kidney	04-02-1921	'L'	£750
Jeremiah Newsome	08-02-1921	'Agreed 50/50'	£150
Alfred Charles Reilly	09-02-1921	'L'	£9,000
William Johnson	09-02-1921	'L – Agreed 50/50'	£4,150
Robert Eady	11-02-1921	'Agreed 50/50'	£2,000
William Sullivan	14-02-1921	Not Stated	£50
Charles Beale	14-02-1921	'Agreed 50/50'	£900
Michael Walsh	18-02-1921	Not Stated	£650
Michael Ryan	19-02-1921	Not Stated	£150
Matt Sweetnam	19-02-1921	'Agreed 50/50'	£100
Michael O'Sullivan	20-02-1921	'L'	£2,000
Alfred Cotter	25-02-1921	'Agreed to accept as British Liability'	£5,000
Henry Murray	25-02-1921	Not Stated	£135
Francis Elliot	04-03-1921	'L – Agreed to accept as British Liability'	£2,600
Brigid Noble	04-03-1921	'British supporter'	£2,000
James Maher	07-03-1921	'Agreed to accept as a British Liability'	£1,500
George Lysaght	07-03-1921	'L – Agreed as British Liability'	£147
Frank McPhillipps	09-03-1921	'Agreed to accept as British Liability'	£410
John Good	10-03-1921	'Agreed 50/50'	£7,000
David Nagle	13-03-1921	'Agreed to accept as British Liability'	£1,400
Michael O'Dempsey	15-03-1921	'Agreed 50/50 Liability'	£4,500
John O'Grady	18-03-1921	'Agreed to accept as British Liability'	£450
James Clarke	19-03-1921	'British supporter'	£200
Dan Lucey	20-03-1921	'L'	£500
Martin Daly	20-03-1921	'L – British supporter'	£600
John Cathcart	25-03-1921	'L'	£8,500

Denis Donovan	29-03-1921	'L'	£2,000
Frederick Stennings	30-03-1921	'Agreed to accept as British Liability'	£5,500
William Latimer	30-03-1921	'Agreed to accept as British Liability'	£5,180
Edward Beirne	05-04-1921	'L – Agreed to accept as British Liability'	£2,500
John Gilligan	06-04-1921	'Agreed British Liability'	£2,000
John Weymes	06-04-1921	'Agreed British Liability'	£1,700
John O'Mahony	07-04-1921	'Agreed to accept as British Liability'	£3,000
John MacNamee	08-04-1921	Not Stated	£1,240
George Johnston	11-04-1921	'L – British supporter'	£1,000
William Moran	13-04-1921	'Agreed British Liability'	£50
Kate Carroll	16-04-1921	'L – British Liability'	£600
Robert Stone	16-04-1921	'L – Agreed to accept as British Liability'	£1,000
John Reilly	21-04-1921	'L – Agreed to accept as British Liability'	£1,200
John Harrison	22-04-1921	'British Liability'	£4.640
Tom Hannon	27-04-1921	'Agreed to accept as full Liability'	£1,150
Michael O'Keefe	30-04-1921	'L – Agreed to accept as British Liability'	£950
Martin Scanlon	08-05-1921	'L – British supporter'	£2,500
Peter Graham	15-05-1921	'L – British supporter'	£500
Michael O'Keefe	17-05-1921	Not Stated	£100
Stephen Barden	19-05-1921	'Accepted as a British supporter'	£25
Patrick Briody	23-05-1921	'Agreed to accept as British Liability'	£3,100
Chris O'Sullivan	27-05-1921	'L – Agreed to accept as British Liability'	£1,850

Michael Hackett	01-06-1921	'L [Liability]'	£400
John Ellard Brady	04-06-1921	Not Stated	£25
Dave Fitzgibbon	08-06-1921	Not Stated	£35
John Donoghue	13-06-1921	'L – Agreed to accept as British Liability'	£350
Michael Power	13-06-1921	'L – British supporter'	£3,300
Philip Dunne	16-06-1921	'Agreed 50/50'	£350
Michael Reilly	17-06-1921	'L – Agreed to accept full Liability'	£1,000
Thomas Cunningham	18-06-1921	Not Stated	£1,250
Robert Pike	18-06-1921	'L'	£40
Patrick D'Arcy	21-06-1921	'Accepted as full British Liability'	£600
Patrick Maher	25-06-1921	'Commission Award'	£935
Thomas Smith	26-06-1921	'L – Agreed British Liability'	£1,000
Hugh Newman	29-06-1921	'Agreed to accept as British Liability'	£2,500
Richard Pearson	01-07-1921	'Accepted as a British supporter'	£500
Abraham Pearson	01-07-1921	'Accepted as a British supporter'	£1,000
Patrick Keelan	02-07-1921	Not Stated	£175
Peter Keyes	05-07-1921	'L – Agreed to accept as British Liability'	£2,500
Andrew Knight	07-07-1921	'L'	£1,250
William Alexander McPhearson	07-07-1921	'Agreed British Liability'	£2,000
David Cummins	09-07-1921	'Agreed 50/50'	£600
George B. O'Connor	10-07-1921	'Accept as British Liability'	£5,000
John Poynton	10-07-1921	'Agreed British Liability'	£1,200
John Begley	11-07-1921	'L'	£1,500

Whether a suspected spy was sentenced to death, executed or punished in some other way often depended on the value of the information he or she had given and whether it resulted in the capture of IRA arms and the deaths of IRA Volunteers. The IRA did not attempt to kill all of those it suspected of spying at the time of the Truce and in a number of cases the advent of the Truce resulted in the death sentences imposed on suspected spies being commuted, or spies being issued with a verbal warning or threatening notice instead. During a mail raid in July 1921, members of the Tipperary No. 3 Brigade IRA discovered the identity of an informer who was writing letters to the RIC. This man, an elderly ex-soldier who lived in Carrick-on-Suir, received a warning to stop corresponding with the RIC but was otherwise unmolested. Denis O'Driscoll, a captain in one of the local IRA companies, believed that the man would have been shot had it not been for the Truce: 'No punitive action was, however, taken against him. I believe that the Truce, coming at the time it did, was what saved him.'[224]

At the same time, the IRA's Longford Brigade had identified, through a mail raid, a woman who was passing accurate intelligence to the British forces in the county. According to the local brigade intelligence officer, Michael Francis Heslin, the suspected spy had 'a good knowledge of our movements, the places at which we stayed and the particular working of the organisation in general'. Heslin believed that the woman's action warranted execution but that the impending ceasefire saved her life.[225]

The advent of the Truce also apparently prevented the execution of a number of suspected spies being investigated by the IRA's East Limerick Brigade. When informing IRA GHQ of the execution of a suspected spy in Limerick before the announcement of the Truce, the local intelligence officer stated: 'A few others would have met the same fate were it not for [the] truce.'[226] A similar situation occurred in Co. Kerry. The IRA's Kerry No. 1 Brigade had killed four suspected spies during the conflict. According to William Mullins, the brigade quartermaster, they were planning to execute several others by July 1921: 'A few more were suspected and proof was being collected and traps set, but the Truce came and saved them … Those few whom the Truce saved still live, some among us, and little do they know how near they were to the same fate of all spies who are caught.'[227]

Acting on the order they had received from the headquarters staff of the 1st Eastern Division to take action against specified targets before the Truce came into effect, the Carnaross Company of the IRA's Meath Brigade organised an attack on the British Army at Moynalty Bridge, Kells, for the morning of 11 July. In conjunction with this they planned to discipline C. W. Chaloner, a suspected spy who lived in the area.[228] Chaloner, a Protestant ex-soldier, was suspected of having given information to the British Army concerning an IRA ambush.[229] The previous month he and his wife had been fired upon because they failed to stop when confronted by an IRA patrol, but they escaped with relatively minor wounds.[230] Having tried Chaloner *in absentia* before the announcement of the Truce, the brigade council of the IRA's Meath Brigade ordered that the car he had used to warn the British Army was to be confiscated as a punishment for his actions.[231] Seán Farrelly led a group of seven armed and masked IRA Volunteers who took Chaloner's car at 10.30 p.m. on 10 July. Before leaving, Farrelly and his comrades mocked Chaloner, advising him to report the incident to the RIC, and saying: 'Perhaps they will help you now as you helped them.'[232] Beyond being held at gunpoint and having his car commandeered, Chaloner was otherwise unmolested.[233]

At 11 p.m. on 10 July IRA Volunteers raided the home of Mrs Harriet Byrne, a Protestant who lived near Maryboro, Co. Laois and accused her of passing information to the British forces. They then tore up a British flag and photographs of the RIC that were in the house and stole a sum of money, but before leaving they made Mrs Byrne sign a statement that she would not report the raid to the British forces and fired a revolver shot in her kitchen.[234] At 1 a.m. on the same night, two armed and masked members of the IRA forced their way into the home of Miss A. Gleeson, a Catholic postmistress, who also lived near Maryboro. The men then forced Miss Gleeson and her nephew, Richard Harvey Cassidy, to sign a statement that in future they would not give any information about the IRA to the British forces.[235] In East Limerick, a group of masked men physically assaulted two women at Timothy Aherne's house and warned them against speaking to the British military.[236] At the time of the Truce, the IRA had also planned to abduct William Ringwood, manager of the Munster & Leinster Bank at Bantry, Co. Cork. Ringwood, a Protestant, was suspected of passing intelligence information to the British forces and was facing execution as a suspected spy, but was saved after a Catholic priest intervened with the local IRA on his behalf.[237]

At 2 a.m. on 11 July the IRA abducted Christopher Farrell, a Catholic labourer who lived at Catherae, Co. Meath:[238]

> At 2 a.m. Paddy Farley Brigade O/C, called and ordered me to go to Carnaross [sic] to arrest a man named Christopher Farrell a suspected spy … We arrested Farrell and took him to a house in Salford where we placed two Volunteers to guard him. I arrived home at 7 a.m. on the morning of the Truce.[239]

Michael Govern does not specify what happened to Farrell, but as there is no record of his death and his name does not appear on 'the missing list' compiled by the British government, it is likely that he was later released unharmed.[240]

On the morning of 11 July Patrick Shannon, a Catholic ex-RIC constable who lived near Castlerea in Co. Roscommon, found a notice posted on the door of his house warning him that he was a convicted spy. Shannon had previously been threatened for failing to force his son to resign from the RIC, and a month earlier his house had been raided by thirteen armed men who tied his daughter to a tree, interrogated her concerning her brother's whereabouts and warned her to cease fraternising with members of the RIC in Elphin and Castlerea.[241]

Just a few hours before the Truce came into effect, the IRA's Mid Limerick Brigade also took non-fatal action against George Ryan, a spy it had unmasked. Ryan, a lieutenant in the Fedamore Company of the IRA, had been caught sending intelligence information by post to the RIC in Limerick city. The local IRA officers court-martialled Ryan *in absentia* and sentenced him to death. In accordance with IRA general orders, the Mid Limerick Brigade sent to IRA GHQ requesting permission to carry out Ryan's execution, but this was refused. Instead, the Mid Limerick Brigade was instructed to fine Ryan £100, destroy his house and sentence him to permanent exile, giving him just twenty-four hours to leave the country.[242] This sentence was carried out at 1 a.m. on 11 July, when a group of armed and masked IRA Volunteers raided Ryan's farm at Fedamore, and burned his farmhouse and its farm buildings to the ground.[243] Ryan's case shows that just because the ceasefire was imminent IRA brigades did not automatically abandon their usual protocols and procedures regarding suspected spies.

At the time of the Truce the IRA's Mid Limerick Brigade was also holding prisoner two suspected spies who had been in IRA custody for up to five months; however, it was felt that there was insufficient evidence of their guilt to warrant their execution and the men were released as soon as the Truce took effect.[244]

Similarly, in Donegal the IRA was holding two suspected spies captive at the time of the Truce, but released them after the ceasefire began. In July 1921 it arrested John Collins, an ex-soldier who worked as a travelling fishmonger and was suspected of supplying to the British forces information that had resulted in a number of arms seizures and the arrest of an IRA Volunteer. Collins had been observed accompanying a party of Auxiliaries conducting house searches in Dungloe, disguised as an Auxiliary and apparently acting as an 'identifier' for the patrol, pointing out active members of the IRA to them for arrest. Following this, Collins was arrested by the IRA and held captive for over a week. Under interrogation he admitted supplying Colonel McClintock, a British intelligence officer in Omagh, Co. Tyrone, with information. Collins also gave the names of others whom he claimed were British agents, including an itinerant named McKeowan, whom he claimed was giving information to the RIC. McKeowan was subsequently arrested and both men were charged with spying at an IRA court martial held about the time the Truce was agreed on 8 July. McKeowan was exiled from the country and Collins was sentenced to death, but the sentence was commuted to permanent exile when news of the Truce reached Donegal.[245]

Two suspected spies who had been held prisoner by the Meath Brigade since October 1920 were also released unharmed once the ceasefire began.[246] After they learned of the Truce, the leadership of the 3rd Battalion, West Waterford Brigade warned three individuals they had been monitoring that, if they continued to associate with members of the British forces, they would be executed as spies.[247]

If the announcement of the ceasefire had been seen as a chance to settle scores on the part of the IRA, as has been argued, there would have been a much larger number of those suspected of spying killed in the final days of the conflict, especially on the night of 10 July and the morning of 11 July 1921, by which time almost every IRA unit in the country knew that the Truce was coming. However, there were only a handful of IRA attempts to kill suspected spies, and these were limited to just five counties: Cork, Dublin, Laois, Offaly and Tipperary. By contrast, in the same period the IRA was responsible for over fifty mail raids across fifteen counties, and since the objective of these raids was to uncover intelligence information, it is clear that after the announcement of the Truce the IRA was far more concerned with gathering fresh intelligence information than with tracking down and attempting to execute those who were already suspected of spying.[248] It is also significant that in the five counties where spies were killed in the days before the Truce, the IRA expended a far greater effort, involving much greater risks, in attacking armed members of the British forces – which seems to rule out the possibility that those shot in the last days of the conflict were innocent civilians selected merely because they were with 'soft targets'.

The evidence just presented clearly indicates that in many cases the announcement of the Truce led IRA units to cancel action they had planned against civilians who were suspected of spying for the British forces. Having learned of the ceasefire, some IRA units limited themselves to warning suspects about their activities, while others were sent threatening notices or were held prisoner for brief periods as a punishment. Death sentences passed by republicans on several loyalists for spying were commuted as a result of the Truce. The IRA released unharmed more suspected spies than were killed in the final days of the conflict. If the IRA had intended to kill as many suspected spies as possible after the announcement of the Truce, it would undoubtedly have killed these instead of releasing them unharmed.

No suspected spies were killed in the IRA's 1st Eastern Division despite the fact that this is the only divisional area where a written IRA order issued after the Truce was announced has survived that directed the local IRA brigade commanders to deal with suspected spies as they saw fit without recourse to higher authority. The available evidence suggests that, while the IRA in Co. Meath took action against spies in its brigade area at the time of the Truce, they were treated far more leniently than suspects in other areas.

Despite previous estimates of up to a dozen suspected spies being executed at the time, as well as hearsay about multiple killings, 'disappearances' and secret burials, the reality is that the IRA shot just six civilians as spies after the announcement of the Truce. This level of violence was not exceptional in comparison to other equally brief periods earlier in the conflict.[249]

The majority of the suspected spies killed in the last days of the conflict had strong links to the British forces and had previously come to the attention of the IRA, which suggests that rather than searching for any available 'soft targets' after the announcement of the Truce, the IRA specifically targeted those of whom they were already suspicious. There is no evidence to support the claim that the announcement of the Truce spurred the IRA nationally into a rash of unwarranted attempts to execute individuals it suspected of spying. In the cases of the six men killed at the time of the Truce, the IRA appear to have acted out of military concern in the belief that their victims were gathering intelligence for the British forces. The available evidence does not suggest that the announcement of the Truce was used as a pretext to carry out sectarian attacks on Protestants. Nor is there much evidence to suggest that the IRA used the announcement of the Truce as a pretext to murder ex-soldiers.

A culture of 'short shrift for spies' had existed among the British forces during the First World War. The British Army in France and Belgium frequently executed civilians it suspected were acting as German spies.[250] Spy mania on the Western Front is thought to have resulted in hundreds of arrests and multiple civilian executions.[251] In some cases the British soldiers executed suspected spies on the basis of dubious evidence; for example, Private B. W. Page of the London Irish Rifles recalled an incident when a telephone was found in the house of a peasant girl who was friendly with British troops on the Western Front. This discovery was considered to be proof that the girl was a German spy and all the occupants of the house were rounded up and executed.[252] When Ivone Kirkpatrick, the British Secret Service's chief spymaster in the

Netherlands during the First World War, was asked what action should be taken to deal with a German agent who had infiltrated his spy network, he replied, 'Bump him off.' The suspected German agent died, having been shot five times at point-blank range while dining in a café.[253]

It is difficult to draw distinctions between the violence used by the British forces in the killing of these alleged spies and the IRA's tactics during the War of Independence. While the IRA operated as a guerrilla army, its standard operating procedure regarding the execution of suspected spies usually mimicked executions conducted by the British Army and other regular military forces. The IRA often used courts martial to try those accused of spying, carried out executions using firing squads with the condemned person tied to a fixed post and, like the British Army on the Western Front, attached spy labels to the bodies of those it shot as spies.[254] The bodies of the majority of those executed by the IRA were deposited in public places with an accompanying label attached to the corpse, reading 'Shot by IRA – Spies and informers beware!' or similar. The labelling of the corpse as a 'spy' took extra effort on the part of the killers and was a public act intended to show proper bureaucratic and judicial processes.[255]

The IRA's sanction of lethal force, threats, warnings and other punitive measures against suspected spies after the announcement of the ceasefire appears to have been based on the degree to which it suspected that an individual was guilty. It was also based on the importance of the information that the IRA believed the suspect had passed to the British forces. As such, the republican treatment of suspected spies immediately before the Truce did not amount to 'giving spies short shrift' or differ significantly from the standard operational procedure throughout the conflict which was, in most cases, based on the military norms, practices and standards of the day.

4

IRA ATTACKS ON
OFF-DUTY BRITISH TROOPS

The 'ceasefire' dispatch issued by the IRA's 1st Eastern Division after the announcement of the Truce ordered 'last-minute' attacks not just on loyalist civilians suspected of spying but also on members of the British forces – with members of the RIC receiving specific mention as the most important target to be attacked at every available opportunity before the Truce began.[1] While not a single loyalist civilian suspected of spying in the IRA's 1st Eastern Division was killed as a result of this order, there were at least ten separate attacks on the British forces in the divisional area before the Truce came into effect and only one of these was made against the British military.[2] The other nine were all against the RIC, with four attacks on RIC barracks, three attacks on RIC patrols and two attacks on RIC constables.[3] None of these attacks produced fatalities.

The specification in the 1st Eastern Division's order that 'the old RIC' should be the primary target of these attacks indicates that the republicans fostered a particular grievance against the Irishmen who continued to serve in that force. This is borne out by James Creegan, adjutant of the IRA's Fingal Brigade:

> Despite their acts of terrorism, we had no real spite towards the Black and Tans or Auxiliaries, whose position we understood. They were an alien force, holding a country for their people. The R.I.C. were in a different category. They were Irish, in the enemy's uniform, and were really uniformed spies. Without them, the other forces of the enemy would have been worthless. We had no love for them.[4]

The specific order to target the 'uniformed spies' of the RIC in the dying hours of the conflict suggests that the IRA's attacks on off-duty members of the British forces were motivated by bitterness and vindictiveness rather than military factors.

During the War of Independence, and for some time after, it was common for British politicians, veterans and military historians to dismiss the IRA's military campaign as a terrorist campaign that relied on barbaric methods, in particular the murder of 'soft targets', which bore no resemblance to 'civilised warfare'. Supporters of this theory often dismiss these attacks as 'acts of terror' or IRA 'terrorism'. The 'soft target' narrative is probably summarised best in John Dorney's book, *The Story of the Irish War of Independence*, in a chapter entitled 'Terror and Counter-Terror':

> By the spring of 1921 the British rarely travelled in convoys of less than two lorries, sometimes accompanied by an armoured car. Their barracks were also by now formidably defended. The IRA simply could not take on these forces in combat. But what they could do was take revenge for the British assassination of their men with assassinations of their own. In Clare for instance three British soldiers were found unarmed apparently having deserted in February 1921. With little hesitation the local IRA men shot them and dumped them on the roadside.[5]

However, Dorney chose a poor example to explain the 'soft target' theory. Local IRA Volunteers believed that the three British soldiers executed in Co. Clare – Privates Morgan, Walker and Williams – were on an intelligence-gathering mission for the British military when they were captured and executed. There is no evidence to suggest that these soldiers were killed in reprisal or as the result of a local vendetta.[6]

In October 1920 Lord Curzon denounced IRA attacks on the RIC as barbaric, telling the House of Lords that the IRA's campaign was 'the warfare of the red Indian, of the Apache'.[7] In

1922 Hugh Pollard condemned the IRA as being a 'small executive body of criminals' with 'the paper formality of a regular force', which shunned the tactics of civilised warfare in favour of a campaign 'far more the nature of an organised murder gang than of an irregular body of patriots'.[8] The following year, the official British Army account of the conflict in Munster echoed Lord Curzon's and Pollard's sentiments, declaring that the IRA 'in most cases, avoided anything in the nature of a pitched battle' and instead favoured the 'murder' of British troops.[9] Some pro-Treaty writers in Ireland, who were uncomfortable with the nature of the IRA violence, also later voiced similar criticism of the IRA's methods. For instance, P. S. O'Hegarty denounced the assassination of Alan Bell in 1920 and Detective Hoey in 1919 by the IRA as the work of 'irresponsible' and 'morally degenerate' gunmen.[10]

Several decades later, Field-Marshal Bernard Law Montgomery, a veteran of the conflict, stated in his memoirs that: 'the Sinn Féin War … developed into a murder campaign'.[11] The British military historian Colonel Walter Leonard Vale dismissed the war as 'a vicious form of large-scale gang warfare' that resulted in the 'wanton shooting of men separated from their comrades'.[12] Another military historian, Sir Arthur Hezlet, denounced the IRA as 'terrorists' and 'ruthless fanatics', who had murdered RIC constables 'in a cowardly manner'. According to Hezlet, RIC constables 'were shot down by a number of concealed gunmen. When even one policeman put up resistance, the IRA generally took to their heels. They [the IRA] preferred to catch their victims unawares or unarmed.'[13]

Some academic scholars have made similar claims in their research. David Fitzpatrick claimed that the last few months of the conflict saw a 'rapid extension of assassination and clandestine killings', and that almost half of those killed during this period were British soldiers or members of the RIC.[14] Peter Hart described the War of Independence as a 'dirty war' in which murder was more frequent than battle.[15] While Hart conceded that a large number of combatants had died in military engagements, he maintained that 'many more people died without a gun in their hands, at their doors, in quarries or empty fields, shot in the back by armed men'.[16] He also claimed that the 'guerrilla war in Cork in 1921 was not primarily an affair of ambushes and round-ups. It was terror and counter-terror, murder after murder, death squad against death squad, fed by both sides' desire for revenge.'[17] Marie Coleman found that the republican military campaign in Longford became increasingly brutal as the IRA adopted more of a hardline stance against Irish RIC constables.[18] William Sheehan has claimed that, by the summer of 1921, the British Army's counter-insurgency measures were so successful that the IRA adopted 'terrorist tactics rather than those of guerrillas'.[19]

Recent popular histories have reiterated these claims. Ernest McCall's book on the RIC Auxiliary Division stated that while the IRA in Dublin had intensified its activities in 1921, the resulting attacks were 'mainly on off-duty members of the Crown Forces when everything was in their favour'.[20] Pádraig Yeates claimed IRA assassinations of members of the British forces were 'more akin to Mafia-style killings' than to conventional warfare.[21]

The 'soft target' theory has gained a foothold in the public consciousness, as evidenced by the claims of retired members of An Garda Síochána who organised an event to mark the ninetieth anniversary of the disbandment of the RIC and DMP.[22] Those organising the event claimed that:

> ... over 500 ... police officers ... were murdered by the IRA during and after the War of Independence and in 1916. These men were for the most part honourable and honest police officers and many were killed while off-duty, often in front of their families ... The circumstances of their deaths were in many cases exceptionally brutal.[23]

In addition to the assertion from various quarters that republicans deliberately chose 'soft targets', the claim that the IRA embarked on a series of reckless attacks following the announcement of the Truce has created the impression that the IRA targeted off-duty British troops engaged in harmless activities in a spate of unjustifiable last-minute killings. In recent years this claim has been embellished by writers who allege that these IRA killings included the execution of four teenage soldiers captured while shopping for sweets, the murder of an RIC constable in his front garden, the shooting of a Black and Tan immediately after his wedding ceremony and the assassination of an RIC sergeant who, being a devout Catholic, was on his way to mass. The proximity of these killings to the Truce has resulted in their becoming so heavily mythologised that the most basic facts relating to them have become either largely obscured or completely lost.[24]

This mythology was constructed chiefly around the deaths of those members of the British forces perceived to have been innocent. The attack on Sergeant King, the last member of the British forces officially killed by the IRA in the conflict, who died less than two hours before the armistice began, has been significantly underplayed in comparison to that on Constable Clarke, who was killed earlier the same day. This is because King's involvement in reprisal killings as the leader of the 'Castlerea Murder Gang' does not fit with the established narrative of republicans bent on gratuitous last-minute violence and attacks launched on supposedly inoffensive members of the British forces like Clarke. The mercy shown by the IRA towards some British soldiers and RIC constables who were captured and released unharmed in the same time period has also been omitted from what has become an overly simplistic and highly propagandised account of pre-Truce killings.

In 1899 and 1907 the Hague Conventions had been negotiated in an attempt to establish internationally accepted 'rules of war' and form a chivalrous military code that would ostensibly be adhered to by all armies. However, while it attempted to regulate the status of militia units fighting an occupying force, the Hague Conventions did not provide a set of unambiguous rules governing the conduct of guerrilla war. The British insisted that the Hague Conventions could not be applied to conditions in Ireland, yet paradoxically they made frequent complaints that the IRA failed to comply with these same terms and protested that their opponents rarely wore uniforms, used prohibited 'dumdum' bullets, did not openly bear arms and failed to adhere to the 'laws of war'.

It is important to note that the British had made the wearing of IRA uniform and the purchase of regular ammunition illegal, that most of the 'dumdum' bullets fired by the IRA had been captured from the British forces and that the unauthorised possession of arms was punishable by death. Furthermore, when Irish republican combatants had attempted to comply with the 'laws of war' during the 1916 Rising, they were refused prisoner-of-war status after capture and their leaders were executed.

Neither the IRA nor the British forces were ever fully compliant with the terms of the conventions and it is difficult to envisage how a military code of conduct that had been intended for use in large-scale conflicts between regular, professional armies could have been applied to a relatively small-scale but intense guerrilla war involving irregular forces on both sides. In fact, the republicans rarely justified their behaviour by referring to the Hague Conventions or international law. Instead, they attempted to explain and justify their actions by referencing local conditions and precedents.[25]

It is worth examining the Hague Conventions in detail to see whether they are relevant to the debate surrounding the legitimacy of IRA attacks on so-called 'soft targets'. Neither the 1899 nor the 1907 conventions make specific reference to attacks on off-duty troops, or afford them any specific protection. The 1907 convention does stipulate that 'it is especially forbidden ... to kill or wound treacherously individuals belonging to the hostile nation or army'.[26] The key word in this phrase is 'treacherously', which implies elaborate deceit or trickery. Subsequent articles expand on this point, specifically referring to the improper exploitation of a flag of truce or the use of the enemy's flag or uniform. The agreement also forbids the killing of unarmed soldiers who have offered an unconditional surrender.[27] Since the Hague Convention of 1907 bestowed no special status or protection on off-duty soldiers, they could be considered legitimate targets unless they qualified for protection through having surrendered unconditionally and verifiably, or having already been taken prisoner.[28]

Cold-blooded attacks on off-duty members of the British forces were a far remove from the lofty ideals of chivalrous warfare envisaged and implemented by the republican leaders of the 1916 Rising.[29] However, a clear distinction must be drawn between the fighting conditions that existed in a short-lived, urban-based insurrection, where the enemy was rarely encountered and the fighting was largely devoid of intimacy and hatred, and guerrilla conflict, where close-quarters combat was the norm, killers were readily identifiable and both sides engaged in reprisals. Michael Collins later claimed that during the War of Independence, the IRA had adhered to the rules of war 'as far as possible'.[30]

In the final stages of the War of Independence, the nature of the conflict became so brutal and intense that Major Bernard Law Montgomery, who served with the 17th Infantry Brigade in Cork, declared: 'My own view is that to win a war of this sort you must be ruthless.'[31] In effect, combatants on both sides did not feel bound by the 'rules of war' so much as the 'customs of war'. They frequently cited the deeds of their opponents as setting a precedent, which they felt justified their own actions. Members of the British forces, such as Lieutenant-Colonel Maxwell Scott, justified their reprisals on the basis that the IRA fought a dirty war: 'Is it to be wondered ... that men ... seeing their comrades shot down in cold blood, sometimes took the law into their own hands and indulged in unofficial reprisals[?]'[32]

In turn, in January 1921 the leadership of the Tipperary No. 3 Brigade, the East Limerick Brigade and three Cork Brigades proposed that drastic measures be taken against off-duty troops and captured British soldiers, citing British actions and reprisals which they felt justified their proposals. They made the following submission to IRA GHQ:

1. That GHQ issue a proclamation to effect: – In areas where hostages are taken by the enemy in lorries and otherwise: the enemy whether armed or unarmed will be shot at sight.

2. That GHQ issue a proclamation to effect: – In view of the enemy proclamation that our troops will be shot if found armed. The enemy will be similarly dealt with by our troops.[33]

The IRA GHQ procrastinated over issuing a response to this proposal and, after growing impatient with their superiors, the IRA officers who had proposed these measures decided to go ahead and implement them without waiting for official approval. The following month members of the IRA's East Limerick Brigade executed two members of the RIC captured after the Dromkeen Ambush.

Tom Barry, who was one of the first IRA officers to sanction such attacks, blamed the actions of his British opponents for forcing a shift in republican attitudes. He claimed that the republicans had no option but to respond in kind to what he believed was the ruthlessness the British forces had introduced into the conflict: 'We were now hard, cold and ruthless, as our enemy had been since hostilities began. The British were met with their own weapons. They had gone down in the mire to destroy us and our nation, and down after them we had to go'.[34] Attitudes like Barry's were not confined to Munster: an IRA Volunteer in Monaghan related how the killings of his comrades in British custody led to increasingly ruthless attacks: 'Through the years of struggle the hangings, and executions, and sufferings had generated in us something unchristian'.[35]

During the War of Independence, IRA brigades had occasionally issued orders for co-ordinated attacks on members of the RIC. Following the death of Terence MacSwiney, the IRA in Kerry received an order that Black and Tans were to be 'shot on sight'.[36] The IRA's Mid Clare Brigade ordered an attack on all available RIC targets for 31 March 1921. The date was chosen specifically because it was the payday for RIC constables and, consequently, it was expected that many members of the force would be spending their time in local public houses.[37] It is significant that in the last days and hours of the conflict, the IRA mounted far more attacks on members of the RIC than on British military personnel. Animosity towards the 'old RIC' was widespread. When Stephen 'Paddy' Vaughan, an IRA veteran from Roscommon, was asked what was his greatest regret arising from the conflict, he replied:

That we didn't kill more of the Irish police. The Irish police knew the land and the countryside as well as you know your own backyard. They are the ones who led the raids. The British Army couldn't have found my house if they'd had a map. We should have gone after the old policemen.[38]

IRA Volunteers in Tralee spent the last night before the Truce pasting notices on lampposts in the town, listing 'Dublin Castle Gunmen'.[39] Those named, whom the notice stated were 'Wanted for Murder', included RIC Constable Patrick Culleton and a French-Canadian Black and Tan known as 'the Jewman de la Roi'. The posters threatened that those listed would be killed.[40] The IRA knew that the Irish RIC constables who remained in the force during the War of Independence were of vital importance to the

British forces and they regarded them as 'the eyes and ears' of the enemy and traitors to their fellow Irishmen.[41] Republican loathing for the members of the 'old RIC' was in many cases because of its effectiveness in intelligence work.

The majority of RIC constables were Irish-born Catholics, and consequently they understood the community they policed and were able to integrate into it far better than the Black and Tans and Auxiliaries, who were mostly recruited in Britain. The RIC practice of minimising transfers ensured that RIC constables spent prolonged periods in the same district, giving them an intimate familiarity with the area.[42] Furthermore, their duties included the collection of agricultural statistics, census enumeration, the regulation of public houses and regular foot patrols, all of which provided them with an in-depth knowledge of the local populace that was vital for intelligence work.[43]

The importance of Irish members of the RIC to British intelligence operations was outlined by the RIC press officer, Hugh Pollard, who pointed out that: 'Effective police work in … Ireland depends largely on one main principle, namely, an efficient local police force whose men know everybody in their area'.[44] Lieutenant Grazebrook, a British military intelligence officer stationed in Cork, also stressed the importance of Irish RIC constables to British intelligence: 'of all the sergeants, Donovan was one of the real old type of the RIC, absolutely invaluable, "the rat" he was called by many of the country folk and he certainly could rat out information impossible to the others in a most wonderful way'.[45] Major General Douglas Wimberley recalled that IRA attacks on the RIC proved effective in neutralising men such as Sergeant Donovan: 'Soon they would no longer identify suspicious rebels we produced … as they knew that to do so meant revenge'.[46] The following anecdote from Patrick O'Brien, an IRA commandant from Cork, sums up succinctly the attitude of many republicans towards the members of the 'old RIC':

Early in August, 1920, the local Military O.C. in Liscarroll [*sic*] (a Lieut. Honeywood) sent a message to me to call up to the Military Post ... He came out and, following a discussion on some general topics, he informed me that he would hold me personally responsible for any attacks being made on the R.I.C. I immediately got my back up and enquired from him whether he had service in the Great War. He stated he had and I then enquired from him what their normal procedure was in dealing with spies. He replied 'Shoot them', and I then politely informed him that we intended to follow similar action with the R.I.C.[47]

IRA GHQ, while approving these killings, was, at the same time, also keenly aware of the public outrage that some of these could incite. Jack Fitzgerald, an IRA officer from Kilbrittain, Co. Cork, recalled that he and his comrades were restricted to targeting only the most active and effective members of the RIC for assassination: 'they [the British military] didn't stir out then without a policeman. He was their intelligence officer and guide. We would only be allowed to shoot a bad RIC man'.[48] For example, IRA GHQ sanctioned the assassination of an RIC sergeant who was actively involved in intelligence work in Bandon. The plan was that the IRA would kill the sergeant when he was en route to Sunday mass. Both Cathal Brugha and Michael Collins (who was not known for his religious piety) expressed outrage that the man was killed at the church doorway, thereby breaching the sanctity of the building.[49]

It is worth noting that some provincial IRA officers, who were perfectly happy to use physical force and mount ambushes on the British forces, objected to the assassination of RIC men on moral grounds. Bill Brennan, an IRA officer in Tipperary, who had refused to carry out the killing of an RIC man, was deprived of his command as a result:

> I objected to it ... taking a life. Just walk in, meet a fellow in a pub or
> the like ... I thought it was very wrong to take the life point blank. I

was prepared to … give them a fair fight rather than the other way. I didn't go along with it … my captainship didn't last … No matter. There was always a hard man somewhere, cared less what he'd do.[50]

Some local IRA leaders adopted a particularly harsh stance when it came to members of the RIC and the Black and Tans. Donnchadh O'Hannigan, leader of the East Limerick Brigade flying column, had two members of the RIC captured after the Dromkeen Ambush, a Black and Tan named Samuel Adams and RIC Constable Patrick Foody, summarily executed.[51] In justification for this action, O'Hannigan cited a directive he claimed to have received from IRA GHQ ordering the court martial and, if necessary, execution of all Black and Tans captured by the IRA. This order was supposedly issued in reaction to the summary execution of IRA Volunteers captured by the British forces.[52] The possibility cannot be discounted that O'Hannigan invented this alleged order because of a division among the participants in the ambush over whether the captured members of the RIC patrol should be executed.[53]

In the days before the Truce was implemented the East Limerick Brigade was not the only one to deliberately focus their attacks on the RIC. Throughout the country RIC men and barracks were targeted, sometimes with fatal results.

THE SHOOTING OF CONSTABLE ALFRED NEEDHAM

Constable Alfred Needham was shot and fatally wounded by the IRA in Ennis on 8 July 1921. Since Needham's death occurred so close to the end of the War of Independence it has been subject to a great deal of embellishment. In *Police Casualties in Ireland 1919–1922*, the historian Richard Abbott incorrectly states that Constable Needham was shot on 10 July – the last full day of the conflict and less than twenty-four hours before the Truce. According to Abbott's narrative, Needham had got married that same morning, and he and his new bride were both attacked by the

IRA.[54] Newspaper columnist Kevin Myers gave a far more colourful account of Needham's killing in an article marking the nine-tieth anniversary of the Truce:

> ... with the Truce just hours away, an RIC man named Alfred Needham, aged 20, clearly thought that finally he could marry his sweetheart. But a clerk in Ennis tipped off the IRA that the groom's profession was 'constable'. So a beaming Alfred and his teenage bride emerged from the registry office, and two gunmen shot him dead.[55]

Most recently, Professor Eunan O'Halpin of Trinity College Dublin has put forward a similar narrative:

> The RIC suffered the most casualties at IRA hands. In March 1920 Constables Charles Healy and James Rock were shot dead as they left devotions at ... Toomevara, Tipperary ... They were the first police to be killed leaving a religious service, but they weren't to be the last ... And what about twenty-year-old RIC Constable Alfred Needham? Who, having just exchanged vows with his bride, was shot dead in front of her, the killing took place on the eve of the Truce.[56]

However, the verifiable facts regarding Constable Needham's shooting bear no relation whatever to these highly fanciful and emotive accounts.

Constable Alfred G. Needham was a Black and Tan from London. He had enlisted in the RIC on 14 December 1920. He was an ex-soldier and worked as a telegraph operator before joining the RIC.[57] He was stationed in Tiermaclane, near Ennis, Co. Clare. On 8 July 1921 Needham was granted eight hours' leave from duty and travelled to Ennis with two other RIC constables. At 4.30 p.m. Needham was standing at the gate of a stable in Upper O'Connell Street, talking with a Miss Corry, when he was attacked. The IRA approached from behind Miss Corry. They were armed with revolvers and fired two shots at Needham, wounding him in the neck. The wounded constable attempted to draw his revolver and return fire but suffered a second gunshot wound to the abdomen before he could do so. His female companion immediately alerted the British military and Needham was removed to the County Infirmary, where two doctors operated on him. He died at 3 p.m. on 10 July and his body was taken to England for burial.[58]

There is no evidence to support the claim that Needham had got married on the morning he was shot. RIC service records indicate that he was single at the time of his death.[59] The Civil Registration Office in Ennis has no record of an Alfred Needham marrying on 8 July 1921.[60] Contemporary police and press reports make no reference to a wedding having taken place before the shooting. Although the RIC county inspector's report of the incident refers to Miss Corry as 'a girlfriend' of Needham's,[61] a detailed report on Needham's shooting, death and funeral arrangements in a local newspaper simply refers to Miss Corry as 'a young lady acquaintance' of the deceased.[62] In October 1921 the Ennis Quarter Sessions awarded the constable's mother £1,200 compensation for his death, plus £25 expenses.[63] In normal circumstances a spouse or fiancée would have been the primary person considered for a compensation payment. The claims of a dependent parent would only have been considered if the deceased was unmarried and there was no other next of kin. The fact that Needham's mother received such a large award is further proof that Constable Needham was single at the time of his death.

The story that Needham had got married just hours before his death appears to have been invented later for propaganda purposes, or melodramatic effect in storytelling, or both. Far from being gunned down leaving a church or registry office immediately after marrying, Needham was actually shot while standing at the entrance to a stable. It is therefore impossible that a clerk processing marriage papers tipped off the IRA as to Needham's profession and arranged the assassination. Moreover, Needham's shooting occurred early on 8 July, before the Truce had been formally agreed or announced. At the time of the shooting, no one among the IRA in Clare knew that a ceasefire had been agreed in Dublin. Michael Brennan, the leader of the IRA's East Clare Brigade and commander of the IRA's 1st Western Division, only discovered that a truce had been agreed when he received a dispatch from IRA GHQ in the days after Needham's assassination.[64] Therefore there is no possibility that the shooting of Constable Needham was a knee-jerk reaction to the advent of the Truce.

THE SHOOTING OF CONSTABLE FREDERICK CORMER

The historian Fr Pat Twohig wrote in effusive terms about the lamentable fate of an anonymous Black and Tan who was supposedly the last victim of the conflict: 'A Black and Tan was shot dead in Enniskerry, Co. Wicklow one hour after the cessation of hostilities. One feels regret, even a twinge of remorse, at such an occurrence. A mother's son, I mean to say, and already a non-combatant, walking the street alone, savouring the new sensation of peace.'[65] However, this incident never happened – there were no members of the RIC killed in Enniskerry or anywhere else in Co. Wicklow on the day the Truce began.

The killing of Constable Cormer at Rathdrum, Co. Wicklow, was probably the basis for this melodramatic fiction.[66] Constable Frederick Cormer was a Black and Tan from Middlesex. He had enlisted in the RIC on 23 November 1920, he was unmarried and had previously been employed as a footman. On completing his training, he was posted to Rathdrum.[67] Shortly after 7 p.m. on 8 July 1921, Constable Cormer, accompanied by RIC Constable Reilly, went to Neary's shop at the Fairgreen in Rathdrum to buy cigarettes and groceries.[68] It is unclear if Cormer and Reilly were armed at the time, but the initial press reports of the incident stated that they were not.[69] On entering the shop they met another

RIC constable, who was armed.[70] Cormer and Reilly called for a round of drinks before ordering groceries. An RIC constable who had been in the bar before them went towards the toilet whilst Mrs Neary was occupied filling the grocery order.[71] Moments later Mattie O'Brien entered Neary's shop accompanied by two other IRA Volunteers. They opened fire on the two RIC constables who were seated, drinking, at the shop counter.[72] The attackers fired approximately six shots, one of which wounded Constable Reilly in the arm. Constable Cormer raced from the shop into the street pursued by the gunmen, who fired a further five shots at him. He was struck by three bullets, which hit him in the forehead, mouth and left clavicle. Cormer collapsed in the street and died instantly.[73] O'Brien and his comrades escaped on a bicycle to Maud Gonne MacBride's cottage in Glenmalure.[74]

Constable Cormer was killed less than two hours after the Truce had been agreed in Dublin; however, his killers would have been completely unaware that a ceasefire had been negotiated. They were motivated to act by local factors and not the political and military developments that had occurred in Dublin. Wicklow was the quietest county in terms of political violence during the War of Independence.[75] For months before July 1921 the IRA's GHQ had been pressurising the brigades in Wicklow to begin a sustained guerrilla offensive. Christopher Byrne, the quartermaster of the IRA's East Wicklow Brigade, claimed that this process had already begun when Seán MacBride was appointed in late June 1921 by the IRA's GHQ to organise the area:

> We were getting things into active shape when Seán MacBride arrived ... and he proceeded to arrange ambushes and shooting of policemen – one in every district – for the following Sunday week. There was to be shooting in every district from Woodenbridge to Greystones ... However the whole thing ended up in the shooting of one policeman.[76]

Despite MacBride's best efforts to launch a co-ordinated republican offensive, only one member of the British forces, Constable John Fitzgerald, was killed in Wicklow on the appointed date of Sunday 3 July. An attempt to ambush an Auxiliary patrol at Cusheen a few days later also ended in failure.

Far from becoming despondent at this lack of success, MacBride proposed that the IRA in Wicklow undertake even larger operations.[77] Local IRA leaders resented MacBride's presence in the area, and Byrne suggested to Mattie O'Brien and his men that they should act on their own initiative by going to Rathdrum, where there was a large RIC garrison, and 'try to get after the Tans'.[78] The result was the attack on the three RIC constables in Neary's shop.

Byrne's account makes it clear that Cormer's shooting, though premeditated, was an opportunistic attack and was not in any way related to the announcement of the Truce.[79] MacBride, who was in overall command of the IRA in Wicklow, appears to have been wholly unaware that a ceasefire was imminent, and there is no evidence to suggest that he had ordered the killing in reaction to the announcement of the Truce.[80] The RIC county inspector for Wicklow's report for July 1921 bears this out: 'Things had been getting worse in the county, and early in July [there had been] two murders of police constables in Wicklow [town] and Rathdrum and there were other signs of attempts to stir up trouble in this county, which up to that period had been comparatively free from very serious outrage.'[81]

THE SHOOTING OF CONSTABLE ALEXANDER CLARKE

Constable Alexander T. Clarke was shot dead by the IRA in Townshend Street, Skibbereen, Co. Cork, a few hours before the Truce began. As with the shootings of Constables Needham and Cormer, the timing of Clarke's killing has ensured that his death has received significant attention, in contrast to other members of the RIC killed during the war. The erroneous claim is frequently made that Clarke was the last casualty of the War of Independence.[82] In fact, the last fatality of the war was a woman who was killed by members of the RIC.[83] The killing of Constable Clarke has been a recurrent feature in opinion columns written by Kevin Myers. In a 1994 article in *The Irish Times*, Myers claimed that Clarke was 'shot in his front garden in Skibbereen' just minutes before the ceasefire. He cited this as part of 'a wave of monstrous violence' preceding the Truce.[84] In an article marking the eightieth anniversary of the Truce, Myers returned to the subject of Clarke's killing:

> Eighty years ago this morning as the seconds to the Truce ticked by, Alexander Clarke, a middle-aged RIC man, was returning to his digs in Townsend [*sic*] Street, Skibbereen … The terms of the Truce had been signed two [*sic*] days before and it was now mere moments away from enactment. Did he perform a little skip of joy as he approached his lodging house, as he felt for his keys? Why not? The promise of peace and retirement into old age lay before him. What Joy! At which point he was shot down, the last [*sic*] formal victim of the Troubles of 1919–1921. In the coming years how did his killer feel? Did he grow warm at the thought of how he had shot a harmless man, for no purpose but for the killing itself? … Did he sit his grandchildren on his knee and tell them how one morning in July 1921 he had gloriously shot a policeman dead yards away from his front door and minutes away from peace?[85]

Marking another anniversary a decade later Myers stated that Clarke was a popular man: 'who always went unarmed … [and] studiously declined to engage in political work'.[86]

Constable Clarke was a native of North Tipperary. He had joined the RIC in 1887 aged eighteen, and had no previous employment. Clarke's father, William, and brother, Samuel, were also members of the force. At the time of his death Clarke was fifty-two and had thirty-four years' service in the RIC. He was married with six children and had been stationed in Skibbereen since 1894.[87] At 8.20 a.m. on 11 July 1921 Constable Clarke left the RIC barracks at High Street, Skibbereen to return to his lodgings in Townshend Street. He walked along Bridge Street, turning left at the junction with Townshend Street and Mardyke Street. Up to four IRA Volunteers were loitering in the Townshend Street area waiting for him.[88] These included Cornelius 'Neilus' Connolly, commander of the local IRA battalion, and Timothy O'Sullivan.[89] At approximately 8.25 a.m. Clarke entered Townshend Street. He was fired on by one of the IRA party and wounded in the face. He attempted to escape his attackers by fleeing into Coffey's shop but was pursued by one of his attackers. The proprietor of the shop, Mrs Ada Coffey, witnessed Clarke's death:

> I heard a noise outside my shop and thought my window had been broken. I then ran from the kitchen into the shop. I then saw a policeman in uniform stagger into the shop from the street. A man was close behind with a smoking revolver in his hand, he fired 3 shots at the Constable in my presence, the Constable then staggered into the inner room & collapsed, the man with the revolver put the revolver back in his pocket and ran out of the shop.[90]

Constable Clarke's attackers rushed back down a laneway and along 98 Street and escaped into the fields bordering the town. The first members of the British forces to arrive at the scene were a group of soldiers from the King's Regiment, who were stationed nearby. They found Constable Clarke's body lying face down in a back room of the shop. He had been shot three times. His remains were placed on a stretcher by the British military and handed over to the RIC a short time later.[91]

The report of the British military inquest into Constable Clarke's killing makes it plain that the story that Clarke was 'shot in his front garden' is incorrect.[92] Furthermore, the assertion that Constable Clarke always went unarmed and refused to carry out his duties in relation to political policing is questionable. The available British records for Clarke's killing do not specify whether he was armed at the time of his death.[93] Neilus Connolly, who led the IRA Volunteers involved in the attack, claimed that Clarke had been targeted specifically because he had been involved in intelligence work. Connolly stated that Clarke was the 'Chief Intelligence man to the British [forces in Skibbereen] and was very much wanted by us'.[94] The circumstances of the shooting support Connolly's assertion that Clarke had been targeted specifically for assassination. The IRA men were waiting in ambush on the street where Clarke lived and appear to have planned their attack in anticipation of his arrival.

Other potential targets were available to the IRA in Skibbereen. Sergeant Michael Lehane had left Skibbereen RIC Barracks unaccompanied just before the attack but was able to walk the streets unmolested. It is unclear if the IRA Volunteers were aware of Sergeant Lehane's movements, but given that they were apparently monitoring Clarke so closely, it seems likely they would have been watching the barracks that morning. If the IRA was searching for any available 'soft target' in Skibbereen, the killing of an RIC sergeant would surely have been a bigger coup than the shooting of a constable.[95] Moreover, Clarke was shot while returning to his lodgings on Townshend Street, less than a hundred yards from the Central Hotel where a garrison of British soldiers from 1st Battalion, King's Regiment was stationed. Had the IRA in Skibbereen been searching for any available 'soft target' in the final hours before the Truce, it would surely have sought a potential victim at a safer distance from this outpost.

If Connolly's assertion that the IRA targeted Clarke because he was involved in intelligence operations is accurate, then Clarke's assassination had as much to do with his activities in the local area over the previous two years as it did with the announcement of the Truce. Nonetheless, the timing of Clarke's shooting suggests that while local republicans might have had cause to target Clarke for some time, the announcement of the Truce probably acted as a catalyst, spurring the local IRA into action once a deadline had been imposed.

THE SHOOTING OF SERGEANT JAMES KING

In stark contrast to Constable Clarke's shooting, the IRA assassination of Sergeant James King has elicited very little comment, despite him being the highest-ranking member of the force killed in the final days of the conflict and the very last member of the RIC killed during the War of Independence. King, a native of Co. Clare, joined the RIC in 1898. He had had no prior employment when he joined the force. King was posted initially to Co. Galway and later transferred to Co. Roscommon after his marriage. In December 1920 he was promoted to the rank of sergeant. He was shot and fatally wounded by two IRA Volunteers on 11 July 1921. At the time of his death King was forty-four years old and had fathered four children. He had twenty-three years' service in the RIC and had spent the previous eight years in Castlerea.[96]

King's long service in Castlerea would have given him an intimate knowledge of the local populace, and this would have proved invaluable to the British forces in the area during the War of Independence. According to local IRA veterans, King used this knowledge with great effect and was the leading member of what was dubbed the 'Castlerea Murder Gang'.[97]

The RIC in Roscommon were aided by Paddy Egan, intelligence officer with the 1st Battalion, South Roscommon Brigade, who was a British intelligence agent.[98] Egan passed information to the RIC which resulted in the capture and summary execution of a number of local IRA Volunteers. The IRA discovered Egan's activities in July 1921 but he fled before retribution could be exacted. Thomas Crawley, the vice-commandant of the 1st Battalion, South Roscommon Brigade IRA, claimed that Egan's activities crippled the republican war effort locally:

We were damned right from the start by having traitors and agents amongst us and in the area and we were never really able to get control over this situation or eliminate that danger. Our Brigade Intelligence officer was found to be an Intelligence agent for the British. He cleared out of the country and was never got. Quite a number of men in the Castlereagh area were either shot in their beds by the R.I.C. and Tans or taken out of their beds and shot, and all of these can be put down to the activities of that ruffian.[99]

Egan's information resulted in the arrest of IRA Volunteer Patrick Conroy at his home at Tarmon, Co. Kerry, in April 1921. Minutes later he was shot dead in a field by members of the RIC.[100] Two months after Conroy's killing, information supplied by Egan led to the capture of IRA Volunteers Michael Carty and Peter Shannon by the RIC at a republican safe house in Aughadrestan, Co. Roscommon. Carty was shot dead and Shannon, though wounded eight times, survived.[101] Local republicans maintained that Sergeant King was involved in these killings.[102]

On 22 June 1921 a force of RIC and Black and Tans led by Sergeant King raided the Vaughan family home at Cloonsuck, surprising three IRA Volunteers inside. Two of these, Ned Shanahan and John Vaughan, were killed by the RIC as they attempted to escape, and the third, Martin Ganly, was taken prisoner.[103] During the search of the house that followed, Sergeant King beat Vaughan's grieving mother unconscious with a rifle butt and before leaving shot dead the family's dog.[104]

As the leader of the 'Castlerea Murder Gang', King would have been the primary target for the IRA's South Roscommon Brigade long before July 1921. According to Thomas Crawley, there had been several attempts to kill King before the Truce: 'Sergeant King of the R.I.C. was the principal man in the murder gang that was organised in the R.I.C. in Castlereagh and was responsible for a number of killings around the area. He was badly wanted by us.

On the morning of the Truce, 11 July, we made a final effort to get this man.'[105] At about 9.30 a.m. Crawley and another IRA Volunteer, Ned Campion, went to Castlerea to mount a last-ditch attempt to kill King. The pair went to a shop in Patrick's Street, a very short distance away from their intended target's home on the opposite side of the street. They had only been there a few minutes when King emerged from his home with a bicycle to attend a 10 a.m. parade at the barracks.[106] Crawley describes what happened next:

> We went into a shop to get a drink of lemonade and when only a few minutes there Sergeant King came out of his own house on the opposite side of the street and proceeded to get on his cycle as if to go to the barracks. We left the shop. Ned Campion and I let him have it. He died immediately.[107]

King was struck in the chest by three bullets and, despite receiving prompt medical attention, died at approximately 10.30 a.m.[108] While King's assassins would have known that the Truce was imminent, had they been in a position to kill King at any other time in the preceding weeks and months they would undoubtedly have taken it. It is clear that this attack was carried out to avenge the deaths of local republicans over the previous three months, in which the sergeant had actively participated. Sergeant King was a long-standing thorn in the side of the Castlerea IRA, and from its perspective he was its most active and dangerous enemy. The attack on King had been planned by the IRA as a deliberate attempt to assassinate one of its leading opponents and not as part of a last-minute effort to kill any available soft target. The fact that the IRA had made repeated efforts to assassinate King shows that while the announcement of the Truce spurred his killers into action, the motivation behind their attack was a long-standing one.

PLANNED ATTACK ON THE SPECIAL CONSTABULARY AT NEWRY AND THE KILLING OF DRAPER HOLMES

Early on the morning of 9 July the IRA set up an ambush at Lisdrumliska, Newry, for a group of off-duty members of the Ulster Special Constabulary – 'B Specials' – who were travelling to work. However, the planned ambush resulted in the death of a civilian who entered the ambush position before the 'B Specials' had arrived, and the operation was abandoned immediately afterwards. According to John Grant, captain of the Mullaughbawn Company of the IRA, who led the botched ambush, the operation was the direct result of an order issued by the leadership of the IRA's 4th Northern Division to kill members of the Special Constabulary in revenge for the killing of four republicans a few days previously.[109]

On 6 July a small group of armed men raided the homes of several Catholic families in the Newry area. These men were not in uniform and travelled in a civilian touring car. They stopped at Cloghoge, calling to the home of John O'Reilly, an ex-RIC sergeant, forced their way inside at gunpoint and abducted two of the family's sons, John O'Reilly Jr and Thomas O'Reilly. The raiders next called at the McGennity family farm a short distance away and arrested Peter McGennity at gunpoint. A few minutes later the McGennity family heard gunfire and went outside and discovered the bodies of all three men lying on the roadside. All had been killed by single gunshot wounds to the head inflicted at point-blank range. At 4.30 a.m. the raiders fired a volley of shots into the McQuaid home at Carnegap, killing Patrick Quinn.[110] An inquest into the killings ruled that the four had been 'murdered by some person or persons unknown', but there can be little doubt that the killings were the work of the British forces.[111] Despite the families of the deceased denying those killed had any political involvement, it appears that all four victims were members of the IRA.[112]

These deaths were the latest in a series of reprisal killings in the Newry area. A member of the 'B Specials', Hugh Gabbie, was killed by the IRA in Newry town on 3 June.[113] The following month, a mixed force of RIC and 'B Specials' arrested, and later killed, William Hickey, a Catholic civilian with no republican connections.[114] On 6 July Teresa McAnuff was shot dead in her brother's home in Newry during another police raid.[115] In the wake of these killings and the reprisal killings of the four republicans in early July, the IRA's 4th Northern Division ordered that a revenge attack on the 'B Specials' should be carried out.[116]

John Grant received specific orders to 'carry out a reprisal for the shooting of our four comrades by shooting a number of "B Specials" from Altnaveigh who were employed as linesmen on the Great Northern Railway'.[117] Early on the morning of 9 July, Grant and six other IRA Volunteers took up ambush positions near the railway line at Lisdrumliska, a mile from Newry.[118] At approximately 7.40 a.m., Draper Holmes, a forty-eight-year-old railway ganger employed by the Great Northern Railway, entered the ambush position.[119] He was a member of Altnaveigh Loyal Orange Lodge No. 37 but was apparently otherwise uninvolved in politics.[120] According to Grant, their initial intention was to keep him prisoner until their intended targets came into range, but Holmes panicked and began shouting. The IRA shot him several times before abandoning its planned ambush and withdrawing from the area. Holmes died from his wounds later that day.[121] Holmes' cries had attracted the attention of at least two passers-by, Samuel McKee and Edward Little.[122]

While Holmes had jeopardised the planned ambush, the IRA's decision to shoot him was counter-productive, as the noise of the shots placed the IRA ambushers in even greater jeopardy and resulted in the abandonment of the planned ambush. Grant later said of Holmes' killing: 'We carried out our orders as far as he was concerned … It was purely accidental that the unfortunate man … came along first and was the only victim.'[123] However, the evidence of Samuel McKee, one of the witnesses to Holmes' shooting, implies that the decision to kill him was more deliberate and calculated. McKee stated that he saw Holmes being held by the throat while a group of men stood over him saying, 'Say your prayers before you die.'[124]

Holmes was a Protestant from a loyalist community. John Grant's justification of the decision to shoot him suggests a nakedly sectarian motivation for the killing:

> There was … ample evidence to prove that he [Holmes] had such an intense hatred for everything republican that he would go to extreme limits to destroy the movement. In this, the man was no different from his other Unionist neighbours in his local village. I wish, however, to record that he suffered not for anything he himself had done but for a deadly danger to the lives and freedom of our companions in arms which men of his class represented.[125]

Grant's assertion that Holmes was shot, 'not for anything he himself had done', but because of the religious and political group he belonged to, seems to confirm that the attack on Holmes was a sectarian killing. Prior to this, the IRA in Newry had been keen to avoid sectarian violence and, with the exception of a number of arson attacks on Protestant-loyalist homes in Killea that April, had refrained from intentionally targeting Protestant-loyalist civilians. In contrast, the Special Constabulary had proved to be an attractive target for the local IRA because they were both members of the British forces and representatives of local unionism.[126]

The significance of the death of Draper Holmes is that it was apparently the first time that the IRA in that area had engaged in a deliberate sectarian killing as a reprisal for the deaths of IRA Volunteers and sectarian attacks on the Catholic-nationalist community. There is no doubt that the aborted ambush at Lisdrumliska which resulted in Holmes' death was planned as a reprisal simply to avenge the killings of local people by the 'B Specials' and had no other tangible military objective. While it is possible that news of the Truce could have reached Newry by the time the attack took place, there is no evidence to suggest that the IRA Volunteers involved had any knowledge of the impending cease-fire. Furthermore, the killing of Draper Holmes appears to have been entirely motivated by local factors and had no relation to political developments nationally, as previously claimed.[127]

NON-FATAL ATTACKS ON OFF-DUTY MEMBERS OF THE RIC

During the last days and hours of the conflict, the IRA mounted a number of non-fatal attacks on off-duty members of the RIC. At 10.30 a.m. on 9 July, in Sarsfield Street, Kilmallock, Co. Limerick, IRA Volunteer Jimmy Costello attacked Constable Charles Bullock, a Black and Tan from Herefordshire. Bullock escaped unharmed and sought refuge in the town's RIC barracks.[128] He was alone and unarmed when Costello attacked him, firing three shots. The evidence suggests that this incident was a haphazard affair; had the IRA set out to assassinate Constable Bullock it is likely that it would have sent several IRA Volunteers and not a single gunman.[129]

The following day an RIC constable was attacked at 1 p.m. in Annacarty, Co. Tipperary.[130] Another off-duty member of the RIC, Constable Massey, was shot near Cappoquin, Co. Waterford on 10 July; he suffered a wound but escaped his attackers and survived.[131] At Tagmon, Co. Wexford, a large group of IRA Volunteers fired shots at a group of RIC constables who were swimming in a pond. The attackers made off with their clothing but none of the RIC suffered any injuries.[132] In the last hour of the conflict, at 11.20 a.m., an RIC constable was shot and seriously wounded in Edenderry, Co. Offaly.[133] Seamus Babington, one of the leaders of the IRA's Tipperary No. 3 Brigade, would later deride an attempt made on the morning of the Truce by a group of IRA Volunteers in Carrickbeg to kill a local RIC man named Prout. A group of IRA Volunteers waited in ambush for him outside a pub he visited daily. Prout appears to have been a relatively inoffensive man, and as far as Seamus Babington was concerned, the unsuccessful plan to kill Prout was: 'A good job [for] he was a Protestant and it would have been said that that was why he was shot.'[134]

THE ATTACK ON CONSTABLE DISHON FARMILOE

On 10 July members of the IRA's Kerry No. 1 Brigade attacked four off-duty Black and Tans as they were returning to Tarbert RIC Barracks. One of the four, Constable Dishon Farmiloe, suffered serious gunshot injuries; his comrade, Constable Dent, received minor wounds.[135] Rather than being a last-minute attack on available 'soft targets', this operation was deliberately premeditated with a view to assassinating Constable Farmiloe. A Black and Tan from Gloucestershire, Farmiloe was a member of the RIC motor patrol that had shot IRA Volunteer John Sheehan in Coilbhee, Listowel, on 26 May 1921. Sheehan had been sitting outside his home with his brother when the patrol approached; he fled in panic, was spotted by the patrol and shot dead.[136] After the incident Farmiloe boasted that he had killed Sheehan and consequently came to the attention of the IRA:

> We subsequently heard through an R.I.C. man that the Tan responsible for his [Sheehan's] death was a man named Farnlow [sic], who was stationed in Tarbert. From then to the Truce we were determined to shoot Farnlow. We received reports of him now and again from the Tarbert Volunteers. Eventually, on the night prior to the Truce, we decided to go into Tarbert and attack the Tans again in the hope that we might get Farnlow.[137]

At 10.30 p.m. on the night of 10 July, a dozen armed IRA Volunteers under the command of John Aherne assembled in Tarbert, Co. Kerry, in the hope of avenging Sheehan's death. The main IRA party remained half a mile outside the town while Con Brosnan and Dan

O'Grady accompanied Aherne into Tarbert.[138] A republican scout, who had been monitoring Farmiloe's movements, informed them that he was drinking in Mulcahy's pub with a handful of other Black and Tans. Aherne ordered Brosnan and O'Grady to summon the main IRA party while he kept watch. Aherne was waiting for reinforcements when Farmiloe and three other Black and Tans left Mulcahy's pub for their RIC barracks at 11 p.m. Fearful that he would miss this opportunity, Aherne opened fire on Farmiloe:

> I was in the open street near the pub on the opposite corner and had to think quickly what to do. There were four of them so I opened fire with the revolver on the four Tans. They did not return the fire but ran for the barracks and opened fire from there, but by this time I was on my way to join my friends. This action took place one hour before midnight on the eve of the Truce.[139]

It is clear from the accounts of Aherne and Brosnan that this attack had the specific intention of killing Constable Farmiloe. Though the attack was made in the knowledge that a truce would shortly come into effect, the operation was undoubtedly motivated by Farmiloe's involvement in the killing of Sheehan six weeks earlier. While the timing of the Tarbert shooting could be interpreted as a haphazard attack on a 'soft target' made in a callous effort to exploit the imminent Truce, the reality is that the attack was a deliberate assassination attempt to kill a specific member of the Black and Tans in order to avenge the death of a local IRA Volunteer. As such, the announcement of the Truce was not the primary motivational factor in the attack.

THE KIDNAP OF CONSTABLES ATWELL AND DOYLE, AND SPECIAL CONSTABLE SINNAMON

On the morning of 11 July 1921 the IRA captured three members of the RIC in Tyrone during a planned IRA operation to burn a loyalist-owned creamery. The Dunamore Company of the IRA's Tyrone Brigade had been planning to burn Doon's Creamery in reprisal for the destruction of Dungate Sinn Féin Hall carried out by the British forces two weeks earlier. The republicans undertook a great deal of planning to ensure that the proposed burning would be a success, since the creamery was situated a mile from the local RIC barracks. Their plans were nearly complete when news reached the Tyrone IRA on 10 July that a truce had been agreed. In spite of this development, the local IRA officers decided to carry out the burning of the creamery before the ceasefire came into effect.[140]

Four IRA Volunteers who had mobilised for the attack were waiting for motor transport to their rendezvous when they saw RIC Constable Doyle approaching from Draperstown on a motorcycle. The four held up Doyle, took him prisoner and commandeered his vehicle.[141] A short time later, the IRA captured a second member of the RIC. As they approached Doon's Creamery, the republicans saw Constable George Atwell, a Black and Tan from Middlesex, standing in front of the building. Initially there was a sense of panic when some of the IRA wrongly assumed that Atwell was part of an RIC protection force guarding the creamery.[142] On seeing Atwell, James McElduff, one of the IRA Volunteers, roared out 'Christ, would you look at that old peeler!' and opened fire. Atwell immediately surrendered and was taken prisoner.[143] The IRA raided the creamery as planned and captured its manager, Henry L. Sinnamon. Sinnamon was a member of the Special Constabulary. Despite being armed when captured, he was not ill-treated by the republicans.[144] The IRA Volunteers immediately withdrew following the destruction of the creamery, taking their captives with them, all of whom were released unharmed a short time later.

There is some conflict in witness accounts as to the manner of Atwell's release. Patrick McKenna, captain of the IRA's Donoughmore Company, stated that the IRA celebrated the operation and the Truce by treating Constable Atwell to a few drinks: 'We kept him in close custody until we had burned the creamery. Afterwards we took him with us to our home area where we gave him both liquor and other refreshments before we allowed him to depart for his home.'[145] Having been held for a short period, Constable Doyle was also released. The IRA kept Doyle's motorcycle but allowed him to keep the £50 he had on his person. One of his captors, Thomas Kelly, recorded that Doyle was released shortly afterwards and parted with his captors on good terms: 'so very relieved that he still had his money he walked back to Draperstown Barracks. He was one of the friendly RIC in Draperstown, and we did not wish to harm him'.[146] It is not recorded whether Sinnamon was afforded similar hospitality to that Atwell and Doyle received. Regardless, all three members of the RIC captured by the Tyrone IRA were released unharmed a few hours after the Truce began.[147]

OTHER IRA ACTIONS TAKEN AGAINST OFF-DUTY MEMBERS OF THE RIC

On the morning of the Truce seven IRA Volunteers from Ballylongford Company laid an ambush near Ballylongford village for a group of Black and Tans stationed in the area. The local IRA unit had monitored their movements for some time and noted that the Black and Tans made regular trips to one section of the River Forde to bathe. A local woman noticed the IRA Volunteers preparing their ambush positions and informed the RIC, and the Black and Tans duly cancelled their daily swim. The republicans waited in ambush for the Black and Tans until noon, when the Truce came into effect. The decision to mount this ambush was made before the announcement of the Truce, and the attack was not planned as a knee-jerk reaction or in response to the order issued by the IRA leadership in Co. Kerry to mount attacks on the British forces before the conflict ended.[148]

Not all of the final actions taken against off-duty members

of the RIC in the final days and hours before the Truce involved physical attacks. On 10 July two RIC constables had their bicycles stolen while attending a religious service at Drumagarner near Coleraine, Co. Derry.[149] A similar incident occurred in Co. Wicklow, where three RIC constables had their bicycles stolen from Hollywood post office.[150] At 10.45 p.m. the same evening four republicans held up two members of the RIC at gunpoint in Market Street, Sligo. Having deprived them of their revolvers, their captors released them unharmed.[151] Had the IRA been acting on instructions to inflict as many fatalities as possible on the RIC before the Truce came into effect, the republicans would have shot these RIC constables instead of releasing them after seizing their firearms and transport.

As with the cases of eight British military personnel released unharmed by the IRA after the announcement of the Truce, the IRA's capture and subsequent release of Special Constable Sinnamon, Constables Doyle and Atwell, and the two RIC constables in Sligo suggests that in many areas the IRA treated its captives mercifully and the announcement of the Truce did not lead to a uniform reaction employing lethal violence against captured British personnel. In particular, the chivalrous treatment afforded to Constable Atwell illustrated that the behaviour towards captured or off-duty members of the RIC varied significantly from area to area, and the levels of IRA aggression used against them depended very much on the local nature and intensity of the conflict.

THE ELLIS QUARRY KILLINGS

Undoubtedly the most controversial incident associated with the Truce was the capture and execution in Cork on 10 July of four off-duty British soldiers: Lance-Corporal Harold Daker, Private Henry Albert Morris, and Sappers Alfred G. Camm and Albert Edward Powell.[152] The incident, remembered locally as the 'Ellis

Quarry killings', is well known in Cork today and has become established in the city's oral tradition and folklore. This is partly because a photograph of the soldiers' bodies has been used in several recent publications.[153]

The practice of targeting off-duty members of the British forces arose in early 1921 in response to the deaths of IRA Volunteers in British custody in Cork about the same time. Before this, attacks on, and the summary execution of, British soldiers had been considered taboo. In January Tom Barry, who held the Essex Regiment responsible for the summary killings of a number of captured IRA Volunteers, issued orders to:

> … shoot every member of the Essex at sight, armed or unarmed, and not to accept their surrender under any circumstances. Up to then those troops were immune from attack when unarmed and off-duty. On their return from a foray where they might have killed unarmed Irishmen and burned out houses, they would go out immune to public houses or promenade outside the suburbs with the few unfortunate women who alone would consort with them. They felt they were safe while unarmed as we had tried to play the game of war by the rules accepted by the civilised world but now immunity was at an end.[154]

On 23 February 1921 the Cork No. 3 Brigade's flying column captured four off-duty members of the British forces in Bandon. Two of those captured, Lance-Corporal Stubbs and Private Knight, both members of the Essex Regiment, were executed.[155] The captured Royal Marines were released unharmed with a communication addressed to the commander of the Essex Regiment, listing eleven republican prisoners said to have been killed while in the custody of the regiment.[156] The message stated that from then onwards, captured members of the regiment would suffer the same fate as Stubbs and Knight if any other republican prisoners were killed in custody.[157]

Five days later the Cork No. 1 Brigade issued orders for wide-spread attacks to avenge the deaths of five IRA Volunteers who had been executed by the British Army in Victoria Barracks, Cork. At nightfall the IRA attacked groups of off-duty soldiers throughout the city, many of whom had left their barracks unarmed to court local girls. Six British soldiers were killed and another ten were wounded.[158] The motivation and timing of the IRA's attack were not lost on British officers such as Major Reginald Graham: 'six men [*sic*] ... [were executed and] that same night the Shinners went out and picked six British soldiers who were courting girls and shot them. So it was tit for tat.'[159] The British military reacted to this new 'policy of murdering unarmed soldiers' by organising units of armed plain-clothes British Army personnel to patrol areas frequented by off-duty soldiers.[160]

However, the IRA attacks did not prevent the British military executing a further two IRA Volunteers who had been captured at Clonmult. In retaliation, the IRA's 1st Southern Division launched a series of co-ordinated attacks on British troops on 14 May 1921.[161] Six off-duty British soldiers were attacked near Castletownbere, Co. Cork; four of them were wounded, three fatally.[162] Private Shepard of the Essex Regiment was killed when members of the Cork No. 3 Brigade machine-gunned a group of soldiers playing a soccer match.[163] Lance-Corporal Madell of the Essex Regiment was killed at Courtmacsherry, Co. Cork.[164] In total, fifteen members of the British forces were killed in a single evening.[165]

On 19 June 1921 Ernie O'Malley ordered the execution of three British officers captured by the IRA as a reprisal for the killings of IRA members captured by the British forces.[166] A similar situation occurred in Dublin, where the IRA mounted the 'Battle of Brunswick Street', an attack that resulted in the deaths of two RIC Auxiliaries.[167]

The Ellis Quarry killings were the last major attack on off-duty soldiers during the War of Independence and they occurred in Cork city the night before the Truce came into effect. This incident differed significantly from previous attacks on off-duty soldiers, since it was entirely opportunistic and was not sanctioned by a senior IRA officer.

At the time, the RIC reported these killings as premeditated mass murder and claimed that the soldiers 'being influenced by the news of the impending truce thought they were safe, but were trapped by the IRA'.[168] The British military claimed the incident as proof of an IRA murder campaign launched in reaction to the announcement of the Truce.[169] During the Civil War, supporters of the Treaty also exploited the incident for anti-republican propaganda and used it to depict members of the IRA as a ruthless band of murderers and criminals. IRA veteran Connie Neenan recalled:

> As a result of this unfortunate incident a priest who had been on our side … turned violently against us during the Civil War. He strongly denounced the shooting of the four soldiers and QUITE RIGHTLY so … In 1924 this same priest came to me asking me if I would use my influence to get our boys back into the Confraternity … I told him straight out that he lionised our [Free State] opponents although he knew perfectly well that those who shot the four soldiers were members of that very opposition of ours (the Civic Guard and Free State Army). Still the priest continued his accusations that we were all murderers, bank robbers and common criminals … It clearly showed the deeply engrained hypocrisy of some of our spiritual leaders.[170]

In the 1950s their detractors taunted republicans in Cork by mention of the Ellis Quarry killings.[171] This was in spite of the fact that the IRA captain who ordered the killings, and his lieutenant who was complicit in the execution, had afterwards been treated as pariahs by the IRA in Cork. Both were stripped of their command and arrested by the IRA after they had applied to join the Civic Guard.[172]

Most IRA veterans seem to have been embarrassed by the

killings and did not write about them in their memoirs. The Ellis Quarry killings were not mentioned in any of the witness statements collected from Cork IRA veterans by the Bureau of Military History. Popular histories of the period, such as *Rebel Cork's Fighting Story*, also ignored the incident.[173] Consequently, knowledge of the incident was beginning to slip from public memory in the 1980s, when Connie Neenan broke ranks with his fellow veterans by publicly discussing and denouncing the killings.[174] Neenan was not involved in the soldiers' executions but was active on the south side of Cork city at the time and immediately set out to secure the soldiers' release after he heard of their capture:

> Around midnight my mother called me to inform me that there were four young British soldiers who had just been taken prisoner by our fellows. I felt alarmed. They were I suppose, out for the first time in months with their guard down. One of them had gone into a shop to buy sweets. With my brother-in-law and a few more I went out and searched the fields from here to Togher. Around two in the morning we met some of our lads. The news is bad, they said; I was astounded. But surely no one would shoot anyone at a time like this? I crept into a house, exhausted and filled with remorse, the chap with me a bundle of nerves.[175]

In his memoirs, Neenan described the act as 'a most senseless, and a deeply regrettable incident, something that did considerable harm to the image of the IRA'.[176]

More recent references to the incident by Peter Hart and Kevin Myers have promoted the idea that the soldiers had been killed as 'soft targets'. Modern accounts of this incident have become increasingly melodramatic and factually inaccurate, mixing elements of Neenan's account with rumour, gossip and folklore. Local historian Richard Henchion wrote in 2003 that the incident was the foulest deed to ever befall the district and implied that the killings were 'evil'.[177] He claimed that the soldiers had been buying sweets at Mrs Martin's shop at No. 49 Bandon Road when captured by four members of the IRA who had left the nearby Fr O'Leary Total Abstinence Hall. According to Henchion's narrative, the soldiers were taken towards Cork Lough and executed in a quarry at Croughtamore. Henchion states that two of the IRA Volunteers he claims were involved, William Barry and Denis Twomey, developed 'qualms of conscience' and refused to take part in the executions, with the result that all four soldiers were executed by a single member of the IRA. Henchion implies that responsibility for the killings ultimately lay with Neenan, and completely dismissed his claim to have attempted to save their lives:

> While Neenan by his own words clears himself of involvement … the traditional story is adamant that he was in the Hall that night playing billiards and was well acquainted with the preliminaries that led to the shooting. His version has never been accepted by the non-aligned general public, it being felt that four ordinary Volunteers would not assume so great a responsibility without some nod of approval from a higher authority.[178]

Gerard Murphy cited the killings in his book *The Year of Disappearances* as an indicator of the 'degradation' to which he claimed the IRA's military campaign had sunk by 1921:

> What idealistic young patriot could imagine, while on a route march to Blarney on a Sunday morning in the autumn of 1919, that a year and a half later he would pick up four unarmed teenage soldiers who had gone out to buy sweets in view of the impending Truce, when all IRA units had been informed of the ceasefire, take them into a field in Togher, shoot them and leave their bodies in the sad rigor of death, to be found the next morning?[179]

More recently, Eoghan Harris described the incident in an article in the *Sunday Independent*. Harris claimed to have received information about the incident from his grandfather, Pat Harris, an IRA veteran, who in turn had supposedly spoken to several eyewitnesses:

> … he was sickened by some of the IRA actions … he would get angry telling me what happened to four young British soldiers on July 9 [*sic*], 1921, the eve before the Truce [*sic*] … At 10.30 p.m. on a fine summer's night, they stopped at a sweetshop on the Bandon Road and bought a bag of bullseyes. They were still sucking on the sweets when they were seized by a party of IRA men and frogmarched towards the Lough. My grandfather, who lived in Barrack Street nearby and got good eyewitness accounts, told me that people on the street called on the IRA party to let the four lads go. But the IRA in Cork was in the grip of a blood lust. The four frightened soldiers were brought to Ellis' Quarry and shot in the head. You can google a grim photo of their four bodies sprawled on the grass. Some mothers' sons.[180]

Harris' version of events is riddled with inaccuracies and errors. His account gets some of the most basic details of the event wrong, including its location, date and timing, but this is hardly surprising since he is reliant on third-hand information from anonymous 'eyewitnesses'. Henchion's account of the incident is also misleading – in particular, his suggestion that Neenan ordered the killing of the four soldiers is wrong. Members of H Company, 1st Battalion, Cork No. 1 Brigade carried out the executions. Neenan was an officer in the 2nd Battalion, Cork No. 1 Brigade, and would have had no command over IRA Volunteers from a different battalion. There is no reliable evidence linking Neenan to these executions.

Murphy's retelling of the incident emphasised the brutality and callousness of killing 'teenage' soldiers. However, none of the soldiers killed were teenagers; all four were over twenty years of age.[181] There was nothing particularly remarkable about the soldiers' youth. The British Army had reduced the age of enlistment from eighteen to seventeen in 1919.[182] Consequently, by 1921 a significant proportion of the British soldiers serving in Ireland would have been aged in their late teens or early twenties.[183] Neither the contemporary RIC reports nor press reports of the killings commented on the soldiers' ages. Furthermore, the relative youth of the four soldiers executed by the Cork IRA does not mean that they were 'raw recruits'. One of the four, Henry Morris, had considerable military experience. In 1914, at the age of fourteen, Morris left his employment as a manual labourer to enlist in the British Army. In 1916 he fought on the Western Front, where he was wounded twice and survived a gas attack.[184] The other member of the South Staffordshires killed, Harold Daker, presumably had even greater military experience, since he was seven years older than Morris and had been promoted to the rank of lance-corporal.[185]

Recent accounts of the killings state that the soldiers were buying sweets at the time they were captured. This detail has been used to emphasise their youth, innocence and supposed childlike demeanours. Murphy stated that all four 'teenage soldiers' left their post to buy sweets. In his memoirs, Connie Neenan recalled that he had been told one of the soldiers was 'carrying some sweets in his hands'; however, Neenan did not witness this himself, and there is no evidence to support the claim that the soldiers had left their barracks specifically to go shopping for sweets when they were captured and killed.[186] One of the earliest accounts of the incident, written by Phillips in 1923, states that the soldiers 'were being "treated" by a friendly publican in celebration of the Truce'.[187] If this account is accurate, then the four soldiers were captured while drinking alcohol and not while buying sweets, but this possibility has been erased from the most recent and highly emotive accounts of the incident.

The verifiable facts are that all four soldiers left the British Army post at Cork jail on 10 July. They were travelling on foot and were unarmed.[188] At 8 p.m. the four soldiers were captured by a patrol of seven IRA Volunteers led by Daniel Hallinan, then captain of H Company, 1st Battalion of the IRA's Cork No. 1 Brigade.[189] Hallinan and his men had been patrolling an area from Donovan's Bridge along the Western Road in search of a suspected civilian informer when they captured the British soldiers. After capture, the four soldiers were searched before being taken to an isolated area and executed at about 9 p.m.[190] The soldiers' bodies were discovered at 10 a.m. the following morning.[191] Three of the four were found blindfolded and all of them had been shot through the head.[192] Neenan had no role in the killings; he had been with Bob Aherne, a fellow IRA officer, when the soldiers were captured, and they had both attempted unsuccessfully to locate the soldiers and free them because they feared their execution would trigger a wave of British reprisals:

> Approaching the Bandon Rd. we were told that H Company, 1st Battalion had captured four young British soldiers attached to the Cork Jail Guard and that they were to be executed. Immediately Bob and I set out to find our IRA men and their four prisoners; I planned to release the soldiers right away since I knew only too well that any harm done to them would result in a wholesale spree of arrests and executions of many of our people and of innocent civilians by the British. We searched everywhere and in several different areas of the city but, unfortunately, we did not find them. Finally, at about 1.30 a.m. we gave up and shortly after met some men belonging to H Company, 2nd Battalion that was in Togher, and the men told us that they had been told that the soldiers had been shot. Bob and I just could not believe it and still hoped it was a false rumour and that the soldiers were still alive … our efforts had been in vain, the soldiers had been executed and we had been unable to prevent it.[193]

The text of a letter written by Captain Hordern of the South Staffordshire Regiment to the family of Private Morris provides a few additional details:

As far as can be found out your son and his friends were shot together. From what I saw myself when they were brought to the barracks, I am convinced that they could not have suffered, but died instantly. Your son was blindfolded and taken to a field about two to three miles from where he had been walking with his friends.[194]

The RIC report on their killings states that Daker, Morris, Camm and Powell, 'being influenced by the news of the impending truce thought they were safe'.[195] This would have been a somewhat fool-hardy assumption, since the situation in Cork city was far from peaceful at that time. A week earlier the IRA had confronted three off-duty British soldiers out walking near Victoria Barracks. The IRA fired on the trio; one of them was killed and the other two were wounded. On 9 July IRA Volunteer Denis Spriggs was taken from his home and killed by British soldiers. That same night British troops also shot a fourteen-year-old boy in the face, criti-cally wounding him. A few hours before the four soldiers made their fatal decision to leave Cork jail, the IRA had raided a house on College Road adjacent to the jail and attempted to kill an ex-soldier they suspected of spying. In the light of these shootings, the four soldiers had completely misread the situation if they assumed they were afforded protection by a ceasefire that had not yet begun and therefore did not grant them any immunity.[196]

The Ellis Quarry killings were an extraordinary event.[197] There is no suggestion that there was an intelligence aspect to the killing of the soldiers. The only event comparable to this shooting on the eve of the Truce happened on 28 February 1921, when the IRA in Cork city attacked off-duty soldiers.[198] However, the February shootings differ from the Ellis Quarry killings, since the former were part of a carefully planned operation, organised by the local IRA leadership and involving dozens of IRA Volunteers from different units.

The only surviving account of the Ellis Quarry executions by an IRA participant is the official report sent to the IRA GHQ by

Daniel Hallinan, captain of H Company, 1st Battalion, Cork No. 1 Brigade.[199] This report gives no indication as to the grounds on which the execution was carried out. It simply reads: 'We held up four soldiers (2 Royal Engineers, 2 Staffs) and searched them but found no arms. We took them to a field in our area where they were executed before 9 p.m.' Hallinan does not explain his rationale for ordering the execution. Given the highly unusual nature of the incident, and the fact that other off-duty British soldiers captured by the IRA that weekend were released unharmed, it must be assumed that there was a definite motivation for such a brutal action. The regiments to which the soldiers belonged may provide a clue to this.

In many districts, vendettas had developed between local IRA units and British regiments operating in the same territory. For example, Tom Barry held the Essex Regiment responsible for the summary killings of a number of his comrades and issued orders that soldiers from the regiment were not to be shown any mercy if arrested. Barry differentiated between the Essex and other British units such as the King's Liverpool Regiment, whom he felt 'had behaved reasonably'.[200] This pattern was repeated throughout Ireland, and regimental identity was often a decisive factor in the treatment meted out to captured British troops by local IRA units. On this account the Cork No. 1 Brigade IRA would have had little reason to target the two younger soldiers executed in the Ellis Quarry killings. Sappers Camm and Powell were both members of the Fortress Company, 33rd Battalion, Royal Engineers. The Royal Engineers had been regarded by the IRA as relatively inoffensive troops engaged on fatigue duties.[201] By contrast, the regimental identity of the two other soldiers executed is more likely to have been a factor in the fate of all four men.

Lance-Corporal Daker and Private Morris were both members of D Company, 2nd Battalion, South Staffordshire Regiment. This regiment had a long and very poor reputation in Ireland. During the 1916 Rising members of the South Staffordshire

Regiment perpetrated the 'North King Street Massacre', during which fifteen unarmed civilians were killed in controversial circumstances.[202] Members of the regiment attempted to cover up the massacre by burying their victims in shallow graves.[203] The South Staffordshires had a particularly odious reputation in Cork city and had been involved in a number of controversial killings. In July 1920 a British military patrol in Cork killed an ex-British soldier named James Burke. This incident sparked a riot between local ex-soldiers and British troops that lasted two days. The rioting was finally quelled in a bloody finale when British soldiers fired on a crowd of unarmed civilians, killing two and wounding twenty others. A body of 5,000 ex-soldiers marched in Burke's funeral cortège.[204] Shortly afterwards, graffiti appeared at the spot where Burke had been killed, reading: 'Murdered by Stafford Regt'.[205] Traditionally, the only explanation offered by local historians as a motivation for the Ellis Quarry killings is that they were a reprisal for the Staffordshire Regiment's role in these riots.[206]

However, the actions of the Staffordshire Regiment a year earlier, while possibly a contributory factor, are unlikely to have been the sole motivation for the abduction and execution of the four soldiers. A more likely explanation is that they were executed in retaliation for several reprisal killings committed by the South Staffordshire Regiment in the preceding weeks. In late June 1921 a civilian named William Horgan was arrested at his home by the South Staffordshire Regiment and shot dead a short time later while allegedly 'attempting to escape from military custody'.[207] On the same night, British soldiers in Victoria Barracks beat IRA Volunteer Charlie Daly to death.[208] Eleven days later, on the night before the Ellis Quarry killings, the South Staffordshire Regiment arrested IRA Volunteer Denis Spriggs at his family home in Strawberry Hill on the north side of Cork city. A short time later, Spriggs was shot dead while supposedly attempting 'to escape from military custody'.[209]

Apart from the fact that soldiers from the South Staffordshire Regiment were involved in both incidents, another link between the shooting of Spriggs and the Ellis Quarry killings is that Hallinan, who ordered the execution of the four soldiers, appears to have known Spriggs personally. As well as being members of the same IRA battalion, both Hallinan and Spriggs were plasterers and they were involved in the Cork plasterers' union. These facts suggest that the Ellis Quarry killings were an IRA reprisal for the killing of Spriggs less than twenty-four hours earlier: on Saturday 9 July members of the South Staffordshire Regiment abduct and kill an IRA Volunteer who works as a plasterer, and the following night an IRA officer who also works as a plasterer orders the abduction and killing of two members of the South Staffordshire Regiment. This explanation fits the established pattern, where all of the previous multiple shootings of off-duty British soldiers in Cork were enacted to avenge the deaths of local IRA men. That these two incidents were entirely coincidental and unrelated is highly unlikely.

Hallinan's report on the incident makes it clear that he was a leading member of his IRA company on an operation to locate a suspected informer when the soldiers were captured.[210] This would have been a routine task for an IRA unit in Cork city and suggests that the killing of the four soldiers was opportunistic rather than premeditated. Despite the callousness of the action, there is no evidence to suggest that the soldiers were deliberately 'trapped by the IRA' and killed as part of a campaign orchestrated to exploit the announcement of the ceasefire as 'an opportunity for attacking and murdering people when ... the murderers could not possibly be punished'.[211]

However, Hallinan and the other IRA Volunteers who carried out the executions would have been fully aware that the Truce had been agreed and was about to come into effect when they captured the four soldiers. In light of this, the IRA Volunteers involved apparently used the opportunity to exact revenge for Spriggs' death and inflict fatalities on the British forces before the war ended. There appears to have been no other military necessity or rationale for the killings and they were militarily unjustifiable, even if carried out as a direct reprisal for the killings of Spriggs and other prisoners by the Staffordshire Regiment. Undoubtedly, the IRA Volunteers involved were enraged when their own comrades were executed after capture by the British forces, and would have insisted on being treated as prisoners of war if captured themselves.

Other IRA attacks targeting off-duty British troops that weekend were of an entirely different nature to the Ellis Quarry killings, in that none of them involved the IRA executing British soldiers who had been taken prisoner.

THE KILLING OF PRIVATE RICHARD EDWARD LARTER

At approximately 7 p.m. on Sunday 10 July, two members of the IRA's Cork No. 2 Brigade shot and killed Private Richard Edward Larter at Doneraile in North Cork.[212] Larter, a nineteen-year-old member of the Machine Gun Corps stationed at Ballyvonaire Military Camp, was out walking with another soldier when they came under fire. Larter was fatally wounded but his comrade managed to escape uninjured.[213] Private Larter was unarmed at the time of his death, but it is not clear whether the soldier accompanying him was.[214] Following the shooting, the British military carried out widespread searches of the area but were unable to capture the attackers.[215] Larter's body was repatriated to England and buried in Swainsthorpe Churchyard, Norwich. There is scant additional information in the accounts of IRA veterans relating to this incident. William C. Regan, the commandant of the IRA's Castletownroche Battalion, told the Bureau of Military History: 'On the same date [10 July 1921] a British soldier was captured in the Doneraile area and executed in the vicinity of Ballyvonaire camp.'[216] While the date and location appear to relate to Larter's killing, the contemporary British accounts cited above suggest that Larter's death occurred as the result of an ambush, and that he was not 'captured and executed' as Regan recalled.

Apart from the nature of the conflict as 'a war of attrition' in which it was necessary to keep up a constant pressure on the enemy by inflicting fatalities, there appears to have been no other military rationale for the attack on Private Larter and his comrade. While Larter was personally unarmed and presumably off-duty at the time of his killing, the fact that he was a belligerent soldier made him a legitimate target under the 'rules of war' as established by the Hague Convention of 1907 and the specific 'conditions of war' as understood by the IRA at that stage of the War of Independence. While Larter's attackers would undoubtedly have been aware that a truce had been agreed, and would soon come into effect, his killing was not exceptional by the standards of warfare that existed in North Cork at the time. Given the lack of additional evidence, it is impossible to say if the attack was premeditated, having been planned in advance of the armistice, or if it was an opportunistic, spur-of-the-moment affair launched in an effort to inflict the maximum number of fatalities on the British forces before the ceasefire took effect.

THE KILLING OF SERGEANT EDWARD MEARS

The very last attack on the British forces in Kerry occurred at 11.45 a.m. on 11 July, just fifteen minutes before the ceasefire was due to start, when the IRA fired on two members of the 1st Battalion Royal Fusiliers, Sergeants Edward Mears and F. G. Clarke, in High Street, Killarney. Both soldiers were apparently unarmed and proceeding to their barracks on mess duty when they were attacked.[217] Sergeant Mears' wound proved fatal and he died shortly afterwards in the Kerry Military Hospital.[218] The assault on Mears and Clarke occurred after two local IRA leaders, Humphrey Murphy and John Joe Rice, issued an order to carry out attacks on the British forces the night before the Truce. However, the order issued by Murphy and Rice related to large-scale assaults on armed members of the British forces, their patrols and their barracks rather than small-scale opportunistic attacks on off-duty soldiers.[219]

The shooting of Sergeant Edward Mears attained a similar level of notoriety in Kerry as the Ellis Quarry killings garnered in Cork. The official history of the British Army's 6th Division cited Mears' killing as an example of the campaign of last-minute murders carried out by the IRA following the announcement of the Truce: 'within fifteen minutes of the Truce, the inhabitants of Killarney, who had never summoned up courage to strike a blow for freedom during the progress of the war, attacked two sergeants of the Royal Fusiliers in the street, one of whom died'.[220] Eoin O'Duffy later used the incident to question the military record of his republican opponents in Kerry.[221]

The attack on Sergeants Mears and Clarke appears to have had no military object other than causing casualties among the enemy. The timing of the attack, just fifteen minutes before a ceasefire was due to come into effect, was callous in the extreme.

ATTACK ON BRITISH ARMY OFFICERS NEAR KILMALLOCK

At 5.20 p.m. on 10 July two British Army officers travelling by car from Kilmallock to Kilfinnane in Co. Limerick came under fire from IRA Volunteers hidden in ambush at Ballingaddy. The officers, who were wearing civilian dress, managed to escape from the ambush, after returning fire.[222] One of them, Lieutenant Harold Brown, an intelligence officer attached to the garrison of the Machine Gun Corps stationed at Kilmallock, was wounded in the attack.[223] He was very effective in gathering intelligence information and the IRA had made several previous attempts on his life.[224] James Malone, the IRA intelligence officer who had plotted Brown's assassination, recalled:

He had a little motor car that had steel plates all round. He travelled about the countryside as if he didn't give a damn about anything. Sometimes a soldier or policeman accompanied him, but often he travelled alone. He was often fired on but always got safely away.[225]

In December 1920 the IRA succeeded in shooting Brown during an ambush at Red Gate in the Kilmallock district, but he emerged unscathed from this attack, apparently because he had been wearing body armour under his clothes.[226] The nature of the attack at Kilmallock on 10 July, and in particular Brown's presence, indicates that this operation was a planned assassination attempt rather than an opportunistic attack on any available 'soft target'. Lieutenant Brown's role as an intelligence officer meant that from an IRA perspective he was a high-profile, legitimate military target, regardless of whether the war was due to end. The clandestine nature of Brown's intelligence activities would have made it impossible for the IRA to tell at any given time if he was off-duty or actively engaged in intelligence work, so there can be little doubt as to the legitimate military nature of this attack, and it appears that its timing and proximity to the Truce were entirely coincidental, though news of the impending ceasefire had probably reached Brown's ambushers by that time.

A POLICY OF LENIENCY

The IRA treated with leniency a number of other British soldiers it captured in the final days and hours before the Truce. In Cork city, the IRA released unharmed William Dickson, a British Army bugle boy captured on 8 July. Dickson was freed from IRA custody a few days after the Truce began and 'deported' to England.[227] With the exception of the one infamous incident when the IRA executed three bandsmen attached to the Manchester Regiment, the republicans generally treated British Army musicians as noncombatants and did not consider them to be legitimate targets.

Bandmaster Frederick Joseph Ricketts and members of the Argyll & Sutherland Highlanders Regimental Band were captured by the IRA near Cobh and released unharmed after they were able to prove their status as musicians.[228]

On the eve of the Truce the IRA captured two off-duty members of the RAF at Ballycottage House near Oranmore, Co. Galway.[229] The pair were courting local girls when they were taken prisoner.[230] Following the disappearance of the soldiers, the British forces raided a number of houses belonging to local republicans but failed to find any trace of the two men, and were still searching for them the following morning when the Truce came into effect. When the ceasefire began, the missing soldiers celebrated in a local pub, having been released by the IRA several hours earlier.[231]

On the morning of 10 July the IRA released three British soldiers it had captured and disarmed during an attack on British forces at Mitchelstown Creamery.[232] Just before the ceasefire began, the IRA in Waterford city held up at gunpoint a British soldier who was conveying mail to a local British Army garrison. The soldier was released unharmed after the IRA seized some of the letters he was carrying.[233]

At the time of the Truce, the Kerry No. 2 Brigade IRA was also holding captive Major Coombes, a British military officer suspected of being on intelligence-gathering duties in the county. Coombes was captured on board a train at Ballybrack station on 7 July.[234] The major was held prisoner for several weeks, but the local IRA brigade intelligence officer did not feel that there was sufficient evidence to sanction an execution.[235] Major Coombes was eventually returned to the British military in exchange for the release of IRA Volunteer Jack Shanahan, who was being held prisoner by the British forces.[236] That this was the only prisoner exchange to take place in Kerry is testimony to the major's importance to the British forces in that county, and a possible indication that he had indeed been involved in intelligence work.

If the IRA had embarked on a policy of killing 'soft targets' at the time of the Truce, these soldiers and Major Coombes would undoubtedly have been killed by their captors. Instead they were shown compassion, and in some cases great generosity and hospitality, by their republican opponents. The mercy afforded to the soldiers in these cases clearly indicates that there was a great dichotomy in the attitudes of local IRA Volunteers towards captured British troops, and that it is folly for historians to talk in terms of a blanket attitude towards, or a co-ordinated national campaign against, off-duty British soldiers in reaction to the announcement of the Truce.

The largest IRA operation planned for the weekend of the Truce was to have been a series of attacks on off-duty members of the British forces in Dublin city centre on 8 July. However, this operation, described by some of the IRA Volunteers detailed to take part as 'a general hit-up', was cancelled at the last moment.[237] This attack had been planned for the date when the Auxiliaries would receive their pay cheques and it was anticipated that the maximum number of British forces would be seen in the streets.[238] The attacks were to have involved dozens of IRA Volunteers from four battalions of the Dublin Brigade as well as the 'Dublin Guard'.[239] The intended action was to have been of such magnitude that it would have dwarfed an IRA attack on off-duty British troops in Grafton Street the previous month, which claimed the lives of two RIC Auxiliaries.[240] The 'general hit-up' could have rivalled the IRA attacks of Bloody Sunday in terms of British fatalities, and the burning of the Custom House in terms of operational scale. Such a vast, co-ordinated surprise attack on off-duty targets would almost certainly have surpassed the Cork IRA's 'shoot-up' of February 1921, which resulted in the deaths of six British soldiers.

While information about this planned operation has been in the public domain for several decades, it has received scant attention from historians. The last-minute cancellation of this onslaught, which would have resulted in attacks on dozens of off-duty members of the British forces, has not been taken into consideration by those who have accused the IRA of mounting a series of unjustifiable attacks on 'soft targets', in reaction to the announcement of the Truce.[241]

The leadership of the IRA's Dublin Brigade had mounted a similar operation a few weeks previously, when at 6 p.m. on 24 June 1921, several groups of IRA Volunteers from the 2nd Battalion of the IRA's Dublin Brigade converged on Grafton Street, a favourite haunt of off-duty British troops. They were armed with revolvers, pistols and grenades and, at a given signal, were to launch a wave of simultaneous attacks on any members of the British forces in sight. Members of the Dublin Brigade ASU, hidden in an armour-plated van disguised as a commercial vehicle and armed with a Thompson machine-gun, were to provide covering fire for the republican gunmen if British reinforcements reached the area before the operation was completed.[242] However, this operation was aborted at the last minute because of a heavy British military presence in the area that prevented most of the IRA Volunteers from taking up their ambush positions. A handful of IRA Volunteers who were already in situ attacked and killed two RIC Auxiliaries before retreating when the attack was cancelled.[243]

It is clear that the 'general hit-up' planned for 8 July 1921 was much larger in scale than its ill-fated predecessor. According to one veteran of the Dublin ASU, the operation: 'was planned on similar lines to that carried out in June … but on a bigger scale. It was designed to cover the entire city and to involve every company of the [Dublin] Brigade'.[244] Members of the 1st Battalion had been ordered to raid the La Scala Theatre, which was popular with members of the Black and Tans, and to shoot any members of the RIC they found attending the evening performance.[245] The 2nd Battalion had been assigned similar targets, including other theatres, pubs, restaurants and cafés frequented by the British troops.[246]

A large number of IRA Volunteers from the 3rd Battalion were to assemble at St Stephen's Green under the guise of playing a football match. As soon as the signal was given, they were to attack every member of the British forces within range. Alphonsus Sweeney, a lieutenant in G Company, 3rd Battalion, was told that his men were not under any circumstances to take prisoners.[247] The sentries on duty at Dublin Castle would be attacked by an IRA force drawn from the 4th Battalion. When this first group of attackers retreated up George's Street, still firing at any visible British troops, a second group of IRA Volunteers armed with grenades was to step forward ready to bomb any motorised patrols and armoured vehicles that might emerge from the Castle to engage in a pursuit.[248] Ship Street Barracks was also due to be attacked in a synchronised operation.[249]

To reduce the risk to the republicans involved, and to prevent British troops from being rushed to the city centre, IRA Volunteers were posted close to the military barracks on the south side of the city. Material for blockading the streets leading to the city centre was prepared and ready to be placed in position at very short notice.[250] IRA riflemen were to be positioned in tenements by the canal to snipe at British patrols attempting to advance over the bridges toward the city centre.[251] A sophisticated ambush for the British forces was set at Crumlin Cross. The IRA planned to deploy two large landmines and three Thompson machine guns in this attack, which was likely to have caused heavy British casualties.[252] At least one Cumann na mBan field hospital had been set up to provide medical assistance for republicans who might be wounded in the operation.[253]

The IRA battalions involved held several rehearsals leading up to the attack, to ensure that each IRA Volunteer knew what position he or she was to occupy, where they would seek their targets and what their escape route would be.[254] The attacks were due to begin at 7 p.m. sharp on 8 July 1921.[255] After the Truce was for-

mally agreed at the Mansion House, Dublin city, de Valera immediately instructed the leadership of the IRA's Dublin Brigade to
cancel the attack.[256] However, the order was delayed in reaching
some of the IRA officers directing the planned attack, and dozens
of armed IRA Volunteers were in position watching their targets
when news of the cancellation reached them with just minutes to
spare before the attack was scheduled to begin.[257]

This decision by de Valera and the IRA's Dublin Brigade to
cancel the operation was significant. Had the IRA been intent on
inflicting the maximum number of fatalities on the British forces in
the final days and hours of the conflict before the Truce came into
effect, the 'general hit-up' would have served as the perfect vehicle
to satisfy any residual bloodlust. Instead, the announcement of the
Truce led the IRA in Dublin to cancel its planned operations, thus
sparing the lives of an unquantifiable number of British troops, IRA
Volunteers and civilians. It is a remarkable testimony to IRA discipline in Dublin that armed IRA Volunteers who had mobilised
for an attack and were within striking distance of off-duty British
troops, received news of the Truce calmly and resisted the urge to
pick off 'soft targets' that were quite literally in their sights.[258]

SOFT TARGETS OR LEGITIMATE ACTS OF WAR?

Nationally there were four separate attacks on off-duty British soldiers and eleven on off-duty members of the RIC after the Truce
was announced. In addition to these, the IRA mounted an ambush
for off-duty members of the 'B Specials', which was called off after
the shooting of a civilian, Draper Holmes. These attacks resulted
in eleven deaths: six British soldiers, four members of the RIC and
one civilian. The fact that the IRA killed ten off-duty members
of the British forces over the weekend before the Truce does not
seem exceptional compared with the numbers of other off-duty
British personnel killed during equally brief periods earlier in the
conflict.[259] There was a far higher occurrence of IRA operations

against off-duty members of the RIC compared with the number of attacks on off-duty British troops after the announcement of the Truce. This may have been because members of the RIC were more readily available as targets, but it seems more likely that they were targeted specifically because they were of greater value to the British forces than the British military and had been the driving force in the fight against the republican guerrillas in most areas. A number of the RIC men attacked were specifically targeted because of their involvement in intelligence work and the reprisal killings of local republicans. In the case of the planned attack at Newry, the off-duty members of the Ulster Special Constabulary were to be killed as a reprisal to avenge killings carried out by members of that force, rather than the specific individuals being targeted.

The assertion that the IRA reacted to the announcement of the Truce by launching a concerted series of attacks on 'soft targets', including unarmed and off-duty members of the British forces, is ill-founded. Of the ten off-duty members of the British forces killed the weekend before the Truce came into effect, at least two, Constables Needham and Cormer, were killed by IRA Volunteers who could not have known that a truce had been agreed. Their deaths were completely coincidental to the announcement of the Truce and not a knee-jerk reaction to it. There is little doubt that some of the IRA's final operations, including the attacks on Private Larter, Sergeant Mears and Constable Bullock were opportunistic attacks on available soft targets made in the knowledge that the Truce had been agreed. However, there is strong evidence to suggest that in a number of the other attacks the IRA was targeting men who had been deliberately marked for assassination for some time because of their military activities.

The majority of attacks on RIC constables that occurred just before the Truce were premeditated and carefully planned legitimate military operations. Constable Clarke's killing may have been motivated by his involvement in intelligence work, and the non-fatal attack on Lieutenant Brown and his companion almost certainly was. Sergeant King's assassination and the attack on Constable Farmiloe were carried out because they were responsible for the deaths of IRA Volunteers and they had been marked for assassination long before the political developments that led to the Truce. While there is evidence that previous attempts had been made on the lives of these men, the timing of the attacks indicates that they were made by IRA Volunteers who were aware that a truce was due to come into effect. These men were probably motivated by a desire to complete their mission before the ceasefire began. In these cases the Truce can be seen as a catalyst – speeding up a process that was already in motion.

The killing of Private Larter and the attack on his comrade appear to have been opportunistic attacks on two 'soft targets'. However, this type of attack had become increasingly common throughout Co. Cork since the spring of 1921 as a direct reprisal for the killing of captured IRA Volunteers. Before this the IRA had not considered off-duty soldiers to be legitimate targets. While the IRA attack on two British NCOs in Killarney, which led to the death of Sergeant Mears, was similar in nature to that on Private Larter, its timing at a quarter of an hour before the start of the Truce puts it in a different context and its use in anti-republican propaganda is not surprising.

Undoubtedly the most questionable action undertaken by the IRA following the announcement of the Truce was the killing of the four British soldiers in Cork. There is an important distinction and significant difference between the death of Private Larter and this incident. Larter and his comrade were attacked while off-duty, regardless of whether they were armed or not, but they had an opportunity to escape their attackers. By contrast, the four British soldiers killed in Cork were definitely unarmed when captured. They had surrendered, were in IRA custody and completely defenceless at the time of their execution. As already discussed, there is a very strong probability that two of the four were executed because their regiment was responsible for the killing of IRA Volunteer Denis Spriggs the previous night in similar circumstances. The additional execution of two other soldiers who were apparently unconnected with Spriggs' death, and the fact that the IRA Volunteers involved knew that a truce was imminent, suggest that the execution of these four soldiers had little or no military justification.

At a national level, the IRA cannot be said to have made an effort to kill as many enemies as possible before the Truce took effect, as claimed by Peter Hart.[260] At least seven members of the British Army and five members of the RIC captured after the announcement of the Truce were released unharmed. Furthermore, the widespread series of co-ordinated attacks against RIC personnel that had been planned in Dublin was cancelled at the last moment because of the Truce. The currently accepted historical narrative is that by July 1921 the IRA nationally had been so weakened by the actions of the British forces that the republicans were incapable of continuing a military campaign against legitimate military targets and had instead switched their focus to 'soft targets'. In fact, there were far more IRA attacks on British Army convoys, RIC curfew patrols and barracks than there were on off-duty members of the British forces in the same time period. These will be examined in detail in the next chapter.

5

Pre-Truce Offensives and IRA Operations, 8–11 July 1921

As outlined in Chapter 4, the IRA mounted sixteen attacks on off-duty members of the British forces after the announcement of the Truce, which resulted in eleven deaths. Writers about the Truce have focused almost exclusively on these killings, yet during the same period the IRA expended a far greater amount of time, effort, manpower and munitions on attacking more regular military targets, resulting in a similar number of fatalities (see Table 5.1) which have been largely ignored by these authors. The dominance and popularity of the 'soft target' theory, and its usefulness as a device in anti-republican propaganda, has ensured that a few IRA attacks on off-duty British troops have received much greater attention than the multitude of large-scale military IRA operations against 'hard targets' that were far more common.

Table 5.1: Fatalities during IRA attacks on 'hard' and 'soft' targets, 8–11 July 1921

Fatalities occurring as a result of IRA attacks on active British troops, 8–11 July 1921	Fatalities occurring as a result of IRA attacks on off-duty British troops, 8–11 July 1921
6 – British Army 1 – Royal Irish Constabulary 4 – IRA Volunteers 1 – Civilian **Total = 12 fatalities**	6 – British Army 4 – Royal Irish Constabulary 0 – IRA Volunteers 1 – Civilian **Total = 11 fatalities**

The IRA made at least sixty-four attacks on the British forces between the announcement of the Truce and its implementation. These included at least twenty-one attacks on British patrols, twenty-seven attacks on British barracks and several other operations. Because of the large number and frequency of these attacks, they have been grouped together, based on their location, in an effort to ascertain whether provincial IRA units launched them in response to the announcement of the Truce.

The official dispatch issued by IRA Chief of Staff Richard Mulcahy announcing the Truce was ambiguous about whether local IRA units should proceed with military operations that had been planned previously. Mulcahy's communication stated that the IRA would cease its military operations as of noon on 11 July and observe in full the ceasefire that was to come into effect at that time. However, it did not specify what action, if any, local IRA units were to take in the interim. Local IRA commanders were free to decide what action they should take and whether they should proceed with planned operations. It also allowed the leadership of each IRA brigade to organise 'eleventh-hour' attacks if they wanted to do so.[1]

The only IRA division to have issued a surviving written command ordering a spate of last-minute attacks against the British forces was the IRA's 1st Eastern Division. The dispatch issued by this division in relation to the Truce stated unambiguously that the ceasefire would have to be obeyed once it came into effect.[2] The wording leaves no doubt that the instructions calling for republican attacks on a wide range of targets were motivated by the announcement of the Truce. While the IRA's 1st Eastern Division failed to kill any suspected spies as dictated by the order, or carry out any attacks on off-duty members of the British forces, there were at least ten separate attacks on active British troops after the order was issued. These included the ambush of a joint British military/RIC patrol, four attacks on RIC barracks, three on RIC patrols and two on RIC constables. None of these attacks proved fatal.[3]

The first of these operations was an IRA ambush of a nine-strong RIC patrol at Streete, Mullingar, Co. Westmeath, at 9.30 p.m. on 9 July. One RIC constable was wounded in the engagement, which lasted about half an hour.[4] The following morning at 3.45 a.m., the IRA ambushed a seven-man RIC patrol at Bailieborough, Co. Cavan, wounding one of them. Two IRA Volunteers were wounded and taken prisoner in the ensuing firefight.[5] Despite this ambush occurring only a few hours before the Truce, the operation had been planned for some time and had been approved at a meeting of IRA officers from the East Cavan Brigade on 4 July.[6] When the local IRA battalion officers learned from a newspaper report on 9 July that a truce was imminent they cancelled the ambush, but this decision was reversed when they discovered that neighbouring IRA units were planning to carry out a series of last-minute attacks.[7] This decision proved costly, however, and the IRA was fortunate not to incur fatalities as the Volunteers were armed with shotguns, which were useless as a military weapon except at point-blank range. The attackers did not have the ammunition for a sustained firefight, and the IRA officers who planned the ambush apparently gave little consideration to the possibility that British reinforcements might arrive unexpectedly. Francis Connell, who took part in the attack, recalled what happened:

> … we took up sniping positions near the barracks – and had just opened fire when we received word that a motor patrol of Tans were approaching the town from Virginia. We immediately retreated … A running fight now ensued in which three of our men were wounded, two of whom were captured … By the time we reached open country, all our ammunition was exhausted.[8]

At 2.10 a.m. on 11 July the IRA mounted an attack on the RIC barracks at Nobber, Co. Meath. The roof and windows of the barracks were pierced by gunshots and the RIC garrison inside the building promptly returned fire. The attack continued for about thirty-five minutes, but neither side suffered any casualties.[9] At about the same time, the Cavan IRA briefly attacked Arva RIC Barracks, firing a few rifle shots and throwing a number of hand grenades at the barracks. Other than the bullet holes in the barracks' windows and protective shutters, the building was not damaged and its garrison was unharmed.[10] A simultaneous attack was launched by the Meath IRA on Longwood RIC Barracks, where the garrison came under sustained rifle and revolver fire for twenty minutes, which caused a minimal amount of damage to the barracks building. The RIC opened a 'vigorous' barrage of rifle fire on their assailants, but did not cause any casualties.[11]

James Maguire, a veteran of the IRA's Mullingar Brigade, stated that he received instructions from Divisional Commander Seán Boylan 'that every barracks in the area was to be attacked on the day of the Truce'.[12] Acting on this order, Maguire organised and led an attack on Castlepollard RIC Barracks, Co. Westmeath, at 11.20 a.m. on 11 July. A handful of IRA Volunteers equipped with just four or five rifles mobilised for the operation.[13] The attack lasted not much more than twenty minutes, ending at around 11.45 a.m.[14] The RIC county inspector for Westmeath claimed that this attack involved a deliberate attempt to assassinate specific members of the garrison and reported: 'fire was directed chiefly on an office occupied by the district inspector and Head Constable showing [a] deliberate attempt to take their lives one hour before commencement of the Truce'.[15] In his account of this operation, Maguire, who led the republicans, made no reference to a plan to kill either of the senior RIC officers at the barracks, simply stating: 'We gave them a royal salute until the bell rang the Angelus, and we went off.'[16]

A six-strong RIC motor patrol was ambushed at Maudlin Bridge near Kells, Co. Meath, when it stopped to collect water.[17] A party of IRA Volunteers armed with shotguns opened fire on the patrol from the cover of a nearby house.[18] The RIC returned fire, escaped from the ambush position and reached their barracks safely. The RIC then returned to Maudlin Bridge with a large body of reinforcements equipped with two machine guns and began searching for their attackers.[19] At 11.20 a.m. that day the IRA shot an RIC constable at Edenderry in Co. Offaly.[20] The IRA's 'parting shot' was aimed at an RIC patrol at Kingscourt, Co. Cavan, at 11.55 a.m. on 11 July and was fired by a group of IRA Volunteers travelling in a car driving through the town in the direction of Carrickmacross.[21] One of the republicans leaned out of the window of the car and fired a single shot at an RIC patrol as it passed Farrelly's Corner. The policemen were initially unaware that they had been attacked, having mistaken the noise of the shot for that of a car backfiring.[22]

While the leadership of the IRA's 1st Eastern Division ordered a spate of fevered last-minute attacks on the RIC in the final days and hours of the conflict, some of its junior officers did just the opposite and responded to the announcement of the Truce by cancelling operations that had been planned for some time.[23] The 5th Mullingar Battalion of the IRA's Meath Brigade cancelled a planned attack on two members of the RIC stationed at Navan.[24] A planned ambush by the IRA's Fingal Brigade on an RIC patrol at Yellow Furze near Balbriggan in Dublin was also abandoned following the announcement of the armistice.[25]

Not all IRA Volunteers in the area were willing to engage in military action once they learned that a ceasefire was imminent, and Joe Lynch led a mutiny when he was ordered to take part in the Maudlin Bridge ambush. During the heated exchange with his commanding officer, Lynch asked, 'Do you think we are mad to go and get killed and a truce being signed tomorrow, after all the fighting we have done[?]' Several of Lynch's comrades sided with him, resulting in a mutiny by members of the Carnaross Company who refused to take part in the attack. Those involved were later disciplined by the IRA for their stand. This incident indicates that some IRA units were motivated by self-preservation rather than bloodlust or the opportunity to exact last-minute retribution on their opponents.[26]

Of the ten attacks the IRA's 1st Eastern Division made against the British forces, at least two had been planned for some time and their proximity to the end of the conflict was entirely coincidental. Of the remainder, there can be little doubt that they were conceived and carried out as a result of the order issued by the 1st Eastern Division. However, all these attacks were relatively brief engagements in which the IRA withdrew before inflicting any fatalities. These 'eleventh-hour' attacks appear to have been organised as a last-minute show of strength, to display military prowess and as a propaganda exercise designed to send the message that the IRA had not been defeated. They were more political than military in their intent; this was in line with the Eastern Division's order, which emphasised that these attacks would ultimately strengthen the hand of republican representatives in the political negotiations they envisaged would take place with the British government.[27]

The 1st Eastern Division was not the only IRA unit to order an increase in activities before the Truce. The Tipperary No. 3 Brigade circulated an order after the announcement of the cessation, calling for attacks on British barracks.[28] Andrew Kennedy, a veteran of the brigade's flying column, recalled:

> On the morning of the 11th July, the general order that was issued to all I.R.A. units was carried out in every Company area. This order was to the effect that intense activity should be shown everywhere, such as sniping enemy posts, or any such operation that would indicate the presence of the I.R.A. up to twelve noon on that day when the

An RIC barracks destroyed by the IRA and daubed with republican slogans. Attacks on RIC barracks led to their evacuation by the British forces and the loss of territory to the IRA. (*Courtesy of Mercier Archive*)

British reprisals at Meelin, Cork in January 1921. The British responded to the IRA's military campaign by carrying out arson attacks and reprisals on the local civilian population. (*Courtesy of Mercier Archive*)

The RIC garrison at Kilmallock, 1920. The sergeant seated in the centre, James Maguire, is one of the few Irishmen in the photo. The scarcity of Irishmen in the force meant they became invaluable for intelligence work. (*Courtesy of Mercier Archive*)

The funeral cortège of Lance Corporal Maddox of the Essex Regiment, who was killed by the IRA in Bandon, Cork. (*Courtesy of Mercier Archive*)

The burning of Custom House on 25 May 1921.
(*Courtesy of Mercier Archive*)

While the IRA in Dublin was on the brink of collapse, their comrades in the provinces were in a much stronger position. The possibility that they could become organised enough to realise their full military potential was a real danger for the British. This photograph of the West Mayo flying column, taken just days before the Truce, shows a well-equipped military unit armed with captured British rifles.
(*Copyright J. J. Leonard, courtesy Anthony Leonard*)

Sir James Craig (*left*) the first Prime Minister of Northern Ireland at the opening of the Northern Irish parliament at Stormont, Belfast, 22 June 1921. (*Courtesy of Kilmainham Gaol Museum, 19PC-IB51-04*)

This crowd outside the Mansion House in Dublin on Friday 8 July anxiously awaits news of the ceasefire negotiations which were taking place inside. (*Author's collection*)

General Neville Macready is greeted by the Mayor of Dublin as he arrives at the Mansion House in Dublin on Friday 8 July 1921 to arrange a truce with the IRA. Note the gun in Macready's pocket. (*Author's collection*)

Short Shrift for Spies at the Battle-Front

'Short shrift for spies' – an illustration from a British propaganda magazine *The War Illustrated*. During the First World War the British Army frequently executed civilians it suspected of being German spies. IRA executions of suspected spies during the War of Independence mimicked regular British Army practice in wartime. (*Author's collection*)

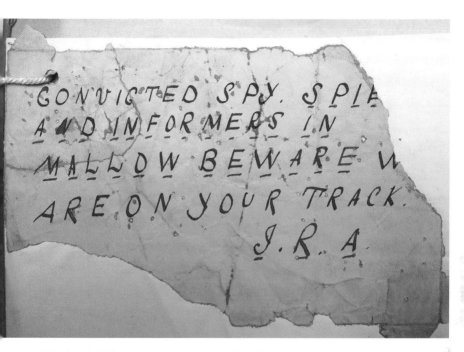

The 'spy label' attached to the body of William Alexander McPhearson, who was killed shortly before the Truce in Mallow, Cork. (*Author's collection*)

Major George B. O'Connor, a former British officer and one of Cork's leading unionist politicians, executed for spying by the IRA. This is the only known picture of O'Connor. (*Author's collection*)

The memorial marking the site of the Kilgobnet Mine Disaster of 9 July 1921 in which one IRA volunteer and five civilians were killed by a British Army booby trap. (*Author's collection*)

Memorial to John Foley, who was shot dead by British soldiers from the West Yorkshire Regiment the night before the Truce began. Foley was largely forgotten until August 2015 when the 'Captain Timothy Kennefick Committee', a Republican Commemorative Group in Cork, erected this memorial plaque marking the site of his killing. (*Author's collection*)

I nOilchuimhne
ERECTED TO THE MEMORY
OF
JOHN FOLEY
LEEMOUNT COACHFORD
MURDERED HERE BY
BRITISH CROWN FORCES
DURING THE
FIGHT FOR FREEDOM
10TH JULY 1921 AGED 38 YEARS

Ar Oheis Dé go raibh
A ANAM Oilis

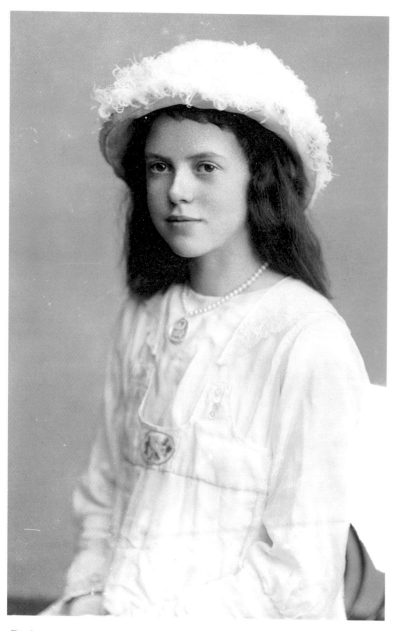

Bridget Dillon, the fifteen-year-old daughter of a former RIC constable, was shot dead at her family home in Kilcash, Co. Tipperary, the night before the Truce, during a botched attempt by the IRA to abduct two of her brothers who were suspected of being British spies.
(*Courtesy of the National Library of Ireland*)

A motorised police patrol in Belfast – note the lorry fitted with bullet-proof armour plates and wire netting roof to prevent grenade attacks. (*Author's collection*)

RIC Constable Thomas Conlon was killed during the IRA attack on an RIC motor patrol in Raglan Street. (*Author's collection*)

The funeral of Mayor of Limerick George Clancy, former Mayor Michael O'Callaghan and Joseph O'Donoghue, who were assassinated by members of the RIC in Limerick city on the night of 6 March 1921. (*Courtesy of Kilmainham Gaol Museum, 19PO-1B14-27*)

Denis Spriggs, a twenty-year-old IRA Volunteer, was taken from his home at Strawberry Hill in Cork by British soldiers from the South Staffordshire Regiment and shot dead a few hours after the Truce was announced.
(*Author's collection*)

Two nights later, just hours before the ceasefire was due to begin, the IRA abducted four unarmed British soldiers (including two from the South Staffordshire Regiment) and executed them at Ellis' Quarry – probably in revenge for the killing of Spriggs.
(*Courtesy of the Imperial War Museum, Q107745*)

RIC Constable Patrick Culleton (*left*) from Cavan and a French-Canadian 'Black and Tan' known as 'The Jewman de la Roi'. The pair were reputed to have been involved in the killing of civilians and IRA Volunteers in Kerry during the War of Independence. (*Courtesy of Mercier Archive*)

College Street, Killarney. The last building visible at the far end of the left-hand side of the street is the Imperial Hotel, where Hannah Carey, the last person killed during the conflict, was shot by an RIC patrol. (*Author's collection*)

As the beginning of the Truce approached, a large crowd gathered at the gates of Dublin Castle expecting a formal announcement or ceremony to mark the occasion. However, all that happened was the appearance of a number of unarmed RIC Auxiliaries, who maintained a tense vigil. (*Courtesy of Mercier Archive*)

Dublin Castle at noon on 11 July 1921, the start of the Truce. (*Courtesy of Mercier Archive*)

Two young boys in Dublin wave orange, white and green flags to celebrate the beginning of the Truce. Note that the boys are barefoot and probably came from the city's slums, the inhabitants of which endured some of the worst social conditions in Europe at that time.
(*Courtesy of Kilmainham Gaol Museum, 19PO-1A33-24*)

Frank Thornton, the IRA's deputy director of intelligence, photographed at IRA intelligence headquarters at the Antient Concert Rooms, Dublin, on 11 July 1921.
(*Courtesy of the Irish Military Archives, Bureau of Military History CD 188/1/2*)

THIS IS WHERE HE WAS IN 1921

THEN THE TREATY CAME
AND THE WIND OF LIBERTY BLEW HIM OUT

UP THE REPUBLIC

1922

NOW THUS IS HE !

'The Trucileer', an anti-Republican cartoon produced by the Irish Free State during the Civil War. This type of propaganda was based on earlier British efforts depicting the IRA as a gang of criminals and cowards who shied away from military tactics to launch a murder campaign against off-duty British troops and Protestant civilians. (*Courtesy of Kilmainham Gaol Museum, 20NO-1D12-06*)

Truce would come into operation. So from daylight until twelve noon on the 11th July, every Volunteer who had a gun sought for means to use it, and the Truce came with intense I.R.A. activity over the area. I understood that this order came from General Headquarters in Dublin and was issued to us by the Brigade Headquarters, but I don't know anything about it except what I have stated. During that morning a lot of shooting at enemy posts took place, it was not a serious affair, as a lot of the shooting was done at long range and the enemy remained strictly indoors.[29]

Kennedy's comment that these last-minute attacks were 'not a serious affair' is a gross understatement. Just three attacks on the British forces took place in the 3rd Tipperary Brigade's operational area, and all of them were ineffective. One RIC constable was fired on by members of the IRA in Annacarty on 10 July but escaped unharmed.[30] That night a fusillade of rifle shots was fired at two RIC men, Constables David Maxwell and John Coyle, from a ruined building about 150 yards from Cappawhite Barracks. Both men escaped injury and their assailants withdrew after fire was returned from the RIC barracks.[31] Dundrum RIC Barracks was the subject of a prolonged IRA sniping attack, which started at 11.45 p.m. on 10 July. One British soldier was wounded in the attack, which was reported to have lasted for two hours.[32]

The republicans also launched simultaneous attacks on two RIC barracks in north-east Tipperary on the morning of 10 July. At 1.30 a.m. the IRA mounted a sniping attack on Gortderrybeg RIC Barracks and the RIC reported that 'Attackers used only rifles and at long range. Damage to barracks slight.' There were no RIC casualties.[33] A short time later, at 2 a.m., a second attack was made on Templetuohy RIC Barracks when the local RIC garrison came under a barrage of sustained rifle, shotgun and revolver gunfire, which it claimed lasted up to fifty minutes. Again, there were no RIC casualties.[34] On the morning of 11 July, a third RIC barracks was attacked at Goulding's Cross in the former county of North

Tipperary. The attack began shortly after midnight and resulted in two members of the RIC being hospitalised with serious wounds.[35]

At 3 a.m. on 11 July the Tipperary IRA began a sustained sniping attack on Annacarty RIC Barracks. The RIC reported that a force of fifty republicans attacked them for a full hour before withdrawing.[36] The IRA returned to Annacarty a few hours later and launched a second sniping attack on the same barracks, which began at 11 a.m. and lasted for approximately forty-five minutes before stopping just a quarter of an hour before the Truce came into effect.[37] Michael Davern, commander of the Republican Police in Cashel, took part:

> We decided that we would give the enemy a farewell party at Annacarty barracks, so we got into position early in the morning, unobserved, and continued to snipe the barracks until 12 o'clock. Although the Truce was to be observed from 12 o'clock on, the R.I.C. and Tans continued to fire at us when they saw us retreating. We observed the Truce and did not reply.[38]

The final IRA operation in Tipperary was literally a last-minute attack when members of the Galtee Battalion determined to make a defiant, if wholly futile, attack on the British forces in Galbally. However, they were equally careful not to breach the letter of the Truce and rigidly observed the ceasefire the second it came into effect. Since none of the local IRA Volunteers possessed a watch, they tasked a local woman with ringing the bell of the local church at 11.45 a.m. sharp as a signal to begin the attack and to stop sounding the bell promptly at noon to indicate the beginning of the Truce.[39] Michael Quirke took part in this and described what happened:

> Some time around 11 a.m. on that day the same 20 men came down from the Galtees in small groups, and took up concealed positions

North, South, East and West around the police and military posts in Galbally, and at about 400 yards range. We lay there under cover until the bell started to toll, and then opened a rapid fire on the windows, sandbags and barbed wire defences for a full ten minutes, then hell was again let loose, with rifle and machine gun fire from the police and military, who made no attempt to get out and locate us. When silence took the place of the machine gun fire we hastily left for the Galtees where we hid our rifles, revolvers and ammunition.[40]

These operations consumed a large amount of ammunition that the IRA could not easily replenish. In later years Seamus Babington, a member of the Tipperary No. 3 Brigade's staff, was critical of the order to launch 'eleventh-hour' attacks:

Bravery appeared to be immediately awakened in the heart and soul of every I.R.A. man, and dozens of them who had been noted for their absence from normal duty were on the warpath for a major attack all day, July 10th, and well up to noon, the Truce hour, seeking the enemy anywhere and everywhere, to top [*sic*] off his head.[41]

The similarities between the attacks on RIC barracks in the counties of North and South Tipperary suggest they had all been organised by the local republican leadership in reaction to the announcement of the Truce. However, while IRA veterans from the South Tipperary Brigade stated that they had received a definite order to launch 'eleventh-hour' attacks on RIC barracks and other targets,[42] similar evidence from North Tipperary is not forthcoming. The final attacks by the IRA in Tipperary were very like those carried out by the 1st Eastern Division.

No county saw so much fevered IRA activity on the eve of the Truce as Kerry. The IRA's Kerry No. 1 and No. 2 Brigades launched eight separate attacks on the British forces after the announcement of the Truce, resulting in eight fatalities: five British soldiers and three IRA Volunteers were killed. These last-minute IRA operations included a sniping attack on a British military barracks, two attacks on RIC barracks, several ambushes of British patrols and two attacks on off-duty members of the British forces. A planned assault on Killorglin RIC Barracks was cancelled at the last moment. In contrast with the actions in Tipperary and the 1st Eastern Division's area, the majority of the final IRA attacks in Kerry targeted the British Army rather than the RIC, but a significant proportion of these had been planned long before the IRA leadership in Kerry knew that a truce had been agreed.

At 1.15 a.m. on 9 July the IRA launched sniping attacks on the two British military outposts in Kenmare.[43] At 3 a.m. it launched a sniping attack on Listowel RIC Barracks, throwing a grenade and firing several rifle shots at the building before withdrawing. After the attack a grenade was found attached to the barracks gate.[44] Another attack occurred at Gortnacoriaga, near Killarney.[45] A ten-strong RIC foot patrol led by a district inspector and an RIC sergeant left Killarney to investigate a report that Farranfore RIC Barracks was under attack. On their return journey to Killarney at 9.30 a.m. on 9 July they were ambushed. The patrol managed to return fire and escape from the ambush unscathed.[46] These operations appear to have been planned for some time beforehand, and their occurrence so close to the Truce was apparently coincidental.

When news of the ceasefire became common knowledge, the IRA in Kerry launched a series of large-scale military operations. Tom O'Connor, commandant of the 6th Battalion, Kerry No. 2 Brigade IRA, recalled that the leaders of the IRA in Kerry planned a series of co-ordinated attacks on the British forces for 10 July 1921: 'The night before the Truce was a Sunday. We were in Kerry 2 Bde [Brigade,] Free [Humphrey] Murphy and John Joe Rice were in charge and they decided to attack [the British forces in] Castleisland, Killorglin and Kenmare.'[47] The meeting decided that at least three large-scale attacks on these targets should be carried out simultaneously.[48] The IRA planned to ambush British military curfew patrols in Kenmare and Castleisland, and to attack the RIC barracks in Killorglin, executing a 'feint attack' on Rathmore RIC Barracks at the same time.[49] However, the ambushes in Kenmare and Castleisland were the result of long-term intelligence work, carried out before the Truce was agreed, involving the observation of British curfew patrols to identify potential targets for future ambushes, and should not be dismissed as a knee-jerk reaction in response to the announcement of the Truce.

Denis Hegarty, commander of the 3rd Battalion, Kerry No. 2 Brigade, led the Kenmare attack. The local IRA had observed the nightly route taken by the British soldiers who patrolled the town enforcing the curfew imposed by martial law, and planned to attack them as they assembled for this duty outside the Lansdowne Hotel.[50] However, the British deviated from their normal routine, and instead of setting out in one large body, split their force into two smaller patrols, probably as a result of IRA attacks on the garrison in the town the previous night. At around 10 p.m. a party of six IRA Volunteers ambushed one of these groups as they passed along Rookery Lane, but the republicans were forced to break off their attack after about half an hour and beat a hasty retreat when they were outflanked by the second section of the curfew patrol, who attacked them with rifle and machine-gun fire.[51] One British soldier, Private William Finch, was wounded.[52]

The planned attack on Killorglin RIC Barracks differed significantly from all of the other barracks attacks because it was the only one that had a tangible military objective – the destruction of the barracks, the capture of war material and the chance of inflicting heavy casualties on the enemy and/or forcing their surrender. All of the others were sniping attacks that served little purpose other than to indicate an active IRA presence in the area and as a test of the morale of those garrisoned at the outpost. In contrast the planned attack on Killorglin was a more ambitious operation modelled on successful barracks attacks at Ballytrain in Co. Monaghan, Kilmallock in Co. Limerick and Rosscarbery in Co. Cork.[53] As a diversion to lure potential British reinforcements away from the Killorglin area, a second group of IRA Volunteers under the command of Captain Jeremiah Kennedy was to mount a simultaneous sniping attack on Rathmore RIC Barracks. The decision to carry out these operations was apparently made in the knowledge that a truce was looming, and consequently proved controversial; at least one of those present at the meeting of the brigade council that approved them, Tom McEllistrim, voiced his concerns about the attacks.[54]

McEllistrim continued to be plagued by doubts about the prudence of the Killorglin attack. The assault on the barracks had been scheduled to begin with the detonation of an improvised landmine made from guncotton explosive, constructed by the local IRA battalion engineer Oliver Mason. When McEllistrim questioned him about the power of the mine and the risk of civilian casualties, Mason replied that it was 'likely to kill anything within 50 yds of it'.[55] McEllistrim was very disturbed at the prospect of an IRA operation causing civilian fatalities in the final hours of the conflict 'because it might have involved the lives of some of the people of Killorglin, and when the Truce was so near the risk to human life would not be justified'.[56] The attack on Killorglin RIC Barracks was cancelled on McEllistrim's orders. There was now no need to proceed with the diversionary attack planned for Rathmore, but it was impossible for a dispatch cancelling that operation to reach the IRA at Rathmore in time. Consequently, about twenty IRA Volunteers, unaware that the operation was by then entirely redundant, carried out their orders to the letter and fired on the barracks without causing any casualties, before withdrawing.[57]

Undoubtedly the most controversial of the 'eleventh-hour' IRA operations against the British forces was the Castleisland ambush, which resulted in the deaths of four British soldiers and three IRA

Volunteers.[58] Several IRA veterans later questioned Humphrey Murphy's judgement for carrying out the attack in the knowledge that a truce was imminent. Tom McEllistrim remembered, 'The Castleisland shooting caused a lot of trouble in the district for it was the last day of the Tan War.'[59] Seamus O'Connor stated, 'it might have been perhaps as well not to bother with it, seeing the Truce was on the following day.'[60] IRA veteran Dan Keating dismissed the operation as a catastrophe: 'It was a complete fiasco. Four [*sic* – actually three] great men killed.'[61] The British historiography has also placed particular emphasis on the Castleisland ambush as an example of IRA guile. The history of the British Army's 6th Division in Ireland cited the Castleisland attack as proof that the IRA exploited the Truce as 'an opportunity for attacking and murdering people when vigilance would obviously be relaxed'.[62] General Macready also pointed to the Castleisland ambush as proof of the IRA's 'campaign of outrage and assassination until the clocks struck twelve on 11th July'.[63]

Andy Cooney, the IRA officer from GHQ who had been sent to Kerry to organise the local IRA brigades, later claimed that the Castleisland ambush was organised by the local IRA Volunteers as a knee-jerk reaction to the announcement of the Truce 'for fear they would not ever get another rap at the British'.[64] However, there is evidence that this attack had been planned for some time and was not merely a last desperate chance to exact vengeance. Though the decision to proceed with it was reached at a council meeting of Kerry No. 2 Brigade some time previously, it was ultimately carried out in the knowledge that a truce was imminent.

The British patrol in Castleisland that the IRA planned to ambush did not vary their route much, generally leaving the barracks at the western end of the town, marching up Main Street to the ruins of the Carnegie Library, and then returning by the same route. The local IRA had burned the library the previous month to prevent it being commandeered by the British forces. The library had held a commanding view of Main Street and the republicans decided to use the ruined building as a vantage point from where they could ambush the curfew patrol.[65] Several failed attempts had been made previously to ambush the patrol and it appears to have been largely coincidental that the night before the Truce was the only night that the British forces strayed into a trap which had been set for them repeatedly.

A foot patrol by members of the North Lancashire Fusiliers left their barracks at 9 p.m. each night, when their commanding officer would fire a single shot in the air from his revolver to signal the beginning of the curfew.

> The battalion had been very active for the past few months, yet the Castleisland garrison were always able to elude the net ... The I.R.A. had tried on a couple of occasions to ambush this patrol but it was a coincidence that the patrol remained indoors whenever the I.R.A. were in the vicinity in strength. It would, of course, have been easy to have one or two of the I.R.A. have a few shots at them on the nights they came out, but both the brigade and battalion were hoping to make a complete job of it if they could get in to the town in strength on a night the patrol came out. For some days prior to July 10th, 1921, battalion intelligence indicated that they were coming out on certain nights, including the night of July 10th. Arrangements were, therefore, made by the brigade to attack the patrol on that night.[66]

The final decision to carry out the attack was made at 3 p.m. on 10 July, when the leadership of the Kerry No. 2 Brigade and the local IRA battalion officers received reliable information that a British military curfew patrol would definitely leave the barracks that night. According to Peter Browne, this information came directly from an IRA mole inside Castleisland Barracks:

The Brigade and Battalion staffs ... were still in the vicinity of Scartaglin village when, at about 3 p.m., another messenger came from Castleisland with word that the patrol was coming out for certain that night. This messenger was no less a person than the informant himself, who had sneaked out of the barracks and taken the risk of being found out by cycling the five miles to Scartaglin with the information.[67]

That evening a group of forty IRA Volunteers under the command of Humphrey Murphy entered Castleisland. Twenty-five volunteers were armed with rifles and the remainder had shotguns. If all went according to plan, the British patrol would be trapped by heavy gunfire in the middle of the street with no cover and would be killed, or forced to surrender, within a matter of minutes. However, the IRA was delayed while entering the town and so some of its men were not in their allocated positions when the British patrol reached the ambush position. One of the IRA sections opened fire prematurely, before the British troops entered the position, so the troops were able to seek cover and engage with their attackers.[68] British reinforcements quickly reached the scene and, after an intense and chaotic battle lasting several minutes, the IRA withdrew. One group of IRA Volunteers attempting to retreat came under sustained rifle and machine-gun fire from the advancing British soldiers and was forced to seek cover in an old quarry. Some of the Volunteers managed to escape under fire, but the remaining three, John Flynn, Richard Shanahan and Jack Prendiville, were trapped and killed by the British forces.[69] Four members of the British forces – Sergeant John Laution Davies, Private George Rankin, Private William Ross and Private William Kelly – were killed in the attack.[70]

Numerous attacks on the British forces were made throughout Ireland in the same period, in areas where the local IRA had not received an order to take last-minute action, suggesting that the majority of the last-minute attacks that occurred all over Ireland in the last days of the war were standard IRA operations no different from hundreds of others except that they coincided with the Truce.

There were three armed clashes between the IRA and the RIC in Co. Clare. The first of these was the shooting of Constable Alfred Needham in Ennis at 4.30 p.m. on 8 July. Later that afternoon members of the East Clare Brigade ambushed an RIC curfew patrol in Sixmilebridge. The final attack on the British forces in Clare occurred at 10.15 p.m. on 9 July, when the Mid Clare Brigade launched a sniping attack on Ballyvaughan Coastguard Station, with the Royal Marines who were occupying the station immediately returning fire with machine guns. The IRA eventually withdrew after a lengthy battle when RIC reinforcements arrived.[71]

In Bunratty, a British soldier, Private R. W. Williams of the 2nd Battalion Royal Welch Fusiliers, was killed as the result of an IRA road-blocking operation. At 2 p.m. on 10 July Williams and another British Army motorcycle dispatch rider were travelling from Limerick towards Ennis when they drove across a bridge spanning the Owengarry River, which the IRA had attempted to destroy with explosives two months earlier. Both soldiers crashed through a breach in the bridge and Private Williams struck his head on the masonry as he fell and was killed.[72] The RIC county inspector claimed these attacks were the result of a deliberate attempt 'to murder as many police and other Crown Forces as possible before the Truce came on'.[73] However, this is impossible, since the three armed attacks in the county occurred before word of the Truce had reached these areas, and Private Williams' death could have happened at any time in the two months since the IRA had mined Bunratty Bridge.

The RIC county inspector for Galway East Riding also claimed that the IRA organised deliberate 'eleventh-hour' attacks to kill members of the RIC before the Truce started. He cited an IRA attack on an RIC patrol at Roxborough near Kilchreest, Co. Galway, on the morning of 11 July as:

> ... a particularly disgraceful affair ... the Truce had been announced in all chapels in the locality on the day before, and it was thought by the police that on the Monday morning nothing would be done ... Very considerable activity was shown by the Sinn Féin and IRA organisations up to the morning of the Truce.[74]

While the IRA Volunteers taking part in this ambush knew that a truce would begin later that day, the ambush had actually been planned the previous month and was not a knee-jerk reaction to the announcement of the Truce. It was carried out by members of the East Clare Brigade's flying column, who had crossed the county border to assist local IRA units. It was just one of a number of ambushes the IRA had been planning for south-east Galway that weekend – but it was the only one that came to fruition. Some of these had been planned weeks in advance as arrangements had to be made to borrow rifles for an attack due to a shortage of arms in the area.[75]

In Cork, at 10.45 p.m. on 9 July, the RIC barracks at Drimoleague was attacked with grenade and rifle fire, which was reported to have lasted for twenty minutes but did not result in any RIC casualties.[76] The following night there was a similar attack on Innishannon RIC Barracks.[77] On the morning of Sunday 10 July, the IRA ambushed a patrol of British soldiers at Mitchelstown.[78] The IRA had been planning an attack there for some time, and Volunteers had occupied ambush positions outside the town for over a fortnight, but no suitable target had presented itself.[79] That Sunday, a thirteen-strong British Army patrol left Mitchelstown Barracks escorting a water wagon to the fountain at the opposite end of the town. They were ambushed by fifteen armed IRA Volunteers who emerged from the town's creamery and called on them to surrender. When challenged, the British troops reached for their rifles and the IRA opened fire; two British soldiers were wounded in the ensuing gunfight and the IRA captured their rifles. Two separate IRA covering parties, each consisting of three riflemen, had been placed near the town's British military and RIC barracks. When the ambush began, they opened fire to prevent reinforcements leaving these outposts. The troops stationed in these barracks replied with machine-gun and rifle fire, and the IRA withdrew once the approach of British military reinforcements from Kilworth camp was signalled.[80]

The republicans also prepared at least six other ambushes in the county, but most of these were abandoned after the British forces did not pass through the prepared ambush positions. The IRA's Cork No. 3 Brigade prepared ambushes at Ardcahan near Dunmanway on 8 July and at Clonakilty Junction the following day, but both of these were abandoned after the British patrols failed to travel through the ambush positions. These ambushes were planned using local intelligence about the movements of the British forces and were mounted before news of the Truce was widespread in Cork.[81]

Cork No. 3 Brigade planned another ambush for 10 July, for a British Army cycle patrol that was expected to pass through Kealkil. The previous day, two local IRA officers had encountered a cycle patrol of ten soldiers dressed in civilian clothing at a local pub. Having made their escape, the two IRA officers immediately organised the manpower and weaponry to attack the patrol. The IRA lay in ambush at Kealkil from 9 p.m. on 10 July until 9 a.m. the following morning, but the ambush was called off as the cycle patrol did not return to the area. In this case it is important to note that a chance encounter and the accidental discovery of a suitable target were the primary motivating factors in planning the attack, and its proximity to the ceasefire was coincidental.[82] The IRA also attempted to ambush the British forces at Clonakilty and

Castlelyons in response to intelligence information gathered locally over several weeks, but both ambushes were abandoned on the morning of 11 July, just hours before the Truce was due to begin.[83]

The largest and by far the most ambitious IRA operation planned for the weekend of the Truce was to be an ambush on a convoy of British military at Barnagh, Co. Limerick, which was planned for Friday 8 July, but was finally abandoned at noon on 11 July. The operation had been planned for weeks and the IRA personnel involved had no knowledge of the political developments in Dublin that led to the Truce. The ambush had originally been scheduled for 1 July, but had to be postponed because of the two weeks it took to accumulate the amount of potassium chlorate needed to make the eight landmines that were to be used in the attack. Around 140 members of the IRA were mobilised at Barnagh, and were equipped with a Hotchkiss machine gun and at least eight landmines, each containing approximately fourteen pounds of explosive, that could be detonated by an electronic charge.[84] The preparation of this ambush was one of the largest IRA operations of the war and it had the potential to eclipse both the Kilmichael and the Crossbarry ambushes in terms of scale and fatalities. Despite the unprecedented mobilisation of IRA manpower, weaponry and equipment, not a single shot was to be fired in anger at Barnagh.

At 7 a.m. on 8 July the IRA engineers had just finished placing the landmines and the riflemen were moving in to occupy their ambush positions when, according to Mossie Harnett, they were taken unawares by the approach of a British convoy from Newcastle West:

> Before we realised what was happening, on they came with a private car in front followed by four transport Crossleys filled with troops and they drove quickly over our mined road and disappeared in the direction of Abbeyfeale.[85]

Patrick O'Brien, who was in overall charge of the operation, made a spur-of-the-moment decision to allow the convoy to pass unchallenged and then attack it on its return journey: 'They had never left at that hour before; it was usually around 3 p.m. before they left for Listowel. We hurriedly decided to let them pass and attack as they were returning.'[86] The convoy failed to return that day or the next. On Saturday evening, Ernie O'Malley, the leader of the IRA's 1st Southern Division, summoned O'Brien to a meeting:

> Late on Saturday evening, July 9th, a despatch arrived from Divisional Headquarters summoning myself and the Battalion O.C. ... to a meeting at Dromahane on Sunday, July 10th. We started immediately and got as far as Freemount that night, where we heard the first rumours of a Truce. On the following day, Sunday, we got to Dromahane and arrived at the venue of the meeting ... It was then we were definitely informed that there was to be a Truce the following day at noon ... We returned to Tournafulla that night and held a Conference with the Section leaders of North Cork and the Officers of the West Limerick Column ... It was unanimously decided that we would go back into the positions evacuated on Friday and remain there until 12 noon.[87]

O'Brien's account makes it clear that before the night of Saturday 9 July, the IRA officers who planned the ambush had no information that a ceasefire was imminent, and the IRA Volunteers at Barnagh knew nothing about the Truce until O'Brien's return the following day. A quarter of an hour before the Truce was due to start, O'Brien cancelled the operation and called on the IRA Volunteers present to form ranks on the roadway. He addressed the men, spelling out the terms of the Truce, and dismissed them at 12 noon sharp when the ceasefire began.[88] At 12.15 p.m., while the IRA engineers were busy dismantling and removing the landmines they had planted for the attack, a convoy of British military from Newcastle West drove into the ambush position at Barnagh. On seeing at first-hand the IRA preparations for an ambush, the British troops initially adopted a hostile attitude, before boarding their vehicles and leaving.[89] They were apparently well informed regarding the IRA's activities and Major Foster, the British officer leading the patrol, confronted them, saying, 'Ye are waiting here for the past week to ambush us.'[90]

In Co. Limerick, aside from the attacks on Lieutenant Brown and Constable Bullock in Kilmallock (see Chapter 4), there were two other republican attacks on the British forces at the time of the Truce. The Mid Limerick Brigade mined the Birdhill to Limerick railway line at Cantor's Bridge near Killonan after it discovered that a full company of the RIC Auxiliaries stationed at Killaloe, Co. Clare, would be transferred by rail to another posting on the morning of 8 July.[91] The Auxiliaries were due to cross the bridge at 8 a.m. that morning; however, shortly before their arrival, the route was searched by the British military, who discovered that the railway was mined. They immediately took cover and the IRA ambushers opened fire on them. After a very brief engagement, the IRA retreated as the sound of gunfire attracted British reinforcements. The Cantor's Bridge ambush was one of the most ambitious operations mounted by the IRA's Mid Limerick Brigade, but its timing on the same day as the Truce was announced was coincidental. The operation had been planned for over a month and Michael Hayes, who took part in the attack, stated that he and his comrades were completely unaware at the time of the political developments in Dublin that led to the signing of the Truce agreement later that day.[92] A second IRA ambush occurred at Dromkeen, where members of the East Limerick Brigade attacked a motorised RIC patrol with a grenade, wounding one RIC constable. Again, it was carried out when IRA personnel in Limerick were still unaware that a ceasefire was imminent.[93]

The RIC county inspector for Waterford claimed that the IRA

in the county 'made a special effort in crime … up to the very hour of the commencement of the Truce. In fact the two days preliminary notice seems to have spurred the local patriots to redouble their exertions, doubtless to let the world see what dashing fellows they are.'[94] However, this claim is not supported by evidence from other sources. According to the Waterford No. 2 Brigade's activity report for July 1921, the IRA in the west of the county spent the final days of the conflict conducting road-blocking operations, with the 1st Battalion being 'confined more or less to early trenching or blocking of roads'.[95] There were just three attacks on the British forces in Co. Waterford after the Truce was agreed. On 8 and 9 July Ardmore Coastguard Station was attacked in IRA sniping attacks. On both nights Royal Marines manning the station returned the republicans' fire and neither side sustained any casualties.[96] On 9 July a grenade was thrown at Dungarvan Castle, which was occupied by the RIC; however, the bomb fell short of the castle wall and exploded harmlessly.[97]

On the eve of the Truce the West Waterford flying column discovered that a column of British soldiers was due to travel through their area of operations the following morning, but according to James Prendergast, vice-commanding officer of the flying column, the republicans decided not to attack 'because of the Truce, which was to take effect at 12 o'clock (midday) the following day'.[98] Despite his claim that the 'two days preliminary notice' of the Truce spurred the IRA in Waterford to redouble their efforts, the RIC county inspector's report for the county recorded just one IRA attack – the shooting of an off-duty RIC constable – during the last two days of the conflict.[99] Given the lack of aggressive IRA activity reported in the county, the IRA in Waterford can hardly be said to have reacted to news of the Truce with an 'eleventh-hour' outburst.

In contrast to the south, there was very little IRA activity in the west of Ireland during 8–11 July. Excluding Co. Galway (examined above), there were just five attacks on the British forces in the province of Connacht, all directed against the RIC. At 9.30 p.m. on 9 July the North Longford flying column ambushed an RIC cycle patrol near Streete in Westmeath; one member of the patrol was wounded in the attack.[100] The following day thirty members of the IRA's Longford Brigade made a sniping attack on the RIC barracks at Ballinalee. This lasted for approximately thirty minutes, but did not result in any RIC casualties.[101] IRA veteran Bryan Doherty dismissed the attack on the barracks as a political gesture rather than a serious military operation: 'The unit did carry out a sort of attack on the stronghold at Ballinalee on the eve of the Truce which I thought was more of a defiant action than a serious attempt to take the fortress.'[102]

On the eve of the Truce the IRA's Roscommon Brigade ambushed an RIC cycle patrol at South Park near Castlerea, but the local IRA unit was ill-equipped to carry out a successful ambush, with a number of the Volunteers mobilised having only two rounds each for their shotguns. They opened fire on the advance party of the patrol, but withdrew after a brief firefight when the main body of approximately fifty RIC arrived, outnumbering them. The RIC suffered no casualties and captured two IRA Volunteers in the immediate aftermath of the ambush.[103] In Co. Mayo, ten rifle shots were fired at the RIC barracks in Swinford on the night of 9 July. The following day, members of the East Mayo Brigade opened fire on a group of Black and Tans who were playing on the sports field in Ballaghaderreen.[104]

News of the ceasefire led to a number of IRA officers in the west cancelling attacks on British forces. The IRA's North Mayo Brigade discovered an RIC convoy stopped at Enniscrone on the night of 10 July. The RIC members had alighted from their vehicles, leaving just one sentry to keep guard. Some members of the brigade suggested attacking the convoy while it could be caught off-guard, but they were informed that 'the Truce was almost on and it was decided that it would be next to dishonourable to attempt it, and in consequence the attack was called off'.[105] Similarly, an IRA attack on the RIC garrison at Cliffoney due to take place the weekend of the Truce was cancelled by the commandant of the IRA's Sligo Brigade, who gave the local IRA unit 'instructions to withdraw our men and not engage in any further activities'.[106]

The IRA's Dublin Brigade had planned a number of large-scale military operations for Friday 8 July, the date that the Truce was agreed. At 1 p.m. that afternoon, members of the Dublin Brigade's ASU under the command of Pádraig O'Connor attacked a train transporting a company of British soldiers from the Gordon Highlanders Regiment at Ballyfermot. One civilian on board the train was mortally wounded by a grenade thrown by the IRA ambushers and died later that day. Despite occurring at the precise time the negotiations to secure a truce were being finalised, the attack had been planned in advance and was based on intelligence reports giving the precise time and date of the troop transport.[107] None of the IRA Volunteers involved knew that a ceasefire was imminent, and they only learned that a truce had been agreed from 'stop press' reports in newspapers in the city that evening.[108]

Once the Truce had been formally agreed and announced, the IRA's Dublin Brigade immediately cancelled all offensive military operations in the capital 'on account of the close proximity of the Truce'.[109] Following this order, there were no other IRA attacks on British troops in the capital, with the exception of a single incident at Dalkey on 9 July, when a British soldier was wounded during an attempt to hijack a British military vehicle parked at the tramway terminus.[110] The final IRA operation in Dublin was a raid on the Inchicore Railway Works to secure materials used in the manufacture of explosives.[111] The raid was carried out on the morning of 11 July but did not involve any contact with the British forces.[112]

Outside Dublin and the IRA's 1st Eastern Divisional area there was relatively little republican military activity in Leinster. The

Kilkenny Brigade attacked two British patrols after the announcement of the Truce. On 9 July a joint British military and police
patrol travelling in two Crossley Tender lorries was attacked at
Clashacrow near Callan.[113] The IRA had made several attempts
to ambush the British forces near Callan in the weeks before the
Truce, so the nature and location of the attack suggest that it was
a standard military operation of the War of Independence.[114]
The following night, members of the Kilkenny Brigade attacked
a British curfew patrol in Mullinahone, Co. Tipperary. They had
been monitoring the routine of this mixed RIC and British Army
curfew patrol for some time. The six-strong patrol departed the
village's RIC barracks each night without varying its routine. It
was attacked with a grenade and revolver fire immediately after
departing the RIC barracks on 10 July. Sergeant John William
Reynolds of the Lincolnshire Regiment was killed and a second
British officer was wounded. The operation was planned before the
agreement of the Truce, and when the local IRA unit learned of
the impending ceasefire it decided to carry out the attack because
it did not consider the ceasefire would be anything other than a
temporary measure.[115]

Wicklow was the only county in east Leinster with no recorded
IRA attacks on British patrols immediately before the ceasefire.[116]
In addition to the shooting of Constable Cormer at Rathdrum,
the British military outpost at Bray came under attack from the
IRA. The barracks suffered three separate sniping attacks after the
announcement of the Truce – at 3.15 a.m. on 10 July and again at
2.30 a.m. and 4 a.m. the following morning. During some of these
attacks the barracks was fired on from two separate locations; there
was some damage to the exterior of the building but no British
casualties.[117]

There was little reaction from the IRA's northern brigades to
the announcement of the Truce in terms of attacks on the British
forces. At 11.15 p.m. on 10 July a group of 'B Specials' on curfew

patrol discovered an IRA unit preparing an ambush at Dun Teague near Omagh, Co. Tyrone. The 'B Specials' opened fire on the republicans, killing IRA Volunteer James McSorely, a twenty-six-year-old ex-soldier.[118] A second attack on the British forces in Ulster occurred in Belfast later that same night, when a police patrol of RIC and Special Constabulary was ambushed in the Falls Road area, and Constable Thomas Conlon was killed in the ensuing firefight with two others seriously wounded.[119] At 10.30 p.m. on 10 July Falcarragh RIC Barracks was attacked with rifle fire. The RIC garrison reported that thirty men were involved in the attack and that they were pursued afterwards but managed to escape. There were no casualties and the barrack building was unscathed except for a few broken windows. On the morning of 11 July, the IRA attempted to burn the Coastguard Station at Greencastle, Co. Down.[120] Apart from these attacks on the British forces, however, the IRA's northern divisions seem to have been concerned primarily with enforcing the 'Belfast Boycott' of loyalist-owned businesses. The night train from Belfast to Derry was held up at Carrickmore, Co. Tyrone, on 10 July by the IRA, who seized a number of bicycles, a large quantity of tobacco and several mail bags before burning several railway carriages containing goods manufactured in Belfast.[121]

A CONTINUATION OF ACCEPTED TACTICS

The 'soft target' narrative maintains that by the end of the War of Independence the IRA was struggling militarily because of the arrival of thousands of extra British reinforcements alongside improvements in British tactics and weaponry; faced with these difficulties, the IRA was apparently increasingly incapable of carrying out military attacks on barracks or ambushes on British patrols and switched instead to 'terrorist' attacks on isolated British troops and their supporters. This narrative has become increasingly popular in recent years with historians such as Peter Hart, who claimed that the Irish War of Independence was a 'dirty war' in which 'murder was more common than battle'.[122]

However, an analysis of the IRA's military campaign in the last five weeks of the conflict (see Table 5.1) shows that the overwhelming majority of republican attacks were standard military operations targeting armed members of the British forces, either ambushed while on patrol or attacked in their barracks.

Table 5.1: Comparison between IRA military operations in June 1921 and on 8–11 July 1921[123]

IRA operations against the British forces, June 1921			IRA operations against the British forces, 8–11 July 1921		
Type	**Number**	**Percentage**	**Type**	**Number**	**Percentage**
'Soft targets'	45	25.7	'Soft targets'	16	25.0
Barracks	49	28.0	Barracks	27	42.2
Ambushes	81	46.3	Ambushes	21	32.8
Total = 175 attacks; fatalities: 58			**Total = 64 attacks; fatalities: 23**		

While the republican military campaign intensified in the last days of the conflict, the IRA did not change its tactics to attack 'soft targets'. The evidence shows that the vast majority of republican attacks continued to be directed against 'hard targets', and the increase in the level of IRA activity was at least in part caused by a general trend that had seen consistent increases in the number of IRA operations throughout the conflict.

The most significant change in the nature of the IRA's campaign immediately before the Truce was a shift away from ambushes in favour of attacks on RIC barracks and British military outposts. This was probably, in part, a result of the number of ambushes cancelled by local IRA leaders after the ceasefire was announced, and of the directives issued by some IRA units calling for last-minute actions against the British forces, which resulted primarily in an upsurge in barracks attacks.

If the IRA had attempted to kill as many people as possible before the Truce began, the republicans would be expected to have halted barracks attacks in the final days and hours of the conflict to concentrate on attacking 'soft targets' and carrying out assassinations and ambushes, which were far more likely to result in enemy fatalities. Yet the opposite occurred – there was a shift in favour of barracks attacks over other types of operations, and the majority of IRA attacks following the announcement of the ceasefire were made on RIC and British military outposts.

The IRA had targeted barracks since the very beginning of the war, but a unique aspect in the final days of the conflict was the IRA practice of launching numerous attacks on a single garrison in one night. Both Annacarty RIC Barracks in Co. Tipperary and the British Army outpost at Bray in Co. Wicklow were attacked twice in the final hours of the conflict. This phenomenon did not occur anywhere in Ireland during the previous month; indeed it was rare for the IRA to attack the same barracks on two successive nights.

Tom Barry, the leader of the Cork No. 3 Brigade's flying column, stated that it was practically impossible for the IRA to capture a British-held barracks without employing explosives:

> Rifle and revolver bullets were about as useful as snowballs against these strong enemy posts. All the garrison had to do was to man the loopholed walls and windows in complete safety and shoot down any attackers who approached.[124]

During the initial stages of the war, the IRA had enjoyed a great deal of success in capturing and destroying RIC barracks, but as the number of IRA attacks increased, so too did British security measures. Consequently, by the summer of 1921 it had become practically impossible for IRA units to penetrate the defences of barracks used by the British forces, except through the deployment of powerful explosive mines. Rosscarbery RIC Barracks in Co.

Cork, which was captured during an IRA attack in March 1921, was the last British barracks destroyed by the republicans, and even after an explosion had demolished part of the building, its garrison managed to resist for several hours before surrendering.[125]

By the summer of 1921 most IRA brigades had stopped planning similar operations because of the chronic shortage of the explosives needed to make them a success. Yet IRA sniping attacks on barracks continued unabated. The IRA's Cork No. 3 Brigade launched regular attacks on RIC barracks, which continued right up to the Truce in spite of a critical shortage of ammunition. According to Barry, who complained of the lack of ammunition: 'Every enemy post was sniped several times, including Innishannon which had five sniping attacks.'[126] The fifth and final attack on Innishannon Barracks happened the night before the Truce.[127] Local IRA leaders knew by the summer of 1921 that these operations were unlikely to force the barracks' garrisons to surrender, or result in the capture and destruction of the outpost. By the end of the conflict they were largely being carried out as an effective means of maintaining IRA morale, as a way of harassing the British forces and because they had important propaganda value.

The *Morning Post* described RIC barracks as 'the block houses of Imperial rule in Ireland' and republicans often attacked these buildings because they were an important local symbol of the British crown's authority.[128] On a more pragmatic level, in many cases the IRA carried out sniping operations because the abandonment of smaller rural barracks and the strengthening of British convoys, by tripling the numbers of troops and vehicles involved, made ambushes of convoys and curfew patrols more difficult. The RIC recorded forty-nine sniping attacks on British barracks in June 1921. By that time republican sniping operations on British outposts were so commonplace that some IRA units in Cork sniped RIC barracks in their area at least twice weekly.[129] Members of the

Tipperary No. 1 Brigade sniped Portroe RIC barracks so often that they lost count of the number of times it was attacked.[130]

In Co. Tipperary the IRA also sniped British barracks because no other feasible targets were available. Jim Leahy of the Tipperary No. 2 Brigade complained that by 1921, 'There were no big engagements in Mid Tipp, but we were always hammering at their posts … The last couple of months only convoys moved through our area, and as they were strong we weren't in a position to attack them.'[131] Another Tipperary veteran, Ned Jordan, recalled that RIC barracks and British Army outposts were the only available targets because the British forces had abandoned rural areas and withdrawn to urban barracks, where they felt safer:

> … the enemy were so quiet that it was hard to keep our men from going down to Carrickbeg [to attack them] … The military and the RIC didn't want to fight. If they could hold their posts that was all they wanted to do … [There was] sniping from Carrickbeg [from] time to time, but we never could learn … the result.[132]

Another reason for the sniping attacks was the harassment of the British forces and the belief that they would have a detrimental effect on enemy morale. IRA veteran James Keating, from Tipperary, recalled that his unit organised sniping attacks 'to worry the enemy forces in the area'.[133] Edward Horgan, from Cork, believed sniping attacks would 'obstruct and confuse' the British forces.[134] Likewise, Michael O'Donnell recalled that the incessant sniping operations kept 'the enemy in a constant state of nerves' and 'the garrisons in these posts were prepared to open fire on hearing the least sound'.[135]

These attacks were usually met with an immediate response from the besieged garrison, which returned its attackers' fire and called for reinforcements by firing signal flares. As a result, sniping operations were also employed by the IRA as a ploy to lure

British troops into ambushes, or as a feint to draw British forces away from the scene of a larger and more sustained operation. In contrast, Ned Jordan and his IRA comrades attacked Glenbower RIC Barracks because of boredom as they were eager 'more to see the Verey Lights [flares] they [the RIC] put up than for anything else'.[136]

IRA sniping attacks required very little effort on the part of a few personnel and became so commonplace that a large number of such attacks occurred during the weekend before the Truce.[137] While it is likely that a number of the twenty-eight IRA attacks on RIC barracks had been planned as routine operations before the announcement of the Truce, it is also clear from the testimony of IRA veterans that some of them were intended as 'parting shots', carried out more with the aim of sending a final defiant message to the British forces in advance of the Truce than as an attempt to achieve a military objective.

Perhaps the most unusual aspect of the IRA barracks attacks to occur following the announcement of the Truce, and the strongest indication that they were not carried out in pursuit of a military goal, were the multiple IRA attacks targeting the same barracks. The IRA attacked Ardmore Coastguard Station on two consecutive nights and the British Army outpost at Bray was sniped three times over two consecutive nights. Annacarty RIC Barracks in Tipperary was fired on twice on the night before the Truce. These actions were undoubtedly designed to make an impression on the Irish public consciousness and to give the British forces the sense that the IRA had not suffered a military defeat, was still militarily active and was capable of taking offensive action. The order issued by the 1st Eastern Division, which called for attacks on the British forces, and in particular attacks on the RIC, stated that these attacks were motivated by the belief that a show of IRA military force would bolster Irish republican negotiators in any political talks that might follow the impending truce.

The rush of combatants to take part in last-minute attacks following the announcement of a ceasefire was not restricted to the Irish War of Independence. The announcement of the Armistice that ended the First World War resulted in similar actions by combatants eager to continue fighting until the moment the ceasefire came into effect. The US Army's 79th Division was due to make an offensive attack on German positions that morning, but the announcement of the ceasefire made these plans redundant. Despite this, the division's commanding officer, Major General Joseph E. Kuhn, ordered 'Hostilities will cease … at 11 hours today … Until that hour, the operations previously ordered will be pressed with vigour.' Likewise, his subordinate, Brigadier General William Nicholson, informed his troops that 'These orders will be strictly complied with, and there will be absolutely no let up in the carrying out of the original plans until 11 o'clock.' It appears that the rank and file of the US Army followed these instructions to the letter. Despite knowing of the 11 a.m. ceasefire, US troops in the 79th Division continued to advance on their enemy's positions as late as 10:59 a.m., while their German counterparts were making frantic efforts to signal to them that the war was about to end.[138]

So many members of the US Army's field artillery were intent on fighting in the dying seconds of the war that dozens of ropes were tied to the lanyards of artillery guns to enable numerous veterans to boast that they had fired the 'final' shot of the war. Many of these soldiers gleefully posed for photographers whilst firing their field guns. Of course they would never know what casualties, if any, their 'parting shots' had inflicted, but those under fire did. Anton Lang, a German soldier with the 2nd Bavarian Artillery Regiment, saw four of his comrades killed by an artillery shell fired by Allied troops at the exact moment the Armistice came into effect:

The battle raged until exactly 11 a.m. and all of a sudden a 'big freeze' set in … The sudden stillness was interrupted by a single heavy shell which exploded … among a platoon of infantry and killed four and wounded about a dozen … this made us sad and mad. Some joker on the other side probably wanted to fire the 'last' shot.[139]

The collection of the Imperial War Museum in London includes a 'sound trace' recorded by a British artillery unit's sound-ranging equipment on 11 November 1918, which shows that artillery units on the Western Front kept firing at their enemy until the very last second before the Armistice began.[140] The legacy of such 'eleventh-hour' fighting zeal was that 10,944 casualties were recorded on the Western Front alone on 11 November 1918. This included 2,738 fatalities, a figure far in excess of the average daily fatality rate of 2,088 troops killed.[141]

Piaras Béaslaí dismissed the final IRA attacks on British troops after the announcement of the Truce as 'belated exhibitions of prowess, with no military objective'. Béaslaí's criticism of the IRA's military campaign seems justified in this case, as the majority of IRA attacks in the final days of the conflict appear to have been launched with little chance of achieving a military objective or affecting the wider military situation, and took place in the knowledge that a truce would shortly come in to effect. However, Hart's claims that the IRA's military campaign during the conflict consisted mainly of attacks on 'soft targets' and that 'murder was more common than battle' are not justified.[142] In the final weeks of the war, the IRA's military campaign was directed primarily against armed and active members of the British forces, their patrols, convoys and barracks, rather than against 'soft targets'. Nor is there evidence to support the claim that there was a deliberate effort by several IRA units to inflict a large number of fatalities before the ceasefire took effect.[143] The increase in IRA activity after the announcement of the Truce was mainly a result of sniping attacks on RIC barracks, which were intended more for propaganda than to cause fatalities.

To date, the historiography of the conflict has centred exclusively on criticism of the IRA's military campaign and the fatalities it inflicted following the announcement of the Truce. By comparison, the actions of the British forces in the same period, which resulted in a significant number of IRA and civilian fatalities, have been ignored. In an effort to redress this imbalance, these fatalities will be examined in detail in the next chapter.

6

FATALITIES INFLICTED
BY THE BRITISH FORCES

Supporters of the claim that the IRA exploited the announcement of the Truce as an opportunity to kill loyalist civilians, off-duty members of the British forces and other 'soft targets' in 'eleventh-hour' attacks have created a highly selective account of the end of the War of Independence. Accounts written in this vein portray members of the British forces as victims of unjustifiable and vindictive republican violence, and conveniently ignore a whole host of killings and reprisal attacks committed by the British forces at the same time. Most of those who have written about the Truce have analysed in detail the IRA killings which occurred after the announcement of the Truce – but all of them have failed to mention the numerous British killings that occurred at the same time.[1] Likewise, newspaper columns about the same time period, including those by Kevin Myers and Eoghan Harris, are similarly selective.[2] Indeed, it could be said that their assessment of history is strikingly similar to the early accounts written by senior British military officers in the 1920s.

The official history of the British Army's 6th Division, written in 1922, juxtaposed the IRA's allegedly 'murderous mentality' with the British military's supposed chivalry and forbearance: 'All pending operations [by British forces] were cancelled immediately, and a state of passive defence was ordered until the actual hour at which the Truce commenced.'[3] The author of the British 5th Division's history described the final days of the conflict in near identical terms: 'All military and police activities in the form of drives, raids, and searches were to cease as soon as orders to this effect could be received by the troops, *without waiting for the official hour on 11th July* ... but attacks by the IRA on the Crown forces and others took place right to the hour of the "suspension of activities".'[4] In his memoirs, General Nevil Macready reinforced the idea that the British forces immediately halted offensive operations, adopted 'a state of passive defence' and abstained as far as possible from taking offensive action against the IRA. Macready lamented that the IRA, who 'continued their campaign of outrage and assassination', abused this British gesture of goodwill.[5] These accounts of the War of Independence were written specifically for a British audience, were largely hagiographical in their treatment of the British forces and were heavily influenced by the anti-republican propaganda employed during the conflict.

However, most of the recent histories that have analysed the last actions of the War of Independence have replicated the pattern set by these pro-British accounts of excluding victims killed by the British forces from any examination of the conflict's final fatalities.[6] This gross imbalance in the historical record has been influential in creating a biased historical narrative that is highly critical of republicanism and gives the impression that, in the final days of the conflict, the IRA engaged in reckless actions that resulted in multiple fatalities, while its British counterparts abstained from violence, adopting a completely passive stance awaiting the beginning of the ceasefire.

Following the announcement of the Truce, the IRA was responsible for the deaths of at least twenty-five people. In the same period, the British forces were responsible for at least nineteen fatalities. Four IRA Volunteers were killed in combat with the British forces, while another ten people – seven civilians, two IRA Volunteers and one member of Cumann na mBan – were assassinated, executed or accidentally killed by the British forces in the south of Ireland. A further five civilians were killed by the British forces during disturbances in Belfast. This chapter will examine the circumstances of, and possible motivations for, the killings in the south; the Belfast deaths will be examined in Chapter 7.

An order giving British Army units formal notice of the Truce arrangements was issued by the British military's GHQ (Ireland) a few hours after the ceasefire was announced on the evening of 8 July. This order informed British troops that, as a result of ongoing negotiations between the British government and the leadership of Sinn Féin, 'an agreement had been made to suspend activities at 12 noon on Monday, 11th July'. Colonel Maxwell Scott wrote that this order instructed:

> All military and police activities in the form of drives, raids, and searches were to cease as soon as orders to that effect could be received by the troops, without waiting for the official hour on 11th July; military action was to be restricted to giving assistance to the police in aid to the Civil Power; all pre-arranged moves of units and detachments in Ireland were to be carried out.[7]

There was a delay in some British units receiving the order, but all sections of the British military in Ireland appear to have received it by the evening of 9 July, twenty-four hours after it was first issued. On the same date, Colonel Campbell, commander of the 15th Infantry Brigade, issued proclamations suspending curfew impositions.[8]

Despite these orders, several sections of the British forces did not suspend offensive actions against the IRA immediately on being informed of the impending Truce, partly because of opposition from some of their members who disapproved of the ceasefire. It is clear from veterans' accounts that combatants on both sides reacted to the announcement of the Truce with a mixture of shock and surprise. Many republicans regarded it as a positive development. For example, Tom Maguire, an IRA leader from

Co. Mayo, initially welcomed the Truce because he thought it signalled a republican victory: 'the English are after this, so we must have won'.[9] Maguire was not alone in reaching this conclusion, and many other republicans felt the agreement of a formal truce acknowledged the IRA's status as a legitimate army by opponents who had previously dismissed it as a 'murder gang'.

For every republican who claimed the Truce as a victory for the IRA there was a member of the British forces who regarded the agreement as a humiliating defeat. In particular, British military officers must have been enraged when they learned that their own intelligence sheet, the *Weekly Summary*, had referred to the Truce as an agreement between the 'British Army' and the 'Irish Army'.[10]

The officers of the British Army's 5th Division felt embarrassed and disappointed 'at the necessity for treating on equal terms with those whom they regarded as callous and treacherous murderers, among whose victims were reckoned many of their friends'.[11] Frederick Clarke, a lieutenant with the Essex Regiment who had been stationed in Cork, felt 'angry' and 'ashamed' at the conclusion of the conflict, because: 'The British politicians had arranged an armistice just when we could have quelled the rebellion.'[12] Captain R. D. Jeune denounced the Truce as Lloyd George 'yielding to threats from the IRA' at the very moment a British victory was assured.[13] The sense that the British government betrayed its troops in Ireland by agreeing to a ceasefire also prevailed among the Black and Tans, including Douglas Duff:

> We could not believe it, we knew only too well that the 'Shinner' resistance was almost finished, we had broken the back of armed rebellion ... Of course we argued this talk of truce is all moonshine, not even Lloyd George would be fool enough to stop when victory is within his grasp.[14]

General dissatisfaction among the RIC was mentioned by Colonel

Maxwell Scott: 'Amongst the RIC there was much uncertainty as to their future and much suspicion that somehow or other they would be "let down".'[15] Eugene Bratton encountered similar dismay among his fellow RIC officers: 'When the Truce came, the officers of the R.I.C. were almost crying. They realised that their good days were over, and they had good days before the troubles began. They were kings in their own areas.'[16] Official reports by senior RIC officers also indicate that members of the RIC rank and file were upset by the Truce. The RIC county inspector for the Galway West Riding wrote that the men under his command 'have considerable apprehensions lest they be let down in the negotiations for a settlement'.[17] His counterpart in Co. Westmeath reported: 'The manner in which it came was also trying on them [RIC constables]'.[18] The RIC inspector in charge of Tipperary North claimed that the sudden announcement of the Truce put a serious strain on RIC discipline:

> The Force of this Riding [Tipperary North] did not receive the Truce announcement and its terms with acclamation. It was only natural that those who had suffered so much during the past twelve months at the hands of the rebels, many of whom were well known murderers, but could not be brought to justice for lack of evidence, felt it difficult to restrain themselves when orders to carry out the 'truce' were received.[19]

While the men of the RIC in Tipperary North did manage to restrain themselves, some members of the British forces in other districts would show considerably less restraint.

The British authorities apparently responded to the announcement of the Truce by reprieving a number of republican prisoners who had been sentenced to death and were due be executed on the morning of Saturday 9 July. John Lenihan, an IRA Volunteer from Listowel, Co. Kerry, had been court-martialled under Regulation

67 of the Restoration of Order in Ireland Act for the killing of RIC District Inspector Sullivan. Subsequently, Lenihan and his co-accused – Edward Carmody, Thomas Deveraux and Daniel O'Carroll – were all sentenced to death for the offence, and all four were due to be executed at 8 a.m. on 9 July alongside four other republican prisoners. According to Lenihan, the final arrangements for the executions were so far advanced at the time the Truce was agreed that the graves of the condemned men had been dug, but the executions were cancelled following the announcement of the Truce.[20]

In contrast to the senior British military officers who cancelled the Cork executions, some lower-ranking members of the British forces in Ireland adopted a less conciliatory attitude and responded to the announcement of the Truce by engaging in reprisals. On the night of 9 July a group of British soldiers was responsible for an outburst of violence in Cork city:

> There was a considerable amount of firing in different parts of the city during curfew hours on Saturday night particularly between ten and eleven o'clock. Shots were fired in Blackpool about 10.15 p.m. it is stated, at a pressman who failed to halt and was subsequently arrested. Military pickets were in the area at the time.[21]

The shop fronts of Grace's grocery store and the post office on Thomas Davis Street were damaged by gunfire. British soldiers shot Augustine Harty, a fourteen-year-old boy, in the face near his home in Grattan Street. He was rushed to the nearby Mercy Hospital in a critical condition but fortunately survived. Shooting was also reported on the northern side of the city, and in the western suburbs.[22] That same night, soldiers from the Devonshire Regiment brawled with local ex-servicemen on Michael Street, Waterford and a British military patrol in full battle kit arrived to clear the thoroughfare.[23]

While the British Army's order to halt immediately all offensive activities appears to have resulted in a significant reduction in their activities, it did not result in a complete cessation. Large-scale round-ups and searches for IRA personnel, arms dumps and safe houses, involving hundreds of British soldiers, cavalry units and Royal Navy vessels, continued apace in Mayo and Waterford. At Durless near Ballygawley, Co. Tyrone, the homes of two local republicans, Patrick McVicker and Francis Donnelly, were destroyed by fire; apparently, this was carried out in reprisal for previous attacks on loyalist-owned properties in the area.[24] In Kildare the British forces raided the home of Stephen Barry-Roche at Monasterevin, arresting his two sons, who were both ex-servicemen, on the pretext that they were suspected of involvement in IRA activities.[25] At Ballon, Co. Kilkenny, British soldiers raided a property belonging to the Nolans, a prominent republican family. Nothing of military significance was found during the search, but members of the Nolan family later accused the British military of having stolen cash from their home.[26]

The activities of the British forces in the wake of the announcement of the Truce were not limited solely to raids and searches; they also killed a number of republicans and civilians in the final days and hours of the conflict.

THE KILGOBNET MINE DISASTER

The most significant action by the British forces following the announcement of the Truce was probably the detonation on 9 July of a booby-trap mine set by the British at Kilgobnet, near Dungarvan, Co. Waterford. This incident, known locally as the 'Kilgobnet Mine Disaster', resulted in six fatalities, with the majority of those killed being civilians.[27]

The incident occurred while the IRA's West Waterford Brigade was preparing to ambush a unit from the Royal East Kent Regiment that was expected to travel through the Cappagh district by bicycle.

As part of the preparations, the commander of the local IRA flying column, George Lennon, sought to have all the roads in the area 'trenched' to make them impassable to the British motor vehicles. One trench, dug across the Chapel Road in Kilgobnet, was to be partially refilled to allow a funeral cortège to pass.[28]

On the morning of 9 July a handful of local IRA Volunteers from H Company, 1st Battalion of the IRA's Waterford No. 2 Brigade began work to reopen the partially filled trench.[29] The IRA was assisted in this task by a large group of local civilians.[30] It is unclear whether the civilians were republican sympathisers who willingly assisted the IRA, or unwilling participants who had been forced to co-operate. The attempt to reopen the trench set off a landmine that had been planted by members of the Royal East Kent Regiment. The booby trap exploded instantly, killing two members of the work party, while a further twelve men were seriously wounded by the blast, four of whom subsequently died.[31] Those killed were Thomas Burke of Inchidrisla, Thomas Cahill of Knockanee, brothers James and William Dunford of Knockanee, Richard Lynch of Kilgobnet and Seán Quinn from Ballymacmague.[32]

The RIC county inspector's report states that those killed were all 'rebels' and claimed that they 'were engaged in laying a landmine when the explosion occurred'. His report concluded, 'It is doubted if the survivors concur in this.'[33] Accounts of the incident written by British military historians have taken a different approach by admitting that the British military were responsible for the blast, but claiming that all those killed were members of the IRA, thus portraying the event as a successful military operation. The official history of the 6th Division of the British Army recorded the incident as follows: '8th [July 1921] Dungarvan. Rebels re-taking road trench blown up; 8 killed, 12 wounded.'[34] The history of the Royal East Kent Regiment states that those killed were all members of the IRA: 'In and around Dungarvan the Buffs had several brushes with the rebels and, in the course of a series of patrols, effected a number of important arrests, whilst one road block was converted into a booby trap, causing many Sinn Fein casualties.'[35]

However, contrary to the British claims, it appears that almost all of the men killed in this incident were civilians. Of the six fatalities named on the monument erected at the site of the explosion, only one, Seán Quinn, is recorded as 'A.P.É.', the abbreviation of Arm Poblachtach na h-Éireann – the Irish language translation of 'Irish Republican Army'. Recent research on the incident confirms Quinn as the only member of the IRA among the fatalities.[36] The British accounts of this incident reflect a trend in British military historiography, which sought to minimise the 'collateral damage' caused by their operations by reclassifying the resulting civilian fatalities as IRA Volunteers.[37]

In the final months of the conflict the use of trap mines became increasingly commonplace. The tactic had developed in a haphazard fashion following experimentation by enterprising British military officers attached to a number of different regiments.[38] In the summer of 1921 republican attempts to disrupt British transport and communications led to a campaign of sabotaging roads and bridges. The British forces initially responded by forcing civilians to repair the damage done to these routes. Later they deployed explosive booby traps in trenches dug by the IRA, which were then wholly or partially refilled, a tactic that often had fatal, or near-fatal, results. On 21 May 1921 IRA Volunteer Patrick O'Brien from Coolacappagh, Co. Limerick, was killed while working to reopen a trench that had been back-filled and booby-trapped by the British forces.[39] In another incident similar to the Kilgobnet Mine Disaster, four IRA Volunteers were wounded while reopening a trench in Co. Roscommon on the road from Roscommon to Lanesboro. The trench had been refilled by members of the British forces, who concealed a booby-trap device incorporating a hand grenade among the earth and rubble.[40]

By 1921 this tactic was so commonly employed by the British

forces that the IRA became highly suspicious of any of their trenches that had been interfered with in any way. In the IRA's Mid Clare Brigade area, the local populace were so suspicious about a wheelbarrow abandoned by the British forces at the scene of a partially refilled trench, that it was left untouched for over a week. The wheelbarrow was eventually removed by some local people, who were so fearful it might be a booby trap that they used several lengths of rope tied together to drag it from the trench.[41] In Co. Cork the British tactic of booby-trapping republican trenches was so readily employed that the local IRA Volunteers, such as Edward O'Sullivan, became experts at dismantling the devices, retrieving the explosives and reusing them against the British forces.[42]

British sources and historiographies denounced the use of trap mines by the IRA as a 'dastardly' and 'shameful' tactic used to 'murder' British soldiers.[43] However, it is beyond any doubt that the British forces employed exactly the same tactic in their efforts to defeat the IRA. British records commonly boasted of their troops' ingenuity in developing and adapting this tactic. The intelligence officer attached to H Company of the RIC's Auxiliary Division boasted in a report to RIC headquarters of how his comrades had rigged the IRA's obstacles they encountered with mines and other explosive devices: 'April 5th. D. I. Durlacher and party patrolled roads to SPA and FENIT. Amongst other obstacles encountered were 8 stone walls about 10 yards apart. These were removed. A booby trap was set by us in a suitable trench and it is to be hoped that the enemy will reopen this particular one. Nil desperandum!'[44] The use of mines by the British forces was an indiscriminate act that endangered civilians and claimed the lives of several. Neither this tactic of the British forces nor the IRA's practice of assassinating off-duty members of the British forces were particularly chivalrous, yet both were legitimate (if deeply unwholesome) methods that were not in violation of the rules of warfare as they were understood at the time.[45]

ATTEMPTS TO KILL REPUBLICANS BEFORE THE TRUCE

Coinciding with the announcement of the Truce, the British government refuted the suggestion by *The Freeman's Journal* that the British authorities had placed a bounty on the head of Michael Collins, then MP for South Cork. On the day before the Truce, Collins pasted a copy of the article into a scrapbook and wrote beneath it: 'Tudor offered £4,000 to any of his men who'd bring me in dead. Even up to 12.30 tomorrow I'm sure the offer will be honoured.'[46] Given Collins' stature, and his importance to the Truce negotiations, the idea that the British forces would have had him assassinated in the final hours of the conflict was fanciful. However, some British troops did seek a final opportunity to attack their opponents as a reprisal for earlier incidents. There were a number of failed attempts to capture and kill IRA Volunteers following the announcement of the Truce.

One such attempt occurred at Lisdoonvarna, Co. Clare, on 9 July. Members of the IRA's Mid Clare Brigade flying column had been waiting for an RIC patrol at Doon near Lisdoonvarna, when the operation was cancelled by their commanding officer, Peader O'Loughlin, who ordered them to cease all offensive actions against the British forces from midnight that night. Several members of the flying column went to Kilfenora in Co. Clare to celebrate this development with a few drinks. Pádraig Ó Fathaigh and a comrade were socialising in a public house in Kilfenora when they received word that a group of Black and Tans was approaching. According to Ó Fathaigh:

> ... the Black and Tans did arrive, and in savage mood. They entered McCormack's shop looking for Sinn Feiners and forced some men they met to tear down Sinn Fein notices. They said they got no order re truce and were in Galway since the previous day. They went there with two of their comrades who were shot down near Doolin.[47]

Having searched the area and forced the local populace to tear down republican proclamations, the Tans departed. Ó Fathaigh and his comrade came out of hiding a short time later but almost immediately received word that the Black and Tans were return-ing, and quickly escaped. Ó Fathaigh interpreted the return of the Black and Tans as a typical ruse used by the British to entrap the IRA: 'It was a favourite trick of the Tans to double back on the expectation that the IRA would become careless.'[48] On this occa-sion the Black and Tans appear to have been enraged by the shoot-ing of two of their comrades near Doolin, Co. Clare, on 7 July, when Constable James Hewitt, a twenty-year-old Black and Tan from Dublin, was killed, while a second Black and Tan, Constable Massey, survived his wounds.[49] It is likely that the Black and Tans' rage at this attack would have been compounded by the announce-ment shortly afterwards of the Truce. Given the circumstances, the reported behaviour of the Black and Tans and their denial that they had been notified of the imminent ceasefire, it seems unlikely that any suspected republicans captured in the raid would have been treated chivalrously.[50]

Members of the RIC made at least two separate attempts to kill IRA officers on 11 July, both occurring after the Truce had come into effect. Péig Malone, wife of Tomás Malone, the adju-tant of the East Limerick Brigade IRA's flying column, worked as a teacher at Boher National School in Tipperary. On the morn-ing of 11 July a party of Black and Tans stationed at Killaloe, Co. Clare, took up positions surrounding the school in the hope that Malone would take advantage of the beginning of the ceasefire as an opportunity to visit his wife at her place of work. They took up ambush positions following the beginning of the Truce at noon and remained there in the forlorn hope that Malone would appear at 3.30 p.m. when his wife finished work, but he did not come.[51]

On the night of 11 July a group of Black and Tans breached the Truce by raiding the home of Patrick O'Reilly, an IRA officer who lived at Moynalty, Co. Meath. All of the raiding party were carrying revolvers and they were accompanied by a local loyalist, who wore a mask to conceal his identity. This raid may have been launched in retaliation for O'Reilly's role in leading the ambush of British soldiers a few hours before the ceasefire began.[52]

THE DEATH OF DENIS SPRIGGS AND PRISONERS 'SHOT TRYING TO ESCAPE'

In Cork city the IRA received word that some members of the British forces were planning a series of reprisals in reaction to the announcement of the Truce, so IRA Volunteers in the city were warned not to sleep in their own homes.[53] A few hours after the Truce was announced, the British military abducted and killed an IRA Volunteer named Denis Spriggs. Spriggs, who was twenty years old and a plasterer and slater by trade, was a member of C Company, 1st Battalion of the IRA's Cork No. 1 Brigade. Spriggs' family home in Strawberry Hill, on the northern side of Cork city, was raided by the 2nd Battalion, South Staffordshire Regiment about midnight on 8 July. According to the British military inquest into the killing, the British Army had planned the raid, having received specific intelligence information, and had launched the operation specifically to capture Spriggs. Spriggs was asleep in his bed when the raid began. He was unarmed and, on being confronted, immediately surrendered to the raiders without offering any resistance. Second Lieutenant A. d'Ydewalle told the military inquest that Spriggs had been shot dead while attempting to escape:

> … acting on information, I proceeded to the house of Denis Spriggs at Strawberry Hill and arrested him … He was placed in a Crossley Tender under an escort. When the Crossley had proceeded about 200 yards down Blarney Street, the tail board either fell down or was released by Denis Spriggs. Spriggs then leaped out of the Crossley and

started to run up Blarney Street. The escort on the Crossley opened fire & he fell. He was apparently dead when picked up. Before putting Denis Spriggs in the Crossley, I personally warned him that he would be shot if he attempted to escape.

The inquest ruled that Spriggs was killed while trying to escape 'and that the deceased was to blame, in as much as he attempted to escape from Military Custody, after having been warned of the consequences'.[54]

David Leeson noted that the cases of captured IRA Volunteers and civilian prisoners being killed by the British forces while allegedly trying to escape were so numerous that the phrase 'shot while trying to escape' had become a euphemism for 'executed'.[55] He concluded that many prisoners were killed by the British forces simply because they were republicans, or connected to republican families.[56]

The practice of British forces summarily executing captured enemy combatants during the Irish War of Independence appears to have had its origins in the First World War. Robert Graves, who had been an officer in the Royal Welch Fusiliers, recalled that, during that conflict, German soldiers taken prisoner by British troops were frequently executed and their deaths were attributed to enemy shellfire:

... nearly every instructor in the mess could quote specific instances of prisoners having been murdered on the way back ... In many of these cases the conductors would report on arrival at headquarters that a German shell had killed the prisoners and no questions would be asked.[57]

The primary motivation for such 'battlefield executions' in both of these conflicts appears to have been the desire to avenge the death of a fallen comrade or comrades. For example, the assassination of Head Constable Peter Burke in Balbriggan, Dublin, on 20 September 1920, sparked widespread reprisals by his comrades that resulted in two killings and the destruction of twenty-five houses. Two days later the deaths of six members of an RIC patrol in the Rineen ambush in Co. Clare were avenged by British forces, who killed six local people and attacked more than seventy properties. A similar cause and effect is evident in British Army reprisals during the First World War. At Bellewaarde, near Ypres, in June 1915, the Royal Scots killed 300 German soldiers they had taken prisoner after their officers encouraged them to avenge their fallen comrades. According to Private Charles Tames, who witnessed the massacre, 'the Scots immediately shot the whole lot, and shouted "Death and Hell to every one of ye shits" and in five minutes the ground was ankle deep in German blood'.[58] In June 1916 members of the Leinster Regiment killed six German prisoners at Vermelles, having discovered the body of one of their own officers who had been killed in battle.[59]

This British military practice of summarily executing enemy combatants and blaming their deaths on the conditions of war appears to have continued unabated into the War of Independence. The main difference was that the explanation 'killed by enemy shellfire' used in Flanders in 1918 was replaced in Ireland with 'shot while attempting to escape'. An examination of the available British military inquest reports reveals that at least forty-two unarmed prisoners were killed in the custody of the British forces while allegedly attempting to escape.[60] However, the true number of prisoners shot by the British forces while supposedly trying to escape is likely to be far higher, because inquest reports for a number of other unarmed prisoners known to have been killed in the same circumstances are not available.[61]

The vast majority of the prisoners killed in alleged escape attempts were IRA Volunteers shot dead within hours of their capture, and there is compelling evidence to suggest that these prisoners were victims of a culture of reprisal killings that existed in several British military and RIC units. Escape attempts were a convenient method of explaining the suspicious circumstances surrounding the deaths of multiple republican prisoners who met violent ends in British custody.

In November 1920 RIC Auxiliaries at Whitegate in Co. Clare arrested three IRA Volunteers – Michael McMahon, Alfred Rogers and Martin Kildea – and a civilian named John Egan. Their captors were aware that McMahon, Rogers and Kildea had been involved in a number of attacks on the RIC in the preceding weeks, some of which had caused RIC fatalities. That night all four prisoners were taken from their holding cells and shot dead on a bridge spanning the River Shannon. The British military inquest into the killings recorded that three of the four had suffered a single gunshot wound to the head and that the fourth suffered a fatal shot to the abdomen.[62] Pat O'Donnell, an IRA Volunteer who assisted with the funeral arrangements for the four, recalled that the men who had suffered a fatal gunshot wound to the head had singed hair near the wounds, indicating that they had been shot at point-blank range, most likely by a revolver placed almost directly against their heads, in the manner of an execution.[63] The official British inquest into their deaths reported that the four, despite being suspected IRA members responsible for a number of RIC fatalities, had not been handcuffed and had been shot after they made a concerted attempt to escape.[64] This explanation is highly unlikely, given that all four men were unarmed prisoners in the custody of a large and very heavily armed guard crossing a bridge that had a permanently manned British military checkpoint at each end. Before the shooting, local people heard the four prisoners pleading to be allowed to see a priest, indicating the men themselves were awaiting execution rather than plotting an escape attempt.[65] The most obvious explanation is that their captors killed all four prisoners as a reprisal killing to avenge the deaths of their fallen RIC comrades.

There were a number of other cases where the British forces were responsible for the multiple deaths of civilians and unarmed IRA prisoners in custody that were recorded as escape attempts. These fatalities included prisoners Dick McKee, Peader Clancy and Conor Clune, who were killed while allegedly attempting to escape from Dublin Castle on 21 November 1920,[66] and the deaths of brothers Stephen and Owen Magill, who were killed at Newry on 13 June 1921.[67] In Counties Limerick and Clare, ten unarmed IRA prisoners were shot dead in British custody during alleged escape attempts.[68] Of these ten, only two, Henry Clancy and Richard Leonard, appear to have been killed during genuine escape attempts. The remaining eight were almost certainly executed in reprisal killings – some of them having been severely ill-treated beforehand.

The largest and most significant multiple killing by members of the British forces to have been officially explained by an alleged escape attempt occurred at Kerry Pike, Co. Cork, on 23 March 1921. On that occasion, six IRA Volunteers were captured during an RIC raid on an IRA safe house and were killed shortly afterwards in suspicious circumstances. According to the official British military inquest, all six republicans were captured while sleeping and surrendered to their captors without offering any resistance. Following this peaceable surrender, the prisoners were alleged by their captors to have launched a simultaneous bid for freedom during which all six were shot down. There were no survivors and none of the prisoners were wounded or recaptured unharmed 'while trying to escape'. The British military inquiry into the incident failed to give any details of the nature of the gunshot wounds or other injuries suffered by the six deceased, but initially recorded that they were 'killed by forces of the Crown in the course of their duty'.[69] However, this finding was subsequently struck out and replaced with a new verdict which completely exonerated the RIC men involved and instead apportioned blame to the deceased IRA Volunteers:

> ... all the deceased, whilst in the custody of the RIC, attempted to escape. The Constabulary in the course of their duty, fired on them, whereby they suffered various gunshot wounds. The deceased were all killed instantly at the above hour. That no blame attaches itself to the RIC or any member thereof.[70]

If, as seems likely, these six prisoners were executed rather than killed during an escape attempt, the alteration of the British military inquest's verdict on the case is a strong indication that some senior British military officers were fully aware of the circumstances of the event, and were willing to turn a blind eye to the excesses, indiscipline, acts of violence and reprisal killings carried out by their subordinates.

The killing of republican prisoners who allegedly tried to escape became so common that the phenomenon began to weigh on the minds of those in command of the British forces. One British officer who served in Cork during the period, Major General Douglas Wimberley, acknowledged in his memoirs that the summary execution of unarmed prisoners troubled him, and he claimed to have used his influence to thwart such killings:

> ... my first action was always to detail two or three of my Jocks [Scottish soldiers] ... and see that they [the Black and Tans and RIC Auxiliaries] did not commit any atrocities such as unlawfully looting or burning houses, when they were acting under my command, or even shooting prisoners, on the grounds that they were attempting to escape.[71]

General Macready, the commander of the British forces in Ireland, became so worried by the number of men being killed in these circumstances that he issued orders that all prisoners must be handcuffed, and if any prisoners who were not handcuffed were killed while allegedly attempting to escape, the senior officer responsible would be held to account.[72] However, senior British officers ignored Macready's decree, and in March 1921 an IRA Volunteer named William McCarthy was taken from a police cell and shot dead by his captors. The British military inquest into his death recorded that McCarthy 'Attempted to escape from custody [of the] RIC *(Not handcuffed).*' Despite Macready's order regarding the shooting of unrestrained prisoners, no punitive action was taken against McCarthy's killers.[73] The following month, the RIC in Tipperary shot dead Thomas Walsh during an alleged escape attempt. The military inquest into Walsh's killing casually recorded it as: 'Another case of handcuffs'.[74]

A unique aspect of the conflict is that not a single member of the IRA in Cork city was killed in action fighting against the British forces; all of them were unarmed when they were killed by British troops. They were assassinated in their homes, killed in grenade attacks by British patrols while walking the city's streets, or 'shot trying to escape' while in British custody.[75] Denis Spriggs was the ninth unarmed IRA prisoner killed by the British forces in Cork city while allegedly trying to escape. Of the other eight killed in similar circumstances, only one, Tadhg O'Sullivan, died during a genuine escape attempt. Six were killed after surrendering to the British forces at Kerry Pike, and Charlie Daly was arrested and beaten to death by British soldiers at Victoria Barracks just twelve days before Spriggs' death.[76]

The same night that Daly was killed, British soldiers also killed an unarmed civilian named William Horgan. Horgan, a twenty-year-old fireman on the Great Southern & Western Railway, was arrested at 2 a.m. at his parents' home at Dillon's Cross and was shot dead a short time later. The British military inquest into his death ruled that he had assaulted a British officer who was searching him for weapons and was killed while attempting to disarm this officer in an effort to escape.

Apart from the explanation that both men were shot 'while

trying to escape', there is another connection between the killing of Horgan in late June and Spriggs on the night the Truce was announced – both were taken prisoner by British soldiers from the 2nd Battalion, South Staffordshire Regiment, who were acting under the direct command of Lieutenant A. d'Ydewalle.[77] Given the circumstances of Denis Spriggs' arrest, the track record of the British officer involved and the explanation proffered for the killing, the probability is that Spriggs was summarily executed by the British military because of his republican activities and not because of any resistance or attempt to escape on his part. It is impossible to establish without further information to what extent, if any, the announcement of the Truce motivated Spriggs' killers.

THE DEATH OF MARGARET KEOGH AND THE BRITISH 'MURDER GANGS'

Margaret Keogh was shot and mortally wounded by unidentified assassins in her home at 20 Stella Gardens in Irishtown, Dublin, at 11.15 p.m. on 9 July. Despite receiving immediate first aid and a direct transfer to Sir Patrick Dun's Hospital, she died of her wounds at 4 a.m. the following day.[78] Keogh was a nineteen-year-old printing assistant employed by Messrs Healy & Co. of Dame Street, Dublin. She was active in Irish language, Gaelic revival, trade union, suffragist and republican circles in the capital. According to press reports at the time, she was 'an ardent Irish Irelander', 'a fluent Irish speaker … [and] a strong supporter of the Irish revival movement'. Keogh was captain of the Croke Ladies Hurling Club, a member of the Irish Clerical Workers' Union and was 'prominently associated with Cumann na mBan'.[79] A year before she was killed, she had been arrested by the British forces for refusing to give her name in English when questioned. At the time of her arrest she had been fund-raising for the Irish language organisation Conradh na Gaeilge (the Gaelic League), which was proscribed at that time.[80]

Keogh was shot after she left her bed to answer a knock at the door of her home.[81] Before she died she told police that 'she answered the door in response to a knock about 11.15 p.m. When she opened it there was no person outside it or about, and as she was in the act of closing the door she heard a single shot and felt a sting in the side and fell back in the hall. She had no idea as to who fired the shot.' Despite making this detailed statement, Margaret Keogh was unable to identify her killers before she died.

Keogh's membership of numerous cultural-nationalist and republican bodies including Cumann na mBan, and her previous confrontation with the British forces, would have made her a target for British reprisals. It appears that the British forces were conducting raids on republican homes in the immediate area at the time she was shot. According to a contemporary press report: 'A short time previous to the shooting of Miss Keogh some persons knocked at the adjoining residence of a man "on the run", but the occupant, an old woman, informed the raiders [that] she would not open the door, and if they wanted admission they should force it.'[82]

The press were refused admission to the British military inquest into Margaret Keogh's killing, which was held in private. A century after her death, the findings of the court of inquiry into her killing have never been published and it appears that this file is one of the records of the War Office papers that is still confidential. Her funeral took place at Glasnevin Cemetery, Dublin, on 14 July.[83] She was buried with military honours in a plot bought by her family. The funeral cortège was reported as being 'of large dimensions … immediately after the hearse marched a large number of young lady friends of the deceased associated with Cumann na mBan, members of the camogie clubs and fellow workers. The coffin was covered with the tricolour.' The following week, the Executive of Cumann na mBan organised a commemorative mass for her at the Star of the Sea church in Sandymount.[84] The inscription on her tombstone indicates that her family blamed the British forces for her death. Keogh is buried with her mother in a pauper's grave. Her headstone reads: 'MARGARET KEOGH – DIED FOR IRELAND'.[85]

The circumstances of Margaret Keogh's death suggest that she was the victim of a British 'murder gang'. The act of killing unarmed republican prisoners in British custody burdened the killers with having to invent a credible explanation that vindicated their actions, or at least concoct a story that was plausible enough to satisfy a British military court of inquiry. In some areas RIC and British military units went as far as to develop a modus operandi of adopting disguises to assassinate known and suspected republicans in their own homes and places of work. These killers never identified themselves as members of the British forces and consequently never had the burden of claiming responsibility for their victims' deaths or explaining their actions to their superior officers and military courts of inquiry. Major General Douglas Wimberley was forthright in admitting that some of his comrades adopted these methods to commit reprisal killings:

> They [the Black and Tans and RIC Auxiliaries] seemed to make a habit of breaking out of their barracks at night, illicitly, and killing men they thought were suspect rebels, and in this way the habit spread surreptitiously even to a few Army officers and men.[86]

During the conflict, republicans alleged that British 'murder gangs', comprising a hard core of RIC and British military personnel, operated throughout Ireland. In some areas the activities of the 'murder gang' overlapped with those of the 'Anti-Sinn Féin Society'. It is generally accepted that the latter was a cover name used as a flag of convenience by British forces' personnel to distance themselves from their more unsavoury activities.[87] There is a record of suspicious behaviour by British raiding parties in the area where Margaret Keogh was killed, which matches the activities of the 'murder gangs' and the 'Anti-Sinn Féin Society'.

Members of the IRA's Dublin Brigade accused British military officers in civilian attire of shooting a number of IRA Volunteers during nocturnal raids on their homes.[88] Joseph Curran, a Sinn Féin councillor living a few doors away from Margaret Keogh, complained of suspicious and aggressive behaviour during British military raids. Members of the Worcester Regiment raided Curran's home at 36 Stella Gardens a few months before Keogh was killed. Curran stated that the leader of the search party 'had two revolvers and a cap pulled down over his eyes [as a disguise] … and went about like a desperado … he was a bit of the Dick Turpin terrorising women and children'. During his court martial for possession of ammunition allegedly found during the raid, Curran raised questions about the identity of this individual. The Worcester Regiment denied that the mystery man was a British soldier and insisted that their troops had been led by 'a [civilian] guide … dressed as a captain'.[89]

The 'murder gang' and 'Anti-Sinn Féin Society' killings began in the spring of 1920, shortly after the IRA killed RIC Constable Luke Finegan. On 20 January 1920 Finegan was shot dead in Thurles, Co. Tipperary, as he was returning home from a night patrol. When the local RIC garrison learned of their comrade's death they ran amok, firing their guns into the homes of local republicans and attacking republican-owned businesses with hand grenades.[90] The 'Sack of Thurles', as the incident became known, was the first occasion that the RIC had reacted to the death of a comrade by going on a rampage. In response to this unprecedented event, Lloyd George wrote to the *Daily Chronicle*:

> Nobody can fail to deplore such occurrences but equally nobody can wonder at them. Indeed it is obvious that if these murderous clubs [the IRA] pursue their course much longer, we may see counter clubs

springing up and the lives of prominent Sinn Feiners becoming as unsafe as prominent officials.[91]

The timing and nature of Lloyd George's letter strongly suggests that senior figures in the British government were aware of the assassination campaign being advocated by some members of the British forces. Comments in Sir Henry Wilson's diary explicitly reinforce the suggestion that members of the British cabinet, senior RIC officers and others knew of the activities of the 'Anti-Sinn Féin Gang' and the identities of those involved:

> Tudor made it very clear that the police and the Black and Tans and the 100 Intelligence officers are all carrying out reprisal murders. At Balbriggan, Thurles and Galway yesterday the local police marked down certain Sinn Feiners as … murderers or instigators and then coolly went out and shot them without question or trial. Winston [Churchill] saw very little harm in this but it horrifies me.[92]

In short, the British authorities at best gave their tacit approval to the combined RIC/British Army campaign of reprisal killings, and in some cases actively encouraged and protected the assassins.

In March 1920, just two months after Lloyd George's unprecedented comments predicting the emergence of 'counter murder clubs', the Mayor of Cork, Tomás MacCurtain, was assassinated by masked gunmen in his home at Blackpool. The inquest into MacCurtain's death ruled that Lloyd George, the British authorities in Ireland and unknown members of the RIC under the command of RIC District Inspector Swanzy were responsible for the killing.[93]

The assassination of active republicans in Cork became increasingly frequent after the recruitment into the RIC of significant numbers of new personnel, mainly British ex-servicemen via the Black and Tans and the RIC Auxiliary Division. On 17 November

1920 IRA Volunteer Eugene O'Connell, Sinn Féin member James Coleman and Patrick Hanley, a seventeen-year-old member of Na Fianna Éireann, the Irish Republican Boy Scouts, were all shot dead in their homes by unidentified men wearing RIC uniforms.[94] The following week IRA Volunteer Patrick O'Donoghue and two civilian friends of his were killed by an RIC constable, who threw a hand grenade at them when they were walking home from work.[95] In December 1920 two brothers, Con and Jeremiah Delaney, both IRA Volunteers, were shot dead in their beds by men in civilian clothing who all spoke with strong English accents.[96] The following February Charlie J. Daly, an IRA officer, was abducted from his workplace by unidentified men, who shot him dead.[97] Another IRA Volunteer, Stephen Dorman, was killed in an almost identical grenade attack to the one that had killed O'Donoghue and his workmates.[98]

A similar spate of reprisal killings attributed to the 'murder gang' occurred in Limerick city at the same time. On 20 November 1920 James O'Neill and Michael Blake were both shot dead, having been held up by armed men while travelling to their homes by car. O'Neill and Blake's brother, Patrick, were returning to the city with their supporters, having been acquitted by a British military court martial of the killing of a Black and Tan named Walter Oakley. Before their court martial, the local RIC county inspector denounced the accused as 'murderers' and 'paid assassins'. Given the circumstances of their deaths and the fact that their killers spoke with a mixture of English and Irish accents, there can be little doubt that members of the RIC who were dissatisfied with the result of the court martial deliberately killed O'Neill. Michael Blake was apparently killed by someone who mistook him for his brother Patrick. Neither of the dead men had any role in Oakley's killing nor any connection to the IRA.[99]

In February 1921 an IRA Volunteer, Thomas Blake, was shot dead in Limerick city by unidentified assassins. British forces had raided Blake's home on a number of occasions and local tradition believes that District Inspector George Montagu Nathan of the RIC Auxiliary Division was involved in Blake's assassination.[100] The following month three members of the IRA – George Clancy, the mayor of Limerick; his predecessor in the office, ex-mayor Michael O'Callaghan; and Joseph O'Donoghue, the manager of a local meat company – were all shot dead at their homes by disguised assassins. O'Callaghan's widow later identified District Inspector Nathan as one of her husband's killers.[101] Nathan apparently confessed to his role in the Limerick killings over a decade later, during the Spanish Civil War, when he was confronted by a group of Irish republicans who had identified him.[102] Given that all three victims were members of the IRA whose homes had previously been raided by the British forces, and that all were killed by men wearing British military-style clothing, there can be little doubt that British forces' personnel, most probably members of an RIC 'murder gang' led by Nathan, were responsible.[103]

Reprisal killings by the British forces were also common in Dublin. Following the killing of RIC Head Constable Bourke at Balbriggan in September 1920, members of the British forces abducted republicans John Gibbons and James Lawless. Their bodies were found the following morning on Quay Street, just a few yards from the local RIC barracks.[104] The following month, Peter O'Carroll, a fifty-six-year-old house-bound invalid, was taken from his home in Manor Street and shot dead by a group of men who had forced their way in and questioned him about his two sons, who were both members of the IRA. O'Carroll's widow refused to give evidence to the British military inquest into his death but instead made a public statement that her husband had been 'murdered by members of the Army of Occupation'.[105]

On 27 October 1920 IRA Volunteer John Sherlock was taken from his home in Skerries and shot dead by unidentified men.[106] Another IRA Volunteer, Thomas Hand, was dragged from his bed at 2 a.m. on 5 December 1920 and shot dead by unidentified men dressed in British uniforms.[107] Two other republicans, Patrick Kennedy and James Murphy, were killed in Dublin on 9 February 1921. Both men had been arrested by the RIC Auxiliaries and taken to Dublin Castle for interrogation; that night a DMP patrol discovered Kennedy's lifeless body in Clonturk Park, Drumcondra. Murphy lay beside him, conscious and mortally wounded, but he lived long enough to dictate a detailed statement identifying his killers. On the basis of Murphy's statement, three members of the RIC Auxiliary Division were court-martialled on a murder charge; however, all three were acquitted, having claimed that both of the victims had been released unharmed after questioning and that neither they nor the British forces were involved in their deaths.[108] On 30 May 1921 Thomas Murphy, a porter for the Dublin South and East Railway, was shot dead in his bed by unidentified assailants. Two days earlier a Black and Tan named Albert Skeats succumbed to his wounds inflicted in an IRA attack, and Murphy was apparently killed by Skeats' comrades in reprisal.[109]

The activities of the 'Anti-Sinn Féin Society' were not confined to Cork, Dublin, Limerick and other large cities. Another group of assassins was responsible for at least seven deaths in North Tipperary. On 28 March 1920 Lieutenant Thomas Dwyer and IRA Volunteer James McCarthy were both shot dead in their homes. The coroner's inquests into their deaths left little doubt as to who the perpetrators were. The jury at the inquest into McCarthy's death ruled that he 'was shot by some person or persons unknown, wearing long black coats and caps similar to those worn by the police'. At Dwyer's inquest, the jury went a step further and returned the verdict 'Thomas Dwyer was wilfully murdered by unknown members of the Royal Irish Constabulary.'[110] Following an IRA attack on the RIC at Shevry, Co. Tipperary, this 'anti-murder gang' struck again in July 1920, shooting Richard Larkin, whose brother was an active member of the IRA. Larkin survived the attack.[111] On 1 October IRA signals officer Michael Cleary was taken from his home and shot a number of times by a group of unidentified gunmen. Despite being left for dead, Cleary also survived, and RIC Sergeant Eugene Igoe was later identified as having led the men who abducted and shot him.[112] Later that month a group of assassins disguised with blackened faces killed another IRA officer, Michael Ryan, by shooting him as he lay in bed.[113] In November Denis Carey, a member of Sinn Féin, was taken from his workplace by masked raiders and interrogated about attacks on the RIC before being shot and mortally wounded; he lived long enough to describe his ordeal and identify his attackers as RIC.[114] Five days after Carey's shooting, armed men raided a house in Thurles where a card game was in progress and shot dead Thomas O'Loughlin. He was a member of the IRA and his killers were believed to have been members of the British forces.[115] The 'anti-murder gang' killings in North Tipperary reached a bloody peak on the night of 10 March 1921, when two members of Sinn Féin, Laurence Hickey and William Loughnane, were shot dead in their homes.[116]

While revenge killings of suspected republicans and attacks on their family homes were commonplace, David Leeson's recent study of the Black and Tans concluded that republican women were not targeted: 'it seems that not a single woman was ever murdered in reprisal [by the British forces]. In the few documented cases where police and soldiers murdered Irish women, their motives were unrelated to the national struggle.'[117] Leeson has stated that the majority of cases of the killing of women committed by British forces during the conflict were not politically motivated. His findings have been reinforced by Charles Townshend, who has suggested that women were 'in no real danger of execution if arrested', and many of the women killed by the British forces were shot unintentionally, innocent bystanders and 'collateral damage'.[118] A minority were the victims of 'crimes of passion' and sexually motivated murders committed by individual British troops.[119] However, Leeson is probably wrong in stating that no woman was ever killed in a British reprisal killing.

The circumstances of Margaret Keogh's death indicate that she was killed by members of the British forces who selected her home, and her neighbour's, as locations where they were likely to find suitable targets for a reprisal killing. Given the available information, it is impossible to know whether Keogh was deliberately targeted for assassination or if another person who lived at the same address was the intended target. The sexism and chivalry of the day meant that the IRA rarely executed women suspected of spying, and the British forces were not in the habit of targeting republican women. The likelihood therefore is that Keogh was fatally wounded by accident, or in a case of mistaken identity, by members of the British forces. Given the timing and location of the incident, Keogh's killers would have been aware that a ceasefire was imminent. Whether the announcement of the Truce was a partial factor, or even the sole motivation, in the decision to launch the fatal attack on the Keogh family home is impossible to establish at this remove.

THE KILLINGS OF JOHN FOLEY AND HANNAH CAREY

On the eve of the Truce British soldiers from the West Yorkshire Regiment shot and killed John Foley, a thirty-eight-year-old farm labourer, in his home at Leemount, Coachford, Co. Cork. Corporal F. J. Smith, who killed Foley, claimed that his patrol had been conducting searches of houses in the district at 6 a.m. that morning and had received orders to arrest any male civilians found in the locality aged between fifteen and forty-five years. According to Smith, he and Lance Corporal W. Pearson called to search Foley's house, but were refused entry. Smith claimed that he had forced his way in, whereupon the occupants of the house (Foley, another man and a woman) barricaded themselves into a bedroom.

When he entered the bedroom alone, Smith claimed that he was trapped inside by the woman and attacked by Foley and his male accomplice, who attempted to disarm him. Pearson was alleged to have then entered the room and, without firing a shot, saved Smith from his attackers. Smith claimed that the he and Pearson were meekly retreating when Foley again attempted to attack him and they fired, fatally wounding Foley. Smith testified that 'He [Foley] staggered past me, left the house and fell into a ditch on the roadside and died.'[120]

Pearson also gave evidence to the inquest, in support of Smith's account, but there are significant inconsistencies between the two accounts. For example Pearson says that Foley attacked Smith with a knife but Smith himself never bothered to mention this important detail. Given that no other witnesses were called to give evidence at the inquest, it is not surprising that the court of inquiry presided over by British Army officers ruled that the troops who had killed Foley were merely carrying out their duty and that 'Foley was himself to blame'.[121]

The British Army inquest into John Foley's killing acknowledged that he had no connections whatsoever to the IRA, but at the same time it ruled that he had launched an unprovoked attack on a force of armed British soldiers. Unsurprisingly local accounts of Foley's killing completely contradict this official version of events. Charlie Browne, a local IRA veteran, stated that Foley was 'an innocent young boy', who had been killed without any provocation and that members of the West Yorkshire Regiment had opened fire on the homes of a number of inoffensive civilians during their search of the area.[122] Local oral accounts of the incident surviving today claim that Foley, his twin brother Tim and their younger sister Margaret were in their family home when a group of armed British soldiers forced their way inside. The soldiers ordered John Foley to dress and, when he turned away to get his coat, he was shot in the back without warning. John Foley attempted to crawl to safety at a neighbour's house and, collapsing en route, was left to die in a ditch by the same British soldiers, who then took his twin brother prisoner in order to beat and humiliate him by leaving him tied to a telegraph pole in Coachford village.[123]

The very last fatality of the War of Independence was Hannah Carey, a forty-eight-year-old civilian shot in Killarney, Co. Kerry, shortly after 11.50 a.m. on the morning of 11 July – just moments before the ceasefire was due to begin. The official Dublin Castle report of the incident attributed Miss Carey's death to the IRA. It stated that she had been killed during the attack on Sergeants Mears and Clarke, which had occurred on High Street a short time earlier. This version of events was repeated in the national and local press. The *Kerry People* reported:

> Killarney Tragedy – 3 Deaths … Dublin Castle reports. At 11.45 a.m. yesterday, Sergeants Mayer [*sic*] and Clarke of the 1st Battalion of the Royal Fusiliers, Killarney, were fired at and wounded by a number of armed men … Hannah Carey, domestic servant employed at the Imperial Hotel Killarney, has died as a consequence of a wound sustained by a stray bullet during the attack on the two sergeants.[124]

The local RIC county inspector also attributed Hannah Carey's death to the actions of the IRA, and his official report stated that Carey was killed when the IRA launched a second attack on an RIC patrol that was rushing to the scene of the earlier ambush:

> At 11.45 a.m. on 11:7:21, Sgt Mears and Sgt F. J. Clarke of 1st Royal Fusiliers, both unarmed, were fired at and badly wounded in High Street, Killarney, by a party of rebels. Military and police visited the scene and were also fired on by the rebels … Hanna [*sic*] Carey, domestic servant who was shot in the neck at the same time, died in a short time.[125]

However, Hannah Carey had not been shot during the IRA attack on the British forces as the British reports claimed: she was shot and fatally wounded by a patrol of RIC/Black and Tans on College Street in a separate incident a short time after the IRA attack on Mears and Clarke.

Carey was an employee of the Imperial Hotel, a domestic servant who had been outside the hotel beating carpets when she was shot, according to the official Dublin Castle report reproduced in the local press.[126] However, this seems unlikely, since her employer stated that she was employed as a waitress at the hotel. The British military inquest into her death was told that a patrol of RIC and Black and Tans left the RIC barracks in Killarney at approximately 11.50 a.m., having learned of the IRA attack on Mears and Clarke five minutes earlier. The members of this patrol were travelling through College Street in two RIC Crossley Tender lorries when a number of shots were fired by the occupants of the first lorry. One member of the RIC patrol testified that two rifle shots had been fired into the air at the time Hannah Carey was shot to clear the street of a group of people who had congregated near the hotel. He was contradicted by the hotel's chef, who was at the front door a few moments before the RIC patrol began firing. The chef testified that while he was standing inside the doorway looking out, and before the RIC patrol arrived and began shooting, College Street had been empty of people. Furthermore, he testified that a British military armoured car had already passed en route to the scene of the IRA attack in High Street, and that its occupants did not fire any shots.

It seems that Hannah Carey was struck by one shot fired by the RIC patrol travelling in the motor lorry. The RIC constable who fired the fatal shot told the inquest into Carey's death that he had shot her by accident as he drove an RIC lorry past her workplace:

> I was holding a revolver in my right hand, and both hands [were] on the steering wheel at the same time, when turning at the end of

College Street I mechanically gripped the wheel tighter, making the turn, and it was then my revolver went off. I suppose I must have pulled the trigger whilst doing so. It was quite unintentional. We were all rather excited at the time, it was just after two military Sergeants had been shot in the street, and we thought it might have been a ruse to get the police out, and we half expected an attack or an ambush. I had no idea anyone had been hit at the time.[127]

The bullet entered Carey's body just above her right collarbone, passed through her neck and exited over her left shoulder blade. After being shot, Carey staggered into the hotel and collapsed in the arms of her employer, saying 'I am done.' She died at the premises about 2 p.m. that afternoon.[128]

The British military inquest into Carey's killing concluded that she was 'Shot by the accidental discharge of a revolver by [a] member of [the] RIC.' None of the members of the British forces who gave evidence at this inquest claimed to have been under attack when she was shot.[129]

Recent academic research has revealed that the British forces were responsible for the largest number of civilian casualties during the War of Independence – the deaths of approximately 42 per cent of civilians killed in the conflict were caused by them. The IRA was responsible for at least 31 per cent of those killed. Given their circumstances, it is impossible to apportion blame for the remainder.[130] The majority – 249 of the 381 civilians killed by the British forces – were slain while allegedly resisting arrest, failing to halt when challenged, or for refusing to put their hands up when ordered to do so.[131] Many of these killings are relatively straightforward affairs in which those killed had not complied with warnings issued by British troops, often because those challenged were drunk or suffered from mental impairments or deafness. However, it was also commonplace for members of the British forces to shoot at inoffensive members of the local populace without warning. British patrols were known to fire on locals for sport, using them for live-target practice, often with fatal results.

On occasion, members of the British forces even boasted of their marksmanship, having fired on, and killed, men in cold blood. During a search of Boyce's farm at Broadford, Co. Limerick, on 28 February 1921, Private Henry Hall of the Warwickshire Regiment shot and killed Richard Boyce, one of the family's sons. Private Hall balanced his rifle on a British Army vehicle and took aim at Boyce, who was tending to his family's horses in a field some distance away. He whistled to attract Boyce's attention and when the young man turned to see where the noise had come from, he was killed by a single shot fired by Hall. Having killed Boyce, Hall walked over to the spot where Boyce's corpse lay, carefully pacing out the distance as he went and then returned to his comrades, boasting, 'Clean through the forehead at 220 paces – not bad shooting.'[132] In a separate incident in Limerick city, an officer from the Oxford and Buckinghamshire Light Infantry shot dead an innocent civilian in reprisal for an IRA attack on an RIC patrol. The regiment's annual magazine wrongly implied that the deceased had been a member of the IRA, recounted the incident in a frivolous fashion and praised the marksmanship of the officer who had fired the fatal shot: 'The dead civilian (one Dan McNamara of Park) was laid low while running by a magnificent shot from a .32 automatic pistol at a range of 40 yards.'[133]

Both John Foley and Hannah Carey were inoffensive civilians shot dead without warning by members of the British forces, but the British authorities offered very different explanations for each of the killings. The British military claimed that Foley was killed deliberately because he had attempted to attack two British officers who had alighted from a vehicle to search his house, and the explanation offered by his killers is not significantly different from that given to justify the death of IRA men taken prisoner and 'shot while trying to escape'. As stated earlier, the alternative account of the killing, that Foley was shot dead in his home without warning by members of a British raiding party, seems more plausible. In contrast to Foley's killing, Carey's death was admitted as having been a tragic accident, but was alleged to have been the unfortunate result of necessary security procedures rather than indiscipline or horseplay.

Another woman had been killed by the RIC in similar circumstances in Galway. Ellen Quinn, a heavily pregnant woman, was shot in the abdomen by a member of a passing RIC patrol as she sat on a wall outside her home cradling her nine-month-old baby. Quinn and her unborn child died a short time later.[134] Although there had been no IRA activity in the area at the time, the British military inquest into the killing returned a verdict of 'death by misadventure', finding that the shot which killed her had been fired as a precautionary measure by the RIC, who feared they might be ambushed.[135] When the IPP MP, Joseph Devlin, raised questions about Ellen Quinn's killing in the House of Commons, the British chief secretary, Sir Hamar Greenwood, stated that Mrs Quinn was killed by members of the British forces who had a right to protect themselves from IRA ambushes.[136] A member of the RIC patrol that killed Hannah Carey offered a similar rationale for her accidental killing – claiming that his comrades had drawn their weapons and fired shots solely to warn people off the streets and thereby frustrate IRA attacks.[137]

A DELIBERATE POLICY

The activities of the British forces in the final days of the conflict show that, contrary to popular accounts, a number of British units did launch aggressive military actions targeting Irish republicans following the announcement, on 8 July 1921, of the Anglo-Irish Truce. The claim that the British forces withdrew to their barracks to adopt a policy of passive defence while awaiting the arrival of the ceasefire is true to the extent that the British military hierarchy in Ireland issued orders to refrain from offensive action and cancelled the executions of a number of republican prisoners who were due to be put to death. However, there were numerous instances where rank-and-file members of the British Army and RIC did not comply with this order. Instead, they continued their standard modus operandi, causing a significant number of civilian and republican fatalities in the process.

The timing and nature of many of these offensive actions, including the Kilgobnet Mine Disaster, indicate that they were regular operations planned in advance of the announcement of the Truce on 8 July. Their occurrence so close to the ceasefire was entirely coincidental, and any resulting fatalities cannot reasonably be considered as evidence of pre-ceasefire 'bloodlust' on the part of the British forces. In other cases, such as the fatal shootings of John Foley and Hannah Carey, it is impossible to say to what extent, if any, news of the Truce motivated the British personnel responsible. The discipline of the British forces at the time was so poor that such killings were commonplace, but it would be wrong to assume that Foley and Carey were killed in premeditated acts by British troops seeking vengeance in the final hours of the conflict. By contrast, the killing of Denis Spriggs, the attack on the Keogh family home which killed Margaret Keogh, and the attempted assassinations of Tomás Malone and Patrick O'Reilly, were apparently premeditated attempts at reprisal killings carried out by members of the British forces who were aware that the Truce was imminent.

The methods, and level of violence, involved in both the final British and republican attacks before the Truce were often comparable. The use of mines by the British forces, as at Kilgobnet, was a reckless and indiscriminate tactic that endangered, and claimed, the lives of a number of innocent civilians. However, it was an effective, if not particularly gallant or chivalrous, method of conducting anti-insurgent warfare. Many of the IRA's methods of warfare, such as its use of improvised mines and explosive booby traps and its attacks on 'soft targets', were equally unwholesome. Despite how loathsome these operations may appear, they were considered legitimate methods of warfare at the time.

Both sides also frequently employed tactics that they knew to be illegal. Members of British forces regularly engaged in reprisal killings, summarily executing unarmed men they had taken prisoner or targeting the homes of republican families and killing unarmed suspects they had captured in their beds. The IRA was guilty of executing unarmed enemies it had taken prisoner who were not suspected of involvement in espionage and whose deaths appear to have been motivated primarily by vengeance.

Despite the questionable morality of actions undertaken by both sides, the trend in Irish and British historiography has been to ignore the killings committed by British troops after the ceasefire was announced. For example Pádraig Yeates focused so much on IRA violence at the time of the Truce that he ignored the deaths of those killed by the actions of the British forces in the same period:

> the IRA mounted a series of attacks around the country before the ceasefire deadline of noon on Monday 11 July. ... The only fatality in Dublin was Andrew Knight, a tram inspector from Clarinda Park, Kingstown, whose body was discovered in Dalkey ... By contrast eight soldiers, two RIC men, three Volunteers and two civilians were killed in the provinces in the last hours of the conflict including the fifteen-year-old daughter of a former RIC man, shot as she tried to protect her father from his attackers, who suspected him of being an informer.[138]

The deaths of Denis Spriggs and Seán Quinn, who were killed by the British forces in non-combat situations, are not mentioned. Yeates' work focuses on Dublin city, yet omits any reference to the death of Margaret Keogh in Dublin city, who was apparently killed there by the British forces.

Another example of this type of narrative comes from Donal J. O'Sullivan's *The Irish Constabularies 1822–1922: A Century of Policing in Ireland*, which gives the following account of the Truce:

> On 9th July, a Truce was agreed between Eamon de Valera and General Macready. Hostilities in Ireland were to officially cease at 12 noon on the 11th. Even though the Truce was signed on 9th July there was a last-minute flurry of activity by the IRA. They shot dead the daughter of a retired RIC man whose house they raided in Tipperary on 9th, and on the same day they fired at and wounded a soldier and an RIC man. Early on 11th July, they kidnapped five British soldiers in Cork city, shot four of them dead and wounded the other. The IRA in Kerry killed three British soldiers on the day the Truce became effective. Serious rioting took place in Belfast during most of the month and several people were killed, including fourteen people on the 11th alone. Military and RIC reinforcements were dispatched by special trains from Dublin in an effort to get the Belfast Riots under control.[139]

In O'Sullivan's account, the IRA is portrayed as the sole aggressor. No mention is made of the numerous cases of British aggression that occurred in the same period and caused a significant number of fatalities.

This type of history is flawed because its inordinate focus on republican violence skews the reality of events at the time. For instance, Alexander Clarke, the RIC constable assassinated by the IRA in Skibbereen, is regularly referred to in books, newspaper articles and on the radio as one of the last victims of IRA violence – 'the last of the "enemy" to die at the hands of the IRA' or 'the last casualty of the War of Independence'.[140] In fact, Clarke was neither. The last member of the RIC killed during the War of Independence was Sergeant James King, but he is frequently overlooked in favour of Clarke because Clarke, unlike King, was not the leader of an RIC 'murder gang'. The final casualty of the war was actually Hannah Carey, an innocent civilian shot dead by the RIC, whose death has never received the same level of public attention as Clarke's.

7

BELFAST'S BLOODY SUNDAY

A total of sixty-one people died as a direct result of political violence in the days between the announcement of the Truce and its implementation. Twenty-two of these fatalities occurred during an intense and extremely violent bout of sectarian rioting in Belfast, which began at midnight on Sunday 10 July and did not abate until the afternoon of Monday 11 July. This death toll gives Sunday 10 July 1921 – Belfast's Bloody Sunday – the dubious honour of having been the bloodiest day in the city's very long and deeply troubled history.

Despite the extremely high number of fatalities, the widespread sectarian rioting and the large-scale destruction of property, these Bloody Sunday riots hardly register in public consciousness today, and are usually reduced to a footnote in histories of the period. Where these riots are mentioned, they are usually linked with the claim that the announcement of the Truce led directly to a series of reckless and foolhardy last-minute IRA attacks. Some contemporary commentators promoted the idea that the riots were solely the result of an unprovoked, cynical and exploitative IRA murder of an inoffensive RIC constable. For instance, in the days following the attack, the *Belfast Telegraph* reported:

> The City of Belfast had an object lesson on Sinn Féin methods yesterday, when the customary quiet of the Sabbath was turned into bedlam by the gunmen … Sinn Féin is evidently taking full value of the few hours remaining before the Truce. There is not the slightest doubt that all the trouble yesterday was commenced and continued by Sinn Féin gunmen. The murder of Constable Conlon and the shooting of

his comrades was the starting point of the turmoil, which would have been infinitely worse but for the admirable restraint of the Loyalists.[1]

Walter Phillips also cited 'the murder of a constable by Sinn Feiners' as the sole cause of the Belfast violence.[2]

This idea has been picked up and built upon by modern commentators. Arthur Hezlet's account of the incident, though somewhat more balanced in acknowledging that Protestant-loyalist attacks also occurred, emphasised that the IRA was to blame for sparking the outbreak and absolved the British forces of any involvement in, or responsibility for, any of the resultant deaths. He suggested that any attempts to link the Special Constabulary to sectarian attacks on Catholics was 'skilful propaganda'.[3] Others, including Richard Abbott and Samuel Trotter, while acknowledging that there was widespread sectarian rioting across the city as the Truce drew near, have identified republican activity and IRA aggression as the root cause of the unrest and its ensuing fatalities.[4]

On several occasions, Kevin Myers has also asserted that the IRA's actions provoked the violence:

> As the hours of the Truce neared, the tempo of the killings increased. Twenty-four hours before the Truce started, the IRA attacked a police patrol on the Falls Road, shooting two Catholic policemen and a Protestant Special Constable. In the chaos and communal riots which followed, a total of 14 [*sic*] people were killed in west and north Belfast.[5]

On the ninetieth anniversary of the Truce, Myers again reiterated his belief that unprovoked IRA violence caused the riots, bizarrely attempting to link this to more recent political violence in the north, blaming the Catholic-nationalist population of Belfast for starting 'their insane war':

... the cycle of psychiatric futility that is Fenianism knows no end ... I've said many, many times that the more we know of the past Troubles, the less likely we are to repeat them ... didn't the nationalist people of West Belfast have all the knowledge that they could possibly have wanted about the futility of violence before they began their insane war in 1971? ... Did they not have the ambush of Raglan Street of July just 90 years ago to tell them of the consequences of violence? This sordid little murder of a Catholic police officer led to an eruption of sectarian violence in which 14 [*sic*] people were killed, 100 injured, and scores of houses burnt out. Did the nationalist people thereby learn of the futility of violence? ... The reverse: 'The Raglan Street Ambush' is cherished in Falls Road folklore.[6]

Myers' analysis of the causes of violence in Belfast may be deeply flawed, but he is correct in stating that the Raglan Street ambush is an important event in the history and folklore of the Falls Road district and is still celebrated by the Catholic-nationalist and republican community there.

THE RAGLAN STREET AMBUSH

On the night of 9 July the IRA attacked a patrol of RIC and 'B Specials' on Raglan Street (today's Ross Street/Road area), in what became known as the Raglan Street ambush. Peter Carleton, who was a member of Na Fianna Éireann in Belfast, spoke of the incident as if it were a premeditated ambush – the high point of the IRA's military campaign in the city and a successful military operation that Belfast republicans were proud of:

The only type of conventional warfare that took place in Belfast and that bore any resemblance to what was then taking place in the South, was the ambush at Raglan Street. Twelve men took part, yet nearly a hundred put in later for Free State pensions ... It was directed against the RIC and B-Specials. There were not a lot of casualties, but they captured some arms and burned the Crossley Tenders.[7]

Another republican also recalled that the IRA had lured the British forces into a trap in Raglan Street, and that so many members of the Belfast IRA later claimed to have been involved that if they 'had really been there, then they could have ate [*sic*] up the cage-car [Crossley Tender], peelers [RIC constables] and all'.[8]

IRA veteran Roger McCorley stated that the ambush was the most successful IRA operation against the British forces in Belfast. According to McCorley, the Belfast IRA seized this opportunity to impose a brutal and just retribution on the British forces for the reprisal killings committed by the 'murder gang', thereby settling the score and restoring the IRA's military reputation with a single deadly blow:

> I had issued a general order that where reprisal gangs were concerned, no prisoners were to be taken. The enemy, after a short time, offered to surrender but our men, in obedience to the order, refused to accept their surrender. The fight continued for about forty minutes and only finished when the last of the reprisal gang was wiped out.[9]

McCorley estimated that the IRA killed up to fifteen members of the British forces in this attack. If this estimate was accurate, it would mean that the Raglan Street ambush was one of the most successful IRA operations of the entire conflict, ranking alongside the attacks at Kilmichael and Crossbarry. One of the participants in the operation, Seán Mac Iomaire, suggested that he and his comrades had killed at least eight RIC constables and that the attack was 'a great victory' for the IRA.[10]

Lore about the Raglan Street ambush was so widespread that some West Belfast bard penned 'The Ballad of the Raglan Street Ambush' to memorialise the event:

Well I'll tell you a tale of a row in the town,
When a lorry went up and it never came down,
It was the neatest oul sweetest row you'd ever meet,
When the boys caught the Specials down Raglan Street.

When Craigavon sent the Specials out to shoot the people down,
He thought the IRA were dead in dear old Belfast town,
But he got a rude awakening with rifle and grenade,
When he met the first Battalion of the Belfast Brigade.

They came cursing and swearing as always before,
And they swore they'd walk knee deep in Sinn Feiners' gore,
But ours was the bullets those bould boys did meet,
And they ran like Hell's blazes down Raglan Street.

Oh the bould Christy Clarke he was there on that night,
Shouting give me a Webbly [*sic*] – I'll put them to flight,
But a Martini bullet cut the bricks at his feet,
And he broke all the records out of Raglan Street.

And the bould Dinkey Campbell, the brother of a man,
With a 'Peter The Painter' clasped in his right hand,
He walked around the corner and a Peeler did meet,
And bang! went the Peeler up Raglan Street.

Well early next morning when dawn it had come,
There was nothing to hear but the sound of a drum,
It wasn't the Orangemen a-walkin the streets,
It was D Company marching up Raglan Street.[11]

Despite the many inconsistencies in the numerous and varied accounts of the incident, all were in agreement that the Raglan Street ambush was at the beginning of the cycle of violence that claimed twenty-two lives in Belfast in just over twenty-four hours. Before the ambush, the RIC in Belfast reported that 'party feeling' (i.e. political and sectarian tension) was running high in early July.[12] It is likely that the announcement of the Truce on 8 July further increased the existing tensions, but both unionist and nationalist newspapers were agreed that the city was peaceable until the night of 9 July. The *Belfast Telegraph* reported that the 'customary quiet of the Sabbath' prevailed, while *The Irish News* stated that 'peace reigned everywhere' in the city up to that time.[13] All contemporary accounts also agree that a force of RIC and 'B Specials' departed Springfield Road Barracks for the Catholic-nationalist Falls Road district approximately one hour after the 10.30 p.m. curfew.

The official RIC account of the incident stated that this was a routine curfew patrol.[14] However, some press reports suggest that the patrol was actually engaged in reprisals. *The Irish News* described the force as a raiding party, which attacked Catholic-nationalist homes on Raglan Street.[15] Similar reports appeared in the *Ulster Herald*: 'After midnight, a Crossley Tender with armed, uniformed, singing men began patrolling Raglan Street. The lorry stopped and when they got out of the car, they battered in a number of doors and called on B----Y Fenians to come out.'[16] IRA Volunteer Jimmy Burns, who was monitoring the patrol's activities, reported that they were drunk and had disguised themselves by painting their faces black, which led the IRA to suspect that the patrol was an RIC 'murder gang' intent on carrying out reprisal killings.[17] Local accounts of the incident support Burns' contention that the RIC constables and 'B Specials' were drunk, and that the curfew patrol's activities were extremely provocative and aggressive.[18]

The IRA had expected British reprisals in the area that night – the targets would appear to have been either Frank Crummey, intelligence officer of the IRA's 3rd Northern Division, who lived at 59 Raglan Street, or Tommy Flynn, captain of D Company, 1st Battalion, who lived at No. 3 Raglan Street. In anticipation of this a force of fourteen volunteers from D Company of the Belfast

Battalion had assembled at their headquarters at No. 3 Raglan Street. Twelve members of this party were armed with rifles, the remaining two had side arms, and the group was under the command of Captain Thomas Flynn. At 11.20 p.m. the residents of the Pound-Loney area near Barrack Street sounded an alarm by blowing whistles and beating bin lids to signal the approach of British forces. The IRA took up positions around Albert Street in expectation of dealing with this threat, but were stood down on the basis that there had been a false alarm. A short time later, the republicans returned to the eastern end of Raglan Street and received a signal flashed from a red lamp, which indicated the approach of British forces. The IRA immediately took up defensive positions near the junction of Peel Street and Raglan Street. Within minutes, an IRA scout arrived with confirmation that an RIC and Special Constabulary patrol was fast approaching.[19]

At 11.50 p.m. the RIC Crossley Tender reached the Raglan Street/Peel Street junction and came under attack from the IRA attackers.[20] The IRA fired at least two co-ordinated volleys of rifle and small arms fire at the Crossley Tender from their defensive positions. The RIC and Special Constabulary returned fire and a chaotic running battle between the opposing forces ensued that lasted for several minutes.[21] RIC Constable Edward Hogan and Special Constable Charles Dunn were wounded in the initial firefight. Four IRA Volunteers attempted to approach the rear of the Crossley Tender and were confronted by Thomas Conlon and two other constables. When Conlon challenged them, shouting 'Halt! Hands up!', IRA Volunteer Jack Donaghy immediately opened fire with an automatic pistol, killing Conlon. The IRA broke off its attack shortly afterwards and retreated to a republican 'safe house' on Baker Street.[22] The attack had rendered the Crossley Tender immobile and a second RIC vehicle was summoned to take the wounded constables to the Royal Victoria Hospital.[23] Constable Conlon was a native of Roscommon, unmarried and thirty-three years old at the time of his death. He had thirteen years' service in the RIC, having been a farmer before enlisting in the force.[24] Conlon was the only member of the British forces killed in the attack. Republican suggestions that the IRA had 'wiped out' the patrol, killing up to fifteen RIC and Special Constabulary are gross exaggerations.[25]

Following the attack a large force of RIC and Special Constabulary was deployed in the area and cordoned off a section of the district bordered by the Falls Road, Panton Street, Cypress Street, McDonnell Street and Albert Street.[26] The first action of the reinforcements was a raid on the Raglan Street Gaelic Athletic Association (GAA) Club. According to the *Belfast Telegraph*, the police found empty rifle ammunition casings strewn outside the club. Inside, they allegedly found over a thousand rounds of ammunition left in plain view on the floor and a German rifle concealed nearby. Having made this discovery, they moved to a motor garage on the ground floor of the premises where, according to the *Belfast Telegraph* 'the police located an outbreak of fire'. However, the *Belfast Telegraph*'s reporter failed to comment on the origins of the mysterious blaze.[27] *The Irish News* reported that the police reinforcements raided a number of Catholic-nationalist homes within the cordoned area, physically assaulting their male occupants, and a number of families in the area had their windows broken and gunshots were fired at their homes. Despite this outbreak of violence, none of the local inhabitants suffered death or serious injury that night.[28]

The probability is that the destruction of the GAA club and the disorder that followed were deliberate acts of revenge carried out by members of the RIC and Special Constabulary to exact retribution on the local populace for the earlier attack on their comrades. While it is conceivable that police reinforcements did discover a rifle and ammunition in the GAA club, though probably not in the quantities and haphazard manner reported in the unionist press, the suggestion that the RIC and Special Constabulary merely stumbled on the fire that eventually destroyed the premises is unlikely, particularly given those forces' record of indiscipline and incendiarism. Tellingly, the RIC account of the disturbances mentions the alleged discovery of the munitions but omits any reference to the subsequent fire and destruction of the premises.[29] *The Northern Whig,* the Liberal newspaper, later published a statement from the Raglan Street GAA Club stating that no arms or ammunition had been found on the premises. *The Northern Whig* also insisted that the destruction of the GAA club and police raids on homes in the district immediately afterwards amounted to state-sponsored attacks on the Catholic-nationalist community.[30]

BELFAST'S BLOODY SUNDAY

The police cordon imposed on part of the Falls Road district in response to the Raglan Street ambush was lifted between 9 a.m. and 10 a.m. the following morning, Sunday 10 July.[31] There had been sporadic outbreaks of shooting and sniping in Cupar Street, Carlisle Street, Lonsdale Street and the Falls Road throughout the early morning, but this appeared to ease after the curfew ended at 5 a.m.[32] At 8 a.m. a loyalist mob assembled in Cupar Street and set fire to five houses occupied by Catholic families. The fire brigade arrived a short time later and extinguished the flames, but had scarcely left the street when it received word that another Catholic home was ablaze. The situation quickly spiralled out of control after the arsonists looted Finnegan's, a Catholic-owned pub at 93 Cupar Street, and afterwards set the business ablaze. Another twenty Catholic homes were destroyed in the wave of simultaneous arson attacks that followed.[33]

At noon there was an outbreak of sniping from the loyalist enclaves of Ashmore Street, Conway Street and Townsend Street.[34] According to *The Irish News:* 'There was a regular ring of unionist snipers commanding the streets abutting on the Falls Road and no person could pass up or down that thoroughfare except at the gravest risk.'[35] By 1 p.m. the violence had spread to adjoining streets and the situation had deteriorated so much that the tram service to the area was halted. At 2.30 p.m. twelve-year-old William Baxter, a Protestant schoolboy, was shot in the chest as he walked to Sunday school in Ashmore Street. Another Protestant youth, Ernest Park, was shot dead on the same thoroughfare as he was taking a kitten to a friend's house. It would appear that both boys were killed by the same nationalist or republican sniper firing from the rear of Ashmore Street School and the Falls Road.[36]

The British forces, protected by armour-plated vehicles, began patrolling sections of the Falls Road. The nationalist press subsequently complained that the British forces deployed a heavy police and military presence in Catholic-nationalist areas, and that these troops raided houses and harassed the occupants while snipers and gunmen in loyalist districts went unmolested.[37] RIC men reported that they had come under sniper fire and that British military and Special Constabulary patrols in armoured vehicles had been deployed on the Falls Road to deal with this threat.[38]

By 3 p.m. RIC and Special Constabulary patrols were running wild, racing through Catholic-nationalist streets in their armoured vehicles and firing indiscriminately at the residents. Large crowds of loyalist onlookers gathered in close proximity to bodies of police and cheered them as they fired each volley. A Catholic ex-soldier named Henry Mulholland was killed at 3.30 p.m., when he was attacked without warning at Clonard Gardens by a gang of armed men who emerged from Cupar Street and shot him in the head. Mulholland lived at 5 Bombay Street, was forty-nine years old and had been employed at Combe's Foundry until the firm's Catholic-nationalist employees had all been expelled by their Protestant-loyalist co-workers.[39]

Loyalist rioters on Cupar Street claimed a second victim shortly after Mulholland's killing, when Alexander Hamilton, a twenty-one-year-old Catholic ex-soldier from Plevna Street, was shot dead.[40] Since early morning there had been attacks on Catholic homes and businesses in that neighbourhood, and before the day ended arsonists had destroyed the homes of at least twenty-six nationalist families and a Catholic-owned pub on Cupar Street. The terror engendered by these attacks on nationalist homes is apparent in the death of Peter Mackey. Mackey was staying in a house on Mary Street at which a gang of unidentified men appeared at night demanding entry. Believing, perhaps correctly, that the men were engaged in sectarian attacks, Mackey fled the building and suffered a fatal fall in his panic-stricken attempt to escape.[41]

Large crowds gathered near the city centre from 4.30 p.m. onwards to watch members of the Orange Order return from a religious service at the Ulster Hall. This Orange parade was attacked at several points by nationalist rioters firing revolvers, and the resulting panic led to a stampede by parade spectators near City Hall. A British soldier, Private C. Hughes, was attacked and wounded by gunmen in Upper Library Street, and a Protestant ex-soldier was wounded near the UVF Hospital.[42] A mixed force of RIC, Special Constabulary and British military, supported by armoured vehicles, rushed to the scene. They responded to the nationalist attacks by pouring rifle and machine-gun fire down the side streets into which they believed the attackers had fled. *The Irish News* gave the following account:

> The side streets were literally swept by rifle and machine-gun fire for over three hours, and during this time not a human being save the Crown forces was to be observed in any of these thoroughfares. Armed forces in motor wagons after a time patrolled the empty streets and there was machine-gun fire at intervals. There was scarcely a second's lull in this intense firing … The plight of the inhabitants was perilous in the extreme. Residents in the fire-swept streets had to

take refuge generally in the back rooms of their homes or lie prone
… on the floor.[43]

By late afternoon the violence had spread to Upper Library
Street, Upper North Street, Millfield, Carrickhill, York Street,
North Queen Street, Stanhope Street and the Old Lodge Road.[44]
Though the violence had reached the city centre and was spread-
ing rapidly, it was still at its most intense between rival mobs and
groups of gunmen along the Falls Road–Shankill Road interface.
The RIC reported that Catholic-nationalist areas were attacked by
Protestant-loyalist mobs, which succeeded in setting fire to a number of houses.[45] *The Irish News* reported that at one point a loyalist
mob, estimated to have been several thousand strong, made a failed
attempt to invade the Falls Road and that many of them carried
petrol, paraffin, rags and other incendiaries.[46]

Bernard Monaghan, a seventy-year-old Catholic, was shot dead
as he stood in the doorway of his house at 69 Abyssinia Street.
James McGuiness, a thirty-five-year-old Catholic, left his home
at 27 McMillan Place to fetch one of his children from Townsend
Street and was shot dead at the corner of McMillan Place and
Durham Street. Another Catholic ex-serviceman, twenty-two-
year-old Frederick Craig, was fatally wounded by a sniper as he
walked home along Clonard Street, and died shortly afterwards
at the Mater Infirmorum Hospital. Dan Hughes, a twenty-eight-
year-old Catholic from McCleery Street, was shot dead by a sniper
from Spamount Street while attempting to reach his home. A
loyalist mob attacked and killed Patrick Hickland in Boyd Street,
kicking and beating him before he was shot. Pat Devlin, a Catholic
from Quadrant Street, was shot by gunmen on Albert Street and
died of his injuries the following April.[47] James Lenaghan, a forty-
eight-year-old Catholic ex-soldier, was shot dead on the corner
of Derby Street and the Falls Road.[48] Daniel Joseph Hughes, a
fifty-year-old Catholic ex-soldier was shot dead while attempting

to bring one of his five children home safely from a neighbour's house.[49] Another Catholic, fifty-six-year-old labourer William Tierney, was shot dead in his home at 15 Osman Street.[50] Mary McGowan, a partially blind Catholic teenager, was crossing Derby Street with her mother when they were both shot without warning by members of the British forces travelling in an armoured vehicle. Mary received a fatal bullet wound to the leg and died the following day.[51] William Mulligan, a fifty-year-old Protestant tailor from James Street, was shot by a Catholic gunman and died of his wounds a short time later in the Victoria Hospital. David McMullan, a nineteen-year-old Protestant who worked as an apprentice engineer, was killed near his home on Lawnbrook Avenue.[52]

The level of violence eased in the early hours of 11 July, but intensified again after daybreak. William Brown, a forty-five-year-old haulage contractor, was shot as he went to work in the nationalist David Street area and died a short time later in Victoria Street Hospital. At 12.45 p.m., three-quarters of an hour after the Truce had come into effect, a nineteen-year-old Catholic, James Ledlie, was fatally wounded by a sniper firing from a Protestant-loyalist enclave.[53]

Ledlie, a native of Plevna Street, was an IRA Volunteer and a member of C Company, 1st Battalion of the Belfast Brigade.[54] Accounts differ as to the circumstances of his death: the official inquiry into Ledlie's death was told by a representative for the family that he had been killed while trying to remove furniture from the home of a Catholic friend who was at risk of sectarian attack. This has since been taken at face value by some historians as proof that Ledlie was not on duty as an IRA Volunteer at the time of his death.[55] However, it was unlikely that Ledlie's family would tell an inquest organised by the British authorities if he had died on active service with the IRA. It is more likely that the alternative narrative espoused by republicans, that Ledlie was mobilised at the time of his death by the IRA for 'outpost duty' in order to prevent further sectarian attacks against Catholics in the Norfolk Street area, is a more accurate version of events.[56]

Regardless of the exact circumstances of Ledlie's death, the nationalist press cited it as an example of loyalist callousness towards the negotiated ceasefire. *The Irish News* stated that his shooting was 'a fitting commentary on the manner in which the Truce was kept by the Orange party in Belfast'.[57] Despite this, the RIC reported that the arrival of the Truce had a positive effect on the situation in Belfast and according to the local RIC district inspector: 'All over the city matters subsided about 12 o'clock noon on Monday, 11th ulto: as arranged by the Truce terms.'[58] The local IRA leader, Roger McCorley, recalled that 'fighting died down immediately' after the Angelus bells sounded at noon on 11 July. However, the advent of the Truce had only a temporary effect on the violence in Belfast. Serious rioting erupted again on 14 July, with outbreaks of sniping, grenade attacks and exchanges of gunfire between rival Catholic-nationalist and Protestant-loyalist mobs, culminating in the shooting of a fourteen-year-old Protestant girl and arson attacks on at least twenty houses.

The cycle of violent events in Belfast that began about midnight on Sunday 10 July and ended around midday on Monday 11 July resulted in at least twenty-one people being killed (one RIC constable, one IRA Volunteer, six Protestant civilians and thirteen Catholic civilians: see Table 7.1). A further eighty people suffered serious injuries.[59] Countless others were made homeless; with the highest estimate claiming that at least 160 Catholic homes were attacked, forcing a thousand homeless Catholics to seek shelter in schools, stores, halls and other makeshift accommodation.[60] Violence in Belfast erupted sporadically, continuing until 1922 and leading Roger McCorley to comment: 'The pogrom lasted two years ... the Truce lasted six hours only.'[61]

Table 7.1   Fatalities in Belfast's Bloody Sunday, 10–11 July 1921

Thomas Conlon	RIC Constable	Killed in IRA attack
William Baxter	Civilian (Protestant)	Killed by nationalist/ republican sniper
Ernest Park	Civilian (Protestant)	Killed by nationalist/ republican sniper
Henry Mulholland	Civilian (Catholic)	Killed by loyalist gunmen
Alexander Hamilton	Civilian (Catholic)	Killed by loyalist gunmen
Peter Mackey	Civilian (Catholic)	Suffered fatal fall fleeing from raiders
Bernard Monaghan	Civilian (Catholic)	Killed by loyalist gunmen
James McGuiness	Civilian (Catholic)	Killed by loyalist gunmen
Frederick Craig	Civilian (Catholic)	Killed by loyalist sniper
Dan Hughes	Civilian (Catholic)	Killed by loyalist sniper
Patrick Hickland	Civilian (Catholic)	Killed by loyalist gunmen
William Mulligan	Civilian (Protestant)	Killed by nationalist/ republican sniper
David McMullan	Civilian (Protestant)	Killed by nationalist/ republican sniper
Patrick Devlin	Civilian (Catholic)	Fatally wounded by loyalist gunmen
James Lenaghan	Civilian (Catholic)	Killed by RIC/Special Constabulary
Daniel Joseph Hughes	Civilian (Catholic)	Killed by RIC/Special Constabulary
William Tierney	Civilian (Catholic)	Killed by RIC/Special Constabulary
Francis Robinson	Civilian (Protestant)	Killed by RIC/Special Constabulary
William Brown	Civilian (Protestant)	Killed by nationalist/ republican sniper
Mary McGowan	Civilian (Catholic)	Killed by RIC/Special Constabulary
James Ledlie	IRA Volunteer	Killed by a loyalist sniper

POLITICAL AND SECTARIAN RIOTING IN BELFAST

While the traditional narrative has attributed the cause of the Bloody Sunday riots to the Raglan Street ambush, the likelihood is that the outbreak of violence was the result of several overlapping factors. The city of Belfast had been a flashpoint for warring communities and ideologies for almost a century before the War of Independence. This was generally the result of two factors, namely negative reaction to political developments that heightened loyalist fears of Home Rule, and tension caused by the annual celebrations on 12 July and Orange Order parades. On 11 July 1921 loyalist opposition to the Truce would have added to escalating sectarian tensions in the city in advance of the 'Twelfth of July'. The resulting riot was not a new phenomenon and there appears to be a definite pattern of nationalist political advances being followed rapidly by violence in the city.

In 1886 loyalist opposition to the First Home Rule Bill resulted in the 'Anti-Home Rule' riots, during which at least thirty people were killed. These riots were sparked by a unionist MP who made a speech denouncing Catholicism as 'a system of sensualism, superstition and sin'. This led immediately to an attack on Protestant-loyalist enclaves by a Catholic-nationalist mob and was followed by gun battles between the RIC and loyalists during which two rioters, a British soldier and an RIC head constable, were killed.[62] Almost a decade later, the Second Home Rule Bill coincided with a spate of sectarian attacks in the Belfast shipyards, which forced hundreds of Catholic workmen from their jobs.[63] Shortly after the Third Home Rule Bill was passed in 1912, a Protestant-loyalist mob rampaged through the Belfast shipyards, forcing out almost 2,000 Catholic workers and a large number of 'Rotten Prods' (i.e. Protestant republicans, socialists and trade unionists).[64]

Belfast's annual 'Twelfth' celebrations stoked sectarian tensions in the city and were often marred by violence. During the 1840s Orange celebrations became so problematic that they were banned temporarily under the Party Processions Act of 1850.[65] In July 1857 an inflammatory anti-Catholic sermon by a Protestant preacher sparked a week of sectarian rioting, which included gun battles between the police and Orangemen that reportedly led to several fatalities.[66] In the 1890s loyalists opened fire on the RIC during 'Twelfth' celebrations because they perceived that the majority of the force were 'Fenian Police', i.e. Catholic RIC constables from the south-west deployed in Ulster to tackle disorder. Constable Thomas Fennell, who served in Belfast at the time, believed that Orange parades were designed to inflame sectarian feeling:

> Orange drumming parties frequently went about ... in the most provocative fashion, sometimes halting opposite Catholic houses, the drummers dancing in circles, something after the fashion of a Negro war dance ... drumming parties ... masqueraded with impunity, leading periodically to assaults and riots.[67]

The 'Twelfth' became even more important during the War of Independence as an occasion to rally the Protestant-loyalist faithful in response to the threat increasingly posed by republicanism. Speeches made at the Orange Order's celebrations on 11 and 12 July became rallying calls for all Protestant-loyalists in the northeast to defend themselves against perceived Catholic aggression. The unionist press carried letters each July warning of the dangers posed by Catholic machinations and urging readers to take swift action to prevent this. The recurring themes and siege imagery of the Orange celebrations served as a call to arms for those in attendance.[68] In many cases, loyalist politicians urged violent resistance against any nationalist or republican advances. On 12 July 1919 Edward Carson promised an assembly of Belfast Orangemen: 'If there is any attempt made to take away one jot or tittle of your rights as British Citizens ... I will call out the Ulster Volunteers.'[69] The following year, with political fears among loyalists reaching a peak, Carson addressed a 25,000-strong 'Twelfth' rally near Belfast, telling his audience: 'Be the consequences what they may, we in Ulster will tolerate no Sinn Féin ... we will take the matter into our own hands. We will reorganise ... throughout the province the Ulster Volunteers ... and these are not mere words. I hate words without action.'[70]

Frederick Dane, a Canadian Orangeman addressing the same rally, used nakedly sectarian rhetoric, blaming Catholics for Ulster's woes and telling his audience that they 'were fighting not an Ulster question alone but a well thought out plan for wrecking the British Empire at the instigation of the Church of Rome'.[71] This sectarian conspiracy theory was repeated at another 'Twelfth' rally by John Bradford, master of the Rathfriland District Orange Order, who launched an anti-Catholic tirade claiming that political violence in Ireland was caused by the machinations of the Pope and the Catholic Church, and it was the duty of every Protestant loyalist in Ulster to combat it and to join the Orange Order.[72] Firebrands addressing similar gatherings in Belfast were alleged to have called for 'a show of revolvers to drive the Fenians out'.[73] After loyalist politicians had increased tensions to a fever pitch with violent rhetoric, the situation spilled over into actual physical violence a few days later when news spread of the assassination of Colonel G. F. Smyth, divisional commissioner of the RIC in Munster, by the IRA in Cork.[74]

A contemporary report in the *Westminster Gazette* alleged that the riots which followed were deliberately orchestrated and premeditated acts of violence planned in advance with the sole aim being 'to drive all the Home Rule workers in the shipyards out'.[75] An estimated 10,000 Catholic workers and up to 2,000 'rotten Prods' were expelled from the shipyards and Belfast's four largest engineering firms.[76] In retaliation, Catholics stoned Protestant shipyard workers en route to the Belfast docks. In revenge for this, Protestant-loyalists burned down several Catholic-owned businesses in the east of the city, the isolated Catholic-nationalist enclaves in Ardoyne and Clonard were attacked by Protestant-loyalist rioters and a 4,000-strong mob attacked St Matthew's Catholic Church and the adjoining convent in the Short Strand.[77] Nineteen civilians (eight Protestants and eleven Catholics) were killed in this outbreak of violence.[78] Incidents like this became so commonplace in Belfast each July that it was standard practice for the British authorities to deploy an additional 1,000 RIC and an equal number of soldiers to the city for the duration of the month, in anticipation of violence.[79] The difficulties of policing sectarian tensions in Belfast were recognised by the RIC, with the result that the political-religious balance of the rank and file in the city was even, which differentiated it from the rest of Ireland.[80]

Aspects of the Bloody Sunday riots appear to have been nakedly sectarian and related to the annual tensions and fear stoked by the Orange celebrations. An elderly Catholic being threatened and harassed by a Protestant-loyalist mob was reported to have appealed to a passer-by for aid, reminding him: 'You have a mother of your own and you would not like to see her murdered.' The man replied: 'I have, but she is a decent Protestant and not a Papist pig or cow' before calling on the mob to kill the woman.[81] Catholics alleged that Orangemen engaged in provocative and offensive behaviour during Orange parades in the city centre, including 'party chants' and 'sash waving'. According to *The Irish News*: 'This did not help to allay the excitement – in fact it added to the turmoil.'[82] Catholic-nationalist gunmen attacked Orangemen returning from Protestant church services that afternoon.[83] The Orange Order's Catholic counterpart, the Ancient Order of Hibernians, was also active that day and led a number of sectarian attacks on Protestants and Protestant-owned business premises in West Belfast.[84]

The violence on Belfast's Bloody Sunday was partly because of a predictable reaction by loyalists to a major political development which threatened their position, and this situation was worsened by the timing, occurring just days before the annual 'Twelfth' celebrations, when sectarian tensions were at their worst. However, the British government had little option but to schedule the Truce at such an inopportune time in mid-July because of political considerations. The timetable for implementation of the Government of Ireland Act demanded that the new parliament of southern Ireland be established by 12 July 1921. The British cabinet decided that, if this assembly had not met by that date, which was impossible given the Sinn Féin boycott, crown colony government and martial law would be imposed throughout the twenty-six counties and a 'surge' against the IRA would be launched by the British military. However, the proposed date for the imposition of martial law and other drastic measures was immediately postponed to 14 July when Lloyd George was reminded of the political and religious significance of the 'Twelfth' in Ireland.[85] Given the propensity for violence at the annual Orange celebrations, the timing of the Truce was far from ideal.

The news that the British authorities had agreed a ceasefire with Irish republicans would be unlikely to receive a welcome among Protestant-loyalists in Ulster, for a whole host of reasons. First, the negotiations that would occur after the Truce began had the potential to establish a hostile republic in the south of Ireland. Second, the Truce effectively bestowed recognition from the British authorities upon the IRA, Sinn Féin and Dáil Éireann, and there were grave loyalist fears that this could lead to an abandonment of partition. Furthermore, loyalists were alarmed that the terms of the Truce were to be applied to the new northern state as well as the twenty-six counties of 'Southern Ireland', especially as this had been agreed without consultation with the Belfast parliament.[86] Loyalists were extremely wary of the British government's negotiations with Irish republicans, complaining that the British had failed to press home their full military advantage over the IRA and suggesting that this was the result of British incompetence, moral cowardice or deliberate treachery.[87]

The mobilisation of tens of thousands of Orangemen and the loyalist faithful in Belfast immediately after the British government announced they had agreed an armistice with the IRA as a prelude to negotiations with Sinn Féin would probably have led to a forceful demonstration of loyalist feeling even if the Raglan Street ambush had not occurred. Thousands of Protestant-loyalist spectators were expected in Belfast city centre to view Orange Order church parades scheduled for Sunday 10 July and the ceasefire would come into effect just a few hours before the 'Eleventh Night' bonfires that were a highlight of the 'Twelfth' celebrations. RIC District Inspector J. J. McConnell, who was based in Belfast at the time, claimed that loyalist dissatisfaction with the news of the Truce was in a large part responsible for the intensity of the rioting. According to him, 'The Northern Loyalists were determined to ignore the Truce, which they regarded as a surrender to the rebels.'[88] Such loyalist militancy was not mindless violence; it had a very definite purpose. The British government's Irish policy was calibrated in response to the balance of forces in Ireland, and violence directed by Belfast loyalists helped to skew the balance in favour of loyalism and served as a reminder to the British public and Conservative politicians in Britain that Protestant-loyalists in the north of Ireland were determined to maintain the union.[89]

THE 'MURDER GANG' AND BRITISH REPRISALS IN BELFAST

Republican accounts of the Raglan Street ambush are adamant that the RIC and Special Constabulary patrol that was attacked was not a regular curfew patrol but a 'murder gang' intent on carrying out reprisal killings. Republicans in Belfast claimed that an RIC 'murder gang', similar to those described in the previous chapter, operated in the city and that this group usually exacted a swift revenge for IRA attacks on the British forces. Recent academic research lends some support to these claims. Robert Lynch found that 'attacks on the Catholic minority were a response to perceived provocations and … largely resulted from the activities of the IRA … IRA members were killed … largely at the hands of RIC murder gangs: extremist secret loyalist groups within the police force'.[90] Timothy Wilson claims that members of the RIC and the Special Constabulary frequently engaged in reprisal killings and acted with impunity: 'A striking feature of the death squads … is the confidence with which they carried out their operations … they did not hide their identity as members of the security forces, but actively flaunted it. They wore police uniforms and caps; they left plenty of female witnesses.'[91]

The first reprisal killings in Belfast occurred on 25 September 1920 in reaction to the shooting of three RIC constables in two separate IRA attempts to disarm the RIC on patrol in Catholic-nationalist districts. One of the wounded constables, Thomas Leonard of the Springfield Road RIC Barracks, died of his wounds a short time later. That night unidentified raiders forced their way into the homes of a number of local republicans and shot dead three members of the IRA. There can be little doubt that members of the RIC garrison stationed at the Springfield Road Barracks were responsible for these killings. Frederick Crawford, the district commandant of the Special Constabulary in South Belfast, identified the assassins as policemen and lauded their actions as a positive step that he believed would prevent future IRA attacks:

> … one policeman shot dead on Saturday night last and two badly wounded. Before morning the police retaliated by shooting three prominent Sinn Feiners. This seems drastic but to my mind it is the only way that we will stop these cold-blooded murders … the patience of the police has been exhausted & … reprisals have taken place, I consider that they are justifiable & right in the eyes of God & man … The Sinn Feiners are quaking as they do not know who will

pay the penalty next amongst them. Several of the leaders have been warned that if there is another policeman or soldier shot they will immediately be shot dead.[92]

Members of the RIC working for IRA intelligence reported that the killers were all members of the RIC led by senior RIC officers, including District Inspector (DI) Nixon. The IRA's informants also claimed that these killings were intended as reprisals for the death of Constable Leonard, that the majority of the killers were stationed at Springfield Road, the same RIC barracks as the deceased, and that the 'murder gang' had gone from there to avenge their comrade.[93] The mother of one of those killed later went to Springfield Road, confronted members of the RIC garrison there and accused them of having murdered her son.[94]

On 26 January 1921 the IRA assassinated two members of the RIC who were staying at Roddy's Hotel.[95] The RIC established that one of the hotel's staff – a barman, Michael Garvey – was involved. In an apparent case of mistaken identity, three masked men in RIC uniform raided the home of a different barman named McGarvey and shot him dead while he lay in bed. RIC constables working for IRA intelligence later identified DI Nixon and members of the 'reprisal outfit' as the killers.[96] On 23 April two RIC Auxiliaries were shot by the IRA in Belfast city centre, and immediately afterwards unidentified gunmen shot IRA Volunteer Dan Duffin and his brother, an innocent civilian, dead in their home at Clonard Gardens. Sympathetic RIC constables again told the IRA that the killers were members of the RIC.[97] District Inspector Ferris of the RIC was implicated in the killings. He had only recently been transferred to Belfast from Cork, where he had been implicated in the assassination of Tomás MacCurtain, the Sinn Féin mayor of the city. At the time of the Belfast killings, Ferris was stationed at Springfield Road Barracks.[98]

Having identified those they believed were members of DI

Nixon's 'murder gang', the Belfast IRA marked them for assassination. Their first attempt to assassinate a member of the group occurred in June 1921, when Constable James Glover was mortally wounded in an IRA attack.[99] Two days later, uniformed members of the RIC abducted Alexander McBride, William Kerr and Malachy Halfpenny from their homes and shot them dead. None of the three was a member of the IRA, and only one, Alexander McBride, was a member of Sinn Féin. McBride's widow identified DI Nixon as the leader of the gang of men in RIC uniform who had abducted and killed her husband.[100] On the same date, Constable Thomas Sturdy was shot dead. He was the first member of the Special Constabulary killed in Belfast, and members of that force ran amok in the Falls Road after his funeral, racing along the thoroughfare in their vehicles, firing indiscriminately at the local populace with rifles and machine guns.[101] One woman, Kathleen Collins, was killed, and three other civilians were wounded.[102]

On 6 July Constable Thomas Galvin was mortally wounded in an IRA attack on Union Street.[103] Constable Galvin's shooting was followed by a serious outbreak of violence in the Catholic-nationalist Union Street, Upper Library Street, North Queen Street and Old Lodge Road district. *The Irish News* denounced this as 'a wild night alarm, much worse than any hitherto experienced … on a terrifying scale … worse than anything previously heard in the city'.[104] The paper reported that the disturbances began when a group of armed and unidentified men, many of whom wore uniform, arrived in the district by vehicle and opened fire on Catholic-nationalist homes. The local populace, fearing the intruders were members of the RIC 'murder gang', raised the alarm by shouting and blowing whistles. Armed locals, either members of the IRA or a rival nationalist group, responded by attacking the intruders with a barrage of revolver fire, and the raiders promptly withdrew. Given that the raiders were armed, arrived by vehicle and wore uniform, the likelihood is that they were members of the RIC and

Special Constabulary intent on exacting revenge for the shooting of Constable Galvin.

There is a definite pattern between IRA attacks on the members of the RIC or Special Constabulary and a succession of swift reprisal killings by members of the so-called 'Nixon Murder Gang', led by a group of RIC officers stationed at Springfield Road RIC Barracks. The successful defence of Catholic-nationalist homes in the Union Street, Upper Library Street, North Queen Street and Old Lodge Road district was the first time that the 'murder gang' had attempted and failed to avenge an IRA attack. Immediately after this failure, two members of the RIC died in quick succession. Constable Glover, an alleged member of the gang stationed at Springfield Road, succumbed to his wounds at the Royal Victoria Hospital on 7 July.[105] The following day Constable Galvin died at the Military Hospital in Victoria Barracks.[106] The failure of the revenge attack in Library Street and the deaths of two comrades would almost certainly have been sufficient motivation for the 'murder gang' to attempt another reprisal. If this were the case, the subsequent announcement of the Truce would have been a further aggravation to any members of the Belfast RIC or Special Constabulary who were considering revenge.

Several hours before the Raglan Street ambush, IRA Volunteer Seán Mac Iomaire reported to Frank Crummey, the local IRA brigade intelligence officer, with the news that a senior RIC officer from Springfield Road Barracks had called on the parish priest at Saint Paul's church and told him that he would be off-duty that night and DI Nixon would take charge. The IRA was aware that a number of the RIC constables wounded in previous IRA attacks were in a critical condition and consequently was on the alert in case of reprisals.[107] The reported presence of Nixon in the area heightened fears of a reprisal. Mac Iomaire recalled, 'when Nixon was there we could guess what for. We returned to Company Headquarters and held a meeting to decide what action to take.

We planned to order all arms and men to report before curfew.'[108] The reported demeanour of the RIC patrol that entered Raglan Street, apparently inebriated, disguised with blackened faces and demanding that 'the bloody Fenians come out' would only have increased republican suspicions that they were facing members of the notorious 'murder gang'.

It has been suggested that Constable Conlon, who is known to have passed intelligence information to the IRA, was not the type of policeman who would have consorted with members of the 'murder gang'.[109] However, republican sympathisers within the RIC in Belfast often attempted to infiltrate the 'murder gangs' to try to gather information about the membership and activities of the group. For example, IRA Volunteer Tom McAnally recalled that a Constable McCarthy, who, like Conlon, was also passing intelligence information to the IRA, often tried to go on patrol with the 'murder gang' so that he could learn more about its membership.[110]

The Raglan Street ambush had little in common with the contemporary IRA ambushes in Munster that still dominate public perceptions of the conflict throughout Ireland. It appears that it was more a haphazard defensive action by the IRA to protect the Catholic-nationalist community in response to a real and present threat from an RIC revenge gang, than a premeditated attack on the British forces. This would have been a typical operation for the Belfast IRA at that time and only differed significantly from the defence of the Upper Library Street–Old Lodge Road district a few days earlier by the fact that an RIC constable was killed and because it coincided with the announcement of the Truce. Its portrayal in the contemporary unionist press and official reports by the British forces as having been part of a wider IRA campaign to inflict as many casualties on the British forces as possible before the Truce took effect has no basis in fact.[111]

THE ULSTER SPECIAL CONSTABULARY IN THE BLOODY SUNDAY RIOTS

At least five of the twenty-two fatalities that occurred during the Bloody Sunday riots were unarmed civilians, killed by members of the RIC or Special Constabulary. Republicans have alleged that these killings were, at least in part, the result of a violent negative reaction on the part of members of the Special Constabulary towards the announcement of the Truce. In the light of these allegations, it is appropriate to examine the origins of the Special Constabulary and the nature of its role in the Bloody Sunday riots.

During the War of Independence Ulster loyalists were deeply sceptical of the loyalties of the RIC, because 82 per cent of the men in the force were Catholic.[112] In 1920 Protestant-loyalists in Ulster still regarded the RIC as the 'Fenian Police'.[113] This attitude was partially the result of naked sectarianism and partially justified, as the RIC developed a practice of transferring constables with suspected republican sympathies to loyalist areas in the north, where it was felt they could inflict minimal damage. Catholic RIC constables already serving in the north were often forced by difficult local circumstances to lend support to republicans as the conflict intensified. Patrick Diamond, a member of the IRA in Derry, stressed that these men were crucial to IRA intelligence in the north and often supplied local IRA units with ammunition and weaponry:

> ... in self preservation the RIC [in the north] were forced into friendship with the IRA. The RIC were in a most difficult position. They were being classified as Black and Tans themselves ... had they resigned and gone back to their native places they would have been shot in the back ... Since conditions were bad it was impossible to get jobs, so all they could do was remain and try and be as friendly as they could to the IRA.[114]

In Belfast Dawson Bates, secretary of the Ulster Unionist Council and Minister for Home Affairs in the parliament of Northern Ireland, complained:

> ... large numbers of the better type of [loyalist RIC] men were drafted to the south and men who could not be trusted ... were sent into Belfast. Over 50 per cent of the force in the city are Roman Catholics, mainly from the south, and many of them are known to be related to Sinn Féin.[115]

In response to these fears about the abilities and loyalty of the RIC, the Ulster Unionist Council passed a motion in June 1920 calling for a revival of the UVF to act as a bulwark against the IRA.[116] Dawson Bates held informal discussions with a number of senior RIC officers and reported to Carson: 'I know they would be delighted with the help which they would receive by enrolling loyalist Special Constables. The old formation of the UVF could be used for this purpose.'[117] The British authorities appeared to agree with this suggestion, and Sir Wilfrid Spender, an Englishman who had commanded the 36th Ulster Division, a force largely recruited from the UVF, was approached by Sir Hamar Greenwood within days of the Ulster Unionist Council's motion and asked to oversee the reorganisation of the UVF. Spender was assured that Lloyd George and the British government approved of the scheme but was also warned that 'it would be politically unwise to announce this publicly'.[118] The following month, Winston Churchill gave his backing to the proposal, suggesting that a large force of armed loyalists raised in Ulster would free up at least seven British Army battalions for action against the IRA in Munster.[119]

The British authorities in Dublin Castle were less enthusiastic about this proposal, warning, 'There would be intense civil war [in Derry] and in other parts of Ulster ... In Belfast Protestants would reduce the Catholics to a state of terror.'[120] Ignoring this warning, the British cabinet decided in September 1920 to 'take the necessary steps through the divisional commissioner of police to organise a force of Special Constables in Ireland'.[121] The original motion referred only to the area of Ulster to be partitioned, but this was later altered to Ireland, camouflaging the fact that the move was specifically intended to arm Protestant-loyalists in the north and no effort was ever made to raise a Special Constabulary elsewhere. The details of the new Ulster Special Constabulary were announced the following month. The force consisted of three sections: 'A Specials' would be full-time recruits aged between twenty-one and forty-five years, whom the authorities hoped would include a large number of ex-soldiers, namely veterans of the UVF and the 36th Ulster Division; 'B Specials' would be a part-time force operating roadblocks, mounting patrols and guarding buildings at night; and 'C Specials' were to be a reserve force with no regular duties, but they could be called on in an emergency.

From the beginning it was clear that the Special Constabulary would reflect the largely sectarian nature of loyalism in Ulster. Catholics were actively discouraged from joining the force and recruitment was almost exclusively from the UVF's membership, which had already been involved in anti-Catholic pogroms in Belfast. The *Belfast Newsletter* carried a special appeal for members of the UVF to enlist in the Special Constabulary.[122] Sir Wilfrid Spender encouraged the membership of the Belfast UVF to enlist in the force and suggested that the 20,000 Special Constables needed in the city should all be recruited from UVF ranks. Spender also proposed that enlistment forms for the force should be held at UVF battalion headquarters and completed 'en masse' by the local UVF membership.[123] Many UVF units were simply transformed into bodies of the Special Constabulary, and many of the new police force's senior officers, including Frederick Crawford and Major Robert Stevenson, were also senior officers in the UVF.[124] Some of them, notably Colonel McClintock in

Tyrone, refused to enrol Catholics.[125] The leadership of the UVF in Tyrone issued a memo to their supporters assuring them that Catholics would not be tolerated as members of the new Special Constabulary and that the British government's 'appeal to "all well disposed citizens" may be looked upon as camouflage'.[126] One Catholic ex-RIC constable and military veteran who applied to join the Special Constabulary in Belfast was told that he would not be accepted because of his religious denomination.[127] A senior member of the new force assured UVF leaders that Catholics would not be admitted to the Special Constabulary; consequently, through harassment and intimidation, it was made abundantly clear to the handful of Catholic loyalists who applied to join the Special Constabulary that they were not welcome in the force.[128] The Special Constabulary became in effect a Protestant-loyalist militia recruited largely from the UVF, leading Sir Henry Wilson to comment that the entire membership of the force consisted of 'Black Protestants'.[129]

The UVF's involvement in anti-Catholic pogroms and the sectarian make-up of the new police force caused Joe Devlin, the IPP MP for West Belfast, to comment: 'The Chief Secretary is going to arm pogromists to murder the Catholics ... Their pogrom is to be made less difficult. Instead of paving stones and sticks they are to be given rifles.'[130] Devlin was not the only voice in the British parliament to denounce the establishment of the Special Constabulary. J. Clynes, a Labour MP, protested that the British government was 'arming ... one faction and making them even more powerful than ever for the sort of mischief which so far they have pursued [a reference to the Belfast shipyard expulsions of July 1920]'.[131] The *Westminster Gazette* commented that the establishment of the Special Constabulary was 'the most inhuman expedient the government could have devised'.[132]

The force had not been established very long when its members began to face accusations of anti-Catholic sectarianism. One of the first companies of 'A Specials' recruited in Fermanagh paraded through Enniskillen singing Orange songs on its way to the training depot and fired shots at a Catholic church.[133] Another platoon of 'A Specials' stationed in Newry was accused of harassing the Catholic populace, firing wildly in the streets and burning down a Sinn Féin hall. Within a few months of their deployment, nine members of the force were court-martialled for looting, and the unit was disbanded shortly after they shot dead a local Catholic youth in suspicious circumstances.[134]

The 'B Specials' in particular gained a reputation for sectarian attacks on the homes of northern Catholics and in some areas this intensified into a campaign of sectarian killings of Catholics and reprisals against suspected republicans.[135] These killings appear to have been actively encouraged by the force's leadership, with officers such as Frederick Crawford suggesting:

> There is only one way to deal with a campaign of murder the rebels are pursuing and that is, where the murder of a policeman or other official takes place, the leading rebel in the district ought to be shot or done away with. If this policy were carried out the murders would soon cease as the whole pack of rebels are a lot of cowards.[136]

In July 1921 the strength of the Special Constabulary stood at 3,500 'A Specials', 15,900 'B Specials' and 1,310 'C Specials'.[137] The creation of the Special Constabulary gave Protestant-loyalists in Ulster a sense of security that the actions of the regular RIC and British Army had not. The level of crossover between the UVF and the Special Constabulary, and its exclusively Protestant membership, meant that Protestant-loyalists were now in control of their own defence. Consequently, the Special Constabulary, and in particular the 'B Specials', were hugely popular with Protestant-loyalists, who saw them as 'their' police, a shield against the 'Fenian' threat that was more reliable than the existing 'Fenian police'. The

'B Specials' came close to squaring the circle between the needs of northern loyalists to identify with the British state while at the same time being deeply distrustful of the intentions of the British establishment.[138]

However, the assurance that the formation of the 'B Specials' gave was quickly eroded by the announcement of the Truce. RIC officers in the north of Ireland issued orders on 10 July that all 'A Specials' were to be disarmed and all 'B Specials' were to be suspended from duty as soon as the terms of the Truce began.[139] News of the Truce was greeted with dismay by loyalists and rumours were rife in Belfast that the Special Constabulary was about to be disbanded. These concerns were reported in the unionist press and expressed by the leadership of the UVF. These fears were further stoked during the 'Twelfth' celebrations.[140] One unionist MP denounced the Truce as a 'nauseating criminal weakness' on the part of the British government, and stated:

> Loyal men were humiliated when they saw the highest servants of the Crown meeting and discussing terms with men who were nothing more than common murderers ... Right through the troubles the hands of the police and soldiers had been tied by a vacillating government.[141]

John Porter, another unionist politician, urged members of the 'B Specials' to resist any attempt to disarm them in the wake of the Truce, assuring them: 'I know the "B" men will hold on to their guns. Hold on to them for as long as you can for we all look to you.'[142] The rank and file of the Special Constabulary were reportedly the section of the Protestant-loyalist community that was the most hostile to the Truce. Sir Hamar Greenwood reported, 'There was grave dissatisfaction on the part of the Ulster loyalists, especially amongst those who had enrolled in the Special Constabulary.'[143] Seán Lehane, commander of the IRA's 1st and

2nd Northern Divisions, later claimed that members of the Special Constabulary had little regard for the Truce and breached it on several occasions by carrying out attacks on Catholic-nationalist communities:

> While the memorable Truce was generally honoured in the South of Ireland, it will be recalled that there was no attempt made to recognise a similar situation in the North, and more especially in the present Six Counties, Eastern Donegal, and the areas close to the … border. The Crown Forces – Tans, Ulster Special Police etc., whether they were supposed to honour their truce or not still backed up the loyal minority of … Ulster in directing their programme in Belfast and their general reign of terror against nationalists.[144]

British forces in Belfast were responsible for the deaths of at least five civilians killed during the Bloody Sunday riots. In many cases, it is difficult to establish precisely which branch of the British forces was involved. Regular RIC constables had by then ceased to wear identification numerals on their tunics and were indistinguishable at a glance from the 'A Specials'. Members of the 'B Specials' frequently did not wear any form of police uniform and were alleged, in some cases, to have led sectarian attacks on Catholics while dressed in civilian clothing.[145] However, in most cases, such as the killing of James Lenaghan, the Special Constabulary were identified as the killers by republicans and members of the Catholic-nationalist community.[146] The Special Constabulary in Belfast was apparently enraged by the announcement of the Truce and this, in combination with the IRA attack in Raglan Street, was alleged to have been a major factor in the Bloody Sunday riots.

Discipline among the Special Constabulary in Belfast was already exceptionally poor before the announcement of the Truce. On 5 July 1921, three days before the Truce was announced, without any apparent provocation or cause for reprisal, members of the Special Constabulary went on a drunken rampage in the loyalist Blyth Street–Sandy Row district. Colonel Frederick Crawford witnessed drunken Special Constables acting aggressively and firing their guns in the air. They continued with a hostile and aggressive attitude towards Crawford, even after he had identified himself as a senior police officer. According to Crawford, one Special Constable was 'considerably the worse of liquor … he smelt strongly of spirits … The active sergeant in charge of the lorry showed he was decidedly the worse of drink'.[147] Given such poor discipline and the highly partisan and sectarian nature of the force, it is not surprising that its members seem to have reacted violently to the announcement of the Truce. Belfast IRA leader Roger McCorley reported that members of the force had run wild in West Belfast and were bent on destruction the night before the Truce:

> The British, especially the Special Constabulary, seemed to be completely out of hand and were bent of [sic] massacre. Armoured cars passed through all our areas and kept up a continuous fire into the houses. Anything moving, man woman or child was fired on … [a] messenger informed me that … judging from the demeanour of the Specials, there would be a massacre of the nationalist population.[148]

Daniel Joseph Hughes' widow witnessed her husband's killing and testified that police opened fire without warning, shooting him dead at point-blank range.[149] The shots that killed William Tierney while he was doing housework in his kitchen were fired by a patrol of Special Constabulary who claimed to have been under attack at the time. The jury at Tierney's inquest found that Tierney 'was shot in the course of a riot by some persons unknown'.[150] At the inquest into Mary McGowan's killing, local residents claimed that the area had been peaceful and quiet before the Special Constabulary arrived. One witness testified that he had seen members of the

'B Specials' fire the shots that killed Mary McGowan from an armoured vehicle as it travelled through Ross Street. The jury at the inquest returned the verdict that the young girl had been killed by 'Crown forces'. Furthermore, the jurors suggested that 'in the interests of peace the Special Constabulary should not be solely deployed to police Catholic areas'.[151] The RIC district inspector objected to this finding and was successful in asking that it be changed to record that McGowan had been killed by the Special Constabulary in particular – not by the regular RIC.[152]

The RIC appears to have been responsible for killing Francis Robinson, a sixty-five-year-old Protestant ex-soldier, who suffered a fatal bullet wound to the head while lying in bed at his home in Brown Street. George Robinson, the son of the deceased, stated he had seen the RIC firing directly into the house from behind a gate about fifteen yards away, and that up to 100 shots had been fired into their home. District Inspector Deignan later admitted that bullets found in the house had been fired by RIC constables.[153]

Attacks by loyalist snipers, mobs and gangs of armed men accounted for the majority of fatalities during the Bloody Sunday riots. Republican veterans insisted that off-duty members of the Special Constabulary, and in particular the 'B Specials', participated in these attacks and in some cases led the mobs. Peter Carleton recalled that The Bone, Carrick Hill and other small Catholic-nationalist enclaves were under constant attack from gangs led by members of the 'B Specials'.[154] Roger McCorley claimed that members of the 'B Specials' frequently used their service rifles to snipe these same areas and were responsible for killing a large number of Catholic civilians.[155] Of course, it is impossible at this remove to verify these specific allegations, or the suggestions that members of the Special Constabulary comprised a hard core of the mobs that attacked Catholic civilians during the Bloody Sunday riots.

THE IRA, HIBERNIANS AND NATIONALIST GUNMEN IN THE BLOODY SUNDAY RIOTS

Contemporaneous reports by the British forces, editorials in the unionist press and statements by British politicians all blamed republicans for the Belfast violence. They accused 'the gunmen of the IRA' of deliberately exploiting the announcement of the Truce for their own ends, and accused 'Sinn Féin snipers' of stoking sectarian tensions by carrying out attacks on defenceless Protestant civilians.[156] The British authorities automatically linked all acts of Catholic-nationalist violence with the IRA. However, these claims are wrong in assuming that the IRA was the sole physical force movement in the wider Belfast Catholic community. So-called 'constitutional nationalists', including members of the Ancient Order of Hibernians, nationalist ex-servicemen's associations and other supporters of Joe Devlin and the IPP played a significant role in the Bloody Sunday riots, including sectarian attacks against the Protestant-loyalist community.

Throughout the War of Independence the Belfast IRA was numerically weak and suffered a crippling shortage of arms. As a result of these weaknesses, in combination with other factors, it never enjoyed the support of the majority of the nationalist populace.[157] Initially, the leadership of the Belfast IRA attempted to remain aloof from the sectarian violence and 'fratricidal strife' in the city. IRA Volunteers were given orders to refrain from attacking loyalist mobs and told that attacks on British troops could only be sanctioned if they were attacking Catholic-nationalist civilians. Not surprisingly, this policy proved unpopular and resulted in the takeover of the IRA's Belfast Brigade by a younger, more restless and more aggressive group of republicans in the spring of 1921.[158] However, the IRA's earlier restraint in the face of sectarian attacks on Catholics in July 1920 allowed other contenders, most notably the Hibernians, to claim the mantle as defenders of the Catholic-nationalist community.[159]

Support for the IPP was particularly strong in West Belfast because the local MP, Joe Devlin, was one of the leading lights of the party and commanded a great deal of local loyalty. Consequently, large swathes of the nationalist community in Belfast were opposed to the re-emergence of republicanism, Sinn Féin and the IRA following the 1916 Rising.[160] In the early 1900s Devlin had presided over the revival of the Ancient Order of Hibernians as an adjunct to the IPP. The Hibernians were frequently employed as a strong arm of the party to harass and obstruct its political opponents. When Sinn Féin emerged as a rival force to the IPP in Belfast, physical confrontation between Hibernians and republicans became increasingly common. The republican leader, Seán MacDiarmada, was physically assaulted by Hibernians in Tyrone in 1906.[161] In the post-Rising period, homes on the Falls Road which flew the republican tricolour, or displayed photographs of the executed 1916 leaders, were attacked by Hibernians.[162] During the 1918 general election, when de Valera challenged Devlin for control of the West Belfast seat, there were frequent outbreaks of violence between their rival supporters. Hibernians and nationalist ex-soldiers attacked election rallies held by de Valera's campaigners and these meetings often had to be abandoned as a result.[163] One Hibernian from the Falls Road recalled that while Joe Devlin 'didn't believe in the gun', his supporters frequently resorted to physical force: 'We used [to] beat the rebels ... We murdered them. Saucepans, pots and everything were fired at them.'[164] Rivalry to secure the political support of the Catholic-nationalist community in Ulster frequently led to bloodshed, and the IRA killed at least nine Hibernians during this period.[165]

There were significant differences between the IRA and its Hibernian-nationalist rivals in how they interpreted the conflict, and this in turn influenced their respective military operations. The IRA regarded loyalists as misguided fellow Irishmen and viewed the British government and its armed forces as its principal enemy.

One republican summed up the situation as: 'our gospel was a simple one; free Ireland from the English'.[166] Republicans feared that local sectarian conflict would distract from the broader struggle for independence, and the Belfast IRA attempted, as far as possible, to defend the nationalist enclaves from attacks by members of the British forces while abstaining from intercommunal sectarian violence.[167] By contrast, Hibernians and other Catholic-nationalist gunmen were more interested in fighting Orangemen than Englishmen and frequently welcomed British troops to their areas as a protective force.[168] Hibernians attempted to mobilise the Catholic-nationalist community to confront Protestant-loyalist mobs and consequently Hibernians and supporters of the IPP led Catholic-nationalist mobs during much of the street violence in Derry and Belfast.[169]

The majority of Catholic rioters in Belfast were Hibernians, not IRA Volunteers, and groups of nationalist ex-servicemen played a predominant role in the violence.[170] A large contingent of the Hibernians and Devlin's supporters were British Army veterans of the First World War and as a result had access to arms and ammunition. Hibernians were also known to have stolen arms from the IRA for their own purposes.[171] These weapons were frequently employed in defence of Catholic enclaves and in attacks on Protestant-loyalist districts during sectarian rioting. In Lurgan, a sectarian attack on the Catholic populace was repelled by armed members of the 'Faugh-A Ballaghs', a group of former British soldiers linked to the IPP.[172] Hibernians and nationalist ex-soldiers' groups which supported the IPP did the most to protect Catholic-nationalist enclaves in Belfast and inflicted the most casualties on their Protestant-loyalist opponents.[173]

There is evidence to suggest that the Hibernians were involved in sectarian attacks during the Bloody Sunday riots. IRA Volunteer Seamus Woods recalled that before the Truce only a quarter of Catholic-nationalists supported the IRA, but 'with the signing of the Truce the Catholic population, believing for the moment that we had been victorious and that the Specials and UVF were beaten, practically all flocked to our standard'.[174] There is no doubt that the agreement of the Truce had a huge impact on the struggle between the IRA and the Hibernians for the support of the Catholic-nationalist community in Belfast. The armistice boosted the status of Sinn Féin and the IRA among the Catholic-nationalists and led to growing fears on the part of Hibernians and supporters of the IPP that they had finally been eclipsed by republicanism. Hibernian involvement in the Bloody Sunday riots was a desperate attempt to prevent the further erosion of the organisation's political support base and undermine Sinn Féin, the IRA and republicanism. According to Roger McCorley, the Hibernians were responsible for looting and a spate of sectarian arson attacks on the morning of the Truce:

> An element of the Nationalists, under the control of the Hibernians, started to loot the Unionist business premises in the Falls Road area. They also set fire to the stabling yard of Messrs. Wordie, Haulage Contractors. It was obvious that this was due to pique at the fact that our people were now accepted by the British as the official representatives of the Irish people. On several occasions during the day our men had to turn out and fire on this mob. They fired over their heads but later on in the evening I gave instructions that if the mob gave any further trouble they were to fire into it. We also sent our patrols with orders to arrest the ring-leaders of this group and bring them to Brigade Headquarters. This was done and we ordered several of the ring-leaders to leave the city within twenty-four hours, otherwise they would be shot at sight. This action ended this Hibernian attempt to break the Truce. It is unfortunate that we did not go after the instigators of this attempt rather than their dupes.[175]

One IRA Volunteer who had attempted to prevent the Hibernian-led mob destroying the business was attacked and beaten by them.[176] The attack on Messrs Wordies & Co. led to the death of William Brown, a forty-five-year-old Protestant from March Street, who worked as a haulage contractor for the company. Brown had been shot in the thigh as he approached his workplace and, despite receiving medical treatment, died a few hours later.[177] Given that the attack on Messrs Wordies was led by Hibernians, it is likely that they were responsible for killing Brown. It is impossible to establish if Hibernians were involved in the sniping attacks on loyalist districts which claimed the lives of other Protestant civilians during the Bloody Sunday riots, but given their role in leading the attack on Wordies and their previous activities, this must be considered a distinct possibility. Consequently, the tendency to link the deaths of all Protestant civilians killed during sectarian violence in Belfast with IRA militancy must be treated with caution. One of the five Protestant civilians who died in the Bloody Sunday riots was killed by the Special Constabulary, and another was probably killed by Hibernians.

WHAT REALLY CAUSED BELFAST'S BLOODY SUNDAY?

The Bloody Sunday riots were the most violent episode that erupted in reaction to the Truce. While the death toll of twenty-two people killed may seem inordinately high, it is not remarkably higher than the number of fatalities caused by the sectarian rioting that occurred in the city the previous year.[178] Furthermore, it is worth noting that Belfast had the highest death rate per capita of any part of Ireland during the conflict, with an estimated 460 fatalities occurring in the city in a two-year period, over 80 per cent of whom were civilians.[179] Just 24.1 per cent of Belfast's population were Catholics, yet Catholics accounted for the overwhelming majority of the victims of political violence in the city.[180] During the rioting following the shipyard expulsions of July 1920, eleven of the nineteen people killed, or 58 per cent of the fatalities, were Catholics. Catholics killed by Protestant-loyalists accounted for fourteen of the twenty-one people who died, or 63.5 per cent of the fatalities.

Despite the fact that the Catholic-nationalist community suffered the most fatalities, arson attacks and forced evictions during the rioting, the British authorities and unionist press interpreted the Bloody Sunday riots as an outburst of IRA violence. This perception has dominated the historiography of these events to date. Although the IRA only killed one member of the RIC and members of the British forces killed far more people in the violence that followed, blame for the Bloody Sunday riots is still levelled at the Belfast IRA, which was widely perceived as the aggressor.

While the Raglan Street ambush was a key factor in sparking the riots, it was not the sole cause of the violence. Its contribution to the subsequent Bloody Sunday riots was in combination with a number of other related factors. These included the annual rise in sectarian tensions as 12 July approached, the activities of Hibernians and nationalist ex-soldiers in expressing opposition to the Truce by conducting sectarian attacks on Protestants, and an existing loyalist tradition of expressing opposition to political change by resorting to violent protest. Loyalist fears about the disarmament of the Special Constabulary, poor discipline within that force, the activities of the RIC 'murder gang' and a desire on the part of the Belfast RIC and Special Constabulary to avenge comrades killed by the IRA were also major contributory factors in making 'Belfast's Bloody Sunday'.

8

CONCLUSION

The overwhelming evidence from the testimony of both IRA and British forces' veterans is that they had no prior knowledge that a truce was imminent. Some combatants had discovered that clandestine peace negotiations between Sinn Féin and British emissaries had taken place. However, the constant press reports from late 1920 onwards continually predicting that peace was imminent had been proved wrong so often that they were dismissed as speculation. The volume of these reports, coupled with the failure of a number of high-profile but ill-advised peace initiatives, had the effect of 'crying wolf', so that when press reports about a ceasefire finally began to have a valid foundation in July 1921 their credibility was thoroughly damaged and the reports were dismissed.

When the Truce was finally agreed, both the British authorities and Irish republican leaders realised there would be practical difficulties in ensuring that their supporters were aware of and prepared to comply fully with the Truce before it took effect. In light of this, a three-day delay was factored in to the agreement to allow for communication of, and compliance with, the ceasefire order. Consequently, many of the combatants who took part in military operations on 8 and 9 July 1921 did so in complete ignorance that the conflict was about to end. These men were motivated primarily by local tactical considerations and completely unaware that any military advantage gained from these exploits would soon be redundant. In some cases IRA units operating in isolated areas in the west of Ireland did not learn that a ceasefire had been agreed until after it came into effect. In these cases it is highly unlikely that any resulting fatalities were deliberately inflicted for vengeful purposes by perpetrators motivated by a belief that they could soon avail of an amnesty.

Both the IRA GHQ and the British military command in Ireland honoured to the letter the Truce agreement by attempting to ensure that its conditions were fully complied with, and they made strenuous efforts to ensure that no combatants under their respective commands engaged in offensive military operations after noon on 11 July 1921. The commanders of both armies also acted in the spirit of the agreement by cancelling planned military operations in the last days before the Truce. Acting on the orders of de Valera, IRA GHQ immediately cancelled the large-scale military offensive that had been scheduled to begin in Dublin, while the British command ordered their troops to cease military operations immediately, without waiting for the ceasefire to begin. The Truce dispatch issued to provincial IRA units ordered them to observe the impending ceasefire, but was ambiguous as to what action was to be taken in the interim. Some IRA commanders opted to cancel all military operations immediately, while others decided to carry out operations that had been planned before the announcement of the Truce. There is no credible evidence to suggest that the IRA GHQ favoured or encouraged a policy of exploiting the advent of the Truce for short-term military advantage, or as a final chance to engage in reprisal killings.

Just three provincial IRA units issued specific orders to launch military offensives following the announcement of the Truce. The order issued by the 1st Eastern Division IRA called specifically for the execution of loyalist civilians suspected of assisting British forces and the assassination of Irish RIC constables. However, these aspects of the orders were clearly ignored by the IRA units in the division, as not a single suspected informer was executed nor a single RIC constable assassinated in the divisional area after the order was issued. The sole result seems to have been an increase in sniping attacks on RIC barracks, which did not result in any fatalities. Unquestionably, there was a surge in IRA activity in Kerry in the final days of the conflict, in particular attacks on British patrols and RIC barracks that resulted in a number of British fatalities. However, IRA veteran testimony suggests that these were intelligence-based operations that had been planned several weeks before, at a time when IRA officers were unaware that a ceasefire was just beyond the horizon. There was no uniform response among the Kerry republicans after the announcement of the Truce as to whether attacks should be carried out in the interim before the conflict ended. In some cases, local IRA officers protested strongly against orders to carry out attacks, arguing that the potential loss of life could not be justified in the light of the impending end of the conflict, and cancelled planned operations. In other cases, such as the shooting of Sergeant Mears in Killarney, the IRA members involved decided to carry out an attack which, given the impending Truce, had no military value. While the decision by some IRA officers in Kerry to follow through with these plans after they learned of the Truce may have been of questionable military value, it did not violate the letter of the agreement.

The Tipperary No. 3 Brigade IRA also reacted to the Truce by issuing orders directing local IRA units to mount sniping attacks on RIC barracks. Again, this resulted in a myriad of barracks attacks in the final twenty-four hours of the conflict. In some cases the same British garrisons were attacked several times within a few hours, suggesting that these operations were not serious attempts to capture the barracks or to kill members of their garrisons, but were launched as a symbolic, psychological and propaganda exercise. They were intended to send a public message that the British forces had not defeated the IRA. Statistical analysis of the IRA's final military operations reveals that, contrary to previous claims, there was no last-minute change in IRA tactics towards attacks on so-called 'soft targets' in an attempt to inflict the maximum number of fatalities on its opponents before the Truce began. In fact, the evidence shows that there was a drop in the level of such attacks in the final days of the conflict as the IRA concentrated instead on symbolic attacks on British barracks, which were less likely to cause fatalities.

Nor does the evidence suggest that the IRA exploited the announcement of the Truce as an opportunity to exercise religious prejudices and kill Protestant civilians on the pretext that they were spies. The number of suspected civilian spies killed by the IRA in the immediate pre-Truce period has been significantly overestimated in previous research, and the actual number of civilians killed as alleged spies following the announcement of the Truce was not inordinately high when compared with similar periods during the conflict. A number of these civilians were killed before their IRA executioners were aware that a ceasefire had been agreed, and therefore knowledge of the Truce could not have been a motivational factor for their killers. Most of those targeted for execution appear to have had recent contact with the British forces and there is evidence to suggest that those killed were suspected by the IRA of having assisted the British forces. Suggestions that sectarianism was often a motivating factor for IRA violence directed against Protestant civilians, and in particular the killing of Protestants whom the IRA later alleged were spies, has dominated this field of research and public discourse on this particular period of Irish history for well over a decade. Yet the evidence provides little corroboration for the claim. The vast majority of suspected civilian spies executed by the IRA during the conflict were Catholics shot by their co-religionists. With specific regard to the claim that anti-Protestant sectarianism was a motivational factor in the killing of civilians by the IRA immediately before the Truce, the available evidence shows that Protestants and Catholics were targeted by the republicans in almost equal numbers.

Regarding allegations of similar prejudice against ex-soldiers suspected of spying by the IRA, it is clear that the case for such prejudice has been overstated and that ex-servicemen joined the IRA in significant numbers during the War of Independence. Many were promoted to senior positions within the IRA leadership. On the other side, there was a strong economic and political incentive for loyalist ex-soldiers to assist the British forces, and they regularly employed local ex-servicemen for intelligence purposes during the War of Independence. All of the civilians executed by the IRA as suspected spies following the announcement of the Truce had strong associations with the British forces, being either ex-soldiers, former RIC constables or RIC applicants. In the cases of Eric Steadman, Major O'Connor, John Poynton and John Begley, it would appear that the IRA was suspicious of them primarily because of their apparent recent contact with the British forces, and all of these men appear to have been under IRA investigation for some time, which suggests that their killings were not the result of opportunistic prejudice. While the timing of the capture of two of these men, William Nolan and John Begley, within minutes of the beginning of the Truce, and their subsequent execution after the Truce came into effect, were breaches of the agreement that were completely unjustifiable from a military standpoint as they happened in peacetime, there is no evidence to suggest that the IRA engaged in a 'rush for justice', attempting to kill as many suspected civilian spies as possible before the Truce came into effect. In many cases, the IRA inflicted non-fatal punishment on those accused of being British intelligence agents; as well as abducting and killing six suspected civilian spies, it released unharmed an equal number whom it had been holding captive.

One of the most controversial aspects of the IRA's military campaign in the immediate pre-Truce period was the assassination of RIC constables, yet an analysis of these killings shows that they were typical of IRA operations carried out during the entire conflict. A number of these killings were perpetrated by IRA Volunteers who were unaware that a ceasefire had been agreed and it is therefore unreasonable to cite the Truce as a factor. Members of the RIC who were attacked by the IRA following the announcement of the Truce were targeted deliberately for assassination, usually because of their involvement in intelligence work or reprisal killings. In these cases, the members of the British forces attacked had been identified for assassination long before the political developments that led to the Truce. Here, the Truce can be seen as a catalyst, speeding up a process that was already in motion. The killing of off-duty British soldiers, such as Private Larter and Sergeant Mears, was different in nature in that these were opportunistic killings with little or no military value. However, they were similar to attacks that had occurred earlier in the conflict and there is no evidence to suggest that they were planned specifically to coincide with the Truce.

By contrast, the execution of four British soldiers taken prisoner by the IRA, at Ellis Quarry on the night before the Truce, was unprecedented in scale, if not in nature. New evidence presented in this book shows that there was a link between this incident and the killing the previous night in similar circumstances of an IRA Volunteer by the British forces, which strongly suggests that the Ellis Quarry shootings were a reprisal killing primarily motivated by local factors and were not a knee-jerk reaction to the announcement of the Truce.

It cannot be said that the IRA made a point of killing as many members of the British forces as possible up to the last minute before the Truce, as has previously been claimed, since at least seven members of the British Army and five members of the RIC captured after the announcement of the ceasefire were released unharmed. Furthermore, the 'general hit-up', a widespread series of co-ordinated attacks against RIC personnel that had been planned, was cancelled at the last moment precisely because of the Truce. The recurring popular historical narrative is that, by July 1921, the IRA nationally had been so weakened by the actions of the British forces that the republicans were incapable of continuing a military campaign against legitimate military targets and had instead switched their focus to 'soft targets'. In fact, there were far more IRA attacks on British Army convoys, RIC curfew patrols and barracks than there were on off-duty members of the British forces from the announcement of the Truce to its implementation.

The Raglan Street ambush has been cited as the cause of sectarian rioting in Belfast the day before the Truce, which resulted in over twenty fatalities, the worst single day of violence in Belfast's long and troubled history. However, the evidence suggests that the 'ambush' was not planned as a last-minute offensive against the British forces, but appears to have been a defensive operation against an aggressive RIC and Ulster Special Constabulary incursion into the Falls Road area. An existing loyalist tradition of expressing opposition to political change by resorting to violent protest was probably equally important in fomenting the pre-Truce violence in the city. Loyalist fears about the disarmament of the Special Constabulary and the activities of Hibernians and nationalist ex-soldiers in expressing opposition to the Truce by conducting retaliatory sectarian attacks on Protestants were also contributory factors. Other causes that were entirely coincidental to the announcement of the Truce included the significant annual increase in sectarian tensions as 12 July approached, poor discipline within the Special Constabulary, the activities of the RIC 'murder gang', and a desire on the part of the RIC in Belfast and the Ulster Special Constabulary to avenge comrades killed by the IRA. While analysis and criticism of this bout of sectarian violence has apportioned blame primarily to the IRA as its instigator, the British forces were also culpable in instigating the violence and were responsible for a number of the subsequent killings.

Analysis of the activities of the British forces in the final days of the conflict shows that, again contrary to popular accounts, a number of military units did launch aggressive military actions targeting Irish republicans following the announcement of the Truce. The established narrative that the British forces withdrew to their barracks to adopt a policy of passive defence while awaiting the arrival of the ceasefire is true to the extent that the British military hierarchy in Ireland issued orders to refrain from offensive action and cancelled the executions of a number of republican prisoners. However, there were numerous examples where rank-and-file members of the British Army and RIC did not comply with this order. Instead, these troops continued their standard modus operandi, causing a significant number of civilian and republican fatalities in the process. The timing and nature of many of these offensive actions, including the Kilgobnet Mine Disaster, indicates that they were regular operations planned before the announcement of the Truce. Their occurrence so close to the ceasefire was entirely coincidental, and any resulting fatalities from these incidences cannot be considered as evidence of pre-ceasefire 'bloodlust' on the part of the British forces.

In other cases, such as the fatal shootings of John Foley and Hannah Carey, it is impossible to say to what extent, if any, news of the Truce motivated the British personnel responsible. The discipline of the British forces at the time was so poor that such killings were commonplace and it would be wrong to assume that Foley and Carey were killed in premeditated acts by British troops seeking vengeance in the final hours of the conflict. By contrast, the killing of Denis Spriggs, the attack on the Keogh family home during which Margaret Keogh was killed and the attempted assassinations of Tomás Malone and Patrick O'Reilly, were apparently premeditated attempts at reprisal killings carried out by members of the British forces who were aware that the Truce was imminent.

The announcement of the Truce caused British personnel to react in a number of different ways. Some welcomed the forthcoming armistice, withdrew immediately from the battlefield and reprieved prisoners whom they had been due to execute. Some of those angered by the announcement of the ceasefire sought opportunities for vengeance, or a final chance to confront the enemy in battle. Others carried out their duties as normal up to the final hour, but were careful not to breach the Truce once it had begun. An equally diverse range of actions and attitudes existed within the IRA at the time, yet the final acts of the republican military campaign have received infinitely more attention than their British counterparts. The allegation that the IRA exploited the immediate pre-Truce period as an opportunity to inflict maximum fatalities on its civilian and military opponents is not borne out by careful study and analysis of historical records. This allegation arose first in the contemporary unionist press as a means of expressing hostility to republicanism and was later reiterated in the memoirs of former British combatants. Subsequently it was used in the Irish Free State as a propaganda device to attack anti-Treaty republican 'Trucileers' during the Civil War, despite the fact that those responsible for some of the most controversial pre-Truce killings, such as the assassination of Constable Clarke and the Ellis Quarry killings, had taken a pro-Treaty stance during the Irish Civil War and were later appointed to senior political and police commands within the new Irish Free State. Subsequent generations of historians and other writers have often repeated the claim that the IRA exploited the advent of the Truce to launch an unwarranted and unprecedented last-minute campaign without examining its veracity. By focusing inordinately on IRA killings in the pre-Truce period, they have produced a biased history of the last days of the war and created a hierarchy of victimhood, lamenting the deaths of those killed in eleventh-hour IRA attacks while consistently ignoring equally important killings committed by the British forces in the same period.

The Irish War of Independence began with two significant events on 21 January 1919: the first meeting of Dáil Éireann in Dublin and the shooting of two RIC constables in Soloheadbeg,

Co. Tipperary. While the Soloheadbeg ambush is inextricably linked in the public consciousness with the national political events in Dublin, the fact is that the ambush was motivated by local factors and its occurrence on the same day that Dáil Éireann held its first meeting was a coincidence. The same applies to the last fatalities of the War of Independence inflicted after the announcement of the Truce. Most of the military operations that caused these fatalities had either been planned in advance, in ignorance of political developments in Dublin, or were the result of immediate local conditions and largely unrelated to the Truce. In short, there is no proof of a concerted military campaign by either side to inflict a maximum number of fatalities following the announcement of the Truce, and the events of the final days of the conflict were not unique.

As we approach the centenaries of the 1916 Rising, the Irish War of Independence and the Civil War, there is much debate about how the Irish Revolution of 1913 to 1923 should be remembered and commemorated. Given the nature of these events and the frequency with which the memory of 'the men of 1916' is invoked in Irish politics, debate about the morality and legitimacy of political violence is bound to continue – such debates are important, healthy and necessary in any society, but they must be based on fact. Myth, propaganda and fabricated 'evidence' have no part in historical and political debate, and historians, politicians, academics, newspaper columnists and media outlets that knowingly employ these devices must not be allowed to go unchallenged.

Appendix

Fatalities Mentioned in the Text that Occurred after the Announcement of the Truce

Frederick Cormer	Black and Tan	Shot by IRA
David Cummins	Civilian	Shot by IRA
Denis Spriggs	IRA Volunteer	Shot by British forces
Eric Steadman	Civilian	Shot by IRA
Draper Holmes	Civilian	Shot by IRA
Alfred G. Needham	Black and Tan	Shot by IRA
Thomas Burke	Civilian	Killed by trap-mine set by British forces
Thomas Cahill	Civilian	Killed by trap-mine set by British forces
James Dunford	Civilian	Killed by trap-mine set by British forces
William Dunford	Civilian	Killed by trap-mine set by British forces
Richard Lynch	Civilian	Killed by trap-mine set by British forces
Seán Quinn	IRA Volunteer	Killed by trap-mine set by British forces
Margaret Keogh	Cumann na mBan	Shot by unknown gunman (suspected British forces)
Bridget Dillon	Civilian	Shot by IRA
Thomas Conlon	RIC Constable	Shot by IRA
William Baxter	Civilian	Shot by nationalist/ republican sniper
Ernest Park	Civilian	Shot by nationalist/ republican sniper
Henry Mulholland	Civilian	Shot by loyalist gunmen
Alexander Hamilton	Civilian	Shot by loyalist gunmen
Peter Mackey	Civilian	Suffered fatal fall fleeing raiders at his home
Bernard Monaghan	Civilian	Shot by loyalist gunmen

James McGuiness	Civilian	Shot by loyalist gunmen
Frederick Craig	Civilian	Shot by loyalist sniper
Dan Hughes	Civilian	Shot by loyalist sniper
Patrick Hickland	Civilian	Shot by loyalist gunmen
William Mulligan	Civilian	Shot by nationalist/republican sniper
David McMullan	Civilian	Shot by nationalist/republican sniper
Patrick Devlin	Civilian	Shot by loyalist gunmen
James Lenaghan	Civilian	Shot by British forces
Daniel Joseph Hughes	Civilian	Shot by British forces
William Tierney	Civilian	Shot by British forces
Francis Robinson	Civilian	Shot by British forces
William Brown	Civilian	Shot by nationalist/republican sniper
Mary McGowan	Civilian	Shot by RIC/Special Constabulary
James Ledlie	IRA Volunteer	Shot by British forces
R. W. Williams	British soldier	Killed by IRA
John Foley	Civilian	Shot by British forces
Richard Larter	British soldier	Shot by IRA
John Flynn	IRA Volunteer	Shot by British forces
Richard Shanahan	IRA Volunteer	Shot by British forces
Jack Prendiville	IRA Volunteer	Shot by British forces
John Davies	British soldier	Shot by IRA
William Kelly	British soldier	Shot by IRA
William Ross	British soldier	Shot by IRA
George Rankin	British soldier	Shot by IRA
Edward Mears	British soldier	Shot by IRA
Hannah Carey	Civilian	Shot by British forces
Alfred Camm	British soldier	Shot by IRA
Albert Powell	British soldier	Shot by IRA
Harold Daker	British soldier	Shot by IRA
Henry Morris	British soldier	Shot by IRA
George B. O'Connor	Civilian	Shot by IRA

John William Reynolds	British soldier	Shot by IRA
John Poynton	Civilian	Shot by IRA
Alexander Clarke	RIC Constable	Shot by IRA
James King	RIC Constable	Shot by IRA
William J. Nolan	Civilian	Shot by IRA
John Begley	Civilian	Shot by IRA

ENDNOTES

1 INTRODUCTION

1   *Irish Independent*, 22 June 2011.

2   Richard Abbott, *Police Casualties in Ireland 1919–1922* (Cork, 2000), p. 265.

3   Eunan O'Halpin, 'In the Name of the Republic', TV3/Title Films Ireland, March 2013.

4   Anon, 'The Irish Rebellion in the 6th Divisional Area', *The Irish Sword*, vol. xxvii, no. 107, Spring 2010, p. 130.

5   W. Alison Phillips, *The Revolution in Ireland 1906–1923* (London, 1923), p. 216.

6   Nevil Macready, *Annals of an Active Life*, Vol. II (London, 1924), pp. 577–8.

7   *Ibid.*, p. 578.

8   Pádraig de Búrca and John F. Boyle (eds), *Free State or Republic?* (2nd edn; Dublin, 2002), pp. 2, 21, 66; Francis Carthy, Bureau of Military History, Witness Statement [hereafter BMH WS] 1040, pp. 27–8.

9   Gavin M. Foster, *The Irish Civil War and Society: Politics, Class and Conflict* (London, 2015), pp. 26–7, 65.

10 P. S. O'Hegarty, *The Victory of Sinn Féin* (2nd edn; Dublin, 1998), pp. 48, 94, 112.

11 Piaras Béaslaí, *Michael Collins and the Making of a New Ireland*, Vol. II (Dublin, 1926), p. 248.

12 T. Ryle Dwyer, *Tans, Terror and Troubles: Kerry's Real Fighting Story, 1913–23* (Cork, 2001), p. 7.

13 Richard Bennett, *The Black and Tans* (5th edn; London, 1970), p. 186.

14 Charles Townshend, *The British Campaign in Ireland 1919–1921: The Development of Political and Military Policies* (London, 1975), p. 198.

15 Joseph M. Curran, *The Birth of the Irish Free State 1921–1923* (Alabama, 1980), p. 61.

16 Tim Pat Coogan, *Michael Collins* (London, 1991), pp. 216–7.

17 Maryann Valiulis, *Portrait of a Revolutionary: General Richard Mulcahy and the Founding of the Irish Free State* (Dublin, 1992), p. 78.

18 Peter Hart, *The I.R.A. at War 1916–1923* (Oxford, 2003), pp. 71–2, 75.

19 *Ibid.*, p. 233.

20 Peter Hart, *Mick: The Real Michael Collins* (London, 2005), p. 277.

21 Marie Coleman, *The Irish Revolution 1916–1923* (New York, 2014), p. 94.

22 In a series of essays in *Irish Historical Studies* entitled 'Historical Revisions' T. W. Moody and Robert Dudley Edwards set out to challenge misconceptions about Irish history which they felt had been exploited for political ends. This took on a new significance following the outbreak of paramilitary violence in Northern Ireland in the 1960s. At the same time the 'official' version of Irish history in the southern Irish state, which held that

the 1916 Rising and War of Independence were the culmination of Irish
national aspirations, became problematic, given the use of lethal violence
by republican paramilitaries. Critics alleged that revisionism was driven by
an ideological agenda hostile to Irish republicanism and served the 'history
needs of the [political] establishment'. The ensuing dispute between supporters and opponents of revisionism brought a complex academic debate
to public attention. Today the term 'revisionist' is generally used to describe
historians, politicians and commentators accused of having a pro-British
and anti-republican bias. Those accused of being revisionists generally reject
the term as pejorative – with the exception of Eoghan Harris, who embraces
the label by using it to describe his political philosophy; Ciaran Brady (ed.)
Interpreting Irish History: The Debate on Historical Revisionism (Dublin,
1994).

23 *Evening Echo*, 14 September 2011; *Sunday Independent*, 18 September 2011.
24 *Sunday Independent*, 31 March 2013.
25 *The Irish Times*, 27 August 1994.

2 THE POLITICAL AND MILITARY ORIGINS OF THE TRUCE

1 William H. Kautt, *Ground Truths: British Army Operations in the Irish War of Independence* (Dublin, 2014), pp. 4–5.
2 David M. Leeson, *The Black and Tans: British Police and Auxiliaries in the Irish War of Independence* (Oxford, 2011) p. 221; *The Illustrated London News*, 29 January 1921.
3 Thomas Jones, *Whitehall Diary, Volume III: Ireland 1918–1925*, ed. Keith Middlemas (London, 1971), p. 9.
4 Irish Situation Committee, note by Mr Long, 29 July 1920 (National Archives United Kingdom, Cabinet Papers [hereafter NAUK, CAB] 24/110, CP 1703).
5 Davies to O'Brien, 19 March 1920 (National Library of Ireland, Art O'Brien Papers [hereafter NLI, AOBP], MS 8427).
6 Paul Bew, *Ireland: The Politics of Enmity 1789–2006* (Oxford, 2007), p. 401.
7 O'Brien to Collins, 8 July, 19 August 1920 (NLI, AOBP, MS 8430).
8 Michael Hopkinson (ed.), *The Last Days of Dublin Castle: The Mark Sturgis Diaries* (Dublin, 1999), p. 46.
9 Thomas, *Whitehall Diary*, p. 27.
10 Michael Hopkinson, *The Irish War of Independence* (Dublin, 2002), p. 180.
11 Dominic Price, *The Flame and the Candle: War in Mayo 1919–1924* (Cork, 2012), p. 171; Patrick Moylett, BMH WS 767, pp. 51–2.
12 Moylett, BMH WS 767, pp. 53, 66.
13 Griffith to Lloyd George (Parliamentary Archives, Lloyd George Papers [hereafter PA, LGP] F/91/7/7-24, 19 November 1920).
14 Ernest McCall, *The Auxiliaries: Tudor's Toughs. A Study of the Auxiliary Division Royal Irish Constabulary 1920–1922* (Newtownards, 2010), p. 62.
15 J. B. E. Hittle, *Michael Collins and the Anglo-Irish War* (Washington DC, 2011), p. 183.

16   C. J. Phillips to Lloyd George, 19 November 1920 (PA, LGP, LG/F/91/7/7–24).

17   Hart, *Mick*, p. 242. Another British officer, Hugh Montgomery, who was mortally wounded on Bloody Sunday, died in December 1920. Available at: http://www.dublin-fusiliers.com/cairo-gang/montgomery.html (accessed 17 August 2014).

18   Peter Cottrell, *The War for Ireland 1913–1923* (Oxford, 2009), p. 97.

19   Moylett, BMH WS 767, p. 68.

20   *Ibid.*, p. 70.

21   Hopkinson (ed.), *The Last Days of Dublin Castle*, pp. 82, 84.

22   Moylett, BMH WS 767, p. 71–2.

23   Abbott, *Police Casualties*, p. 157.

24   There has been a lengthy debate between academic and popular historians about what actually happened at Kilmichael. It has been questioned whether Tom Barry, the IRA officer who led the attack, committed a war crime by ordering his men to 'take no prisoners' following an apparent 'false surrender' by the RIC Auxiliaries. Barry had served in the British Army during the First World War and his actions at Kilmichael reflected his army training, which dictated that soldiers did not have to accept an enemy's 'surrender' until it had been established as genuine. For example, General Sir Lancelot Kiggell issued an order in June 1916: 'In the case of apparent surrender, it lies with the enemy to prove his intention beyond the possibility of misunderstanding, before the surrender can be accepted as genuine'; Niall Ferguson, *The Pity of War: Explaining World War One* (New York, 1999), pp. 385–6.

25   Jones, *Whitehall Diary*, p. 41.

26   Hopkinson, *The Irish War of Independence*, p. 148.

27   Anon, *An Officer's Wife in Ireland* (London, 1994), p. 73.

28   Hopkinson (ed.), *The Last Days of Dublin Castle*, p. 85.

29   Hopkinson, *The Irish War of Independence*, p. 181.

30   Royal Irish Academy, *The Dictionary of Irish Biography* [hereafter DIB], Vol. 9 (Cambridge 2009), p. 187.

31   Moylett, BMH WS 767, p. 70.

32   *Connacht Tribune*, 11 December 1920.

33   Haverty's motives in proposing the resolution are unclear, as his memoir was influenced by bitter local rivalries, personal disputes and Civil War politics. Haverty's political career was ruined by controversy about the 'Peace Resolution' and for decades afterwards he threatened legal action against anyone who published an account of the incident he objected to; 'Memoirs of an Ordinary Republican' (BMH, CD 72).

34   *Connacht Tribune*, 11 December 1920.

35   Tomás Bairead, BMH WS 408, p. 1.

36   Alice M. Cashel, BMH WS 366, p. 8.

37   Pádraic Ó Fathaigh, *Pádraic Ó Fathaigh's War of Independence: Recollections of a Galway Gaelic Leaguer*, ed. Timothy G. MacMahon (Cork, 2000), p. 61.

38   *Ibid.*

39   Michael Brennan, *The War in Clare 1911–1921: Personal Memoirs of the Irish War of Independence* (Dublin, 1980), p. 65.

40   Cabinet Conclusions, 8 December 1920 (NAUK, CAB 23/23, ff. 206–7).

41   Dorothy Macardle, *The Irish Republic* (5th edn; London, 1968), p. 380.

42   DIB, Vol. 7, p. 475.

43   Moylett, BMH WS 767, p. 70.

44   DIB, Vol. 7, p. 474.

45   Fearghal McGarry, '1916 and Irish Republicanism: Between Myth and History', in John Horne and Edward Madigan (eds), *Towards Commemoration: Ireland in War and Revolution 1912–1923* (Dublin, 2013), pp. 46–53.

46   Hopkinson (ed.), *The Last Days of Dublin Castle*, p. 103.

47   Jones, *Whitehall Diary*, p. 52.

48   Hittle, *Michael Collins and the Anglo-Irish War*, p. 183.

49   Hart, *Mick*, pp. 270–1.

50   Jerry Ryan (Ó Fiaich Library, Louis O'Kane Papers [hereafter LOKP], IV B 05).

51   Clune was a monarchist supporter of Home Rule and the British war effort during the First World War. He had also advocated conscription for Australia while serving as Catholic chaplain to the Australian forces. DIB, Vol. 2, pp. 602–3.

52   There were previous attempts by the Catholic hierarchy to halt the IRA's military campaign. Archbishop Gilmartin of Tuam attempted to prevent the IRA acting in his diocese and declared a 'Truce of God' in his diocese following an IRA ambush at Gallagh, Co. Galway in July 1920. Gilmartin denounced the IRA as 'murderers' and summoned an IRA officer to a meeting in an effort to dissuade him from starting a flying column; P. Murray, *Oracles of God: The Roman Catholic Church and Irish Politics 1922–37* (Dublin, 2000), p. 409.

53   Rev. J. T. McMahon, BMH WS 362, p. 1.

54   Collins to Griffith, 2 December 1920 (National Archives Ireland, Dáil Éireann Papers [hereafter NAI, DÉ], 234 A).

55   Collins to Joe McDonagh, 2 December 1920 (NAI, DÉ 234 A).

56   Brian Barton, *The Secret Court Martial Records of the Easter Rising* (Stroud, 2010), p. 91.

57   Michael Staines, BMH WS 944, p. 16.

58   Quoted in McMahon BMH WS 362, p. 14.

59   *Ibid.*, p. 15.

60   Dr Fogarty, *The Irish Press*, 20 June 1935.

61   Hittle, *Michael Collins and the Anglo-Irish War*, p. 183.

62   Coogan, *Michael Collins*, p. 197.

63   Hopkinson (ed.), *The Last Days of Dublin Castle*, p. 183.

64   McMahon, BMH WS 362, pp. 16–24.

65   Jones, *Whitehall Diary*, p. 44.

66   *Ibid.*, pp. 45–6.

67   *Ibid.*, p. 45. The bishop's decree was published in *The Cork Examiner*.

'DECREE OF BISHOP OF CORK IN REFERENCE TO AMBUSHES, KIDNAPPING AND MURDER Beside the guilt involved in these acts by reason of their opposition to the law of God, anyone who shall within these spaces of Cork, organise or take part in an ambush or kidnapping or otherwise be guilty of murder or attempted murder shall incur by the very fact the censure of excommunication. [Signed] Daniel Cohalan, Bishop of Cork'; *The Cork Examiner*, 12 December 1920. Emphasis in the original.

68   Hopkinson (ed.), *The Last Days of Dublin Castle*, p. 91.

69   *Ibid.*

70   Béaslaí, *Michael Collins and the Making of a New Ireland*, Vol. II, pp. 123–5.

71   Collins to Griffith, 14 December 1920 (NAI, DÉ 2/234B).

72   Hopkinson (ed.), *The Last Days of Dublin Castle*, p. 94.

73   Jones, *Whitehall Diary*, p. 47.

74   *Ibid*, pp. 47–8.

75   McMahon, BMH WS 362, p. 24.

76   Greenwood to Lloyd George, n/d December 1921 (PA, LGP LG/F/19/2/31).

77   Hopkinson, *The Irish War of Independence*, p. 184.

78   Jones, *Whitehall Diary*, pp. 57–67.

79   McMahon, BMH WS 362, p. 27.

80   Interview with Liam Deasy (Ernie O'Malley Notebooks, University College Dublin Archives [hereafter EOMN UCDA], P17b/086).

81   Hopkinson (ed.), *The Last Days of Dublin Castle*, p. 193.

82   Jones, *Whitehall Diary*, p. 51.

83   *Ibid.*, p. 54.

84   Jones to Bonar Law, 24 April 1921, cited in Jones, *Whitehall Diary*, p. 55.

85   Jones, *Whitehall Diary*, pp. 53–5.

86   *Ibid.*, p. 57.

87   *Ibid.*, p. 58.

88   *Ibid.*, pp. 60–1.

89   Thomas Jones to Bonar Law, 24 April 1921, cited in Jones, *Whitehall Diary*, p. 65.

90   Jones, *Whitehall Diary*, p. 70.

91   *Ibid.*, p. 66. Emphasis in the original.

92   Thomas Jones to Bonar Law, 24 April 1921, cited in Jones, *Whitehall Diary*, p. 65.

93   Hopkinson, *The Irish War of Independence*, p. 193.

94   Alan F. Parkinson, *Belfast's Unholy War* (Dublin, 2004), p. 125.

95   *Ibid.*, p. 121.

96   Hopkinson, *The Irish War of Independence*, p. 193.

97   *Ibid*, pp. 193–4.

98   Philip Knightley, *The First Casualty: The War Correspondent as Hero and Myth-Maker from the Crimea to Iraq* (London, 1975), p. 93.

99   Hugh Martin, *Ireland in Insurrection: An Englishman's Record of Fact* (London, 1921); Wilfrid Ewart, *A Journey in Ireland 1921* (London, 1922).

100 Barry Keane, *Massacre in West Cork: The Dunmanway and Ballygroman Killings* (Cork, 2014), p. 32.

101 Maurice Walsh, *The News from Ireland: Foreign Correspondents and the Irish Revolution* (London, 2008), p. 101.

102 *Ibid.*, p. 183.

103 Keane, *Massacre in West Cork*, pp. 31–2.

104 Robert B. Self (ed.), *The Austin Chamberlain Letters: the Correspondence of Sir Austin Chamberlain with his Sisters Hilda and Ida 1916–1937*, Vol. V (Cambridge, 1995), pp. 138–9.

105 Coleman, *The Irish Revolution*, p. 52.

106 *Ibid.*, p. 54.

107 *Ibid.*, p. 51.

108 William Sheehan, *British Voices from the Irish War of Independence 1918–1921* (Cork, 2005), p. 151.

109 Brian Inglis, *West Briton* (London, 1962), p. 31.

110 Bennett, *Black and Tans*, p. 70.

111 Coleman, *The Irish Revolution*, p. 50.

112 Jones, *Whitehall Diary*, p. 66.

113 *Ibid.*, p. 69.

114 William G. Fitzgerald, *The Voice of Ireland: A Survey of the Race and Nation from All Angles* (London, 1925), p. 5.

115 Keith Jeffery, *The British Army and the Crisis of Empire 1918–1922* (Manchester, 1984), p. 52.

116 John Pimlott, *The Guinness History of the British Army* (Enfield, 1993), p. 12.

117 Monthly Returns of the Distribution of the Army (NAUK, War Office Papers [hereafter WO] 73/1134).

118 Pimlott, *The Guinness History of the British Army*, p. 121.

119 Jeffery, *The British Army*, p. 1.

120 William H. Kautt, *Ambushes and Armour: The Irish Rebellion 1919–1922* (Dublin, 2010), p. 58.

121 Jeffery, *The British Army*, pp. 28, 54, 59–60.

122 Monthly Returns of the Distribution of the Army (NAUK, WO 73/114).

123 Jeffery, *The British Army*, pp. 127–8.

124 *Ibid.*, p. 12.

125 Cabinet Papers (NAUK, CAB 23/26/17–21); Jeffery, *The British Army*, p. 29.

126 Jeffery, *The British Army*, p. 16.

127 Jones, *Whitehall Diary*, p. 27.

128 Cabinet Papers (NAUK, CAB 23/26/47–21).

129 Jeffery, *The British Army*, p. 158.

130 Memorandum by General Staff, 20 January 1922 (NAUK, CAB 24/132 C.P. 3619).

131 William H. Kautt, 'Studying the Irish Revolution as Military History: Ambushes and Armour', *The Irish Sword*, vol. XXVII, no. 108, Summer 2010, p. 254.

132 *Ibid.*

133　Application for a bonus for District Inspectors: DI Ryan, Lurgan, Co. Armagh, 13 January 1921 (NAUK, PRO T 351/81).

134　Private Sibthorpe, Private Connelly, Private Hamilton and Private Dailly. Dailly's death was reported in the *Nenagh Guardian* as an 'accidental killing' even though he had shot himself through the mouth with a rifle.

135　Cabinet Papers (NAUK, CAB 24/123 C.P. 2965).

136　Monthly reports on desertion (NAUK, WO 35/172).

137　Jones, *Whitehall Diary*, pp. 17, 42, 51, 54–5.

138　Jeffery, *The British Army*, p. 90.

139　Richard Abbott, *Police Casualties in Ireland 1919–1922* (Cork, 2000), pp. 48, 169, 272. Abbott gives a figure of fifteen RIC fatalities in 1919, 178 in 1920, and 235 in 1921, before the Truce. Of the last figure, 176 occurred before June 1921. While Abbot's research is the most authoritative to date, his figures are not absolute. For example, he attributes the deaths of Constables John Kearney and Joseph Bourke to the IRA, when in fact both men were killed by other members of the RIC. I have adjusted Abbot's figures to exclude these two fatalities.

140　Available at www.cairogang.com/soldiers-killed/list-1921.html (accessed 17 August 2014).

141　The Chief Secretary's Office: Inspector General's Confidential Monthly Reports (NAUK, CO 904/108–115); Abbott, *Police Casualties*, p. 7; available at www.cairogang.com/soldiers-killed/list-1921.html (accessed 17 August 2014).

142　Abbott, *Police Casualties*, p. 169.

143　Available at www.cairogang.com/soldiers-killed/list-1921.html (accessed 17 August 2014).

144　Abbott, *Police Casualties*, p. 272; figures for soldiers available at www.cairo-gang.com/soldiers-killed/list-1921.html (accessed 17 August 2014).

145　*Weekly Summary*, 6 June 1921.

146　For a lengthy, full and in-depth analysis of the balance of the military situation in Ireland at the time of the Truce, see 'Appendix 3: The IRA's Military Capability at the Time of the Truce', in Ó Ruairc, 'The Anglo-Irish Truce: An Analysis of its Immediate Military Impact 8–11 July 1921', PhD thesis, University of Limerick, 2014.

147　Sheehan, *British Voices*, p. 192.

148　B. L. Montgomery to Lt General A. C. Percival 14 October 1923, quoted in Sheehan, *British Voices*, pp. 151–2.

149　Home Office report on revolutionary organisations in the UK, 19 May 1921 (NAUK, Cabinet Papers 2952).

150　Jones, *Whitehall Diary*, p. 80.

151　*Foreign Affairs*, vol. 48, no. 2, January 1969, p. 214.

152　Hopkinson, *The Irish War of Independence*, pp. 194–5.

153　Tom Casement Diary (University College Dublin, de Valera Papers [hereafter UCDA, DeVP] 1321).

154　*Ibid.*

155　Hopkinson, *The Irish War of Independence,* p. 195.

156　*Ibid.*, p. 194.

157 Jones, *Whitehall Diary*, p. 76.
158 Macready to Miss F. Stevenson, 20 June 1921 (PA, LGP LG/F/36/2/19).
159 Jones, *Whitehall Diary*, pp. 78–9.
160 Sheehan, *British Voices*, p. 91.
161 Jones, *Whitehall Diary*, p. 60.
162 Earl of Midleton Papers (NAUK, PRO/30/67/45/2652).
163 Dáil Éireann official correspondence relating to the peace negotiations (BMH, CD 120/3).
164 Coogan, *Michael Collins*, p. 215.
165 Valiulis, *Portrait of a Revolutionary*, p. 79.
166 Midleton Papers (NAUK PRO/30/67/45/2650).
167 *Ibid.* (NAUK PRO/30/67/45/2657).
168 Valiulis, *Portrait of a Revolutionary*, p. 79.
169 Midleton Papers (NAUK, PRO/30/67/45/2652).
170 Macready, *Annals*, Vol. II, pp. 571–7.
171 *Ibid.*
172 For more, see: 'Appendix 2: Analysis of the Reasons for the Failure of the December 1920 Truce Negotiations', in Pádraig Ó Ruairc, 'The Anglo-Irish Truce: An Analysis of its Immediate Military Impact 8–11 July 1921', PhD thesis, University of Limerick, 2014.
173 Kautt, *Ground Truths*, pp. 4–5.
174 O'Hegarty, *Victory of Sinn Féin*, p. 44.
175 *An t-Óglach*, 22 July 1921.
176 Kautt, *Ground Truths*, pp. 5–6.
177 *The Record of the Rebellion, Volume IV: '5th Division History'*, Appendix XXI, 'Interpretation of the "Agreement" of 11th July 1921 by GOC 5th Division', p. 120, in Jeudwine Papers, Imperial War Museum.
178 Macready, *Annals*, Vol. II, p. 583.
179 Kautt, *Ground Truths*, p. 6; Keane, *Massacre in West Cork*, pp. 30–1.
180 Kautt, *Ground Truths*, p. 179.
181 William Murphy, *Political Imprisonment and the Irish 1912–1921* (Oxford, 2014), p. 246; Kautt, *Ground Truths*, pp. 4–5.
182 *Weekly Summary*, 11 July 1921.
183 Tomás Kenny, *Galway: Politics and Society 1910–23* (Dublin, 2011), p. 35. Kenny claims that there were no British reprisals after the Ballyturin Ambush in Galway, commenting: 'Strangely given the relatively high ranking of the Army and RIC men [killed], there was no retaliation, perhaps indicating the perception that a truce was not far away.' However, the ambush was followed by widespread British reprisals, including the killing of an RIC constable who had republican sympathies and the destruction of several houses and a local business; Cormac Ó Comhraí, *Revolution in Connacht: A Photographic History 1913–1923* (Cork, 2013), p. 117.
184 Townshend, *The British Campaign in Ireland*, p. 197.
185 Macready, *Annals*, Vol. II, pp. 571–7.
186 Joseph E. Persico, *Eleventh Month, Eleventh Day, Eleventh Hour: Armistice Day 1918, World War 1 and Its Violent Climax* (London, 2005), p. 360.

187 Edward Paice, *Tip & Run: The Untold Tragedy of the Great War in Africa* (London, 2007), p. 387.

188 William Sheehan, *Hearts & Mines, The British 5th Division, Ireland 1920–1922* (Cork, 2009), p. 103.

189 'The 52nd in Ireland', *Regimental Chronicle* 1921 (Soldiers of Oxfordshire Trust Archives).

190 Summary of Outrages Reported by the Police, July 1921 (NAUK, CO 904/146).

191 Douglas V. Duff, *Sword for Hire: The Saga of a Modern Free-Companion* (London, 1934), pp. 83–4.

192 Castletownroche Detachment Log, 9 July 1921 (The National Army Museum).

193 Sheehan, *Hearts & Mines*, p. 104.

194 C. S. Andrews, *Dublin Made Me: An Autobiography* (Cork, 1979), p. 154.

195 Seán Prendergast, BMH WS 755, pp. 538.

196 James Fulham, BMH WS 630, p. 24.

197 Joseph O'Connor, BMH WS 487, pp. 58–9.

198 Seán Prendergast, BMH WS 755, pp. 537–8.

199 Tom Barry, in K. Griffith and T. E. O'Grady (eds), *Curious Journey: An Oral History of Ireland's Unfinished Revolution* (London, 1982), p. 238.

200 Interview with Paddy Donoughue (EOMN UCDA P17b/112).

201 James J. Comerford, *My Kilkenny IRA Days 1916–1922* (Kilkenny, 1980), p. 817.

202 Michael Ó Droighnáin, BMH WS 1718, p. 37.

203 Patrick Butler, BMH WS 1187, p. 20.

204 Seamus Babington, BMH WS 1595, p. 149.

205 Brennan, *The War in Clare*, p. 104.

206 Daniel Ryan, BMH WS 1007, p. 24.

207 Connie Neenan (Cork City and County Archives [hereafter CCCA], Neenan Memoir, p. 70); Ted O'Sullivan, BMH WS 1478, p. 43; Tom Barry, in Pat Twohig, *Green Tears for Hecuba* (Cork, 1994), p. 79.

208 James O'Toole, BMH WS 1084, p. 19; Patrick McKenna, BMH WS 911, p. 10.

209 Comerford, *My Kilkenny IRA Days*, pp. 817–23.

210 Michael Doherty, BMH WS 1583, pp. 11–12.

211 Dónal Ó hÉalaithe, *Memoirs of an Old Warrior* (Cork, 2014), pp. 219–20.

212 The only veteran who claimed to have had prior knowledge of the Truce was Seamus Finn, adjutant of the IRA's 1st Eastern Division. Finn said that the IRA Meath Brigade had received about a week's notification of the forthcoming Truce and were ordered to kill suspected spies before the ceasefire began. However, none of the other IRA veterans from the 1st Eastern Division or the Meath Brigade have supported his claim and no spies were killed in Meath in the week before the Truce. What Finn was most probably referring to was the ceasefire order he issued on 9 July 1921, which specified that action should be taken against suspected spies before the Truce began; Seamus Finn, BMH WS 1060, p. 58.

213 BMH CD 284.

214 James Durney, *The Volunteer: Uniforms, Weapons and History of the Irish Republican Army 1913–1997* (Naas, 2004), p. 31. Emphasis in the original.

215 This order is signed 'Divisional Adjutant'– this was Finn's rank; see 'IRA Officers and Units, 11 July 1921: The Bureau of Military History List', in Noelle Grothier and Anthony Kinchella (eds), *The Irish Sword*, vol. XXVII, no. 110.

3 THE EXECUTION OF SUSPECTED SPIES

1 The anger generated by reprisals meant that the British forces often had to gather intelligence from a local population that was isolated and alienated from them. By contrast, the IRA operated using intimate local knowledge and information gleaned from a population that was generally supportive of it. Major General Douglas Wimberley stated that 'we were now in what was largely a hostile country, and … maybe 75 per cent of all local inhabitants … viewed us with enmity'; Sheehan, *British Voices*, pp. 98, 173.

2 In general, the IRA seems to have used the labels 'spy' and 'informer' as interchangeable terms. IRA leader Tom Barry maintained that 'informers' were typically unpaid, independently wealthy loyalists: 'big landlords, gombeen men and all these types … quite a number of what was called the ascendancy were informers'. Barry defined spies as 'paid scoundrels' who came from more impoverished backgrounds. A more accurate definition might be that an informer was a member of a local community who, motivated by political or personal factors, breached the popular policy of boycotting the British forces by volunteering information, whereas spies were usually strangers to an area who employed clandestine methods, disguises and false identities to gather information in return for financial reward; Charles Townshend, *The Republic: The Fight for Irish Independence* (London, 2013), p. 263.

3 For example, the various French resistance organisations are estimated to have killed around 9,000 people in extra-judicial executions during what is termed the *épuration sauvage*. The majority of those executed were policemen accused of aiding the Nazis, suspected civilian informers and collaborators; Matthew Cobb, *The Resistance: The French Fight Against the Nazis* (London, 2009), pp. 185, 280.

4 Caoimhe Nic Dháibhéid, *Seán MacBride: A Republican Life 1904–1946* (2nd edn; Liverpool, 2014), p. 43.

5 The figure given here only includes those killed up to the end of the War of Independence in July 1921. This figure is higher than that in recent research by Eunan O'Halpin, who gives a figure of 181 civilians killed by the IRA as spies between February 1920 and January 1922. O'Halpin includes a number of men in his study such as Bell and Byrne (aka Jameson) who I have excluded from my total as they were employed by the British authorities as professional intelligence agents at the time of their deaths, rather than being civilians who engaged in intelligence work of their own volition; Eunan O'Halpin, 'Problematic Killing during the War of Independence and its

Aftermath: Civilian Spies and Informers', in James Kelly and Marian Lyons (eds), *Death and Dying in Ireland, Britain and Europe: Historical Perspectives* (Dublin, 2013), pp. 328–9.

6   H. B. C. Pollard, *The Secret Societies of Ireland: Their Rise and Progress* (2nd edn; Kilkenny, 1998), p. 182.

7   Anon, 'The Irish Rebellion in the 6th Divisional Area', pp. 85, 99.

8   Arthur Hezlet, *The 'B' Specials: A History of the Ulster Special Constabulary* (Belfast, 1997), p. 35.

9   Jane Leonard, 'Getting Them at Last: The IRA and Ex-servicemen', in David Fitzpatrick (ed.), *Revolution? Ireland, 1917–23* (Dublin, 1990), p. 121.

10   *Ibid.*, p. 125.

11   David Fitzpatrick, *The Two Irelands 1912–1939* (Oxford, 1998), p. 95.

12   It is an astonishing suggestion that a century later a historian could discern with any degree of certainty the private life, sexual orientation and activities of the IRA's victims, especially given that homosexuality was illegal in the 1920s and adulterers generally kept their affairs a secret. Others have attributed similarly bizarre and unreliable motives to IRA killings. For example, Charles Townshend claimed that moral outrage led the IRA to kill Patrick O'Gorman, a Limerick farmer, because he was involved in an extramarital sexual relationship. In fact, the Limerick IRA did not succeed in killing O'Gorman, and there is ample evidence which suggests that he was targeted because he had passed intelligence to the British forces that led to the killing of an IRA officer; Townshend, *The Republic*, p. 266; Tom Toomey, *The War of Independence in Limerick 1912–1921* (Limerick, 2010), pp. 295–7.

13   Peter Hart, *The I.R.A. & Its Enemies: Violence and Community in Cork, 1916–1923*, pp. 304–15; Hart, 'Definition: Defining the Irish Revolution' in Joost Augusteijn (ed.), *The Irish Revolution, 1913–23* (London, 2002), p. 26; Hart, 'The Protestant Experience of Revolution in Ireland', in Richard English and Graham Walker (eds), *Unionism in Modern Ireland* (Dublin, 1996), p. 89.

14   Hart, *The I.R.A. at War*, pp. 19, 235.

15   Hart, *Mick*, p. 277; Hart, *The I.R.A. at War*, p. 19.

16   O'Halpin, 'Problematic Killing', in Kelly and Lyons (eds), *Death and Dying in Ireland, Britain, and Europe*, pp. 327–31.

17   Marie Coleman, *County Longford and the Irish Revolution 1910–1923* (Dublin, 2006), p. 154.

18   Coleman, *The Irish Revolution*, p. 94.

19   Provisional Military Court of Inquiry in lieu of Coroner's Inquest [hereafter PMCILCI] on Andrew Knight (NAUK, WO 35/153B); on John Moloney (NAUK, WO 35/155B); on William Alexander McPhearson (NAUK, WO 35/153B).

20   *The Irish Times*, 27 August 1994.

21   Patrick Mannix, BMH WS 502, p. 4. Mannix, a DMP constable who was secretly working for IRA intelligence, claimed that Knight was a spy: 'I supplied information that Andrew Knight, a tram inspector on the Dalkey

line, was a very active anti-IRA man and that he was supplying information about IRA activities to the British military.'

22 *The Irish Times*, 27 August 1994.

23 RIC County Inspector's Reports (NAUK, CO 904/116).

24 Valiulis, *Portrait of a Revolutionary*, p. 78.

25 Executions by IRA, 1921 (National Library of Ireland, CP, Microfilm 920); only three of those named at the end of the document were listed under July 1921 – George B. O'Connor, Eric Steadman and John Poynton – were actually killed in the final days of the conflict.

26 Gerard Murphy, *The Year of Disappearances: Political Killings in Cork 1921–1922* (Dublin, 2010), pp. 300–6, 323.

27 *Ibid.*, pp. 101, 181, 225–6.

28 Interview with Connie Neenan (EOMN UCDA P17b/112); Murphy, *Year of Disappearances*, pp. 300–6.

29 O'Malley's son Cormac K. H. O'Malley, custodian of the O'Malley notebooks, has confirmed the accuracy of my transcription of the account, which shows that Neenan referred to two spies killed before the Truce and not three Protestant teenagers killed afterwards as Murphy alleged. When questions were raised about the accuracy of Murphy's transcription he initially defended it. However, Murphy later conceded that his transcription was inaccurate and corrected it in the second edition of his book. Despite admitting to this error, Murphy continues to insist that Neenan's interview with O'Malley supports his claim that three Protestant teenagers were abducted by the IRA and killed. For more see: *Sunday Tribune*, 16 January 2011; Murphy, *Year of Disappearances*, p. 173; *History Ireland*, November/December 2011.

30 Murphy, *Year of Disappearances*, p. 302.

31 Summary of Outrages Reported by the Police, July 1921 (NAUK, CO 904/146).

32 Murphy, *Year of Disappearances*, pp. 229–30.

33 *The Southern Star*, 18 February 1922.

34 Barry Keane, 'Ethnic Cleansing? Protestant Decline in West Cork between 1911 and 1926', *History Ireland*, March /April 2012.

35 *Observer-Reporter*, a Washington county newspaper, 3 December 1979.

36 Eunan O'Halpin, 'In the Name of the Republic' (TV3/Title Films, March 2013). For a review of the programme, see *History Ireland*, May/June 2013.

37 *The Irish Times*, 22 August 1921.

38 Activity report of O/C G. Coy for Month of July 1921 (UCDA, Richard Mulcahy Papers [hereafter RMP], P7/A/23); Borgonovo, John, *Spies, Informers and the Anti-Sinn Féin Society* (Dublin, 2007), p. 69.

39 *The Irish Times*, 22 August 1921; Jasper Ungoed, *Jasper Wolfe of Skibbereen* (Cork, 2008), p. 122.

40 Ungoed, *Jasper Wolfe*, p. 122.

41 *The Irish Times*, 22 August 1921.

42 Summary of Outrages Reported by the Police, July 1921 (NAUK, CO 904/146).

43   Timothy Tierney, BMH WS 1227, pp. 12–13.

44   Paul Mulcahy, BMH WS 1434, p. 14.

45   *The Irish Times*, 11 July 1921.

46   Paul Mulcahy, BMH WS 1434 pp. 14; Timothy Tierney, BMH WS 1227, p. 12.

47   Timothy Tierney, BMH WS 1227, p. 12.

48   Paul Mulcahy, BMH WS 1434, p. 14.

49   Coleman, *County Longford and the Irish Revolution*, p. 154.

50   T. Ryle Dwyer, *Michael Collins: The Man Who Won the War* (Cork, 2009), pp. 153, 161.

51   Compensation Commission Register of Cases (NAUK, CO 905/15).

52   Paul Mulcahy, BMH WS 1434, p. 14.

53   Ernie O'Malley, *On Another Man's Wound* (4th edn; Dublin, 2008), p. 380.

54   PMCILCI on an unknown man found at Puttaghaun, Tullamore (NAUK, WO 35/159B).

55   RIC County Inspector's Report for Offaly, July 1921 (NAUK, CO 904/115); PMCILCI on an unknown man found at Puttaghaun, Tullamore (NAUK, WO 35/159B).

56   Interview with Jim Harris (EOMN UCDA P17b/120).

57   PMCILCI on an unknown man found at Puttaghaun, Tullamore (NAUK, WO 35/159B).

58   Interview with Seán Magennis and Jim Harris (EOMN UCDA P17b/120).

59   *Ibid.*

60   'Military Intelligence in the Black and Tan Days', O'Donoghue Papers (NLI, MS 31/443).

61   Thomas Earls Fitzgerald, 'The Execution of Spies and Informers in West Cork, 1921', in David Fitzpatrick (ed.) *Terror in Ireland 1916–1923* (Dublin, 2012), p. 184.

62   IRA Intelligence Department, November 1920, O'Donoghue Papers (NLI, MS 31/202).

63   Wilfrid Ewart, *A Journey in Ireland 1921* (London, 1922), pp. 127–9.

64   Kenneth Strong, *Intelligence at the Top: The Recollections of an Intelligence Officer* (London, 1969), p. 1.

65   Casualties – British Military and Police (IMA, A/0614).

66   Interview with Seán Magennis (EOMN UCDA P17b/120).

67   PMCILCI on an unknown man found at Puttaghaun, Tullamore (NAUK, WO 35/159B).

68   *Ibid.*

69   RIC County Inspector's Report for Cork, July 1921 (NAUK, CO 904/115).

70   *The Cork Examiner*, 12, 15, 17 October 1921.

71   Connie Neenan (CCCA, Neenan Memoir, pp. 70a–71).

72   Colman O'Mahony, *Maritime Gateway to Cork: A History of the Outports of Passage West and Monkstown, 1754–1942* (Cork, 1986), p. 104.

73   *Cork Constitution*, 21 April 1921.

74   O'Mahony, *Maritime Gateway to Cork*, p. 104.

75   Interview with Mick Murphy (EOMN UCDA P17b/112).

76 *Cork Constitution*, 10 February 1921; *The Cork Examiner*, 15 February 1921.

77 Mick Murphy, BMH WS 1547, p. 36.

78 Cork East Riding Criminal Injury Book, February–October 1921 (NAI, Cork Crown and Peace Officers Records). It is unclear whether this was a separate attempt on O'Connor's life or if it was a reference to Reilly's killing. The former seems more likely.

79 Interview with Florrie O'Donoghue (EOMN UCDA P17b/96).

80 Compensation Commission Register of Cases (NAUK, CO 905/15).

81 PMCILCI on John Poynton (NAUK, WO 35/157B).

82 RIC Register (NLI, Microfilm).

83 *Ibid.*

84 Michael Rafter, *The Quiet County: Towards a History of the Laois Brigade IRA and Revolutionary Activity in the County 1913–1923* (Naas, 2005), p. 96.

85 Executions by IRA, 1921 (NLI, CP, Microfilm 920).

86 *Ibid.*

87 *Ibid.*

88 Edward Brennan, BMH WS 1514, pp. 4–5.

89 Compensation Commission Register of Cases (NAUK, CO 905/15).

90 RIC County Inspector's Report for Cork, July 1921 (NAUK, CO 904/115).

91 John Borgonovo, *Spies, Informers and the Anti-Sinn Féin Society* (Dublin, 2007), p. 69.

92 Robert Ahern, BMH WS 1676, p. 8.

93 Liam Ó Duibhir, *The Donegal Awakening: Donegal and the War of Independence* (Cork, 2009), pp. 128–9.

94 Tom Toomey, *The War of Independence in Limerick 1912–1921* (Limerick, 2010), p. 467.

95 East Clare Brigade, Report to IRA GHQ (UCDA, RMP, P7/A/17).

96 Pa Scannell, IRA Pension Application, quoted by Gerard Murphy; available at https://www.year-of-disappearances.blogspot.ie/2011/10/ response1-to-padraig-og-o-ruairc.html?m=1 (accessed 17 August 2014). Scannell's pension application, like those of other War of Independence veterans, is currently a sealed file in the Irish Military Archives. However, some scholars have been given privileged access and have been able to quote details from these files, although they are currently inaccessible to the general public. John Borgonovo, review article, 'Revolutionary Violence and Irish Historiography' in *Irish Historical Studies*, xxxviii, no. 150 (November 2012).

97 Activity report of O/C G. Coy for Month July 1921 (UCDA, RMP, P7/A/23).

98 Seán O'Connell, BMH WS 1706, p. 9.

99 Annie Begley to Minister of Defence, 6 October 1922 (DOD Series, A/07360).

100 Interview with Connie Neenan (EOMN UCDA P17b/112).

101 *Ibid.*

102 Denis Mulchinock, Michael Courtney and Jeremiah Murphy, BMH WS 744, p. 14.

103 F. O'Donoghue, Intelligence Officer (IO) First Southern Division report to Chief of Staff, 24 June 1921 (UCDA, RMP, P17A/20); Denis Mulchinock, Michael Courtney and Jeremiah Murphy, BMH WS 744, pp. 14–15.

104 Anonymous, 'The Irish Rebellion in the 6th Divisional Area', p. 82.

105 Mulchinock, Courtney and Murphy, BMH WS 744, pp. 15–16.

106 Anon, 'The Irish Rebellion in the 6th Divisional Area', p. 82.

107 Michael O'Connell, BMH WS 1428, pp. 14–15.

108 John Moloney, BMH WS 1036, p. 17.

109 *Ibid.*, 'It was found essential that the police or other "identifiers" should not be seen, otherwise, if recognised as identifiers, they became marked men and liable later for assassination', Sheehan, *British Voices*, p. 93.

110 F. O'Donoghue, Intelligence Officer (IO) First Southern Division report to Chief of Staff, 24 June 1921 (UCDA, RMP, P17A/20).

111 Saunders and McPhearson were neighbours. Saunders lived at 3 Broom Lane, Mallow, while McPhearson lived just 200 yards away at 4 Bridge Street, Mallow. The 'spy label' attached to McPhearson's body indicated that the IRA suspected he was associated with a network of spies in the town; PMCILCI on William Alexander McPhearson (NAUK, WO 35/153B).

112 Interview with Owen Hayes (EOMN UCDA P17b/123); Mulchinock, Courtney and Murphy, BMH WS 744, p. 15.

113 Mulchinock, Courtney and Murphy, BMH WS 744, p. 15.

114 Seán O'Connell, BMH WS 1706, p. 9.

115 'Activity report of O/C G Coy for Month July 1921' (UCDA, RMP, P7/A/23).

116 Compensation Commission Register of Cases (NAUK, CO 905/15).

117 For example, on 10 July IRA Volunteers raided the home of Thomas Goulding, a Catholic ex-soldier, who lived at College Road, Cork city. Goulding escaped through the back door unnoticed and sought refuge in the adjacent RIC barracks. He had previously been shot and wounded in an attempt on his life; RIC County Inspector's Report for Cork, July 1921 (NAUK, CO 904/115).

118 Interview with Mick Burke (EOMN UCDA P17b/103).

119 Interview with Andrew Kennedy (EOMN UCDA P17b/114).

120 *The Cork Examiner*, 12 July 1921.

121 Seamus Babington, BMH WS 1595, pp. 110–28.

122 Michael Dillon Snr application to the Irish Grants Commission (NAUK, CO 762/3).

123 Michael-Thomas Dillon application to the Irish Grants Commission (NAUK, CO 762/119).

124 Seamus Babington, BMH WS 1595, pp. 123–5.

125 Information from Phil Flood, local historian, Ballypatrick, Kilcash, Co. Tipperary.

126 Seamus Babington, BMH WS 1595, p. 123.

127 *Ibid.*

128 Seamus Babington, BMH WS 1595, p. 124; alternatively, Andrew Kennedy

stated that he was in charge of this operation and that it was conducted by members of the IRA's Carrick-on-Suir Company; interview with Kennedy (EOMN UCDA P17b/114).

129 Seamus Babington, BMH WS 1595, p. 128.

130 PMCILCI on Bridget Dillon (NAUK, WO 35/149A).

131 *Ibid.*

132 As claimed by Kilmartin, BMH WS 881, pp. 19–20; interview with Andrew Kennedy (EOMN UCDA P17b/114); Kilmartin claimed that Michael Dillon had opened fire from inside the house, and that Bridget Dillon was killed when the IRA returned fire. Kennedy made a similar claim. Michael Dillon Snr told the British Military inquest into his daughter's death that he threw the glass jug at a member of the IRA who was attempting to break in through the window of his home. A possible explanation is that the IRA Volunteers interpreted the noise of the jug smashing as gunshot, and opened fire; PMCILCI on Bridget Dillon (NAUK, WO 35/149A).

133 PMCILCI on Bridget Dillon (NAUK, WO 35/149A).

134 Seamus Babington, BMH WS 1595, p. 125.

135 Michael Dillon Snr application to the Irish Grants Commission (NAUK, CO 762/3); William Dillon's body was discovered buried in the grounds of Tollomain Castle at Fethard, Co. Tipperary the following October. It was alleged that his remains had been mutilated. Michael Dillon Snr apparently blamed members of the Free State Army for this and stated to the Irish Grants Committee in 1929 that: 'It wasn't the Rebels that destroyed the remains of my son but the people put in power in Ireland by British Act of Parliament.' Following the discovery of William Dillon's body, the remaining members of the family left Ireland for East Sheen in London.

136 Michael-Thomas Dillon application to the Irish Grants Commission (NAUK, CO 762/119).

137 *The Irish Times*, 27 August 1994.

138 For O'Hanlon and Smyth, see RIC County Inspector's Report for Armagh, June 1921 (NAUK, CO 904 /115).

139 For Doyle, see Thomas Ryan, BMH WS 1442, p. 9; for Kennedy, see PMCILCI on William Kennedy (NAUK, WO 35/157A); for O'Dempsey, see PMCILCI on Michael J. O'Dempsey (NAUK, WO 35/157A); for O'Donoghue, see RIC County Inspector's Report for Carlow, June 1921 (NAUK, CO 904/115); for Hackett, see Executions by IRA, 1921 (NLI, CP, Microfilm 920).

140 For Briody, see Séan Sheridan, BMH WS 1613, p. 17; for Newman, see PMCILCI on Hugh Newman (NAUK, WO 35/155B).

141 RIC County Inspector's Report for Clare, October 1920 (NAUK, CO 904/113); PMCILCI on J. Reilly (NAUK, WO 35/157B); PMCILCI on P. D'Arcy (NAUK, WO 35/147B); Pádraig Óg Ó Ruairc, *Blood on the Banner: The Republican Struggle in Clare* (Cork, 2009), pp. 186–7, 237–8, 250–3, 331. D'Arcy's execution was controversial and some IRA veterans later stated he was innocent; interview with John Burke (EOMN UCDA P17b/130). Liam Haugh mentions a fourth Clare man supposedly shot as

a spy in December 1920, but does not name him. This may be a reference to the killing of Joe Greene of Toonavoher in January 1921. However, contemporary reports suggest Greene's killing was agrarian, so he has not been included here; Liam Haugh, BMH WS 474, p. 26.

142   For Quinlisk, see Michael Murphy, BMH WS 1547, pp. 12–18; for Herlihy, see Jeremiah Keating, BMH WS 1657, p. 6; for Gordon, see Timothy O'Sullivan, BMH WS 719, p. 7; for O'Callaghan, see IRA Executions 1921 (NLI, CP, Microfilm 920); for Hawkes, see RIC County Inspector's Report for Cork, October 1920 (NAUK, CO 904/113); for Downing, see *The Cork Examiner*, 26 November 1920; for Blemens, see Seán O'Hegarty to Adj. General O'Sullivan (IMA, A/0535); for Horgan, see Emmet Dalton to Richard Mulcahy (IMA, A/0535); for Dwyer, see PMCILCI on Michael Dwyer (NAUK, WO 35/149A); for Bradfield, see RIC County Inspector's Report for Cork WR, January 1921 (NAUK, CO 904/114); for Rae, see IRA Executions 1921 (NLI, Collins Papers, Microfilm 920); for Bradfield, see PMCILCI on Thomas Bradfield (NAUK, WO 35/146A); for Kidney, see RIC County Inspector's Report for Cork WR, February 1921 (NAUK, CO 904/114); for Reilly, see RIC County Inspector's Report for Cork ER, February 1921 (NAUK, CO 904/114); for Johnson, see RIC County Inspector's Report for Cork WR, February 1921 (NAUK, CO 904/114); for Eady see RIC County Inspector's Report for Cork WR, February 1921 (NAUK, CO 904/114); for O'Leary, see *Cork Constitution*, 10 February 1921; for Sullivan, see *Cork Constitution*, 15 February 1921; for Beale, see *Cork Constitution*, 16 February 1921; for Walsh, see *The Irish Times*, 21 February 1921; for Sweetnam, see RIC County Inspector's Report for Cork WR, February 1921 (NAUK, CO 904/114); for Connell, see RIC County Inspector's Report for Cork WR, February 1921 (NAUK, CO 904/114); for Mohally, see RIC County Inspector's Report for Cork ER, February 1921 (NAUK, CO 904/114); for O'Sullivan, see RIC County Inspector's Report for Cork ER, February 1921 (NAUK, CO 904/114); for Alfred Cotter, see RIC County Inspector's Report for Cork WR, February 1921 (NAUK, CO 904/114); for Thomas Cotter, see RIC County Inspector's Report for Cork WR, March 1921 (NAUK, CO 904/114); for Noble, see *The Irish Times*, 22 August 1921; for John Sheehan, see RIC County Inspector's Report for Cork ER, March 1921 (NAUK, CO 904/114); for Good, see RIC County Inspector's Report for Cork WR, March 1921 (NAUK, CO 904/114); for Nagle, see IRA Executions 1921 (NLI, CP, Microfilm 920); for Lindsay, see *The Irish Times*, 22 August 1921; for Clarke, see *The Irish Times*, 22 August 1921; for Cornelius Sheehan, see Compensation Commission Register (NAUK, CO 905/15); for Lucey, see Edward Neville, BMH WS 1665; for McCarthy, see RIC County Inspector's Report for Cork ER, March 1921 (NAUK, CO 904/114); for Cathcart, see RIC County Inspector's Report for Cork ER, March 1921 (NAUK, CO 904/114); for Good, see RIC County Inspector's Report for Cork WR, March 1921 (NAUK, CO 904/114); for Denis Donovan, see RIC County Inspector's Report for Cork ER, April 1921 (NAUK, CO

904/115); for Stennings, see Compensation Commission Register (NAUK, CO 905/15); for Denis Finbar Donovan, see PMCILCI on Denis Finbar Donovan (NAUK, WO 35/149A); for John Sheehan, see Compensation Commission Register (NAUK, CO 905/15); for O'Callaghan, see RIC County Inspector's Report for Cork ER, April 1921 (NAUK, CO 904/115); for McCarthy, see IRA Executions 1921 (NLI, CP, Microfilm 920); for Harrison, see IRA Executions 1921 (NLI, CP, Microfilm 920); for O'Keefe, see IRA Executions 1921 (NLI, CP, Microfilm 920); for Saunders, see Florence O'Donoghue to Richard Mulcahy (UCDA, RMP, P17A /20); for Purcell, see RIC County Inspector's Report for Cork ER, May 1921 (NAUK, CO 904/115); for Lynch, see PMCILCI on James Lynch (NAUK, WO 35/153B); for Collins, see *The Irish Times*, 9 May 1921; for Walsh, see IRA Executions 1921 (NLI, CP, Microfilm 920); for Hawkins, see RIC County Inspector's Report for Cork ER, May 1921(NAUK, CO 904/115); for McMahon, see RIC County Inspector's Report for Cork ER, May 1921 (NAUK, CO 904/115); for O'Sullivan, see RIC County Inspector's Report for Cork ER, May 1921 (NAUK, CO 904/115); for Peacock, see RIC County Inspector's Report for Cork WR, May 1921 (NAUK, CO 904/115); for Fitzgibbon, see RIC County Inspector's Report for Cork WR, June 1921 (NAUK, CO 904/115); for O'Callaghan, see PMCILCI on Daniel O'Callaghan (NAUK, WO 35/156); for Crowley, see IRA Executions 1921 (NLI, CP, Microfilm 920); for Lynch, see RIC County Inspector's Report for Cork ER, June 1921 (NAUK, CO 904/115); for Patrick Sheehan, see RIC County Inspector's Report for Cork ER, June 1921 (NAUK, CO 904/115); for John Sullivan, see RIC County Inspector's Report for Cork WR, June 1921 (NAUK, CO 904/115); for Francis Sullivan, see RIC County Inspector's Report for Cork ER, July 1921 (NAUK, CO 904/116); for McPhearson, see RIC County Inspector's Report for Cork ER, July 1921 (NAUK, CO 904/116); for O'Connor, see RIC County Inspector's Report for Cork ER, July 1921 (NAUK, CO 904/116); for Nolan, see RIC County Inspector's Report for Cork ER, July 1921 (NAUK, CO 904/116); for Begley, see RIC County Inspector's Report for Cork ER, July 1921 (NAUK, CO 904/116). This list does not include Samuel Shannon, who died on 13 October 1920 having resisted an unidentified group of men who attempted to force their way into his home. Peter Hart has claimed that Shannon was executed by the IRA for spying, but it seems just as likely that Shannon was killed in a botched IRA arms raid or a bungled burglary by a criminal gang. Gilbert Fenton was also fatally wounded when armed men tried to force their way into his home. He died of his wounds six months later. His attackers cannot be identified and consequently their motives cannot be accurately ascribed. George Woodward and Joseph Boynes were killed near Mallow on 10 April 1921. The local RIC claimed the IRA was responsible, but did not clarify if the men had been killed on suspicion of being spies or for some other reason. William Bransfield, killed on 8 May 1921, was described at the inquest into his death as a 'Sinn Féiner'. A witness said that the masked men who killed him 'did not speak like men from Cork' and this seems to indicate that he was killed by members of the British forces and was not executed by the IRA on suspicion of spying.

143 For Straw, see *The Freeman's Journal*, 1 November 1920; for Herbert-Smith, see Hittle, *Michael Collins and the Anglo-Irish War*, p. 167; for McGrath, see Executions by IRA, 1921 (NLI, CP, Microfilm 920); for Doran, see Hittle, *Michael Collins and the Anglo-Irish War*, p. 226; for Ryan, see Executions by IRA, 1921 (NLI, CP, Microfilm 920); for O'Neill, see Executions by IRA, 1921 (NLI, CP, Microfilm 920); for Graham, see Patrick J. Brennan, BMH WS 1773, p. 22; for Barden, see Patrick J. Brennan, BMH WS 1773, p. 22; for Frasier, see *The Irish Times*, 24 May 1921; for Brady, see Executions by IRA, 1921 (NLI, CP, Microfilm 920); for Halpin, see Executions by IRA, 1921 (NLI, CP, Microfilm 920); for Pike, see Pádraig Yeates, *A City in Turmoil, Dublin 1919–1921* (Dublin, 2012), p. 180; for Knight, see Executions by IRA, 1921 (NLI, CP, Microfilm 920). This figure for Dublin does not include John Charles Byrne (aka Jameson), Alan Bell and Leonard Aldie Wilde, all of whom appear to have been in the full employment of the British intelligence services when killed.

144 For Fourvargue, see Hittle, *Michael Collins and the Anglo-Irish War*, p. 202.

145 D. M. Leeson, *The Black & Tans: British Police and Auxiliaries in the Irish War of Independence* (Oxford, 2011), pp. 48, 61. Leeson claimed that two other Galway men, Tom Malloy and Tom McKeever, were executed by the IRA, but both men were killed by the British forces. Leeson admitted this was a possibility in Malloy's case, but not that the same was true of McKeever; Thomas Manion, BMH WS 1408, pp. 15–16.

146 For Jasper, see Patrick McKenna, BMH WS 1205, p. 8; for Daly, see PMCILCI on Martin Daly (NAUK, WO 35/147B); for Nagle, see T. Ryle Dwyer, *Tans, Terror and Troubles*, p. 295; for O'Mahony, see *Ibid.*, p. 299; for Vicars, see *Ibid.*, p. 301; for O'Sullivan, see RIC County Inspector's Report for Kerry, April 1921 (NAUK, CO 904/115); for Fitzgerald, see T. Ryle Dwyer, *Tans, Terror and Troubles*, p. 308; for Kane, see RIC County Inspector's Report for Kerry, June 1921 (NAUK, CO 904/115).

147 For Power, see PMCILCI on Michael Power (NAUK, WO 35/157B); for Dunne, see PMCILCI on Phillip Dunne (NAUK, WO 35/149B).

148 For Kenny, see *The Irish Times*, 22 August 1921; for Cassidy, see *Irish Independent*, 7 January 1921; for O'Keefe, see Thomas Treacy, BMH WS 1093, p. 70; for Dermody, see Executions by IRA, 1921 (NLI, CP, Microfilm 920).

149 For Keyes, see PMCILCI on Peter Keyes (NAUK, WO 35/153A); for Poynton, see PMCILCI on John Poynton (NAUK, WO 35/157B).

150 For Latimer, see PMCILCI on Will Latimer (NAUK, WO 35/153A); for Harrison, see PMCILCI on John Harrison (NAUK, WO 35/151A).

151 John O'Callaghan, *Revolutionary Limerick: The Republican Campaign for Independence in Limerick, 1913–1921* (Dublin, 2010), pp. 171–84; Dalton appears to have been killed as the result of an internal IRA feud and it is likely that the allegation he had been a spy was later invented by his killers; Toomey, *War of Independence in Limerick*, pp. 283–91.

152 Coleman, *County Longford and the Irish Revolution,* pp. 153–4.

153 Stephen O'Donnell, *The Royal Irish Constabulary and Black and Tans in County Louth 1919–1922* (Louth, 2004), pp. 109–10.

154 For Bradley, see *The Irish Times,* 22 August 1921; for Donoghue, see Executions by IRA, 1921 (NLI, CP, Microfilm 920); for Smith, see Compensation Commission Register (NAUK, CO 905/15); for Keelan, see *The Irish Times,* 22 August 1921. William Gordon, who was executed by the IRA in Meath in June 1920, has not been included in the above list as he was sentenced to death as a murderer, having shot a young man named Clinton in an agrarian dispute.

155 Fearghal McGarry, *Eoin O'Duffy: A Self-Made Hero* (Oxford, 2005), pp. 64–73. It is unclear whether Hugh Duffy was killed solely because of the suspicion that he was a spy, or whether his membership of the USC was also a motivating factor. A ninth suspected spy, John McCabe, a Catholic ex-soldier, was shot by the IRA near Carrickmacross in April 1921 but apparently survived.

156 *The Irish Times,* 20 June 1921; RIC County Inspector's Reports, May–July 1921 (NAUK, CO 904/116).

157 For Canning, see interview with Frank Simmons (EOMN UCDA P17b/107, 137); for Ward, see Compensation Commission Register of Cases (NAUK, CO 905/15); for Heavy, see Luke Duffy, BMH WS 661, p. 31; for Elliot, see *Irish Independent,* 9 March 1921; for Gilligan, see Kathleen Hegarty Thorne, *They Put the Flag a-Flyin': The Roscommon Volunteers 1916–1921* (Oregon, 2005), p. 79; for Weymes, see *Ibid.,* p. 79; for Scanlon, see Frank Simmons, BMH WS 770, p. 32; for McCalley, see *Ibid.,* p. 32; for Maher, see Seamus O'Meara, BMH WS 1505, p. 50.

158 Michael Farry, *Sligo 1914–1921: A Chronicle of Conflict* (Trim, 1992), pp. 288–9; Michael Farry, *The Aftermath of Revolution: Sligo 1921–1923* (Dublin, 2000), pp. 192–3.

159 For Kirby, see *The Irish Times,* 7 September 1990; for Looby, see Patrick Butler, BMH WS 1187, pp. 13–14. In January 1921 the body of an unidentified man was found near Cahir, Co. Tipperary. The likelihood is that this unidentified man was the same person that Butler identified as Looby; RIC County Inspector's Report for Tipperary SR, January 1921 (NAUK, CO 904/114). For Ryan, see RIC County Inspector's Report for Tipperary SR, February 1921 (NAUK, CO 904/114); for Maher, see James Leahy, BMH WS 1454, pp. 67–8; for Meara, see James Leahy, BMH WS 1454, pp. 67–8. Lysaght was shot by the IRA on 7 March 1921 and died on 20 May 1921; PMCILCI on George Lysaght (NAUK, WO 35/153A); Joseph Brady RIC County Inspector's Report for Tipperary SR, March 1921 (NAUK, CO 904/114); Seán Hogan, *The Black and Tans in North Tipperary: Policing, Revolution and War 1913–1922* (Nenagh, 2013), p. 331. For Stone, see *The Irish Times,* 22, 26 June 1921 and Seán E. Walshe, BMH WS 1363, p. 8; for Cranley, see *The Irish Times,* 27 April 1921; for Boyle, see *The Irish Times,* 16 June 1921 and Seán E. Walshe, BMH WS 1363, p. 8; for Wallis, see Seán E. Walshe, BMH WS 1363, p. 8; for Healy see

Ibid.; for Maher, see Hogan, *The Black and Tans*, p. 383; for Cummins, see *The Irish Times*, 11 July 1921. Two suspected spies, Jerry Brien and Brian Turpin, were killed by the IRA in Tipperary on an unknown date in 1921, although it seems they were killed during the War of Independence rather than in the Truce period: 'The Upperchurch lads killed and buried two tramps, one of them was Jerry Brien a tinker from Newport … they shot Brian Turpin who had a lame step and some said he was shot wrong', interview with Paddy Dwyer (EOMN UCDA P17b/119).

160 Tommy Mooney, *Cry of the Curlew: A History of the Déise Brigade IRA and the War of Independence* (Dungarvan, 2012), p. 258.

161 For Lyons, see County Inspector's Report for Westmeath, November 1920 (NAUK, CO 904/113); for Blagriff, see Michael McCormack, BMH WS 1488, p. 33; for Johnston, see McCormack, BMH WS 1500, pp. 13, 45; for Lee, see Executions by IRA, 1921 (NLI, CP, Microfilm 920); for unidentified man, see RIC County Inspector's Reports May–July 1921 (NAUK, CO 904 / 116).

162 For Newsome, see Thomas Doyle, BMH WS 1041, p. 67; for the Skeltons, see James O'Toole, BMH WS 1084, pp. 14–15; for Morrisey, see Doyle, BMH WS 1041, p. 68.

163 In this case, the term 'Protestants' includes members of the Church of Ireland, Presbyterian and Methodist churches. It could be argued that the number of Protestants was highest in the historical province of Ulster, where the IRA shot very few spies and so Protestants were over-represented in terms of the proportion of the civilian population killed as alleged spies. However, it should be noted that Protestants in Ireland were given preferential treatment by the British authorities (the Church of Ireland was the established church until 1871) and also that the close links between the Protestant community and the British Army meant that Protestants were more likely to be loyalists.

164 Peter Hart (ed.), *British Intelligence in Ireland 1920–1921: the Final Reports* (Cork, 2002), p. 49.

165 León Ó Broin, *Protestant Nationalists in Revolutionary Ireland: The Stopford Connection* (Dublin, 1985), p. 177.

166 Interview with Flor Begley (EOMN UCDA P17b/111).

167 Anonymous, 'The Irish Rebellion in the 6th Divisional Area', p. 99.

168 Paddy Heaney, Pat Muldowney and Philip O'Connor (eds), *Coolacrease: The True Story of the Pearson Executions – an Incident in the Irish War of Independence* (Cork, 2008), p. 178.

169 *The Irish Times*, 14 January 1924.

170 Strong, *Intelligence at the Top*, p. 1.

171 Surnames have traditionally been used in Ireland as a means of ascertaining a person's religious denomination. The 1911 census records for Co. Tipperary show that 429 people named Cummins lived in the county at the time – of whom 419 were Catholic, so it would not be surprising if Byrne had assumed that David Cummins was a Catholic (NAI, 1911 Census).

172 PMCILCI on John Poynton (NAUK, WO 35/157B).

173 Interview with Seán Magennis (EOMN UCDA P17b/120).

174 Tom Crawley, BMH WS 718, p. 11.

175 Theological insight supplied by Fr Brian Murphy OBM, Glenstal Abbey, Co. Limerick.

176 Seán Farrelly, BMH WS 1734, p. 48; Michael Govern, BMH WS 1625, p. 7.

177 Thomas Morris in Galway is not included in this figure as he has already been counted as an ex-soldier.

178 Leonard, 'Getting them at last', p. 119.

179 Michael J. Whelan, *Allegiances Compromised. Faith, Honour and Allegiance: Ex-British Soldiers in the Irish Army 1913–1924* (Dublin, 2010).

180 Hittle, *Michael Collins and the Anglo-Irish War*, p. 96.

181 Borgonovo, *Spies, Informers and the Anti-Sinn Féin Society*, p. 82.

182 Ó Ruairc, *Blood on the Banner*, pp. 99, 157–63.

183 C. Browne, BMH WS 873, p. 10.

184 Neil Richardson, *A Coward if I Return, a Hero if I Fall: Stories of Irishmen in World War One* (Dublin 2010), pp. 328–31.

185 Phil Tomkins, *Twice a Hero: From the Trenches of the Great War to the Ditches of the Irish Midlands* (Gloucestershire, 2012), p. 88.

186 Borgonovo, *Spies, Informers and the Anti-Sinn Féin Society*, p. 82.

187 Hogan, *The Black and Tans*, p. 220.

188 File on Patrick Barnes, Ministry of Home Affairs, Public Record Office of Northern Ireland (PRONI, HA/5/2182).

189 Seamus McKenna, BMH WS 1016, p. 41.

190 Gerard Noonan, *The IRA in Britain 1919–1923: 'In The Heart of Enemy Lines'* (Liverpool, 2014), p. 75.

191 Sinn Féin, the Irish Volunteer Army (NAUK, WO 141/40).

192 Florence O'Donoghue, *No Other Law* (Dublin, 1954), p. 145.

193 Yeates, *A City in Turmoil*, p. 57. Emphasis in the original.

194 Peter Hart – 'Interview', *History Ireland*, March/April 2005, p. 50.

195 Paul Taylor, 'Heroes or Traitors? Experiences of Returning Irish Soldiers from World War One', unpublished PhD thesis, University of Oxford, 2012, quoted in Myles Dungan, *Irish Voices from the Great War* (2nd edn; Kildare, 2014), p. 285.

196 Hittle, *Michael Collins and the Anglo-Irish War*, pp. 101–10.

197 Interview with Tadg Kennedy (EOMN, UCDA, 17b/102).

198 Yeates, *A City in Turmoil*, p. 56.

199 Hogan, *The Black and Tans*, p. 110.

200 Yeates, *A City in Turmoil*, p. 101.

201 Borgonovo, *Anti-Sinn Féin Society*, pp. 78, 98.

202 Whelan, *Allegiances Compromised*, p. 45.

203 *The Cork Examiner*, 20 June 1921.

204 H. S. Jeudwine, quoted in Sheehan, *Hearts & Mines*, p. 211.

205 W. J. Lowe, 'Who Were the Black and Tans?', *History Ireland*, vol. 12, no. 3, Autumn 2004, p. 48.

206 McCall, *The Auxiliaries: Tudor's Toughs*, p. 51.

207 Ryle Dwyer, *Tans, Terror and Troubles*, pp. 304–5.

208 Toomey, *The War of Independence in Limerick,* pp. 261–3. One of the four, Thomas Hanley, was later captured by the IRA, executed and secretly buried; *Limerick Leader*, 4 November 1928.

209 *The Irish Times*, 10 February 1921.

210 Richardson, *A Coward if I Return*, pp. 328–34.

211 W. J. P. Agget, '*The Bloody II*', Vol. 3: *History of the Devonshire Regiment 1914–1969* (Exeter, 1995), p. 205.

212 John Moloney, BMH WS 1036, p. 17.

213 *The Irish Times*, 7 September 1990.

214 Borgonovo, *Anti-Sinn Féin Society*, pp. 58–9, 89.

215 RIC County Inspector's Reports, July 1921 (NAUK, CO 904/116).

216 PMCILCI on John Poynton (NAUK, WO 35/157B).

217 Borgonovo, *Anti-Sinn Féin Society*, pp. 82, 99; O'Callaghan, *Revolutionary Limerick*, p. 184.

218 Brian Hanley, *The IRA: A Documentary History 1916–2005* (Dublin, 2010), p. 16.

219 *Irish Examiner*, 30 October 2010.

220 Letter from Barry Keane in *History Ireland*, May/June 2015, Vol. 23, No. 3, p. 13.

221 Many of the quotes and information cited as evidence here come from IRA veteran testimony recorded by Ernie O'Malley and the Bureau of Military History. As these statements were collected between twenty and thirty-five years after the events described they must be treated with caution, since they may contain inaccuracies, contradictory evidence or personal bias. However, they are often the only surviving evidence detailing the supposed guilt or innocence of a suspected spy from the perspective of those who were directly involved in, or familiar with, their cases.

222 Gemma Clark, *Everyday Violence in the Irish Civil War* (Cambridge, 2014), p. 22.

223 Elizabeth Latimer, Irish Grants Committee Claims (NAUK, CO 762/4).

224 Denis J. O'Driscoll, BMH WS 1159, p. 11.

225 Michael Francis Heslin, BMH WS 662, pp. 16–17.

226 East Limerick Brigade Intelligence Report to GHQ for July 1921, 29 July 1921 (UCDA, RMP, P7a/8).

227 William Mullins, BMH WS 801, p. 10.

228 Seán Farrelly, BMH WS 1734, pp. 50–1.

229 *Ibid.*, p. 48.

230 Summary of Outrages Reported by the Police, June 1921 (NAUK, CO 904/146).

231 Seán Farrelly, BMH WS 1734, p. 48.

232 *Ibid.*, p. 51. Chaloner recovered his car after it had been abandoned by the IRA. It was commandeered again by the IRA after the implementation of the Truce but was later returned to Chaloner intact.

233 Summary of Outrages Reported by the Police, July 1921 (NAUK, CO 904/146).

234 *Ibid.* (NAUK, CO 904/150).

235 *Ibid.*

236 *Ibid.*

237 Hart, *The I.R.A. & Its Enemies*, p. 313.

238 *The Cork Examiner*, 13 July 1921.

239 Michael Govern, BMH WS 1625, p. 7.

240 List of Missing Persons, Department of Justice Files (NAI, H16, 1922–1926).

241 Summary of Outrages Reported by the Police, July 1921 (NAUK, CO 904/150).

242 Seán Clifford, BMH WS 1279, p. 3. He mistakenly reported this as happening in 1920.

243 Summary of Outrages Reported by the Police, July 1921 (NAUK, CO 904/146).

244 Thomas Moynihan, BMH WS 1452, p. 9.

245 Liam Ó Duibhir, *The Donegal Awakening: Donegal and the War of Independence* (Cork, 2009), pp. 295–9; Denis Houston, BMH WS 1382, pp. 17–19; Patrick Breslin, BMH WS 1448, pp. 31–4; Major General Joseph A. Sweeney, *Capuchin Annual* (Dublin, 1970), pp. 444–5; Collins remained in the area and was killed by the IRA in April 1922; Liam Ó Duibhir, *Donegal and the Civil War* (Cork, 2011), pp. 94–5.

246 Patrick O'Reilly, BMH WS 1650 p. 14.

247 Mooney, *Cry of the Curlew*, p. 315.

248 The mail raids were in Carlow, Cavan, Clare, Cork, Dublin, Kerry, Kilkenny, Limerick, Monaghan, Offaly, Tipperary, Tyrone, Waterford, Wexford and Wicklow; Summary of Outrages Reported by the Police, July 1921 (NAUK, CO 904/146); Summaries of DMP Reports (IMA, Oscar Traynor Collection, CD 120/3, CD 120/4).

249 For example, the IRA in Co. Cork alone killed five suspected spies over the weekend of 18–20 February 1921 – Michael Walsh, Matthew Swetnam, Richard Connell, William Mohally and Michael O'Sullivan.

250 James Morton, *Spies of the First World War: Under Cover for King and Kaiser* (London, 2010), p. 74.

251 Ian Penberthy (ed.), *The First World War in Pictures* (Lewes, 2013), p. 114.

252 William Sheehan, *The Western Front: Irish Voices from the Great War* (Dublin, 2011), p. 45.

253 Morton, *Spies of the First World War*, pp. 94–7.

254 See, for example, the depiction of a British military execution entitled 'Short Shrift for Spies at the Battle Front', *War Illustrated*, 20 November 1915.

255 In the minority of cases where the IRA chose instead to secretly bury the bodies of suspected spies it had killed, this suggests that the killing would not have been approved by the wider community (e.g. the shooting of a woman – Mrs Lindsey). It may also have been done as a purely pragmatic measure to obscure evidence of the killing; T. K. Wilson, *Frontiers of Violence: Conflict and Identity in Ulster and Upper Silesia 1918–1922* (Oxford, 2010), pp. 152–3.

4 IRA ATTACKS ON OFF-DUTY BRITISH TROOPS

1   Durney, *The Volunteer*, p. 31.
2   Michael Govern, BMH WS 1625, pp. 7–8.
3   Summary of Outrages Reported by the Police, July 1921 (NAUK, CO 904/146).
4   James Creegan, BMH WS 1395, p. 27.
5   John Dorney, *The Story of the Irish War of Independence* (e-book, 2010).
6   Pádraig Óg Ó Ruairc, 'The Woodford Incident', in *Bugle & Sabre: Military History in Oxfordshire & Buckinghamshire*, Vol. IV (Oxford, 2010), pp. 24–6.
7   Chris Ryder, *The Fateful Split: Catholics and the Ulster Constabulary* (London, 2004), p. 14.
8   Pollard, *The Secret Societies of Ireland*, pp. 152, 157.
9   Anonymous, 'The Irish Rebellion in the 6th Divisional Area', p. 73.
10 O'Hegarty, *The Victory of Sinn Féin*, p. 123.
11 Bernard Law Montgomery, *The Memoirs of Field-Marshal The Viscount Montgomery of Alamein, K.G.* (London, 1958), pp. 39–40.
12 Colonel Walter Leonard Vale, *The History of the South Staffordshire Regiment* (London, 1969), p. 399.
13 Hezlet, *The 'B' Specials*, p. 4.
14 David Fitzpatrick, 'Militarism in Ireland 1900–1922', in Thomas Bartlett and Keith Jeffery (eds), *A Military History of Ireland* (Cambridge, 1996), p. 405.
15 Hart, *The I.R.A. & Its Enemies*, p. 18.
16 *Ibid.*, p. 18.
17 *Ibid.*, p. 96.
18 Coleman, *County Longford and the Irish Revolution*, p. 132.
19 William Sheehan, *A Hard Local War: The British Army and the Guerrilla War in Cork 1919–1921* (Stroud, 2011), p. 164.
20 McCall, *Tudor's Toughs*, p. 165.
21 Yeates, *A City in Turmoil*, p. 50.
22 It is remarkable that former members of An Garda Síochána would denounce the Irish War of Independence as a 'murder' campaign since it ultimately led to political independence for southern Ireland and the creation of the modern Irish state and the police force in which they themselves had served. One wonders if such former gardaí recognise the legitimacy of Dáil Éireann – the Irish government, its department of justice and courts or the Irish Defence Forces, since all of these, like An Garda Síochána, emerged from the War of Independence and were founded by IRA veterans of that conflict.
23 *The Irish Times*, 22 August 2012.
24 See the accounts of Needham's killing in Abbott, *Police Casualties*, p. 265, and Kevin Myers, *Irish Independent*, 22 June 2011.
25 Kautt, *Ground Truths*, pp. 94–5, 194–5; Sönke Neitzel and Harald Welzer, *Soldaten. On Fighting, Killing and Dying: The Secret Second World War Tapes of German POWs* (London, 2012), pp. 77–8.

26   Hague Convention 1907 (Hague IV), Laws and Customs of War on Land, Section II, Chapter I, Article 23.

27   *Ibid.*

28   *Ibid.*

29   Fearghal McGarry, 'Violence and the Easter Rising', in David Fitzpatrick (ed.), *Terror in Ireland 1916–1923*, pp. 39–57.

30   John A. Murphy, in the Béal na mBláth Ninetieth Anniversary Commemoration booklet (Cork, 2012), p. 70.

31   Sheehan, *British Voices*, p. 151; General Patton, Montgomery's contemporary in the US Army, put the brutal necessities of war more bluntly: 'remember that no son of a bitch ever won a war by dying for his country. He won it by making the other poor dumb son of a bitch die for his country', *Association of the United States Army Journal*, Vol. 15, Part 1 (Washington, 1964), p. 32.

32   Sheehan, *Hearts & Mines*, pp. 41–2.

33   John M. McCarthy, BMH WS 883, Appendix G.

34   Barry, *Guerilla Days in Ireland* (5th edn; Dublin, 1981), p. 112.

35   McGarry, *Eoin O'Duffy*, pp. 76–7.

36   Interview with Tom O'Connor (EOMN UCDA P17b/132).

37   Ó Ruairc, *Blood on the Banner*, p. 232.

38   Interview with Stephen Vaughan, 6 February 1995, conducted by Kathleen Hegarty Thorne. Transcript in author's possession.

39   Summary of Outrages Reported by the Police, July 1921 (NAUK, CO 904/146).

40   Ryle Dwyer, *Tans, Terror and Troubles*, p. 320.

41   Brian Hughes, 'Persecuting the Peelers', in David Fitzpatrick (ed.), *Terror in Ireland 1916–1923*, p. 206.

42   Hogan, *The Black and Tans*, p. 9.

43   *Ibid.*, p. 8.

44   Pollard, *The Secret Societies of Ireland*, p. 181.

45   Grazebrook Diary, 7 April 1921 (Soldiers of Gloucestershire Museum).

46   Sheehan, *British Voices*, p. 178.

47   Patrick O'Brien, BMH WS 764, p. 15.

48   Interview with Jack Fitzgerald (EOMN UCDA P17b/112).

49   Interview with Liam Deasy (EOMN UCDA P17b/086).

50   Hogan, *The Black and Tans*, pp. 279–81.

51   Toomey, *War of Independence in Limerick*, pp. 515–16.

52   The only other possible reference to this alleged GHQ directive comes from an interview with IRA veteran Broddie Malone, conducted by Ernie O'Malley, during which O'Malley declares, 'The Tans should have been shot anyhow for that was a General Headquarters order'. In this case it is not clear whether O'Malley is referring to an order he had received himself at the time, or heard of later from another interviewee. Other than this fleeting reference by O'Malley, there is no record of IRA GHQ issuing such an order as outlined by O'Hannigan. Furthermore, IRA GHQ issued a booklet during the Truce which contained the text of all twenty-eight

'General Orders' issued by IRA GHQ, and none of these orders directs IRA Volunteers to court martial and execute captured members of the RIC. Cormac K. H. O'Malley and Vincent Keane (eds), *The Men Will Talk to Me: Mayo Interviews by Ernie O'Malley* (Cork, 2014), p. 187; General Orders, IRA (BMH, CD 105/02/19); Toomey, *The War of Independence in Limerick*, pp. 515–6.

53 O'Callaghan, *Revolutionary Limerick*, p. 140.
54 Abbott, *Police Casualties*, p. 265.
55 *Irish Independent*, 22 June 2011.
56 O'Halpin, 'In the Name of the Republic'.
57 RIC Register (NLI, Microfilm).
58 *The Clare Champion*, 16 July 1921.
59 RIC Register (NLI, Microfilm).
60 Information from the Civil Registration Office, Ennis.
61 RIC County Inspector's Report for Clare, July 1921 (NAUK, CO 904/115).
62 *The Clare Champion*, 16 July 1921.
63 *Saturday Record*, 5 November 1921.
64 Brennan, *The War in Clare*, p. 104.
65 Twohig, *Green Tears for Hecuba*, pp. 335–6.
66 *Ibid.*
67 RIC Register (NLI, Microfilm).
68 PMCILCI on Frederick Cormer (NAUK, WO 35/148).
69 *The Irish Times*, 9 July 1921.
70 PMCILCI on Frederick Cormer (NAUK, WO 35/148).
71 *Ibid.*
72 Christopher M. Byrne, BMH WS 1014, pp. 15–16; PMCILCI on Frederick Cormer (NAUK, WO 35/148).
73 PMCILCI on Frederick Cormer (NAUK, WO 35/148).
74 Christopher M. Byrne, BMH WS 1014, p. 16.
75 O'Halpin, 'Counting Terror, Bloody Sunday and the Dead of the Irish Revolution', in David Fitzpatrick (ed.), *Terror in Ireland 1916–1923* (Dublin, 2012), p. 152.
76 Christopher M. Byrne, BMH WS 1014, p. 14.
77 *Ibid.*, p.15.
78 *Ibid.*
79 *Ibid.*
80 Nic Dháibhéid, *Seán MacBride*, p. 50.
81 RIC County Inspector's Report for Wicklow, July 1921 (NAUK, CO 904/115).
82 Diarmuid Kingston, *Beleaguered: A History of the RIC in West Cork during the War of Independence* (Cork, 2013), p. 191.
83 Jasper Ungoed-Thomas, *Jasper Wolfe of Skibbereen* (Cork, 2008), p. 123.
84 *The Irish Times*, 27 August 1994.
85 *Ibid.*, 11 July 2001.
86 *Irish Independent*, 22 June 2011.
87 RIC Register (NLI, Microfilm).

88   Summary of Outrages Reported by the Police, July 1921 (NAUK, CO 904/146).

89   Cornelius Connolly, BMH WS 602, p. 2. Connolly took the pro-Treaty side during the Civil War and was elected TD for pro-Treaty Sinn Féin in West Cork. He resigned his seat after a short period in office and returned to work as a farmer. O'Sullivan took the pro-Treaty side during the Civil War and later joined An Garda Síochána. He was killed by an IRA trap-mine in Co. Clare on 11 June 1929; Brendan K. Colvert, *On My Honour: One Man's Lifelong Struggle to Clear His Name* (Cork, 2011), p. 12.

90   PMCILCI on Alexander Clarke (NAUK, WO 35/147A).

91   *Ibid.*

92   *Ibid.*

93   *Ibid.*

94   Cornelius Connolly, BMH WS 602, p. 2.

95   PMCILCI on Alexander Clarke (NAUK, WO 35/147A).

96   RIC Register (NLI, Microfilm).

97   Thomas Crawley, BMH WS 718, p. 13.

98   Interview with Stephen Vaughan, 4 June 1996.

99   Thomas Crawley, BMH WS 718, pp. 14–15.

100 Hegarty Thorne, *They Put the Flag a–Flyin'*, p. 92.

101 *Ibid.*, p. 101.

102 Micheál O'Callaghan, *For Ireland and Freedom: Roscommon's Contribution to the Fight for Independence*, p. 136.

103 Hegarty Thorne, *They Put the Flag a–Flyin'*, p. 106.

104 Interview with Stephen Vaughan, 6 February 1995.

105 Thomas Crawley, BMH WS 718, p. 13.

106 Kevin Myers' assertion that King, being motivated by his deep religious faith, was en route to mass in the local Catholic church at the time of his shooting is incorrect; *The Irish Times*, 27 August 1994.

107 Thomas Crawley, BMH WS 718, p. 13.

108 PMCILCI on James King (NAUK, WO 35/153 A).

109 John Grant, BMH WS 658, pp. 15–16.

110 PMCILCI on Patrick Quinn, John O'Reilly, Thomas O'Reilly and Peter McGennity (NAUK, WO 35/158).

111 *Ibid.*

112 Edward Fullerton, BMH WS 890 p. 18; Jack McElhaw, BMH WS 634, p. 27.

113 Sam Trotter, *Constabulary Heroes 1826–2011: Incorporating the RUC GC/PSNI and Their Forebears in the USC* (Coleraine, 2012), p. 26.

114 Edward Fullerton, BMH WS 890, pp. 18–19.

115 RIC County Inspector's Report for Down, July 1921 (NAUK, CO 904/116).

116 John Grant, BMH WS 658, pp. 15–16.

117 *Ibid.*, p. 16.

118 *Ibid.*, p. 16. Grant mistakenly dates this to 11 July.

119 PMCILCI on Draper Holmes (NAUK, WO 35/152).

120 *The Irish Times*, 2 June 1995.

121 PMCILCI on Draper Holmes (NAUK, WO 35/152).

122 *The Cork Examiner*, 11 July 1921.

123 John Grant, BMH WS 658, pp. 16.

124 PMCILCI on Draper Holmes (NAUK, WO 35/152).

125 John Grant, BMH WS 658, pp. 15–17.

126 E-mail correspondence with Dr William Matthew Lewis, Queen's University Belfast, 13 October 2009.

127 *The Irish Times*, 27 August 1994.

128 *Ibid.*,11 July 1921.

129 Mainchín Seoighe, *The Story of Kilmallock* (Kilmallock, 2012), p. 285.

130 Summary of Outrages Reported by the Police, July 1921 (NAUK, CO 904/146).

131 RIC County Inspector's Report for Waterford, July 1921 (NAUK, CO 904/116).

132 Summary of Outrages Reported by the Police, July 1921 (NAUK, CO 904/146).

133 *Ibid.*

134 Seamus Babington, BMH WS 1595, p. 149.

135 Summary of Outrages Reported by the Police, July 1921 (NAUK, CO 904/146); John Ahern, BMH WS 970, p. 7.

136 J. Anthony Gaughan, *Listowel and Its Vicinity* (Kildare, 1973), p. 393.

137 Con Brosnan, BMH WS 1123, p. 7.

138 *Ibid.*, pp. 7–8.

139 John Ahern, BMH WS 970, p. 7.

140 Patrick McKenna, BMH WS 911, p. 10.

141 Thomas J. Kelly (Ó Fiaich Library, Armagh, Fr Louis O'Kane Papers [hereafter OFL, LOK], Section IV, Part B 06, pp. 2–3).

142 Patrick McKenna, BMH WS 911, p. 10.

143 Uinseann MacEoin, *Survivors* (Dublin, 1980), pp. 175–6.

144 *Ibid.*

145 Patrick McKenna, BMH WS 911, p. 11. Another participant in the attack, Patrick Diamond, has given a conflicting account of Atwell's release. Diamond states that he had been ordered to execute Atwell. He claimed that as he was about to carry out the execution he discovered that Atwell, an English Protestant, was wearing a 'Sacred Heart' scapular given to him by his Irish Catholic girlfriend. Diamond claims that he decided, based on his strong personal religious convictions, that he could not kill his prisoner and released him after they shared a quantity of brandy; Patrick Diamond (OFL, LOK IV B 01, pp. 29–31).

146 Thomas J. Kelly (OFL, LOK IV B 06, pp. 2–3).

147 RIC County Inspector's Report for Tyrone, July 1921 (NAUK, CO 904/116).

148 Thomas Carmody, BMH WS 996, p. 11.

149 Summary of Outrages Reported by the Police, July 1921 (NAUK, CO 904/146).

150 *Ibid.*

151 *Ibid.*

152 Daker was a member of the 2nd Battalion, South Staffordshire Regiment. His military service number was 4905129. He was born in 1893 and lived at Chasetown, Staffordshire, England. He is buried in Saint Ann's Churchyard, Chasetown. Morris was a member of the 2nd Battalion, South Staffordshire Regiment. His military service number was 4905221. He was born on 20 January 1900, the eldest son of Henry Alfred Morris and his wife Lucy (née Williams) of 57 Pool Street, Walsall, England. He is buried in Ryecroft Cemetery, Walsall. Camm was a member of the Royal Engineers. His military service number was 1856603. He is buried in Cork Military Cemetery. Powell was a member of the Fortress Company, 33rd Battalion, Royal Engineers. His military service number was 1853916. He was the son of Henry Arthur and Jane Powell of 28 Abbott Road, Poplar, London. He is buried in Nunhead (All Saints) Cemetery in South London.

153 See, for example, the cover of Sheehan's *A Hard Local War* and in McKenna's *Guerrilla Warfare in the Irish War of Independence 1919–1921*. Eoghan Harris references this photograph in his account of the killings in the *Sunday Independent*, 31 March 2013.

154 Barry, *Guerilla Days*, p. 99.

155 Anonymous, 'The Irish Rebellion in the 6th Divisional Area', p. 87.

156 William McCarthy, BMH WS 1255, p. 7.

157 Barry, *Guerilla Days*, pp. 103–4.

158 Borgonovo, *Anti-Sinn Féin Society*, p. 88.

159 Sheehan, *British Voices*, pp. 211–12.

160 Anonymous, 'The Irish Rebellion in the 6th Divisional Area', p. 87.

161 Borgonovo, *Anti-Sinn Féin Society*, p. 88.

162 *Irish Independent*, 16 May 1921.

163 *Ibid.*

164 *The Irish Times*, 16 May 1921.

165 Anonymous, 'The Irish Rebellion in the 6th Divisional Area', p. 147; Abbott, *Police Casualties*, pp. 237–40.

166 O'Malley, *On Another Man's Wound*, p. 371.

167 Nic Dháibhéid, *Seán MacBride*, pp. 44–7.

168 RIC County Inspector's Report for Cork ER, July 1921 (NAUK, CO 904/115).

169 Anonymous, 'The Irish Rebellion in the 6th Divisional area', p. 130.

170 Connie Neenan's memoir (CCCA, Neenan Memoir, pp. 70a–71).

171 Information from personal recollection related by Criostoir de Baroid, Cork.

172 Diary of Liam de Roiste TD, 23 March 1922 (CCCA, De Roiste Papers).

173 Various, *Rebel Cork's Fighting Story 1916–1921* (Cork, 2010).

174 MacEoin, *Survivors*, p. 241.

175 *Ibid.*

176 Neenan (CCCA, Neenan Memoir, pp. 70a–71).

177 Richard Henchion, *The Land of the Finest Drop: The Story of Life, Love*

and Labour in the Districts of the Lough, Togher, Pouladuff, Friars Walk and Ballyphehane over a Period of 400 years (Cork, 2003), pp. 81–2.

178 *Ibid.*

179 Murphy, *The Year of Disappearances,* p. 16.

180 *Sunday Independent,* 31 March 2013.

181 Camm and Powell were both aged twenty, Morris was twenty-one and Daker twenty-eight years old.

182 Jeffery, *The British Army,* p. 16.

183 Sheehan, *A Hard Local War,* p. 49.

184 Morris' service number when he joined the British Army was 4905221. Details of his early military career are available online at: www.cairogang.com/soldiers-killed/cork-jul-21/morris/morris/.html (accessed 17 August 2014).

185 Further details of Daker's military service are not available, since the South Staffordshire Regimental records giving the enlistment details of recruits at the time Daker enlisted are incomplete. Register of enlisted men, Ref: 8416 (Staffordshire Regimental Museum Library).

186 Connie Neenan's memoir (CCCA, Neenan Memoir, pp. 70a–71).

187 Phillips, *The Revolution in Ireland,* p. 216.

188 RIC County Inspector's Report for Cork ER, July 1921 (NAUK, CO 904/115).

189 Activity report of O/C, H Company, 1st Battalion, Cork No. 1 Brigade to IRA GHQ, July 1921 (UCDA, RMP P7/A/23).

190 *Ibid.* The British forces' official account of the incident issued by Dublin Castle on 11 July 1921 stated that the soldiers were kidnapped at 10.30 p.m. but it is likely that this refers to the time the alarm was raised about their disappearance when they failed to return to their posts. The commanding officer of H Company, who ordered the men's execution, would undoubtedly have been better placed to recall accurately what time the men were captured and killed. There is some debate as to the location of the execution site but it appears to have been somewhere between St Finbarr's Cemetery and 'The Lough'. The 1900 Ordinance Survey Map for Cork shows several gravel pits in fields in that area. One of these pits, located where the Ashwood Estate and Hillside Grove meet today, was apparently known as 'Ellis' Quarry'; Plan of Cork city 1900 (Cork 1989). Information from local resident and author Barry Keane to author by email, 6 May 2014.

191 Summary of Outrages Reported by the Police, July 1921 (NAUK, CO 904/146).

192 *The Cork Examiner,* 12 July 1921; Summary of Outrages Reported by the Police, July 1921 (NAUK, CO 904/146).

193 Connie Neenan's memoir (CCCA, Neenan Memoir, pp. 70a–71).

194 Available at: www.cairogang.com/soldiers-killed/cork-jul-21/morris/morris/.html (accessed 17 August 2014).

195 RIC County Inspector's Report for Cork ER, July 1921 (NAUK, CO 904/115).

196 *Ibid.*; PMCILCI on Denis Spriggs (NAUK, WO 35/159A); *The Cork Examiner,* 11 July 1921.

ENDNOTES

197 It was the only occasion during the conflict when four off-duty British soldiers were captured and killed together. A similar multiple execution occurred at Ovens, Co. Cork, the previous month, when three off-duty members of the Manchester Regiment were captured by the IRA, executed and secretly buried. However, this incident is not directly comparable with the Ellis Quarry killings, since the executions of the Manchester bandsmen were carried out on the assumption that they were on an intelligence-gathering mission when captured; Fergus A. D'Arcy, *Remembering the War Dead: British Commonwealth and International War Graves in Ireland since 1914* (Dublin, 2007), p. 50.

198 Borgonovo, *Anti-Sinn Féin Society*, p. 88.

199 Activity report of O/C, H Company, 1st Battalion, 1st Cork Brigade to IRA GHQ, July 1921 (UCDA, RMP P7/A/23).

200 Barry, *Guerilla Days*, p. 99.

201 Hittle, *Michael Collins and the Anglo-Irish War*, p. 121; Jane Leonard, 'English dogs or poor devils?: the dead of Bloody Sunday morning', in David Fitzpatrick (ed.) *Terror in Ireland 1916–1923*, p. 116.

202 Fergal Tobin, *The Irish Revolution: An Illustrated History 1912–1925* (Dublin, 2014), pp. 120–1; Fearghal McGarry, *The Rising: Ireland, Easter 1916* (Oxford, 2010), p. 187.

203 Séan Enright, *Easter Rising 1916: The Trials* (Dublin, 2014), pp. 18, 32.

204 Borgonovo, *Anti-Sinn Féin Society*, p. 82.

205 Goddard Lieberson, *The Irish Uprising 1916–1922* (New York, 1968), p. 133.

206 Henchion, *The Land of the Finest Drop*, pp. 81–2.

207 PMCILCI on William Horgan (NAUK, WO 35/152).

208 Borgonovo, *Anti-Sinn Féin Society*, p. 110.

209 PMCILCI on Denis Spriggs (NAUK, WO 35/159A).

210 Activity report of O/C, H Company, 1st Battalion, Cork No. 1 Brigade to IRA GHQ, July 1921 (UCDA, RMP P7/A/23).

211 Anonymous, 'The Irish Rebellion in the 6th Divisional Area', p. 130.

212 Cork No. 2 Brigade, Operations Report for July 1921 (UCDA, RMP, P7/A/20).

213 RIC County Inspector's Report for Cork ER, July 1921 (NAUK, CO 904/115).

214 Summary of Outrages Reported by the Police, July 1921 (NAUK, CO 904/146).

215 *The Cork Examiner*, 13 July 1921.

216 William Regan, BMH WS 1069, p. 13.

217 Summary of Outrages Reported by the Police, July 1921 (NAUK, CO 904/146); PMCILCI on Hannah Carey (NAUK, WO 35/147A).

218 *Kerry People*, 16 July 1921.

219 Interview with Tom O'Connor (EOMN UCDA P17b/132).

220 Anonymous, 'The Irish Rebellion in the 6th Divisional Area', p. 130.

221 Ryle Dwyer, *Tans, Terror and Troubles*, p. 7.

222 Summary of Outrages Reported by the Police, July 1921 (NAUK, CO 904/146).

223 Toomey, *The War of Independence in Limerick*, p. 471.

224 Various, *Limerick's Fighting Story* (Cork, 2009), pp. 194–5.

225 James Malone, *Blood on the Flag: Autobiography of a Freedom Fighter*, ed. Patrick J. Twohig (Cork, 1996), pp. 117–18.

226 Ned Tobin, BMH WS 1451, pp. 71–2; Toomey, *The War of Independence in Limerick*, p. 471.

227 Activity report of O/C, F Company, Cork No. 1 Brigade to IRA GHQ, July 1921 (UCDA, RMP P7/A/23).

228 Information from John Wade, grandson of Frederick Ricketts, lodged at Charles Fort National Monument, Kinsale, Cork; John Trendall, *Colonel Bogey to the Fore* (London, 1991).

229 Summary of Outrages Reported by the Police, July 1921 (NAUK, CO 904/146).

230 Frederica Sophie Cheevers, *The Cheevers of Killyan* (National University of Ireland, Galway Archives, LE 20 1), p. 20.

231 *Ibid.*, p. 21.

232 William Roche, BMH WS 1362, pp. 7–9.

233 Summary of Outrages Reported by the Police, July 1921 (NAUK, CO 904/146).

234 *The Irish Times*, 22 August 1921; Michael J. O'Sullivan, BMH WS 862, pp. 30.

235 Daniel Mulvihill, BMH WS 938, p. 14.

236 Information from Dr Tim Horgan, Ballycarthy, Ballyseede, Tralee.

237 James Fulham, BMH WS 630, pp. 23–4.

238 McKenna, *Guerrilla Warfare*, p. 108.

239 Various, *The Dublin Brigade Review* (Dublin, 1939), pp. 20, 24, 52, 82.

240 Abbott, *Police Casualties*, p. 258.

241 Despite detailed accounts of the planned operation being published in *The Dublin Brigade Review* (Dublin, 1939), it is not mentioned in the vast majority of subsequent studies, including Townshend's, *The British Campaign in Ireland 1919–1921*; Valiulis' *Portrait of a Revolutionary*; Fitzpatrick's 'Militarism in Ireland 1900–1922'; Francis Costello's *The Irish Revolution and Its Aftermath 1916–1923*; or Peter Hart's *Mick*.

242 Abbott, *Police Casualties*, p. 258; Patrick McCrae, BMH WS 413, pp. 42–3.

243 Abbott, *Police Casualties*, p. 258.

244 Pádraig Ó Conchubhair and Paddy Rigney, 'The Active Service Unit', *The Dublin Brigade Review*, p. 82.

245 John Kenny, BMH WS 1693, p. 21.

246 Various, *The Dublin Brigade Review*, p. 24.

247 Alphonsus Sweeney, BMH WS 1147, pp. 8–9.

248 James Fulham, BMH WS 630, pp. 23–4.

249 Various, *The Dublin Brigade Review*, p. 52.

250 Joseph O'Connor, BMH WS 487, pp. 58–9.

251 Moira Kennedy O'Byrne, BMH WS 1029, pp. 12–13.

252 Joseph O'Connor, BMH WS 813, p. 44.

253 Moira Kennedy O'Byrne, BMH WS 1029, pp. 12–13.

254 Various, 'The Fourth Battalion', *The Dublin Brigade Review*, p. 52.

255 Joseph O'Connor, BMH WS 487, pp. 59.

256 Various, 'The Fourth Battalion', *Dublin Brigade Review*, p. 52.

257 Alphonsus Sweeney, BMH WS 1147, pp. 8–9.

258 According to a veteran of the Dublin Brigade ASU the operations were cancelled because 'it was thought that an operation of the magnitude of that contemplated would stop any overtures for peace'. IRA veterans who had mobilised for the 'general hit-up' later held divergent attitudes as to the wisdom of the proposed attacks. Colonel Joe Leonard took the view that the Dublin IRA was so critically short of ammunition that those taking part in the attacks would have been embarking on a suicide mission: 'we had not enough ammunition to fill our guns and would of necessity have all been wiped out by their fire, but for the job being called off at the last minute there would have been no Truce'. John Kenny, F Company, 1st Battalion, was given 'a meagre supply' of ammunition in preparation for the attack, and was ordered to collect the side arms of members of the British forces killed in the attack – presumably with the intention of using these to secure their retreat. A lieutenant in the 3rd Battalion, Alphonsus Sweeney, believed that the prospects for the attack's success were much greater and that the 'hit-up' was 'an operation which, if carried out completely, was well calculated to be the most sensational and sanguinary since the Rebellion of 1916'; Leonard, BMH WS 547, p. 24; Kenny, BMH WS 1693, pp. 21; Sweeney, BMH WS 1147, p. 9.

259 For example, at least fifteen off-duty British troops, six British soldiers and nine members of the RIC were killed by the IRA between Friday 13 and Monday 16 May 1921: Private J. Hunter, Private R. McMillan, Private D. Chalmers, Private F. Sheppard, Lance-Corporal R. Maddell, Gunner B. Francis, Gunner W. Parker, Constable J. Kenna, Sergeant E. Coleman, Constable R. Redmond, Constable T. Bridges, Head Constable F. Benson, District Inspector H. Biggs, Constable H. McClean, Constable J. Nutley, District Inspector A. Blake. For details, see *Irish Independent*, 16 May 1921; *The Irish Times*, 16 May 1921; *The Freeman's Journal*, 16 May 1921; Abbott, *Police Casualties*, pp. 237–42. While many of these fatalities were the result of the order issued by the IRA's 1st Southern Division to launch a series of co-ordinated attacks on British troops on 14 May in retaliation for the execution of a number of IRA Volunteers in Cork, fatal attacks also occurred in Dublin, Galway, Limerick and Tipperary.

260 Hart, *Mick*, p. 277.

5   PRE-TRUCE OFFENSIVES AND IRA OPERATIONS, 8–11 JULY 1921

1 Patrick Dunleavy Collection (IMA, BMH, CD 248/1/16, Group 1).

2 Durney, *The Volunteer*, p. 31.

3 Summary of Outrages Reported by the Police, July 1921 (NAUK, CO 904/146); Seán Farrelly, BMH WS 1734, pp. 51–2.

4   Summary of Outrages Reported by the Police, July 1921 (NAUK, CO 904/146).

5   *Ibid.*

6   Francis Connell, BMH WS 1663, p. 10.

7   *Ibid.*

8   *Ibid.*

9   Summary of Outrages Reported by the Police, July 1921 (NAUK, CO 904/146).

10   *Ibid.*

11   *Ibid.*

12   James Maguire, BMH WS 1439, p. 29.

13   *Ibid.*

14   *The Cork Examiner*, 13 July 1921.

15   RIC County Inspector's Report for Westmeath, July 1921 (NAUK, CO 904/116).

16   James Maguire, BMH WS 1439, p. 29.

17   Summary of Outrages Reported by the Police, July 1921 (NAUK, CO 904/146).

18   Michael Govern, BMH WS 1625, p. 7.

19   Summary of Outrages Reported by the Police, July 1921 (NAUK, CO 904/146).

20   *Ibid.*

21   O'Donnell, *Royal Irish Constabulary and the Black and Tans in County Louth*, p. 181.

22   Summary of Outrages Reported by the Police, July 1921 (NAUK, CO 904/146).

23   Seamus Finn, BMH WS 1060, p. 58, says 'operations had been planned' but RIC reports indicate that no such plans took place.

24   *Ibid.*, p. 70.

25   Michael Rock, BMH WS 1398, pp. 20–1.

26   Seán Farrelly, BMH WS 1734, pp. 51–2.

27   Durney, *The Volunteer*, p. 31.

28   Andrew Kennedy, BMH WS 963, p. 30; interview with Bertie Scully (EOMN UCDA P17/102).

29   Andrew Kennedy, BMH WS 963, p. 30.

30   Summary of Outrages Reported by the Police, July 1921 (NAUK, CO 904/146).

31   *Ibid.*

32   *Ibid.*

33   Summary of Outrages Reported by the Police, July 1921 (NAUK, CO 904/146).

34   *Ibid.*

35   *Ibid.*

36   *The Cork Examiner*, 13 July 1921.

37   Summary of Outrages Reported by the Police, July 1921 (NAUK, CO 904/146).

38   Michael Davern, BMH WS 1348, p. 56.

39   Michael Quirke, 'My Life and Times', p. 36 (unpublished memoir, Cashel War of Independence Museum).

40   *Ibid.*

41   Seamus Babington, BMH WS 1595, p. 149.

42   Andrew Kennedy, BMH WS 963, p. 30.

43   Summary of Outrages Reported by the Police, July 1921 (NAUK, CO 904/146).

44   *Ibid.*; Gaughan, *Listowel and Its Vicinity*, p. 394.

45   Summary of Outrages Reported by the Police, July 1921 (NAUK, CO 904/146).

46   RIC County Inspector's Report for Kerry, July 1921 (NAUK, CO 904/116).

47   Interview with Tom O'Connor (EOMN UCDA P17b/132).

48   Thomas McEllistrim, BMH WS 882, p. 33; interview with Tom O'Connor (EOMN UCDA P17b/132).

49   *Ibid.*

50   Daniel O'Sullivan, BMH WS 1191, p. 12.

51   *Ibid.* pp. 12–13; Kerry No. 2 Brigade IRA Operations Report, July 1921 (UCDA, RMP, P7/A/20).

52   RIC County Inspector's Report for Kerry, July 1921 (NAUK, CO 904/116); War Office Papers (NAUK, WO 141/54). Lieutenant Frederick Coleman and Private William Finch were both decorated for their role in repelling the IRA's attack at Kenmare.

53   Hopkinson, *The Irish War of Independence*, pp. 147, 113, 119.

54   Interview with Tom McEllistrim (EOMN UCDA P17b/102).

55   *Ibid.*

56   Daniel Healy, BMH WS 1067 pp. 16–17.

57   Jeremiah Kennedy, BMH WS 1192, p. 18.

58   Sergeant Davis, Private William Kelly, Private William Ross and Private George Rankin of the 2nd Battalion North Lancashire Regiment, British Army, and IRA Volunteers John Flynn, Jack Prendiville and Richard Shanahan.

59   Interview with Tom McEllistrim (EOMN UCDA P17b/102).

60   Seamus O'Connor, *Tomorrow Was Another Day: Irreverent Memories of an Irish Rebel Schoolmaster* (Tralee, 1970), p. 55.

61   'Last Man Standing – An Interview with Dan Keating', *History Ireland*, May/June 2008.

62   Anonymous, 'The Irish Rebellion in the 6th Divisional Area', *The Irish Sword*, vol. XXVII, no. 107, Spring 2010, p. 130.

63   Macready, *Annals*, pp. 577–8.

64   Interview with Andy Cooney (EOMN UCDA P17b/107).

65   Denis Prendiville, BMH WS 1106, p. 9.

66   Peter Browne, BMH WS 1110, pp. 54–5.

67   *Ibid.*, p. 56.

68   John O'Connor, BMH WS 1181, pp. 25–6.

69   Denis Prendiville, BMH WS 1106, p. 10; Peter Browne, BMH WS 1110, pp. 60–2.

70   War Office Papers (NAUK, WO 141/54).

71   Summary of Outrages Reported by the Police, July 1921 (NAUK, CO 904/146); *The Irish Times*, 12 July 1921.

72   Claremorris Command to GHQ Dublin (IMA, A/07304).

73   RIC County Inspector's Report for Clare, July 1921 (NAUK, CO 904/116).

74   RIC County Inspector's Report for Galway ER, July 1921 (NAUK, CO 904/116).

75   Patrick Connaughton, BMH WS 1137, pp. 15–16.

76   *The Irish Times*, 10 July 1921; Summary of Outrages Reported by the Police, July 1921 (NAUK, CO 904/146).

77   Frank Neville, BMH WS 443, p. 16.

78   Leo Skinner, BMH WS 940, pp. 5–7.

79   Various, *Rebel Cork's Fighting Story*, pp. 270–1.

80   RIC County Inspector's Report for Cork ER, July 1921 (NAUK, CO 904/116); Various, *Rebel Cork's Fighting Story*, pp. 270–2.

81   Seán Murphy, BMH WS 1445, pp. 16–17; Dan Corkery, BMH WS 1719, p. 26.

82   William Norris, BMH WS 595, p. 14.

83   Daniel Canty, BMH WS 1619, p. 34; James Brennock, BMH WS 1113, p. 19.

84   Patrick O'Brien, BMH WS 764, pp. 57–8.

85   Mossie Harnett, *Victory and Woe: The West Limerick Brigade in the War of Independence* (Dublin, 2002), pp. 109–17.

86   James Collins, BMH WS 1272, pp. 39–40.

87   Patrick O'Brien, BMH WS 764, pp. 58–9.

88   *Ibid.*, pp. 59–60.

89   *Ibid.* p. 60; Daniel Browne, BMH WS 785, pp. 11–12; Harnett, *Victory and Woe*, pp. 109–17.

90   John J. O'Riordan, *Kiskeam versus the Empire* (Cork, 2010), p. 121.

91   Liam Forde, BMH WS 1710, p. 25; McCall, *Tudor's Toughs*, pp. 210–13.

92   Michael Hayes, *The Irish Republican Struggle in Limerick: Diary of a 16-year-old Volunteer*, ed. Michael Ó hAodha (Dublin, 2013), p. 62.

93   *The Irish Times*, 11 July 1921.

94   RIC County Inspector's Report for Waterford, July 1921 (NAUK, CO 904/116).

95   1st Battalion Waterford No. 2: Brigade report to GHQ, July 1921 (UCDA, RMP, P7/A/23).

96   3rd Battalion Waterford No. 2: Brigade report to GHQ, July 1921 (UCDA, RMP, P7/A/23).

97   *The Irish Times*, 10 July 1921.

98   James Prendergast, BMH WS 1655, pp. 14–15.

99   Attack on Constable Massey near Cappoquin on 10 July. RIC County Inspector's Report for Waterford, July 1921 (NAUK, CO 904/116).

100   *The Irish Times*, 13 July 1921; Seamus Conway, BMH WS 440, p. 28.

101 Michael Francis Reynolds, BMH WS 438, pp. 19–20.

102 Bryan Doherty, BMH WS 1292, p. 14.

103 Hegarty Thorne, *They Put the Flag a-Flyin'*, pp. 110–12.

104 Summary of Outrages Reported by the Police, July 1921 (NAUK, CO 904/146); Patrick Cassidy, BMH WS 1017, p. 15.

105 William J. O'Hara, BMH WS 1554, p. 20.

106 Martin Bernard McGowan, BMH WS 1545, p. 13.

107 Pádraig O'Connor, BMH WS 813, pp. 43–4.

108 Patrick McCrae, BMH WS 413, p. 45.

109 Pádraig O'Connor, BMH WS 813, p. 44.

110 *The Irish Times*, 12 July 1921.

111 Pádraig O'Connor, BMH WS 813, p. 44.

112 Summaries of DMP reports, Oscar Traynor Papers (BMH, CD 120/4).

113 RIC County Inspector's Report for Kilkenny, July 1921 (NAUK, CO 904/115).

114 Thomas Meagher, BMH WS 1672, p. 7.

115 Jim Maher, *The Flying Column: West Kilkenny 1916–21* (Kilkenny, 1988), pp. 151–3.

116 RIC County Inspector's Report for Wicklow, July 1921 (NAUK, CO 904/115); Summary of Outrages Reported by the Police, July 1921 (NAUK, CO 904/146).

117 Summary of Outrages Reported by the Police, July 1921 (NAUK, CO 904/146).

118 *The Irish Times*, 11 July 1921; *The Irish News*, 15 July 1921; *Ulster Herald*, 16 July 1921; PMCILCI on James McSorley (NAUK, WO 35/154).

119 RIC Inspectors Report for the City of Belfast, July 1921 (NAUK, CO 904/115); Abbott, *Police Casualties*, p. 265.

120 Summary of Outrages Reported by the Police, July 1921 (NAUK, CO 904/146).

121 *The Irish Times*, 12 July 1921; William J. Kelly, BMH WS 893, p. 25.

122 Hart, *The I.R.A. & Its Enemies*, p. 18.

123 Summary of Outrages Reported by the Police, June–July 1921 (NAUK, CO 904/146); Abbott, *Police Casualties*, pp. 216–17; Trotter, *Constabulary Heroes*, pp. 23–8; www.cairogang.com (accessed 17 August 2014).

124 Barry, *Guerilla Days*, pp. 75–6.

125 Abbott, *Police Casualties*, pp. 216–17.

126 Tom Barry, *The Reality of the Anglo-Irish War 1920–21 in West Cork: Refutations, Corrections and Comments on Liam Deasy's Towards Ireland Free* (Tralee, 1974), p. 49.

127 Frank Neville, BMH WS 443, p. 16.

128 Townshend, *The Republic*, p. 8.

129 Michael O'Donnell, BMH WS 1145, p. 8.

130 Martin Grace, BMH WS 1463, p. 6.

131 Interview with Jim Leahy (EOMN UCDA P17b/100).

132 Interview with Ned Jordan (EOMN UCDA P17b/103).

133 James Keating, BMH WS 1528, p. 8.

134 Edward Horgan, BMH WS 1644, p. 13.

135 Michael O'Donnell, BMH WS 1145, p. 8.

136 Interview with Ned Jordan (EOMN UCDA P17b/103).

137 Only two of the planned barracks attacks following the announcement of the Truce appear to have had a tangible military goal. The attack on Kenmare RIC Barracks was supposed to employ an explosive mine and involve an attempt to storm the barracks, which could potentially have resulted in the capture of the barracks and its destruction. The sniping attack on Listowel Barracks appears to have been a ruse to attempt to draw out the RIC garrison and cause it to trigger a 'booby trap' mine attached to the barracks gate.

138 Persico, *Eleventh Month, Eleventh Day, Eleventh Hour*, pp. 133–6.

139 Max Arthur, *The Road Home: The Aftermath of the Great War told by the Men and Women Who Survived It* (London, 2010), p. 5.

140 Imperial War Museum, Photographic Archive (Q 47886).

141 Persico, *Eleventh Month, Eleventh Day, Eleventh Hour*, p. 308.

142 Hart, *The I.R.A. & Its Enemies*, p. 18.

143 Hart, *Mick*, p. 277.

6   FATALITIES INFLICTED BY THE BRITISH FORCES

1   Anonymous, 'The Irish Rebellion in the 6th Divisional Area', p. 130; Sheehan, *Hearts & Mines*, pp. 104–5; Phillips, *Revolution in Ireland*, p. 216; Macready, *Annals*, pp. 577–8; Béaslaí, *Collins and the Making of a New Ireland*, p. 248; Townshend, *The British Campaign*, p. 198; Curran, *Birth of the Irish Free State*, p. 61; Coogan, *Michael Collins*, pp. 216–7; Hart, *The I.R.A. at War*, pp. 71–2, 75; Hart, *Mick*, p. 277; Donal J. O'Sullivan, *The Irish Constabularies 1822–1922: A Century of Policing in Ireland* (Kerry, 1999), p. 361; Murphy, *Year of Disappearances*, pp. 16, 300–6; Sheehan, *A Hard Local War*, p. 160.

2   *Irish Independent*, 22 June 2011; *Sunday Independent*, 31 March 2013.

3   Anonymous, 'The Irish Rebellion in the 6th Divisional area', p. 130.

4   Sheehan, *Hearts & Mines*, p. 103. Emphasis in the original.

5   Macready, *Annals*, pp. 577–8.

6   Only one killing attributed to the British forces has been afforded specific mention in histories of the period which discuss the immediate pre-Truce fatalities. Robert Kee and Russell Rees mistakenly claim that Major G. B. O'Connor was killed by British forces. The origin of the erroneous claim comes from a newspaper report, which appeared in *The Irish News* a few days after the Truce. One of that newspaper's correspondents, using the pen-name 'Belfast Commercial', wrongly implicated the British in the killing; Robert Kee, *The Green Flag, Vol. III: Ourselves Alone* (London, 1972), p. 143; Russell Rees, *Ireland 1905–1925, Vol. I: Text & Historiography* (Newtownards, 1998), p. 270; *The Irish News*, 13 July 1921.

7   Sheehan, *Hearts & Mines*, pp. 104–5.

8   *The Irish News*, 13 July 1921.

9   Ruairí Ó Brádaigh, *Dílseacht: The Story of Comdt. General Tom Maguire and the Second Dáil* (Dublin, 1997), p. 10.

10   *Weekly Summary*, 11 July 1921.

11   Sheehan, *Hearts & Mines*, pp. 104–5.

12   *Ibid.*, pp. 39, 42.

13   *Ibid.*, pp. 90–1.

14   Duff, *Sword for Hire*, p. 84.

15   Sheehan, *Hearts & Mines*, p. 104.

16   Eugene Bratton, BMH WS 467, p. 11.

17   RIC County Inspector's Report for Galway WR, July 1921 (NAUK, CO 904/116).

18   *Ibid.*

19   *Ibid.*

20   John Lenihan, BMH WS 968, p. 6.

21   *The Cork Examiner*, 11 July 1921.

22   *Ibid.*; *Kerry People*, 16 July 1921.

23   Michael Ryan, BMH WS 1709, p. 30.

24   RIC County Inspector's Report for Tyrone, July 1921 (NAUK, CO 904/115).

25   *The Cork Examiner*, 11 July 1921.

26   Nan Nolan, BMH WS 1441, p. 11.

27   Mooney, *Cry of the Curlew*, p. 313.

28   Seán Murphy and Síle Murphy, *The Comeraghs: Gunfire and Civil War. The Story of the Deise Brigade IRA 1914–1924* (Waterford, 2003), pp. 109–10.

29   IRA Report to GHQ Waterford No. 2 Brigade, July 1921, Richard Mulcahy Papers (UCDA, P7/A/23).

30   Mooney, *Cry of the Curlew*, p. 313.

31   PMCILCI on Quin, Burke, Lynch (NAUK, WO 35/158); *The Irish Times*, 11 July 1921; Murphy and Murphy, *The Comeraghs*, pp. 109–10.

32   Murphy and Murphy, *The Comeraghs*, pp. 109–10.

33   RIC County Inspector's Report for Waterford, July 1921 (NAUK, CO 904/116).

34   Anonymous, 'The Irish Rebellion in the 6th Divisional Area', p. 151.

35   Colonel C. R. B. Knight, OBE, *Historical Record of the Buffs 1919–1948* (London, 1951), p. 3.

36   Mooney, *Cry of the Curlew*, p. 313.

37   For example, Cecil and Aidan O'Donovan, two unarmed teenage brothers, were shot dead by British forces at Parteen, Co. Clare, in February 1921. The British officers who conducted the military inquiry into their deaths accepted that the brothers were innocent civilians; nonetheless the RIC report on their killing states that they had been armed with a grenade and two revolvers. The inquest into their deaths made no mention of any such weaponry. Furthermore, the official British Army history compiled a short time later describes the O'Donovan brothers as active IRA Volunteers. Anonymous, 'The Irish Rebellion in the 6th Divisional Area', p. 143; Toomey, *The Blackwater Tragedy 20th February 1921: Commemorative Booklet* (Meelick, 2013).

38 Hart, *The I.R.A. at War*, p. 94.

39 Toomey, *The War of Independence in Limerick*, pp. 607–8.

40 Hegarty Thorne, *They Put the Flag a-Flyin'*, p. 418.

41 Liam Haugh, BMH WS 474, p. 28; David S. Daniel, *The Royal Hampshire Regiment 1918–1954* (Hampshire, 1955), p. 7.

42 Edward O'Sullivan, BMH WS 1501, pp. 5–6.

43 Summary of Outrages Reported by the Police, June 1921 (NAUK, CO 904/146); Anonymous, 'The Irish Rebellion in the 6th Divisional Area', p. 113.

44 O'Donoghue Papers, 'Intelligence Summary, H Company Auxiliaries' (NLI, MS 31,225).

45 In the later stages of the conflict, the IRA developed the tactic of using hidden landmines during attacks on British patrols. However, these were deliberately detonated by command wire/electrical current during attacks. During the War of Independence republicans seldom used 'booby trap' devices that were abandoned and could easily be triggered accidentally by civilians.

46 Margaret Forester, *Michael Collins: The Lost Leader* (London, 1972), p. 201.

47 Ó Fathaigh, *Ó Fathaigh's War* p. 79.

48 *Ibid.*, pp. 79–80.

49 Abbott, *Police Casualties*, p. 264.

50 Ó Fathaigh, *Ó Fathaigh's War*, pp. 79–80.

51 Thomas Malone Jr., *Alias Seán Forde: The Story of Commandant Tomás Malone, Vice O.C. East Limerick Flying Column, Irish Republican Army* (Dublin, 2000), p. 88.

52 Michael Govern, BMH WS 1625, pp. 7–8.

53 Valiulis, *Portrait of a Revolutionary*, p. 78.

54 PMCILCI on Denis Spriggs (NAUK, WO 35/159A).

55 Leeson, *The Black & Tans*, p. 182. The same phrase was used by the German forces in their attempts to conceal the execution of fifty captured Allied airmen in March/April 1944. Twenty German officers involved in these killings were tried by the British for war crimes and fourteen were executed for the murder of prisoners who were allegedly 'shot while trying to escape'; Simon Read, *Human Game: The True Story of the Great Escape Murders and the Hunt for the Gestapo Gunmen* (New York, 2013), pp. 16, 31, 231.

56 Leeson, *The Black & Tans*, p. 189.

57 Robert Graves, *Goodbye to All That* (London, 1960), p. 153.

58 Malcolm Brown, *The Imperial War Museum Book of the Western Front* (London, 1993), p. 176.

59 *Ibid.*, p. 178.

60 Provisional Military Inquest reports (NAUK, WO 35/147A–159B) and RIC County Inspector's Reports (CO 904/145–146).

61 The total number of those killed by the British forces while allegedly trying to escape is likely to be far in excess of fifty. This does not include more than 200 civilians who were killed by the British forces for allegedly 'refusing to

halt', or IRA members who had not been taken prisoner and were shot dead while attempting to evade arrest.

62   PMCILCI on Martin Kildea, Alfred Rogers, Michael McMahon and John Egan (NAUK, WO 35/153A).

63   Henry O'Mara, BMH WS 1653, p. 18.

64   PMCILCI on Martin Kildea, Alfred Rogers, Michael McMahon and John Egan (NAUK, WO 35/153A).

65   Henry O'Mara, BMH WS 1653, p. 14.

66   Hopkinson, *The Irish War of Independence*, p. 91.

67   PMCILCI on Owen and Stephen Magill (NAUK, WO 35/155A).

68   Michael McMahon, Alfred Rogers and Martin Gildea, 16/11/1920; Michael McNamara and William Shanahan, 22/12/1920; Martin Conway, 27/12/1920; William Slattery, 30/12/1920; Richard Leonard, 31/12/1921; Henry Clancy, 1/5/1921; Seán Wall, 6/5/1921.

69   PMCILCI on W. Deasy, D. Murphy, J. Mullane, M. Sullivan, T. Dennehy and D. Crowley (NAUK, WO 35/149A).

70   *Ibid.*

71   Sheehan, *British Voices*, p. 188.

72   Handcuffs for Prisoners: RIC Circular C.562/1291, 30 March 1920 (NAUK, Home Office 184/125, f. 235).

73   PMCILCI on William McCarthy (NAUK, WO 35/153B). Emphasis in the original.

74   PMCILCI on Thomas Walsh (NAUK, WO 35/160).

75   Borgonovo, *The Anti-Sinn Féin Society*, pp. 112–13.

76   *Ibid.*, p. 115.

77   PMCILCI on William Horgan (NAUK, WO 35/152).

78   *The Cork Examiner*, 13 July 1921; BMH CD 120/3–CD 120/4.

79   *The Irish News*, 13, 14 July 1921.

80   *Ibid.*, 14 July 1921.

81   *The Cork Examiner*, 13 July 1921.

82   *The Irish News*, 13 July 1921.

83   *Ibid.*, 14 July 1921.

84   *Irish Independent*, 15 July 1921.

85   Grave MI 276, Saint Bridget's, Glasnevin Cemetery, Dublin.

86   Sheehan, *British Voices*, p. 188.

87   There is also the possibility that in some areas with a significant loyalist population, the 'Anti-Sinn Féin Society' recruited active loyalists to gather intelligence information, act as 'identifiers' for raiding parties, or assist the British forces in conducting anti-republican reprisals.

88   Charles Dalton, *With the Dublin Brigade* (Cork, 2014), pp. 90–1.

89   *Irish Independent*, 11 September 1920.

90   Hogan, *The Black and Tans*, pp. 156–61. Official reports blamed these killings on the 'Anti-Sinn Féin Society'.

91   Abbott, *Police Casualties*, p. 51.

92   Hogan, *The Black and Tans*, p. 465.

93   Hopkinson, *The Irish War of Independence*, p. 109.

94   Borgonovo, *Anti-Sinn Féin Society*, p. 107.

95   *Ibid.*, p. 107.

96   *Ibid.*, pp. 107–8.

97   *Ibid.*, p. 110.

98   *Ibid.*, p. 111.

99   Toomey, *The War of Independence in Limerick*, pp. 458–65.

100   *Ibid.*, pp. 508–9.

101   *Ibid.*, pp. 537–53.

102   Maurice Levine, *Cheetham to Cordova: A Manchester Man of the Thirties* (Manchester, 1984), p. 39.

103   Toomey, *The War of Independence in Limerick*, pp. 537–53.

104   Ross O'Mahony, 'The Sack of Balbriggan', in David Fitzpatrick (ed.), *Terror in Ireland 1916–1923*, p. 64.

105   Yeates, *A City in Turmoil*, p. 185.

106   *Ibid.*, p. 172.

107   *Ibid.*

108   *The Freeman's Journal*, 15 April 1921; *Irish Independent*, 16 April 1921.

109   Séamus Mac Ciarnáin (ed.), *The Last Post: The Details and Stories of Republican Dead 1913–1975* (Dublin, 1976), p. 88.

110   Hogan, *The Black and Tans*, pp. 176–83.

111   *Ibid.*, p. 463.

112   *Ibid.*, p. 263.

113   *Ibid.*, p. 264.

114   *Ibid.*, pp. 282–3, 464–5.

115   *Ibid.*, pp. 464.

116   *Ibid.*, pp. 331–4.

117   Leeson, *The Black & Tans*, p. 178.

118   Townshend, *The Republic*, p. 251.

119   For crimes of passion, see the case of Kathleen Kelleher, who was shot dead by her boyfriend, RIC Constable John McCansh. McCansh claimed that his pistol had accidentally discharged while they were alone together. He was acquitted of her murder by a British military court of inquiry. For sexually motivated murders, see the case of Kate Maher, who was found unconscious, bleeding to death from serious internal wounds to her vagina. Found next to her was a heavily intoxicated British soldier, Private Thomas Bennett of the Lincolnshire Regiment. Bennett was later acquitted of her murder by a British military court of inquiry; PMCILCI on Kathleen Kelleher (NAUK, WO 35/160); PMCILCI on Kate Maher (NAUK, WO 35/155B).

120   PMCILCI on John Foley (NAUK, WO 35/150).

121   *Ibid.*

122   Charlie Browne, *The Story of the 7th: A Concise History of the 7th Battalion, Cork No. 1 Brigade IRA from 1915–1921* (Cork, 2007), p. 87.

123   Information from Peggy Murphy Leemont, Coachford, Co. Cork, who now lives in John Foley's home, and her son-in-law Michael Dilworth, July 2015.

124   *Kerry People*, 16 July 1921.

125 RIC County Inspector's Report for Kerry, July 1921 (NAUK, CO 904/115).

126 *Kerry People,* 16 July 1921.

127 PMCILCI on Hannah Carey (NAUK, WO 35/147A).

128 *Ibid.*

129 *Ibid.*

130 O'Halpin, 'Counting Terror', in *Terror in Ireland*, p. 154.

131 O'Halpin, 'Problematic Killing during the War of Independence', in Kelly and Lyons (eds), *Death and Dying in Ireland, Britain and Europe*, p. 318.

132 Toomey, *War of Independence in Limerick*, p. 529; Harnett, *Victory and Woe*, p. 166.

133 'Summary of 1st Battalion Diary', in *Regimental Chronicle 1921* (Soldiers of Oxfordshire Trust Archives).

134 William Henry, *Blood for Blood: The Black and Tan War in Galway* (Cork, 2012), pp. 126–8.

135 *Galway Observer*, 6 November 1920.

136 *Irish Independent*, 5 November 1920.

137 PMCILCI on Hannah Carey (NAUK, WO 35/147A).

138 Yeates, *A City in Turmoil*, p. 285.

139 O'Sullivan, *The Irish Constabularies*, p. 361.

140 See Kee, *The Green Flag, Vol. III*, p. 143; *Irish Independent*, 22 June 2011.

7   BELFAST'S BLOODY SUNDAY

1 *Belfast Telegraph*, 11 July 1921.

2 Phillips, *The Revolution in Ireland*, p. 216.

3 Hezlet, *The 'B' Specials*, pp. 23, 46.

4 Abbott, *Police Casualties*, p. 265; Trotter, *Constabulary Heroes*, p. 28.

5 *The Irish Times*, 27 August 1994.

6 *Irish Independent*, 22 June 1921.

7 MacEoin, *Survivors*, p. 305.

8 Gerry Adams, *Falls Memories: A Belfast Life* (Colorado, 1994), pp. 66–7.

9 Roger McCorley, BMH WS 389, pp. 22–3.

10 Seán Mac Iomaire, in Geraldine McAteer (ed.), *Down the Falls. Book One: The Old Falls* (Belfast, 1983), p. 17.

11 Lyrics recorded by Hugh McAteer and reproduced in *Down the Falls*. The additional verse (verse two) is from local historian Jim McDermott. This song is a reworking of 'A row in the town' written about the 1916 Rising; McAteer (ed.), *Down the Falls*, p. 17; Jim McDermott, *Northern Divisions: The Old IRA and the Belfast Pogroms 1920–22* Belfast 2001), pp. 100–1; Frank Harte, *Dublin Street Songs* (Dublin, 2004).

12 RIC County Inspector's Report for Belfast, July 1921 (NAUK, CO 904/115).

13 *Belfast Telegraph*, 11 July 1921; *The Irish News*, 11 July 1921.

14 RIC County Inspector's Report for Belfast, July 1921 (NAUK, CO 904/115).

15 *The Irish News*, 11 July 1921.

16 *Ulster Herald*, 16 July 1921.

17   McAteer (ed.), *Down the Falls*, p. 16.
18   McDermott, *Northern Divisions*, p. 99.
19   McAteer (ed.) *Down the Falls*, pp. 15–16.
20   *Belfast Telegraph*, 9 August 1921.
21   RIC County Inspector's Report for Belfast, July 1921 (NAUK, CO 904/115); Seán Mac Iomaire in McAteer (ed.) *Down the Falls*, p. 16.
22   McDermott, *Northern Divisions*, p. 103; McAteer (ed.) *Down the Falls*, p. 16.
23   Trotter, *Constabulary Heroes*, p. 28.
24   Abbott, *Police Casualties*, p. 265.
25   Interview with Roger McCorley (EOMN UCDA P17b/98).
26   McDermott, *Northern Divisions*, p. 101.
27   *Belfast Telegraph*, 11 July 1921.
28   *The Irish News*, 11 July 1921.
29   RIC County Inspector's Report for Belfast, July 1921 (NAUK, CO 904/115).
30   McDermott, *Northern Divisions*, p. 101.
31   *The Irish News*, 11 July 1921.
32   *Belfast Telegraph*, 11 July 1921; *The Irish News*, 11 July 1921.
33   *The Irish News*, 11 July 1921.
34   RIC County Inspector's Report for Belfast, July 1921 (NAUK, CO 904/115).
35   *The Irish News*, 11 July 1921.
36   Parkinson, *Unholy War*, p. 155.
37   *The Irish News*, 11 July 1921.
38   RIC County Inspector's Report for Belfast, July 1921 (NAUK, CO 904/115).
39   *The Irish News*, 11 July 1921.
40   Parkinson, *Unholy War*, p. 154.
41   *The Irish News*, 11 July 1921.
42   *Belfast Telegraph*, 11 July 1921.
43   *The Irish News*, 11 July 1921.
44   Parkinson, *Unholy War*, p. 154.
45   RIC County Inspector's Report for Belfast, July 1921 (NAUK, CO 904/115).
46   *The Irish News*, 12 July 1921.
47   Parkinson, *Unholy War*, p. 155; *The Irish News*, 11 July 1921.
48   McDermott, *Northern Divisions*, p. 102.
49   Parkinson, *Belfast's Unholy War*, p. 154.
50   *Belfast Telegraph*, 9 August 1921.
51   *Ibid.*, 21 August 1921.
52   McDermott, *Northern Divisions*, pp. 101–2.
53   *The Irish News*, 12 July 1921.
54   McDermott, *Northern Divisions*, p. 103.
55   *Belfast Telegraph*, 9 August 1921; Parkinson, *Unholy War*, p. 155.
56   Belfast National Graves Association, *Antrim's Patriot Dead 1919–1993* (Belfast, undated); McDermott, *Northern Divisions*, p. 102.

57　*The Irish News*, 12 July 1921.

58　RIC County Inspector's Report for Belfast, July 1921 (NAUK, CO 904/115).

59　RIC County Inspector's Report for Belfast, July 1921 (NAUK, CO 904/115).

60　Macardle, *The Irish Republic*, p. 437.

61　Interview with Roger McCorley (EOMN UCDA P17b/98).

62　Stanley H. Palmer, *Police and Protest in England and Ireland 1780–1850* (Cambridge, 1988), p. 527; Andrew Boyd, *Holy War in Belfast* (Tralee, 1969), pp. 142–9.

63　Boyd, *Holy War*, p. 174.

64　McDermott, *Northern Divisions*, p. 6.

65　Boyd, *Holy War*, p. 9.

66　*Ibid.*, pp. 10–32.

67　Thomas Fennell, *The Royal Irish Constabulary* (Dublin, 2003), pp. 86–9.

68　Robert Lynch, 'The People's Protectors? The Irish Republican Army and the "Belfast Pogrom" 1920–1922', *Journal of British Studies*, vol. 47, no. 2 (April, 2008), p. 379.

69　*Belfast Newsletter*, 14 July 1919.

70　*Ibid.*, 13 July 1920.

71　*The Irish News*, 13 July 1920.

72　*Banbridge Chronicle*, 24 July 1920.

73　Tim Pat Coogan, *The IRA* (4th edn; London, 1995), p. 26.

74　Michael Farrell, *Arming the Protestants: The Formation of the Ulster Special Constabulary and the Royal Ulster Constabulary 1920–27* (London, 1983), p. 25.

75　Coogan, *The IRA*, p. 26.

76　Lynch, *The Northern IRA and the Early Years of Partition* (Dublin, 2006), p. 28; McDermott, *Northern Divisions*, p. 37.

77　Michael Farrell, *Northern Ireland: The Orange State* (London, 1976) pp. 28–9.

78　Lynch, 'The People's Protectors?', p. 380.

79　Palmer, *Police and Protest*, p. 528.

80　Elizabeth Malcolm, *The Irish Policeman 1822–1922: A Life* (Dublin, 2006), pp. 155–6.

81　*The Irish News*, 16 July 1921.

82　*Ibid.*, 11 July 1921.

83　*Belfast Telegraph*, 11 July 1921.

84　Roger McCorley, BMH WS 389, p. 25.

85　Hopkinson, *The Irish War of Independence*, pp. 194–5.

86　Farrell, *Arming the Protestants*, pp. 60–1.

87　Wilson, *Frontiers of Violence*, pp. 85–6.

88　J. J. McConnell, BMH WS 509, p. 6.

89　Wilson, *Frontiers of Violence*, pp. 92–3.

90　Lynch, 'The People's Protectors?', pp. 378–81.

91　Wilson, *Frontiers of Violence*, p. 107.

92　Diary of Frederick Crawford (PRONI, D640/11/1).

93   Confidential file on DI Nixon, Ernest Blythe Papers (UCDA, P24/176).

94   McDermott, *Northern Divisions*, pp. 60–1.

95   Trotter, *Constabulary Heroes*, p. 15.

96   Confidential file on DI Nixon, Blythe Papers (UCDA, P24/176).

97   McDermott, *Northern Divisions*, pp. 76–7.

98   Kieran Glennon, *From Pogrom to Civil War: Tom Glennon and the Belfast IRA* (Cork, 2013), pp. 27–8, 62.

99   *Ibid.*, p. 88.

100   McDermott, *Northern Divisions*, pp. 88–9.

101   McCorley, BMH WS 389, p. 20.

102   McDermott, *Northern Divisions*, p. 90.

103   Trotter, *Constabulary Heroes*, p. 27.

104   *The Irish News*, 8 July 1921.

105   Trotter, *Constabulary Heroes*, pp. 24–5.

106   *Ibid.*, pp. 26–7.

107   Interview with Roger McCorley (EOMN UCDA P17b/98).

108   McAteer (ed.), *Down the Falls*, p. 17.

109   McDermott, *Northern Divisions*, p. 100.

110   Interview with Tom McAnally (EOMN UCDA P17b/99).

111   See *Belfast Telegraph*, 11 July 1921; RIC County Inspector's Report for Belfast, July 1921 (NAUK, CO 904/115).

112   Hezlet, *The 'B' Specials*, p. 25.

113   Malcolm, *The Irish Policeman*, pp. 155–6.

114   Audio recording of Patrick Diamond (OFL, LOK IV, B 01).

115   Farrell, *Arming the Protestants*, pp. 13–14.

116   Ryder, *The Fateful Split*, p. 12.

117   Bates to Carson, 14 May 1920 (PRONI, Carson Papers D1570/1/3/39).

118   Ryder, *The Fateful Split*, p. 12.

119   *Ibid.*, p. 10.

120   Farrell, *Arming the Protestants*, p. 33.

121   *Ibid.*, p. 39.

122   *Belfast Newsletter*, 2 November 1920.

123   Spender to Belfast Regiment UVF Battalion Commanders, 29 October 1920 (PRONI, D1295/2/12).

124   Spender to Rev B. Ingram (PRONI D1295/2/16).

125   Interview between S. G. Tallents and General Ricardo, June 1922 (NAUK, CO 906/26).

126   Memo to Tyrone UVF Battalion Commanders, September 1920 (PRONI, D1678/6).

127   Statement by Sergeant John Murphy, 22 March 1922 (State Papers Office, Dublin).

128   Farrell, *Arming the Protestants*, pp. 49–50.

129   Ryder, *The Fateful Split*, p. 20.

130   United Kingdom Parliamentary Debates (Hansard), House of Commons, 5th Series, vol. 133, cols 1504–05, 25 October 1920.

131   *Ibid.*, vol. 133, cols 1487–8, 25 October 1920.

132 *Westminster Gazette*, 16 September 1920.

133 Peader Livingstone, *The Fermanagh Story* (Enniskillen, 1969), p. 302.

134 United Kingdom Parliamentary Debates, House of Commons, 5th Series, vol. 133, cols 1291–2; vol. 138, col. 93; vol. 139, cols 22–3 and 1678–82; 20 December 1920; 16 February 1921; 7–17 March 1921.

135 See, for example, the killings of the O'Reilly brothers, P. McGennity, P. Quinn and T. McAnuff in Chapter 6.

136 Crawford Diary, 29 September 1920 (PRONI, D640/11/1).

137 Weekly returns of Special Constabulary strength, 1921 (PRONI, FIN 18/1/13).

138 Wilson, *Frontiers of Violence*, p. 90.

139 Abbott, *Police Casualties*, p. 267.

140 *Belfast Telegraph*, 12 July 1921; Sir Wilfrid Spender to W. Kennedy, 12 July 1921 (PRONI, CAB 6/21/1).

141 *Belfast Telegraph*, 12 July 1921.

142 *Fermanagh Herald*, 19 July 1921.

143 Sir Wilfred Spender's interview with Sir Hamar Greenwood, 10 August 1920 (PRONI, CAB 4/14/7).

144 Interview with Seán Lehane (EOMN UCDA P17b/108).

145 Pearse Lawlor, *The Outrages: The IRA and the Special Constabulary in the Border Campaign 1920–1922* (Cork, 2011), p. 189.

146 McDermott, *Northern Divisions*, p. 102.

147 Frederick Crawford Diary, 5 July 1921 (PRONI, D640/11/1).

148 McCorley, BMH WS 389, p. 23.

149 *The Irish News*, 13 July 1921.

150 *Belfast Telegraph*, 9 August 1921.

151 *Ibid.*, 21 August 1921.

152 McDermott, *Northern Divisions*, p. 102; *The Irish News*, 11 July 1921; *Belfast Telegraph*, 21 August 1921.

153 *Belfast Telegraph*, 9 August 1921.

154 MacEoin, *Survivors*, p. 305.

155 Roger McCorley, BMH WS 389, p. 26.

156 RIC County Inspector's Report for Belfast, July 1921 (NAUK, CO 904/115); *The Irish News*, 12 July 1921.

157 McDermott, *Northern Divisions*, p. 36.

158 Lynch, *The Northern IRA*, pp. 29–30.

159 Lynch, 'The People's Protectors?', p. 382.

160 *Ibid.*

161 Brian Feeney, *Seán MacDiarmada* (Dublin, 2014), p. 167.

162 McAteer (ed.) *Down the Falls*, p. 15.

163 Jack McNally, *Morally Good – Politically Bad* (Belfast, 1987), p. 5.

164 McAteer (ed.), *Down the Falls*, p. 15.

165 Wilson, *Frontiers of Violence*, p. 129.

166 *Ibid.*, p. 125.

167 Lynch, *The Northern IRA*, pp. 29–31; Wilson, *Frontiers of Violence*, p. 129.

168 Wilson, *Frontiers of Violence*, p. 125.

169 *Ibid.*, p. 128.
170 *Ibid.*
171 John McCoy, BMH WS 492, p. 114.
172 *The Cork Examiner*, 26 July 1921.
173 Lynch, 'The People's Protectors?', p. 382.
174 Woods to Mulcahy, 27 July 1922 (UCDA, RMP, P/7/B/77).
175 Roger McCorley, BMH WS 389, pp. 25–6.
176 Operations Report, 3rd Northern Division, 12 July 1921 (UCDA, RMP, P7/A/22).
177 *Belfast Telegraph*, 9 August 1921; *The Irish Times*, 12 July 1921.
178 Lynch, 'The People's Protectors?', p. 380.
179 *Ibid.*, p. 375.
180 McDermott, *Northern Divisions*, p. 44.

Bibliography

Archival Sources

Armagh
Cardinal Tomás Ó Fiaich Library and Archive
Fr Louis O'Kane Collection [OFL, LOKP]

Belfast
Public Records Office of Northern Ireland
Carson Papers
Frederick Crawford Diaries
Ministry of Home Affairs Files

Bicester
The Soldiers of Oxfordshire Trust Archive
Lieutenant J. B. Jarvis Intelligence Papers
Oxford and Buckinghamshire Light Infantry Regimental Record

Chelmsford
Essex Regimental Archive
Lieutenant Coleman Trollope Papers
Captain I. Paton Papers
Harry John Staff Papers

Cork
Cork City and County Archives [CCCA]
Connie Neenan Papers
Liam de Roiste Papers
Plan of Cork City (West) 1900

Dublin
Irish Military Archives
Bureau of Military History Contemporaneous Documents
Department of Defence Series
Military Service Pension Records IRA Nominal Roll
Oscar Traynor Collection

National Archives
1901 Census Returns
1911 Census Returns
Bureau of Military History Witness Statements [BMH, WS]
Cork Crown and Peace Officers Records
Dáil Éireann Papers [NAI, DÉ]
Department of Justice Files
Royal Irish Constabulary Register [microfilm]

National Library of Ireland
Michael Collins Papers [microfilm]
Art O'Brien Papers [NLI, AOBP]
Florence O'Donoghue Papers
Ernie O'Malley Papers

University College Dublin Archives
Ernest Blythe Papers
Richard Mulcahy Papers
Ernie O'Malley Military Notebooks [EOMN UCDA]
Ernie O'Malley Papers
Éamon de Valera Papers [UCDA, DeVP]

State Papers Office
Sergeant John Murphy Papers

Ennis
Civil Registration Office
Local Register of Births, Deaths and Marriages

Galway
National University of Ireland Archives
Chevers Papers

Gloucester
Soldiers of Gloucestershire Museum
R. M. Grazebrook Papers

Lichfield
Staffordshire Regimental Museum
Register of Enlisted Men

Limerick
Mary Immaculate College Library
'The British in Ireland, 1914–1921': CO 904 Papers [microfilm]
RIC County Inspectors' and Inspector General's Reports: CO 904 Papers [microfilm]

London
Imperial War Museum
Sir Hugh Jeudwine Papers
General Sir Peter Strickland Papers
Lieutenant Colonel J. B. Jarvis Papers
Photographic Archive

National Army Museum
Digest of service of the 1st Battalion Lancashire Fusiliers
East Kent Regiment – Castletown Roche Detachment Log
Brigadier M. H. ap Rhys Pryce Tapes
General Sir Edmond Allenby Papers
Lieutenant Colonel Peter F. Fitzgerald Papers

National Archives
Cabinet Papers [NAUK, CAB]
Colonial Office Papers
Earl of Midleton Papers
Home Office Papers
War Office Papers [NAUK, WO]

Parliamentary Archives
David Lloyd George Papers

Oxford
Bodleian Library
Lieutenant J. B. Jarvis Diary

Stirling
The Argyll and Sutherland Highlanders Regimental Museum
R. C. B. Anderson Manuscript – History of the 2nd Batt. Argyll and Sutherland Highlanders

Newspapers and Periodicals

An t-Óglach
The Atlantic Monthly (now Atlantic
    magazine)
Banbridge Chronicle
Belfast Newsletter
Belfast Telegraph
Capuchin Annual, The
Clare Champion, The
Connacht Tribune
Cork Constitution
Cork Examiner, The (now Irish
    Examiner)
Dublin Brigade Review
Evening Echo
Fermanagh Herald
Foreign Affairs
Freeman's Journal, The
Galway Observer
History Ireland
Irish Daily Mail
Irish Independent
Irish News, The
Irish Times, The
Kerry People
Limerick Leader
Illustrated London News, The
Morning Post
Nenagh Guardian, The
New York Times, The
Northern Whig, The

Observer-Reporter
Saturday Record
Southern Star, The
Sunday Independent
Sunday Tribune
Times, The
Ulster Herald
War Illustrated, The
Weekly Summary
Westminster Gazette, The

Private Collections

Kathleen Hegarty Thorne Interviews
Michael Quirke Papers, c/o Martin O'Dwyer, Cashel War of Independence
    Museum
George Lennon Manuscript, *From Ulster to the Deise*, Extract in author's posses-
    sion

PUBLISHED SOURCES

Abbott, Richard, *Police Casualties in Ireland 1919–1922* (Cork, 2000)

Adams, Gerry, *Falls Memories: A Belfast Life* (Colorado, 1994)

Agget, W. J. P., *The Bloody Eleventh, History of The Devonshire Regiment Vol. 3: 1914–1969* (Exeter, 1995)

Andrews, C. S., *Dublin Made Me: An Autobiography* (Cork, 1979)

Anonymous, 'The Irish Rebellion in the 6th Divisional Area', *The Irish Sword*, vol. xxvii, no. 107 (Spring 2010)

Anonymous, *An Officer's Wife in Ireland*, eds Caroline Woodcock and Tim Pat Coogan (London, 1994)

Arthur, Max, *The Road Home: The Aftermath of the Great War Told by the Men and Women Who Survived It* (London, 2010)

Augusteijn, Joost (ed.), *The Irish Revolution, 1913–23* (London, 2002)

Barry, Tom, *The Reality of the Anglo-Irish War 1920–21 in West Cork: Refutations, Corrections and Comments on Liam Deasy's Towards Ireland Free* (Tralee, 1974)

Barry, Tom, *Guerilla Days in Ireland* (5th edn; Dublin, 1981)

Bartlett, Thomas and Jeffrey, Keith (eds), *A Military History of Ireland* (Cambridge, 1996)

Barton, Brian, *The Secret Court Martial Records of the Easter Rising* (Gloucester, 2010)

Béaslaí, Piaras, *Michael Collins and the Making of a New Ireland* (2 vols, Dublin, 1926)

Belfast National Graves Association, *Antrim's Patriot Dead 1919–1993* (Belfast, undated)

Bence Jones, Mark, *Twilight of the Ascendancy* (London, 1987)

Bennett, Richard, *The Black and Tans* (5th edn; London, 1970)

Bew, Paul, *Ireland: The Politics of Enmity 1789–2006* (Oxford, 2007)

Boghardt, Thomas, *Spies of the Kaiser: German Covert Operations in Great Britain during the First World War Era* (Basingstoke, 2004)

Borgonovo, John, *Florence and Josephine O'Donoghue's War of Independence: A Destiny that Shapes Our Ends* (Dublin, 2006)

— *Spies, Informers and the Anti-Sinn Féin Society* (Dublin, 2007)

— 'The Guerrilla Infrastructure: IRA Special Services in the Cork Number One Brigade 1917–1921', *The Irish Sword*, vol. XXVII, no. 108 (Dublin, 2010)

— 'Revolutionary Violence and Irish Historiography', *Irish Historical Studies*, vol. xxxviii, no. 150 (November 2012)

Boyd, Andrew, *Holy War in Belfast* (Tralee, 1969)

Brady, Ciaran (ed.) *Interpreting Irish History: The Debate on Historical Revisionism* (Dublin, 1994)

Brennan, Michael, *The War in Clare 1911–1921: Personal Memoirs of the Irish War of Independence* (Dublin, 1980)

Brown, Malcolm, *The Imperial War Museum Book of the Western Front* (London, 1993)

Browne, Charlie, *The Story of the 7th: A Concise History of the 7th Battalion, Cork No. 1 Brigade IRA from 1915–1921* (Cork, 2007)

Burleigh, Michael, *Blood & Rage: A Cultural History of Terrorism* (London, 2008)

Campbell, Fergus, *Land and Politics: Nationalist Politics in the West of Ireland 1891–1921* (Oxford, 2005)

Chamberlain, Austin, *The Austin Chamberlain Diary Letters: The Correspondence of Sir Austin Chamberlain with His Sisters Hilda and Ida, 1916–1937,* Vol. V, ed. Robert B. Self (Cambridge, 1995)

Cobb, Matthew, *The Resistance: The French Fight against the Nazis* (London, 2009)

Coleman, Marie, *County Longford and the Irish Revolution 1910–1923* (Dublin, 2006)

— *The Irish Revolution 1916–1923* (New York, 2014)

Collins, Jude, *Whose Past is it Anyway? The Ulster Covenant, the Easter Rising & the Battle of the Somme* (Dublin, 2012)

Collins, M. E., *Ireland 1868–1966* (Dublin, 1993)

Colvert, Brendan K., *On My Honour: One Man's Lifelong Struggle to Clear His Name* (Cork, 2011)

Comerford, James J., *My Kilkenny IRA Days 1916–1922* (Kilkenny, 1980)

Coogan, Oliver, *Politics and War in Meath 1913–23* (Dublin, 1983)

Coogan, Tim Pat, *Michael Collins* (London, 1991)

— *The IRA* (4th edn; London, 1995)

Costecalde, Claude and Walker, Brian (eds) *The Church of Ireland: An Illustrated History* (Dublin, 2013)

Costello, Francis, *The Irish Revolution and Its Aftermath 1916–1923* (Dublin, 2003)

Cottrell, Peter, *The War for Ireland 1913–1923* (Oxford, 2009)

Coyle, Stephen, *High Noon on High Street: The Story of a Daring Ambush by the IRA in Glasgow in 1921* (Glasgow, 2008)

Curran, Joseph M., *The Birth of the Irish Free State 1921–1923* (Alabama, 1980)

Dalton, Charles, *With the Dublin Brigade* (Cork, 2014)

Daniel, David S., *The Royal Hampshire Regiment 1918–1954* (Hampshire, 1955)

D'Arcy, Fergus A., *Remembering the War Dead: British Commonwealth and International War Graves in Ireland since 1914* (Dublin, 2007)

De Burca, Padraig and Boyle, John F., *Free State or Republic? Pen Pictures of the Historic Treaty Session of Dáil Éireann* (2nd edn; Dublin, 2002)

Dooley, Terence, 'IRA Activity in Kildare during the War of Independence', in William Nolan and Thomas McGrath (eds), *Kildare: History and Society* (Dublin, 2005)

Dorney, John, *The Story of the Irish War of Independence* (e-book, 2010)

Duff, Douglas V., *Sword for Hire: The Saga of a Modern Free-Companion* (London, 1934)

Dungan, Myles, *Irish Voices from the Great War* (2nd edn; Kildare, 2014)

Durney, James, *The Volunteer: Uniforms, Weapons and History of the Irish Republican Army 1913–1997* (Naas, 2004)

English, Richard and Walker, Graham (eds), *Unionism in Modern Ireland* (Dublin, 1996)

Enright, Séan, *Easter Rising 1916: The Trials* (Dublin, 2014)

Evans, Bryce, *Seán Lemass: Democratic Dictator* (Dublin, 2011)

Ewart, Wilfrid, *A Journey in Ireland 1921* (London, 1922)

Farrell, Michael, *Northern Ireland: The Orange State* (London, 1976)

— *Arming the Protestants: The Formation of the Ulster Special Constabulary and the Royal Ulster Constabulary 1920–27* (London, 1983)

Farry, Michael, *Sligo 1914–1921: A Chronicle of Conflict* (Trim, 1992)

— *The Aftermath of Revolution: Sligo 1921–1923* (Dublin, 2000)

— *Sligo: The Irish Revolution 1912–23* (Dublin, 2012)

Feeney, Brian, *Seán MacDiarmada* (Dublin, 2014)

Fennell, Thomas, *The Royal Irish Constabulary* (Dublin, 2003)

Ferguson, Niall, *The Pity of War: Explaining World War One* (New York, 1999)

Fitzgerald, Thomas Earls, 'The Execution of Spies and Informers in West Cork, 1921', in David Fitzpatrick (ed.) *Terror in Ireland 1916–1923* (Dublin, 2012)

Fitzgerald, William G., *The Voice of Ireland: A Survey of the Race and Nation from all Angles* (London, 1925)

Fitzpatrick, David (ed.), *Revolution? Ireland, 1917–23* (Dublin, 1990)

— 'Militarism in Ireland 1900–1922', in Thomas Bartlett and Keith Jeffrey (eds), *A Military History of Ireland* (Cambridge, 1996)

— *Politics and Irish life: 1913–1921: Provincial Experience of War and Revolution* (2nd edn; Cork, 1998)

— *The Two Irelands 1912–1939* (Oxford, 1998)

— (ed.), *Terror in Ireland 1916–1923* (Dublin, 2012)

Forester, Margaret, *Michael Collins: The Lost Leader* (London, 1972)

Foster, Gavin M., *The Irish Civil War and Society: Politics, Class and Conflict* (London, 2015)

Gallagher, Ronan, *Violence and Nationalist Politics in Derry City 1920–1923* (Dublin, 2003)

Gaughan, J. Anthony, *Listowel and Its Vicinity* (Kildare, 1973)

Glennon, Kieran, *From Pogrom to Civil War: Tom Glennon and the Belfast IRA* (Cork, 2013)

Graves, Robert, *Goodbye to All That* (London, 1960)

Griffith, Kenneth and O'Grady, Timothy (eds), *Curious Journey: An Oral History of Ireland's Unfinished Revolution* (London, 1982)

Hanley, Brian, *The IRA: A Documentary History 1916–2005* (Dublin 2010)

Hannigan, Dave, *Terence MacSwiney: The Hunger Strike that Rocked an Empire* (Dublin, 2010)

Harnett, Mossie, *Victory and Woe: The West Limerick Brigade in the War of Independence* (Dublin, 2002)

Hart, Peter, 'The Protestant Experience of Revolution in Ireland', in Richard English and Graham Walker (eds), *Unionism in Modern Ireland* (Dublin, 1996)

— *The I.R.A & Its Enemies: Violence and Community in Cork 1916–1923* (Oxford, 1998)

— (ed.), *British Intelligence in Ireland 1920–1921: The Final Reports* (Cork, 2002)

— 'Definition: Defining the Irish Revolution', in Augusteijn, Joost (ed.), *The Irish Revolution, 1913–23* (London, 2002)

— *The I.R.A. at War 1916–1923* (Oxford, 2003)

— *Mick: The Real Michael Collins* (London, 2005)

— 'Interview', *History Ireland*, March/April 2005

Harte, Frank, *Dublin Street Songs* LP (Dublin, 2004)

Hayes, Michael, *The Irish Republican Struggle in Limerick: Diary of a 16-year-old Volunteer*, ed. Michael Ó hAodha (Dublin, 2013)

Heaney, Paddy, Muldowney, Paddy, O'Connor, Philip and others (eds), *Coolacrease: The True Story of the Pearson Executions – an Incident in the Irish War of Independence* (Cork, 2008)

Hegarty Thorne, Kathleen, *They Put the Flag a-Flyin': The Roscommon Volunteers 1916–1921* (Newberg, Oregon, 2005)

Henchion, Richard, *The Land of the Finest Drop: The Story of Life, Love and Labour in the Districts of the Lough, Togher, Pouladuff, Friars Walk and Ballyphehane over a Period of 400 Years* (Cork, 2003)

Henry, William, *Blood for Blood: The Black and Tan War in Galway* (Cork, 2012)

Hezlet, Arthur, *The 'B' Specials: A History of the Ulster Special Constabulary* (Belfast, 1997)

Hittle, J. B. E., *Michael Collins and the Anglo-Irish War: Britain's Counterinsurgency Failure* (Washington DC, 2011)

Hogan, Séan, *The Black and Tans in North Tipperary: Policing, Revolution and War 1913–1922* (Nenagh, 2013)

Hopkinson, Michael (ed.), *The Last Days of Dublin Castle: The Mark Sturgis Diaries* (Dublin, 1999)

— *The Irish War of Independence* (Dublin, 2002)

Horne, John and Madigan, Edward (eds), *Towards Commemoration: Ireland in War and Revolution 1912–1923* (Dublin, 2013)

Inglis, Brian, *West Briton* (London, 1962)

James, Lawrence, *Warrior Race: A History of the British at War* (London, 2002)

Jeffery, Keith, *The British Army and the Crisis of Empire 1918–1922* (Manchester, 1984)

Jones, Thomas, *Whitehall Diary, Vol III: Ireland 1918–1925*, ed. Keith Middlemas (London, 1971)

Joy, Sinéad, *The IRA in Kerry 1916–1921* (Cork, 2005)

Kautt, William H., *Ground Truths: British Army Operations in the Irish War of Independence* (Dublin, 2014)

— *Ambushes and Armour: The Irish Rebellion 1919–1921* (Dublin, 2010)

— 'Studying the Irish Revolution as Military History: Ambushes and Armour', *The Irish Sword*, vol. XXVII, no. 108 (Summer 2010)

Keane, Barry, 'Ethnic cleansing? Protestant Decline in West Cork between 1911 and 1926', *History Ireland* (March/April 2012)

— *Massacre in West Cork: The Dunmanway and Ballygroman Killings* (Cork, 2014)

Kee, Robert, *The Green Flag, Vol III: Ourselves Alone* (London, 1972)

Kenny, Tomás, *Galway: Politics and Society 1910–23* (Dublin, 2011)

Kingston, Diarmuid, *Beleaguered: A History of the RIC in West Cork during the War of Independence* (Cork, 2013)

Knight, Colonel C. R. B., *Historical Record of the Buffs 1919–1948* (London 1951)

Knightley, Philip, *The First Casualty: The War Correspondent as Hero, Propagandist and Myth Maker* (London, 1975)

Lawlor, Pearse, *The Burnings 1920* (Cork, 2009)

— *The Outrages: The IRA and the Special Constabulary in the Border Campaign 1920–1922* (Cork, 2011)

Leeson, David M., *The Black & Tans: British Police and Auxiliaries in the Irish War of Independence* (Oxford, 2011)

Leonard, Jane, 'Getting Them at Last: The IRA and Ex-servicemen', in David Fitzpatrick (ed.), *Revolution? Ireland, 1917–23* (Dublin, 1990)

— 'English Dogs or Poor Devils? The Dead of Bloody Sunday Morning', in David Fitzpatrick (ed.), *Terror in Ireland 1916–1923* (Dublin, 2012)

Levine, Maurice, *Cheetham to Cordova: A Manchester Man of the Thirties* (Manchester, 1984)

Lewis, Matthew, 'The Newry Brigade and the War of Independence in Armagh and South Down 1919–1921', *The Irish Sword*, vol. XXVII, no. 108 (2010)

Lieberson, Goddard, *The Irish Uprising 1916–1922* (New York, 1968)

Livingstone, Peadar, *The Fermanagh Story* (Enniskillen, 1969)

Lowe, W. J., 'Who Were the Black-And-Tans?', *History Ireland*, vol. 12, no. 3 (Autumn 2004), pp. 47–51

Lynch, Robert, *The Northern IRA and the Early Years of Partition* (Dublin, 2006)

— 'The People's Protectors? The Irish Republican Army and the "Belfast Pogrom" 1920–1922', *Journal of British Studies*, vol. 47, no. 2 (April 2008)

Macardle, Dorothy, *The Irish Republic* (5th edn; London, 1968)

Mac Ciarnáin, Séamus (ed.), *The Last Post: The Details and Stories of Republican Dead 1913–1975* (Dublin, 1976)

MacEoin, Uinseann, *Survivors* (Dublin, 1980)

Macready, Nevil, *Annals of an Active Life* (2 vols, London, 1924)

Maher, Jim, *The Flying Column: West Kilkenny 1916–21* (Kilkenny, 1988)

Malcolm, Elizabeth, *The Irish Policeman 1822–1922: A Life* (Dublin, 2006)

Malone, James, *Blood on the Flag: Autobiography of a Freedom Fighter*, ed. Patrick J. Twohig (Cork, 1996)

Malone, Thomas Jr., *Alias Seán Forde: the Story of Commandant Tomás Malone, Vice O. C. East Limerick Flying Column, Irish Republican Army* (Dublin, 2000)

Martin, Hugh, *Ireland in Insurrection: an Englishman's Record of Fact* (London, 1921)

Matthews, Ann, *Renegades: Irish Republican Women 1900–1922* (Cork, 2010)

McAteer, Geraldine (ed.), *Down the Falls. Book One: The Old Falls* (Belfast, 1983)

McCall, Ernest, *The Auxiliaries: Tudor's Toughs: A Study of the Auxiliary Division Royal Irish Constabulary 1920–1922* (Newtownards, 2010)

McCluskey, Fergal, 'The "Tan War" in Tyrone 1920–1921: A Comparative Analysis of the Violence of the IRA and Crown forces', *The Irish Sword*, vol. XXVII, no. 109 (2010)

McDermott, Jim, *Northern Divisions: The Old IRA and the Belfast Pogroms 1920–22* (Belfast 2001)

McGarry, Fearghal, *Eoin O'Duffy: A Self-Made Hero* (Oxford, 2005)

— *The Rising: Ireland, Easter 1916* (Oxford, 2010)

— *Rebels: Voices from The Easter Rising* (Dublin, 2011)

— 'Violence and the Easter Rising', in David Fitzpatrick (ed.) *Terror in Ireland 1916–1923* (Dublin, 2012)

— '1916 and Irish Republicanism: Between Myth and History', in John Horne and Edward Madigan (eds), *Towards Commemoration: Ireland in War and Revolution 1912–1923* (Dublin, 2013)

McKenna, Joseph, *Guerrilla Warfare in the Irish War of Independence 1919–1921* (Jefferson, 2011)

McNally, Jack, *Morally Good – Politically Bad* (Belfast, 1987)

McNamara, Michael, *Unveiling of a Memorial to Commemorate the Glenwood Ambush of 20 January 1921: Commemorative Booklet* (Sixmilebridge, 2011)

Milne, Kenneth, 'A History of the Church of Ireland', in Claude Costecalde and Brian Walker (eds), *The Church of Ireland: An Illustrated History* (Dublin, 2013)

Montgomery, Bernard Law, *The Memoirs of Field-Marshal, the Viscount Montgomery of Alamein K.G.* (London, 1958)

Mooney, Tommy, *Cry of the Curlew: A History of the Déise Brigade IRA and the War of Independence* (Dungarvan, 2012)

Morton, James, *Spies of the First World War: Under Cover for King and Kaiser* (London, 2010)

Mulcahy, Risteard, *My Father the General: Richard Mulcahy and the Military History of the Revolution* (Dublin, 2009)

Murphy, Brian P., *The Origins and Organisation of British Propaganda in Ireland 1920* (Cork, 2006)

Murphy, Donie, *The Men of the South and Their Part in the Fight for Irish Freedom* (Cork, 1991)

Murphy, Gerard, *The Year of Disappearances: Political Killings in Cork 1921–1922* (Dublin, 2010)

Murphy, Séan and Murphy, Síle, *The Comeraghs: Gunfire and Civil War. The Story of the Deise Brigade IRA 1914–1924* (Waterford, 2003)

Murphy, William, *Political Imprisonment and the Irish 1912–1921* (Oxford, 2014)

Murray, P., *Oracles of God: The Roman Catholic Church and Irish Politics 1922–37* (Dublin, 2000)

Neitzel, Sonke and Welzer, Harald, *Soldaten on Fighting, Killing and Dying: The Secret World War Tapes of German POWs* (London 2012)

Nic Dháibhéid, Caoimhe, *Seán MacBride: A Republican Life 1904–1946* (2nd edn; Liverpool, 2014)

Nolan, William and McGrath, Thomas (eds), *Kildare: History and Society* (Dublin, 2005)

Noonan, Gerard, *The IRA in Britain 1919–1923: 'In The Heart of Enemy Lines'* (Liverpool, 2014)

Ó Brádaigh, Ruairí, *Dílseacht: The Story of Comdt. General Tom Maguire and the Second (All-Ireland) Dáil* (Dublin, 1997)

Ó Broin, León, *Protestant Nationalists in Revolutionary Ireland: The Stopford Connection* (Dublin, 1985)

O'Callaghan, John, *Revolutionary Limerick: The Republican Campaign for Independence in Limerick, 1913–1921* (Dublin, 2010)

O'Callaghan, Mícheál, *For Ireland and Freedom: Roscommon's Contribution to the Fight for Independence 1917–1921* (Boyle, 1991)

O'Connor, Seamus, *Tomorrow Was Another Day: Irreverent Memories of an Irish Rebel Schoolmaster* (Tralee, 1970)

O'Donnell, Ruán, Meehan, Niall and Murphy, Brian P., *Troubled History: A 10th Anniversary Critique of Peter Hart's 'The IRA and Its Enemies'* (Cork, 2008)

O'Donnell, Stephen, *The Royal Irish Constabulary and Black and Tans in County Louth 1919–1922* (Louth, 2004)

Ó Duibhir, Liam, *The Donegal Awakening: Donegal and the War of Independence* (Cork, 2009)

— *Donegal and the Civil War: The Untold Story* (Cork 2011)

Ó Fathaigh, Pádraic, *Pádraic Ó Fathaigh's War of Independence: Recollections of a Galway Gaelic Leaguer*, ed. Timothy G. MacMahon (Cork, 2000)

O'Halpin, Eunan, 'Problematic killing during the War of Independence and its aftermath: Civilian Spies and Informers', in *Death and Dying in Ireland, Britain and Europe: Historical Perspectives* (Dublin, 2013)

— 'Counting Terror, Bloody Sunday and the Dead of the Irish Revolution', in David Fitzpatrick (ed.) *Terror in Ireland 1916–1923* (Dublin, 2012)

Ó hÉalaithe, Dónal, *Memoirs of an Old Warrior: Jamie Moynihan's Fight for Irish Freedom 1916–1923* (Cork, 2014)

O'Hegarty, P. S., *The Victory of Sinn Féin* (2nd edn; Dublin, 1998)

O'Mahony, Colman, *The Maritime Gateway to Cork: A History of the Outports of Passage West and Monkstown 1754–1942* (Cork, 1986)

O'Mahony, Ross, 'The Sack of Balbriggan', in David Fitzpatrick (ed.), *Terror in Ireland 1916–1923* (Dublin, 2012)

O'Malley, Cormac K. H. and Keane, Vincent (eds), *The Men Will Talk To Me: Mayo Interviews by Ernie O'Malley* (Cork, 2014)

O'Malley, Ernie, *On Another Man's Wound* (4th edn; Dublin, 2008)

O'Riordan, John J., *Kiskeam versus the Empire* (Cork, 2010)

Ó Ruairc, Pádraig Óg, *Blood on the Banner: The Republican Struggle in Clare* (Cork 2009)

— 'The Difference is a Fine but a Real One': Sectarianism in Clare during the Irish War of Independence 1919–21', *The Other Clare: Journal of the Shannon Archaeological and Historical Society* (Shannon, 2010)

— 'The Woodford Incident', in *Bugle & Sabre: Military History in Oxfordshire & Buckinghamshire*, Vol. IV (Oxford, 2010)

— *Revolution: A Photographic History of Revolutionary Ireland 1913–23* (Cork 2012)

— 'Missing in Action', *History Ireland* (November/December 2012)

— 'TV Eye: In the Name of the Republic', *History Ireland*, May/June 2013

— *The Anglo-Irish Truce: An Analysis of Its Immediate Military Impact 8–11 July 1921*, PhD Thesis (University of Limerick, 2014)

— Book review: *The Black and Tans: British Police and Auxiliaries in the Irish War of Independence.* Available at www.theirishstory.com

Paice, Edward, *Tip & Run: The Untold Tragedy of the Great War in Africa* (London, 2007)

Palmer, Stanley H., *Police and Protest in England & Ireland 1780–1850* (Cambridge, 1988)

Parkinson, Alan F., *Belfast's Unholy War* (Dublin, 2004)

Penberthy, Ian, *The First World War in Pictures* (Sussex, 2013)

Persico, Joseph E., *Eleventh Month, Eleventh Day, Eleventh Hour: Armistice Day 1918, World War One and its Violent Climax* (London, 2005)

Phillips, W. Alison, *The Revolution in Ireland 1906–1923* (London, 1923)

Pimlott, John, *The Guinness History of the British Army* (London, 1993)

Pollard, H. B. C., *The Secret Societies of Ireland: Their Rise and Progress* (2nd edn; Kilkenny, 1998)

Price, Dominic, *The Flame and the Candle: War in Mayo 1919–1924* (Cork, 2012)

Rafter, Michael, *The Quiet County: Towards a History of the Laois Brigade IRA and Revolutionary Activity in the County 1913–1923* (Naas, 2005)

Read, Simon, *Human Game: The True Story of the Great Escape Murders and the Hunt for the Gestapo Gunmen* (New York, 2013)

Rees, Russell, *Ireland 1905–1925. Vol. I: Text & Historiography* (Newtownards, 1998)

Regan, John M., 'The Bandon Valley Massacre as a Historical Problem', *History: The Journal of the Royal Historical Society*, vol. 97, no. 1, January 2012

Richardson, Neil, *A Coward If I Return, A Hero If I Fall: Stories of Irishmen in World War One* (Dublin, 2010)

Royal Irish Academy, *The Dictionary of Irish Biography* (Cambridge, 2009)

Ryder, Chris, *The Fateful Split: Catholics and the Royal Ulster Constabulary* (London, 2004)

Ryle Dwyer, T., *Tans, Terror and Troubles: Kerry's Real Fighting Story 1913–23* (Cork, 2001)

— *Michael Collins: The Man Who Won the War* (Cork, 2009)

Self, Robert B. (ed.), *The Austin Chamberlain Diary Letters: The Correspondence of Sir Austen Chamberlain with His Sisters Hilda and Ida, 1916–1937*, Vol. V (Cambridge, 1995)

Seoighe, Mainchin, *The Story of Kilmallock* (Kilmallock, 2012)

Sheehan, William, *British Voices from the Irish War of Independence 1918–1921* (Cork, 2005)

— *Hearts & Mines: The British 5th Division, Ireland 1920–1922* (Cork, 2009)

— *A Hard Local War: The British Army and the Guerrilla War in Cork 1919–1921* (Stroud, 2011)

— *The Western Front: Irish Voices from the Great War* (Dublin, 2011)

Stanley, Alan, *I Met Murder on the Way: The Story of the Pearsons of Coolacrease* (Carlow, 2005)

Strong, Kenneth, *Intelligence at the Top: The Recollections of an Intelligence Officer* (London, 1969)

Talbot, Hayden, *Michael Collins' Own Story Told to Hayden Talbot* (2nd edn; Dublin, 2012)

Taylor, Paul, 'Heroes or Traitors? Experiences of Returning Irish Soldiers from World War One' (unpublished PhD thesis, University of Oxford, 2012), quoted in Myles Dungan, *Irish Voices from the Great War* (2nd edn; Kildare, 2014)

Tobin, Fergal, *The Irish Revolution: An Illustrated History 1912–1925* (Dublin, 2014)

Tomkins, Phil, *Twice a Hero: From the Trenches of the Great War to the Ditches of the Irish Midlands* (Stroud, 2012)

Toomey, Tom, *The War of Independence in Limerick 1912–1921* (Limerick, 2010)

— *The Blackwater Tragedy – 20th February 1921: Commemoration Booklet* (Meelick, 2013)

Townshend, Charles, *The British Campaign in Ireland 1919–1921: The Development of Political and Military Policies* (London, 1975)

— *The Republic: The Fight for Irish Independence* (London, 2013)

Trendall, John, *Colonel Bogey to the Fore* (London, 1991)

Trotter, Samuel, *Constabulary Heroes 1826–2011: Incorporating the RUC GC/PSNI and their Forebears in the USC* (Coleraine, 2012)

Twohig, Pat, *Green Tears for Hecuba: being a superficial, brief but appreciative study of the troubled times in Ballyvourney* (Cork, 1994)

Ungoed-Thomas, Jasper, *Jasper Wolfe of Skibbereen* (Cork, 2008)

Vale, Colonel Walter Leonard, *The History of the South Staffordshire Regiment* (London 1969)

Valiulis, Maryann, *Portrait of a Revolutionary: General Richard Mulcahy and the Founding of the Irish Free State* (Dublin, 1992)

Various, *Béal na mBláth Commemoration Ninetieth Anniversary Booklet 1922–2012* (Cork, 2012)

Various, *Limerick's Fighting Story* (Cork, 2009)

Various, *Rebel Cork's Fighting Story* (Cork, 2009)

Various, *The Dublin Brigade Review* (Dublin, 1939)

Walsh, Maurice, *The News from Ireland: Foreign Correspondents and the Irish Revolution* (London, 2008)

Whelan, Michael J., *Allegiances Compromised: Faith, Honour and Allegiance Ex-British Soldiers in the Irish Army 1913–1924* (Dublin, 2010)

Wilson, T. K., *Frontiers of Violence: Conflict and Identity in Ulster and Upper Silesia 1918–1922* (Oxford, 2010)

TELEVISION DOCUMENTARIES

Eunan O'Halpin, 'In the Name of the Republic', TV3/ Title Films Ireland, March 2013

WEBSITES

http://gcd.academia.edu/NiallMeehan/Papers

www.cairogang.com

www.theirishstory.com

www.icrc.org

INDEX